THE GRUNTS AND VIETNAM: THE OTHER WAR

THE GRUNTS AND VIETNAM: THE OTHER WAR

Charles R. Anderson

PRESIDIO PRESS · CALIFORNIA

THE GRUNTS
© 1976 by Presidio Press

VIETNAM: THE OTHER WAR
© 1982 by Presidio Press, 31 Pamaron Way,
Novato, California 94947

PRINTED IN THE UNITED STATES OF AMERICA

THE GRUNTS AND VIETNAM: THE OTHER WAR

THE GRUNTS

DEDICATION

This book is for Sam,
and for
Chief, D. J., Red Mountain, Beck,
Day Tripper, Big Dipper,
L. C., Old Man, Hair,
Brother Books, Pooch, Whitey,
and all the rest.

Contents

Epilogue

Acknowledgements

In the course of my own tour in Vietnam, I met several hundred persons whose actions and comments contributed in some measure to this book. However, I would like to cite in particular Bruce Williams, Herman Wimbush, George Webb, James Sloban, Hector Perez, Archie Morton III and Michael McCloskey for offering their own descriptions and interpretations of Vietnam. Special thanks is extended to Professor Charles C. Moskos, Jr. of Northwestern University who did so much to help this work across that broad gulf which separates written manuscripts from published books. I am further indebted to my manuscript typists of two cultures—Joyce Brown Duesing, Catherine Havelick, Nancie A. Wood and Kiyomi Sugawara.

Introduction

This book is an attempt to describe the Vietnam War as it was experienced by the individual infantryman, the grunt. This personal account of the war shares that purpose with several previous efforts. But in fulfilling its purpose this work moves in different directions than others, because it incorporates a different view of the experience of the Vietnam War. Earlier accounts have presented the war as a one-dimensional experience; only that which occurred in the war zone was recounted. This account, however, presents the Vietnam War as a two-dimensional experience. Both that which the participant did in the war zone and what he found on his return to America are examined. Such a definition of the total experience of the Vietnam War requires that the account make a radical change of focus, from the microcosmic to the macrocosmic. But that is a change of focus which must be made if the account is to be true to its purpose, for the experience it describes includes the same change of focus.

In experiencing the war and then his postwar hometown, the participant was forced to rapidly expand the focus of his action and concern from an environment small and concentrated to one large and diffuse. In Vietnam the infantryman could afford only to be concerned with survival and its related questions. The environment allowed no more. But back in America, where survival has a completely different definition, he could not afford to be concerned with only one issue. The home environment forced an expansion of perception and concern. Thus the total experience of the Vietnam War amounted to a forced move from a microcosm to a macrocosm. This account makes the same change of focus.

Existing accounts of the war concentrate on the microcosmic aspect of the experience—the war in Vietnam. The macrocosmic aspect—the readjustment to American society—has been largely ignored in spite of the fact that it was for many veterans as wrenching an experience as the war. Thus there persists an unbalanced understanding of what those who went to and returned from the war experienced. This account is an attempt to redress that imbalance.

Part One of this account details the actions of one U.S. Marine infantry company on a 58-day combat operation. All incidents happened as related. The events described are those encountered by only 160 men, though the adversity recounted is representative of that experienced by all grunts in Vietnam. The chronology of the account is interrupted by brief descriptions of what a few Americans far from the war were doing. The juxtaposition of grunts in Vietnam and civilians in America is used to illustrate how, to the former, the seemingly innocuous actions of their countrymen appeared at various times hilarious, absurd, maddening, even threatening—anything but normal or logical.

Part Two differs from Part One in two respects. First, the scope of analysis is much wider. Postwar and select prewar experiences of all the grunts, not only those of one infantry company, are examined against a background much larger than that of the war—American society of the late 1960s. Before they went to Vietnam, the grunts had a particular set of experiences which equipped them with certain expectations about war and one's return from it. But those who went to and returned from this war found that previous experience was poor preparation for what Vietnam and the American public presented them. Part Two also differs from Part One in that it manifests a conglomerate character. In addition to a consideration of the society which the grunts came from and returned to, there is presented in Part Two an investigation into those actions of the grunts which contributed nothing toward the accomplishment of their official mission in Vietnam. Herein is a discussion of the causation behind two such actions: atrocities against Vietnamese civilians and fraggings, the attempted murder of unit leaders by some of their troops. American troops in Vietnam displayed a very human mix of the admirable and the questionable. While there was heroism and compassion, there was also fear and indifference, cowardice and brutality.

Before this account begins, several persistent misconceptions should be countered in order that the overall experience of the war on the ground in Vietnam will be better understood. First, many distant observers believed during the war years—and somehow still believe—that American troops in Vietnam outnumbered their enemy. In fact, however, there were never more than one-fifth as many Americans in the field as the Viet Cong/North Vietnamese Army. The organization of communist forces was such that their ratio of troops in the field to total personnel in uniform was much higher than that of the American force. Total field strength of the VC/NVA was usually estimated at 300,000 to a half million. In contrast, the American Military Assistance Command, Vietnam, was top-heavy with rear-echelon staff personnel, much more so than any previous military force America sent to war. The ratio of troops in the field to personnel in Vietnam was consistently between one to six and one to eight. Applying that ratio to the 540,000 Americans in uniform in Vietnam at the height of the American involvement, we find that only 67,000 to 90,000 were assigned to front-line combat units. Pushing that figure even lower was the normal attrition of personnel caused by malaria, rest and recreation leave, heat exhaustion and combat. Thus, there were never more than about 80,000 American ground troops actually looking for and fighting over 400,000 VC/NVA. The American force was of course augmented by the South Vietnamese Army, which numbered about 800,000 in 1969, but that force was for several reasons not nearly as effective as its size would indicate. While American grunts did enjoy certain advantages over their enemy, numerical superiority in the field was definitely not one of them.

Second, the great contrast between the war experience of troops in the field and that of rear-echelon staff and support personnel is still not appreciated among those who did not see the war. By the mid-1960s American military science had so developed that less than twenty percent of the personnel in the U.S. Military Assistance Command, Vietnam, were infantrymen. The majority were engaged in a myriad of support activities. Incredibly, for that majority life could be as secure and comfortable as it was for those assigned to a base in the States. In the rear-echelon bases there were all those things the troops in the field were denied. There were movies, free time, dry beds with clean sheets, mail and showers every day and plenty to eat and drink. And there were the clubs, the clubs with their air conditioners, pool tables, slot machines, floor shows, steak dinners and, "would you care to see the wine list, sir?" The comforts enjoyed by those in rear-echelon bases were a constant source of resentment for the grunts.

Finally, even among troops in the field, the adversity encountered was not uniform; time and region influenced the grunts' experience of war. The war in the hills of the northern provinces of South Vietnam, of which this is a partial description, was much different from the war in the rice paddies of the Mekong Delta region, or the war in the urban centers. And, the war in 1969 was almost as different from the war in 1965 as was the Vietnam War from the Korean War.

None of the incidents described herein is merely true to the spirit of the experience of Vietnam. All dates, place names, unit designations, and events in this account are factual. However, in accordance with the wishes of certain participants, or their survivors, all names have been changed.

Vocabulary Note

Like most wars, the Vietnam War provoked a vocabulary of its own. Many of the hundreds of words and phrases coined during the war appear in this book and require explanation.

After they had been in their branch of the military for awhile, the marines rarely referred to their organization as the Marine Corps. They preferred terms less officious and more descriptive of their experiences with the workings of the Corps. They decided on terms decidedly uncomplimentary—the *green machine*, the *crotch*, the *green weenie*, and *this green mother*.

In *the Nam*, the grunts spent most of their time in the *bush*, the field, far way from towns and cities. In the bush the grunts *humped*, walked, after two enemies, the *VC*, the Viet Cong, and the *NVA*, the North Vietnamese Army. In their humping after the VC and NVA, the grunts were sometimes assisted by the South Vietnamese Army, the Army of the Republic of Vietnam, *ARVN*, pronounced *arvin*. The humps and search and destroy operations carried out by the grunts were planned and supervised by high-ranking staff personnel and unit commanders, the *heavies*, of the military hierarchy. However, when the grunts said they were *busting heavies*, they were working hard, not doing anything to their commanders. Unlike most grunts, most heavies were *lifers*, they were making a career of military service.

The number *six* was the designation for the commander of any unit larger than a platoon, and was preceded by a codified term for a particular unit: *Bravo Six, Mustang Six,* etc. The term *Sky Six* was a slang designation for God. Unit commanders wanted their troops to carry out directives and missions *ASAP,* as soon as possible, and according to the *SOP,* standing operating procedure.

During both offensive and defensive operations the grunts occasionally encountered Vietnamese civilians. The Vietnamese were almost always referred to in the most derogatory terms—*gooks, gooners, zipper-heads* or *zips, slopes, dinks,* and *slant-eyes.* In contrast to the last term, *round-eyes* designated westerners.

Life in the bush was generally a *bummer,* an adverse experience, which was only rarely broken by the *bennies,* benefits like warm beer and letters from the *World,* the United States. When they appeared, the bennies were delivered by a *bird* or *chopper,* a helicopter. Whenever possible, the grunts *cut each other a hus,* did favors for each other, to relieve the adversity.

The grunts had much to fear in the bush. Some of the most common fears were of being wounded, being denied the bennies for several days, receiving *office hours,* and hearing about *Jody* back in the World. Office hours was an expedient form of dispensing punishment for minor violations of the Uniform Code of Military Justice. Jody was the guy who stole a grunt's girl friend back in the World while the latter was serving a tour in the war. The grunts' greatest fear, of course, was of being killed, the most common terms for which were *dinged, zapped, greased, blown away, caught his lunch,* and *bought the ranch.*

part one
The Tour

It's a small war, God, but
it's the only one we've got.

anonymous, sign over chaplain's
bunker at Con Thien, 1967

With America's newest war heating up in the mid-1960s, draft calls were raised and standards for volunteers were lowered. Existing training facilities were expanded; new camps and schools opened. By the summer of 1968, dozens of training camps and specialist schools were turning out thousands of troops and junior officers every month. They learned how to fly helicopters at Fort Rucker, Alabama; load napalm and bombs on fighters at Lackland Air Force Base, Texas; lead infantry platoons at Quantico, Virginia, and Fort Benning, Georgia; and drive tanks and trucks at Camp Pendleton, California. They were taught to cook mess hall food at Camp Lejeune, North Carolina; run an Army photographic lab at Fort Monmouth, New Jersey; fire aircraft carrier boilers at Norfolk, Virginia; treat combat wounds at Great Lakes, Illinois; conduct counter-guerilla warfare at Fort Bragg, North Carolina; and fly Phantom fighter-bombers at Pensacola, Florida. Their training complete, these new warriors were given thirty days leave before reporting to one of several military air terminals on the West Coast. There they boarded civilian jets, complete with inflight meals and smiling stewardesses, for the flight to Da Nang or Saigon.

1 Hotel Twenty-Nine

Travis Air Force Base is about an hour-and-a-half drive up Interstate 80 from San Francisco. The highway roams over and between those low hills linking the Bay Area with California's vast agricultural interior. Tract housing creeps obscenely up some of the slopes. An occasional billboard claims too much of the view; one screams "Impeach Earl Warren!" To the west is that huge red sun falling into the Pacific. The reason they call it "Golden California" becomes obvious on this road at this time of day. Before it moves out of sight, the red ball turns everything a glowing, fluid gold—the rolling hills wearing a soft grassy mantle and a few clumps of trees and mounds of rocks; the highway, black most of the day; even the oncoming cars bearing natives in deep tans, outrageous colors, and—always—the sunglasses. You squint at the goldness of everything, but it's not like squinting at the glare of midday sun off a new snowfall—this feels good, warm, almost makes one desire sleep. So you squint to expose more of your eyelids to that golden warmth, and you want to stay—*goddam, you want to stay all of a sudden—did I really volunteer for this thing?*

Soon the gold ball leaves to tend to Hawaii, the thousands of mini-islands farther west, then on to that part of the planet misnamed the Far East. In *the Nam* the same gold ball drives the colonels and generals into their air-conditioned headquarters offices. It drives the supply *pogues* in the rear bases to their Coke machines and fans. And it drives the grunts into bunkers at fire support bases or into streams in the bush, the streams with their leeches and black water fever.

Signs come out of the dusk, reporting one's progress on the way to war:

> . . . Fairfield 11, Sacramento 52 . . . Fairfield 4, Sacramento 45 . . . Welcome Fairfield Suisun . . . Fairfield Beauty Academy . . . HiFi Steakburgers . . . Bank of America . . . Armijo High School . . . George's House of Liquor . . . WOW Discount Market . . .
>
> United States Air Force
> Travis A.F. Base
>
> . . . Attention Visitors . . . Assist Us in Assisting You . . . Please Present Proper Identification . . . Headquarters 22d Air Force . . . Military Airlift Command . . . Pride in Professional Performance . . . An Equal Opportunity Employer . . . .
>
> *Evening, Sir. Go straight ahead to the stop sign after the next light, turn right, and go all the way to the end of the road. That'll be the parking lot. You'll see a lotta people and the operations tower. That's it.*

In the waiting room, one meets those selected to man the frontiers of freedom. Two white-haired colonels mumble in military officialeze near the row of phone booths. Clusters of soldiers, sailors, and airmen play cards on suitcases or just wander around: staring out at the flight line, waging and losing battles against the discomfort of military uniforms, leafing through a phonebook, chewing on a candy bar. Most of those assigned to this flight, Hotel Twenty-Nine, sit in those pale green or tomato soup-red fiberglass chairs that violate all laws of comfort and seem to grow in herds wherever air terminals are built. No parents come into the waiting area; only a handful of girl friends are there.

A long night of nothing to do, nowhere to go, begins. Conversations are born, then allowed to die. Faces and expressions are studied, then ignored as they take on the uniform look of resignation. Eyes bound around the clinic-like terminal, from plastic signs to stainless steel signs to plastic signs:

. . . Passenger Processing . . . Men . . . Ladies . . .
Terminal Base Exchange . . . Cafeteria . . . Men . . .
Firehose . . . Ladies . . . Lost and Found Luggage
. . . In-Flight Meals . . . Are You Shipping Your
Car Overseas? . . . Flight Insurance . . . .

Men fight for sleep in the impossible chairs; in most cases the chairs win. Giant jets nose up from the darkness a few hundred yards away, roaring engines pushing the earth down, rattling windows, chairs, teeth, baggage lockers.

. . . Space Available Roster . . . U.S. Army Pacific Personnel Liaison Team . . . Warning: 1. It Is a Crime to: A. Carry Concealed Weapons Aboard Aircraft, B. Interfere with Flight Crews, Including Any Steward or Stewardess, C. Transport Explosives, D. Seize an Aircraft . . . .

Your attention in the terminal, please. Attention in the terminal, please . . . will all passengers manifested on Continental Airlines government contract flight Yankee One Zulu Five for Anchorage, Alaska, and Honolulu, Hawaii, please check the name on their boarding pass . . . Mrs. Shrieber has lost her boarding pass. That is, Mrs. Shrieber has lost her boarding pass . . . .

. . . Things Go Better with Coke . . . No Admittance . . . Foreign Student Liaison . . . Army/Air Force VIP Lounge . . . Gate 2 . . . Entry for the Following Passenger Categories . . . No Visitors/Spectators Beyond This Point . . . .

Eight hours ago the sun slid down behind the venetian blinds. Now that same sun creeps back in through loading gate door frames and passenger entrances. B-52 bombers walk up onto the flight line and plow through the new day's heat waves, up and up to assume their Strategic Air Command vigil for a few hours.

. . . Coffee . . . cement-filled roll on a formica table . . . cold water shave . . . .

And then the long-awaited liberation:

May I have your attention in the terminal, your attention in the terminal, please. Travis Air Force Base announces the immediate departure of World Airways government contract flight Hotel Twenty-Nine for Da Nang, Vietnam, via Anchorage, Alaska, Atsugi, Japan, and Kadena Air Force Base, Okinawa. Passengers will board the aircraft through gate four in the following manner: all officers and civilians of equivalent rank, followed by all staff NCOs, followed by other enlisted personnel. You are reminded to retain one copy of your orders on your person at all times. Please extinguish all cigarettes at this time. No photographs are permitted on the flight line. Thank you.

All get up, join the somnolent hassle for a place in the hierarchy of the line, all except one very young soldier who wears the look of never having been farther away from home than boot camp. A girl clings to his left arm, dropping tears on his khaki shoulder. His is the only girl who stayed the night on those maddening chairs, stayed to be near him. He fights a trembling lip and growing embarrassment. Both are afraid he'll be killed, of course; but they can't know yet how good the chances are that he'll return. Next year they'll have to get to know each other all over again, and that might prove more painful than adjusting to death. He might not want to forget that warm girl he will meet on his R & R in Hong Kong or Tokyo, the girl who will make him feel like a man and beg him to take her with him to the States.

Hi, fellas, where you going?

Boo . . . Hiss . . . Oh, wow! Look at the set on her . . . Jesus Christ, lady . . . .

I'd like to introduce the crew and staff to you now. Our pilot today is Captain Thomas, the co-pilot is Lieutenant Rosen—he's the one with the curls, guys! And your flight engineer is Captain James. Please keep your seats as I introduce the girls now. Ha, ha, you're so cute, Colonel. Way in . . . .

Pinch her on the ass, Colonel . . . Fuck the lifers!

. . . the back is Carol, from Detroit. A little farther up is Dianne, from New Orleans. Behind me here is Suzie. She used to work at the Playboy Club in San Francisco—how about that one, men! In the galley is Janie, from Kansas City; and I'm Shirley from beautiful downtown Burbank—no guys, actually I'm from Los Angeles. If there is anything at all we can do for you, just let us know. Well, almost anything! Come on now, be nice. Oh, you're all so sweet, you sure don't look like killers! Now, Dianne and I will demonstrate the life jacket you'll find over each of your seats. If there's a chance we'll have to ditch over water, just reach straight above . . . .

Here we go to hell, escorted by the tight-hipped, Mabellined, hard-smiling, round-eyed stews from Never-Never Land. There's not much you can say about sixteen hours in a 707. It's just there and has to be endured. There's an exhilaration at take-off despite the night before, and, what the hell, you're still 10,000 miles from it!

Above the clouds, excited conversation at many locations in the cabin gradually gives way to a general quiet. It is the quiet born of a train of mutual comprehensions—of female bodies under airline uniform camouflage, of the meaning of one's first foreign country, of the resemblance of clouds to known forms. There is an advancing numbness, first fought and then allowed supremacy in certain areas—the first to lose is your ass. One long and two short articles in a *Time* magazine after the first in-flight meal and:

Gentlemen, may I have your attention please. This is Captain Thomas speaking. Our flight plan has been changed since our departure from Travis. We will not be going to Anchorage, Alaska, but will go directly to Atsugi, Japan. I'll be keeping you posted on any further developments as they might occur.

By the time the second meal is consumed, all stewardesses have lost the capacity for bouncy comment and automated smiling. Service is now by the comatose, and the trivial again receives undue study:

. . . Live Vest Under Seat . . . Gilet de Sauvetage Sous Seige . . . No Smoking . . . Defense de Fumer . . . Fasten Seat Belt . . . .

Four meals, two magazines, and three naps later, Captain Thomas arrives with the cavalry to break the ordeal:

Gentlemen, we'll be landing at Atsugi very shortly. If you will look out the left side of the aircraft as we move into our landing pattern, you can see the snow-capped Mount Fuji through the clouds. We will have about a two-hour layover before going on to Okinawa. You will be allowed off the aircraft but you are restricted to the passenger terminal area. Your stewardess will give you further instructions.

In long lines at urinals and snack bars, the attrition rate on Hotel Twenty-Nine is obvious. It will be days before 165 metabolic rates recover from the assault of the International Dateline. A cold face-wash, a Coke, and aching positions are resumed.

Gentlemen, please fasten your seat belts as soon as you've taken your seats. Only a couple more hours and you'll be on dry, solid ground for a few days.

Instructions, seat belts, lift-offs, had taken on the familiarity and naturalness of body functions these last few hours or days or whatever.

Looks like this is your first tour in the Nam?
Yeah. My first tour. Hope it's not as bad as this damn flight.

This is a lot better than when I went the first time. We was on a ship out of San Diego. Took twenty-two days, and most of us were sick the whole time but about two days. This is the only way to go over, believe me! I just think about that first steam bath I'm going to get on Oki.

Gentlemen, we'll be touching down at Kadena Air Force Base in about ten minutes . . . please put out all cigarettes and fasten your seat belts, please . . . the local time is eleven in the morning on the fourth . . . the ground temperature is eighty-five degrees with clear skies . . . .

Okinawa. So this is Okinawa. The last battle of the big war. Here. Sake, kamikazes, samurai swords, harakiri—the whole show. Right here. Khaki forms file past painted stewardesses into an environment holding new possibilities for discomfort. A glaring sun forces eyelids into a tight squint; JP-4 fumes flare out noses and lungs; and humidity clamps over every pore. Western bodies—black and white, young and old—recoil from the latest assault of the endless day.

Civilian 707s in bright colors—World Airways, Continental, TWA, National—sit in a cluster near the control tower. A little farther out is a perimeter of squat C-130s—the slow, droning birds with black bulbous noses and squint-eyed windows—some silver, some in tan and dark brown camouflage patterns. Next to the C-130s rest a pack of sleek, screaming fighter bombers and that most beautiful and awesome piece of military technology, the Phantom. At the farthest reaches of the flight line, segregated from the others, the lord of the strip, the B52, relaxes between missions.

It is difficult to get lost in this airport. There are only two kinds of people here, those on the way home and those on the way to Vietnam. In addition to a different uniform, those home-bound wear the victor's gait and a look of obvious relief. The new guys stand awkward, silent, self-conscious, suddenly feeling a little immature, uninitiated, and wonder what kind of an experience could cause an appearance so apparent on those across the waiting room.

Men are always somewhat short of maturity until they have

tasted the deep uncertainty bred only by combat. And though they may still be less than mature after seeing war, they will thereafter need no such base experience to erase that deficiency. On Okinawa, the mature and the incomplete were passing each other going in opposite directions. Here in the humid air was a dichotomy: absolute confidence resting beside absolute uncertainty. Half were "going south," as they would learn to say in the next few days; they were not at all sure they would survive the experience. The other half, since they had already been there, were certain of their survival; they were headed for the fantasyland of the Big PX, the *World,* Man—Stateside!

Find a seat on the first three buses, gentlemen.

Four short round-faced men begin to move four green army buses out of a parking lot that looks like any airport parking lot of any middle-sized American city. The only difference is the humid air.

Hey, what's that, Gunner?

That's a turtle-back tomb. They don't build them much any more, just the older people now. Japs used them for machine gun positions. Lotta my buddies got zapped from them back in forty-five, lot of them.

. . . Welcome to Camp Sukiran . . . United States Army, The Ryukus . . . Bolt Sell Store . . . Koza City . . . Honeymoon Hotel . . . .

In Koza City, the green caravan with faces pressed to windows provokes a cheer from the group of GIs on liberty.

Keep your head and ass close to the deck, Sweetheart—Ha!

. . . Chibana . . . Asahi Beer . . . Bar Mary . . . Steam Bath and Cocktail Laungh Special Everything . . . Club Tennessee . . . Come see . . . We Have Special State-side Nudie Show from Australia . . . Ishikawa . . . .

Look at that, a damn horse and wagon!

. . . Jewely Beuty Shop . . . Special Japan Bed Floor

Look Show Every Night . . . Yaka Beach R & R Center . . . Little Tailor Specialize For Custom Shirt . . . Combat Range 6 . . . Kin Sanitarium . . . Camp Hansen . . . .

Come right in, gentlemen. Move toward the front. Take the seats toward the front. Please, move it on up . . . Gentlemen, you should find on your desk two sheets of white paper stapled together, a blue card, and a white card. Please fill out the top half of the blue and white cards at this time—only the top half, gentlemen; do not write below the dotted line. Please follow directions; we don't want to keep you here any longer than necessary. Gentlemen, when you've finished filling out your card, please pass it toward the center aisle. Keep the blue cards separate from the white; blue cards in this pile, Lieutenant. Gentlemen, as your papers are being endorsed, I want you to read this form very carefully. Then, when you're finished, I'll have some final word to pass before we get you out of here. We have more people who get delayed or into trouble because they can't follow these simple directions. Gentlemen, I call your attention to item seven. You must store all uniforms except the set you'll wear on the flight south in Building Twenty-six Fifty-four. All you'll have with you when you go is the uniform you'll wear, one set of civilian clothes for R & R, and your orders. That's all. Don't try to take all kinds of crap. Store it here, gentlemen, it's free. Your flight can store uniforms Friday morning from zero-nine to fifteen hundred. Do I have any questions? Good. Now some final word. Gentlemen, you are tentatively on Flight Hotel Twenty-Nine leaving the eighth, but check it when you sign in at the desk across the street in Building Twenty-six Thirty-six each day at ten hundred and at sixteen-thirty. E-six and above have all night liberty; E-four and E-five, until zero-two hundred; and E-three and below until midnight. E-five and below must have a liberty card. Civilian attire is authorized for all grades.

Tomorrow between zero-nine and twelve hundred, all of you will report to sickbay to have your shot cards checked. Don't lose the goddam thing. E-four and above may draw pay in advance not to exceed fifty dollars. Disbursing is in

Building Twenty-six Nineteen. Day after tomorrow, all E-six and above will report to G-three, Building Twenty-two Fifty-one, for a tactical briefing, with documents proving you have a secret clearance. If anybody gets in trouble in town some night, we have MPs and a brig here, too, just like back in the World. And I would remind you that the VD rate on Oki is currently at ninety-seven percent. Good evening, gentlemen.

All the new arrivals on Oki wonder what their first veterans will look like, the ones who've been there. Like high school athletes curious about adversaries in a tentative way, they wonder how they will measure up next to the blooded. "They call them grunts, you know, the guys from the bush in Nam, and they're supposed to be the gungiest mothers around. You can't miss 'em." Do they stick out because they have more starch in their uniforms, or less? Are they bigger, do they look older? The first ones seen are remembered. They amble out of the barracks at about nine in the morning and take a direct route across the grass (in violation of Base Order 4010.2b) to the snack bar in the bowling alley, then on to the PX, with its stereo corner, its magazine rack. Watching them you see why they don't need to wear medals or bandages to make it known where they've been the past year. Once-black boots have turned white from the sun and paddies. The cover rests on the back of a thick wad of hair, and out from under it creep the beginnings of sideburns to challenge more regulations. Hair rests on the back of the collar, hair keeps the nose and lower lip spaced properly. Hair, hair—it pisses off the lifers! The saluting hand is in a pocket, the other flips a lighter top open and shut. The eyes—no thousand-yard stares here. Instead, an intense darting that bores through to an evaluation in seconds. And the walk, an exclusive and temporal possession from the experience. They will lose it some day, as Vietnam recedes into two years, five, ten. They don't quite swagger or strut, but they are beyond conforming to anyone's cadence but their own. It comes from two things: months of trying to move one's body and about thirty-five or seventy pounds through paddies and over hills while using as little energy as possible, and the final jubilation of each nerve and muscle cell in the realization that it's all over at last—they'll never have to carry that fucking pack or radio again. Move into their path and pick up the vocabulary, the interests . . .

an' it surprised me too, ya know, gettin' tight with a gunny but he was all right . . . helped me get the R & R I wanted . . . She still writes me, too—you seen her pitcher yet? . . . If I can draw some advance pay this afternoon I'm gonna get me them speakers we was lookin' at yesterday, the Panasonics, you know . . . hey, you remember that guy used to try and make it to sickbay every day we had a hike on Parris Island? The son of a bitch got a Silver Star on that Operation Liberty Two! A guy out in the vill told me last night—he was with him when he did it . . . .

But the picture is still incomplete. One discovers, as the result of tired and aimless wandering about the camp, the place where the young veterans let it all hang out. Building 2412 is the base library, and it is one of the very few comfortable buildings available to the junior enlisted man both day and night. Its popularity rests on one characteristic.

Hey, Man, where we goin' today?

Got any jing?

I told you. They fucked up my pay record in Nam.

Well, I got some, but not enough for the vill again. We'll go to the library.

To the what? Who in the fuck you trying to jack anyway?

A guy told me in the mess hall today—it's fucking air-conditioned. Open till ten every night. And it ain't just for the heavies. It's for everybody, and it's free!

Air-conditioned? You mean slope air conditioning, or Stateside air conditioning?

They got real Stateside machines in there, Tripper, the real motors.

The troops make no pretense of scholarly pursuit. Here they come to be by themselves, to crawl into themselves, to inch cautiously back to the thought patterns of a peaceful, pleasurable existence. Here they have none of the attitudinal adornments displayed in the presence of civilians. In the morning, they come in, head straight for the reading tables, the stacks, and just crash —sleep—until Okinawa cools off. Places nearest the air conditioning ducts go first, then the cushioned chairs and couches, then the floor spaces in between. Nothing but wall-to-wall green marines, crashed out in beautiful dreams. Very rarely does one snore. It's as if they want to be in the deepest possible state of relaxation while maintaining just enough consciousness to preserve an awareness of the cool luxury in the air. Nor is the stereo room off-limits. Some stay all day, plugged into the soul sounds, the country and western, the acid rock or the "Golden Oldies"—eyes closed, lips forming the words of peace and love, heads bobbing to a new beat, absorbed inward in dreams of the cars they'll buy at home, the girls they'll chase and win, the homecoming parties without end . . . .

> *I been sweating for a year, Man. In here you don't even sweat! It's outa sight, Man, fucking outa sight!*

Though they were still 1,400 miles from the war farther south, young Americans on the way to it got an introduction to some of its direct effects at places like Kin Village and Koza City on Okinawa. During the 1960s the term "camp follower" implied a greater variety of activities and businesses than ever before, but central to it all was still the timeless theme of lonely boy far from home meets pretty girl. In places like Kin and Koza, soldiers and marines found girls refreshingly uninhibited but maddening and depressing in their relentless drive for the American dollar. If anyone ever invents a machine to do nothing but separate a human being from his legal tender, surely it will resemble the town across from the main gate of any military base the world over. In any one of the hundreds of bars, the story is the same.

Well, hello, and what's your name?
Me, Sachiko, wha's you name?
You can call me Bob, I'm from Denver—how 'bout you, Sachiko?
I from Henoko—that way—this you firs' time Okinawa, Bob-a-san?
Ha! Bob-a-san—ja hear that D. J.?
Yeah, this is my first time in Okinawa. I think I like Oki very much. How 'bout you showing me around the island some time?
Sure, I show you. Say, you want drinky now, Bob-a-san?
Yeah, I'll have a beer, Sachiko, an' get whatever you want, too.
Campai. Bob-a-san . . . hey, Bob-a-san, you like me? Maybe we hab many drinky, hab good time tonight—maybe pray honeymoon rater, eh?
Yeah, sounds good, Sachiko. Yeah, I like you jus' fine.
Let's go, Pal, we can do better than this.

Soon, over and over:

Hey, you big han'some GI, maybe we go pray honeymoon apter tweb 'crock, eh?
Well, how did you do last night, Pal? I lost you after the Napoleon Club.
Oh, Man, she was something else. "I show you number one Japanese way tonight," she said. I gotta find her again!
Hey, you hear about George? Dropped a hundred-thirty last night, on the same broad, and all he got outa the deal was a steam bath. She wouldn't go honeymoon with him. He'll probably do it again, though. He's definitely got no brains and a lotta bread.

Days and nights turn into a barhopping routine having damn little variety and less logic. Out of money, the uneasiness about the future becomes sharper to the privates first class and the lance corporals. They kill time wandering around the base, looking over stereos and tape decks in the PX, or lying in the heat of the barracks studying the intricacies of springs under mattresses overhead. Okinawa is not the end of this trip. Their time too drawing near, the new lieutenants retreat to the Officers' Club to wrestle with facts and thoughts getting heavier each day.

What the hell, I didn't come over here to screw every slant-eyed broad I could find.

Over seven-sevens and whiskey sours they remind each other in silence where they're going, that many other lives will soon depend on their abilities to read a map, reach a quick decision.

What if I screw up?

Each little fragment of doctrine thrown at them in the last seven months becomes the most important class they ever received, just like the instructors used to say;

Maybe they shoulda given us a class on how to write letters of condolence?
Hey, ferget it, Man, here have another one . . . .

Finally, long after the you-buy-me-drinky-we-play-honeymoon swindle has lost all novelty, troop handlers walk briskly through barracks buildings around the sickbay and base headquarters.

Fall out! Hey, git that guy outa the rack there, Hotel Twenty-Nine on the road!

It is an order eagerly followed. The young warriors-to-be move quickly through the heat. Ranks form, bodies are counted, buses are boarded. And 500 yards away at the "O" Club on the coral mound:

May I have your attention in the club, your attention please. All officers manifested on Hotel Twenty-Nine please muster at the main entrance to the club, that is . . . .

A few of the 165 have found a new girl these past six days. For them, there would be an additional source of mail during the next year, but now on the buses back to Kadena, most thoughts were 1,400 miles beyond Camp Hansen or the "Lucky Hearts Club." Of the journey to war by jet, only three hours remained.

Welcome back, men! Aw, come on, don't look so glum—we'll all be back together again next year. At this time I'd like to introduce . . . our flying time will be two hours forty-three minutes . . . we will serve beverages during the flight but no meal . . . will demonstrate the life preservers to be found . . . . Good afternoon, gentlemen, this is your captain speaking. This afternoon we'll be flying at an altitude of approximately twenty-two thousand feet . . . we expect excellent weather all the way . . . .

No one slept this time. All were quiet and alert, none betraying his last revel in the vill the night before. As time and distance ran out, a nervous anxiety was manifested. Finally, about an hour from the destination, soft voices broke the tense silence. The hard reality was upon all now; its terrible possibilities no longer seemed far-away, not-me things. Stewardesses were no longer stared at, though some worked hard at hearing an American female voice right up to the last minute. There were only two sailors on the entire plane. Both were very young and both were going to be medical corpsmen with the marines in the field. One began turning white as the big jet dropped into its landing pattern over Da Nang.

Ah, 'scuse me, Sir. Who you, ah, gonna be with when we get there?

I'm not sure yet. I could stay in Da Nang for awhile or go right out with a company as soon as I report in. How about yourself?

Well, my buddy here and I, we're both corpsmen and we'll be with some Marine unit somewhere—probably in the field . . . you, ah, know what it's like out there?

Well, I've never been there, of course, but it's not that bad —not as bad as the veterans in the bars tell it.

I sure hope so. But I heard a lotta corpsmen get it when they're helpin' guys that got hit—an' the VCs look to knock out the corpsman, the corpsman and the radioman.

Well, there's no sense worrying too much now. You've had good training, you'll do all right, Doc.

Yeah, it shouldn't be too bad, I'll be plenty busy . . . it shouldn't be too bad.

The men, the kids—joking, talking, staring—didn't seem so foolish in their vanities, their pretensions. They didn't know what was about to happen to them and they were a little happy in their ignorance. All were certain their lifestyle would be drastically changed; many, however, would soon be amazed when they realized how many of the safe, hometown routines could be preserved. But parents, of course, knew that every son was dodging bullets and pungi stakes every day—". . . in the bush. That's what my kid Ronnie calls the front lines. Yeah, he's right up there, right up there! Got a letter just yesterday, says he saw his first dead body!"

Gentlemen, we'll be touching down in Da Nang, Vietnam in about ten minutes. The local time is now two in the afternoon on the twelfth, and the ground temperature is ninety-six degrees with a clear sky. Please extinguish all cigarettes and fasten your seat belts, please. On behalf of the entire crew and staff, I'd like to say we've enjoyed having you with us on World Airways government contract flight Hotel Twenty-Nine, and we hope to see all of you again next year on your way home. Good-bye and good luck.

2 Bravo One-Three

In a branch of the armed forces most conscious of its history and image before the public, 1st Battalion of the Third Marine Regiment is comparatively unknown outside its own ranks. Though consistently manned by a fair share of heroic individuals, the unit has rarely been a headline-maker. But while there was less glory, there is a history. After chasing Dominican rebels and Mexican bandits, One-Three sat out all of World War I and was disbanded in the early 1920s. Twenty years later it was reactivated and bore a major share of the fighting in the Bougainville and Guam campaigns of World War II. During the Korean War the battalion and the entire parent Third Marine Division cruised around the Far East, pulling liberty in Manila and Hong Kong, sailing around the Korean peninsula waiting for an emergency. General MacArthur never called. During the next twelve years the only casualties the battalion sustained were those from brawls in the bars and bordellos of various liberty ports in the Pacific.

Twelve years after the ceasefire in Korea there was a call. President Johnson landed American ground troops at Da Nang, Vietnam on the morning of March 8, 1965. The first ashore were from 3d Battalion 9th Marines and 1st Battalion 3d Marines. In the next four and one-half years, One-Three would see more action than in her previous thirty-four years.

On April 19, 1969, "B" Company, 1st Battalion, 3d Marines was taken off Operation Maine Crag after forty-five consecutive days in the field near the Laotian border, twenty-eight miles south of the Demilitarized Zone. Maine Crag had been embarrassingly fruitless for Bravo Company: only six North Vietnamese soldiers sighted and four killed in those forty-five days. Beyond that action there was nothing but too much boredom, exhaustion, thirst, immersion foot and jungle rot, the painful skin eruptions that fester and never heal in the bush.

During the first week in April the regimental commander had flown out to inspect the fire support base Bravo Company had just built. He was not impressed by the ragged, exhausted appearance of the troops and directed a three-day rehabilitation for the entire Company at the division's in-country R & R center. After a six-hour trip by helicopter, truck, and U.S. Navy river boat, the troops walked onto the white coastal sands at the mouth of the Cua Viet River on the South China Sea. They dropped packs and rifles, and learned to smile and laugh again in the cool surf, cold beer in one hand, steak in the other. And on their third afternoon on the beach, the troops got to see again what a real round-eye looked like when the Division Special Services Office scheduled a show with four real live Australian girls and a band.

> "Wow! Look at them knockers, and that long hair, and can you imagine what it'd be like having them long, long legs wrapped around you, and her working out for all she's worth? Jeez, Man, someday . . . ."

A rehab normally lasts only three days but this one had stretched to ten; plenty of time for the jungle rot to dry out and heal, even enough time to get a suntan. It was definitely over, though. A couple days before, people had begun to sense it in the air. Soon the mutual sensation became a freely-voiced rumor: "Oh, yes Sir, that's straight skinny right from the Colonel's radioman!" But there were really only two things to do until confirmation of the new "operation" came through: drink beer and crash on the beach.

"Operation" is probably the biggest misnomer of all. There is nothing antiseptic, nothing surgically precise about a search and destroy sweep, nothing predictable like some anatomical structure or disorder. They usually start on the designated "H-hour" as planned, but thereafter blunder on, in something closer to chaos than plan, to either a bloody climax or a quiet and uneventful conclusion. And there are days on which the worst enemies of an American field unit are exhaustion, stupidity, and the shortsightedness of its own leaders and troops.

In any event, every operation begins with an "Op Order," an officiously-worded document of some forty-two or seventy-seven or one hundred nine typed pages of intelligence estimates, logistics appendices, and tactical concepts. The best reading is usually found in the paragraph labeled "Mission." Here the general's wordsmiths go all out to inject the fighting spirit into the lower-echelon commanders: "1st Battalion (Reinforced) will, on order, occupy and defend designated objectives in the assigned Tactical Area of Responsibility, and thereafter, by the maximum use of supporting arms and aggressive patrolling techniques . . . ." Such blushing prose always provides a short respite from the boredom and nagging fear in war. "Make sure your troops run aggressive patrols now, not just them regular old SOP jobs—Ha!"

On the afternoon of April 27, 1969, the company commander and four platoon commanders of Bravo One-Three were sitting in their tent on the beach, drinking beer and looking over the newest operation order. Here was the final word, the dreaded confirmation of the dreaded rumor. It was to be called Operation Virginia Ridge and it would start at six in the morning the day after tomorrow. Participating units would be the 1st and 2d battalions of the 3d Marine Regiment and the 37th ARVN Ranger Battalion. "Well, at least they didn't name the damn op after the general's wife's parakeet."

"Yeah, looks like it's in a pretty good area, too . . . about twenty miles west of here . . . Be sure and tell your people to get rid of their beer tonight, we don't want to give any of it back."

Each man could feel this fat document burn a little in his hands as it was read, passed around, discussed. A whole new series of unexpected incidents would be faced in the next few weeks, and since war rarely duplicated its tangled challenges, past experience was not an infallible guide. New decisions with new consequences would have to be made. The responsibility for timely decisions and for life itself was underlined, renewed. But to other people this document meant other things.

Here in this op order was the unpublicized counter to the highly publicized *esprit de corps* of the United States Marine Corps. It was the ages-old animosity between front-line infantrymen and the staff and support personnel farther back—the "pogues," those "rear-echelon motherfuckers!" Those who wrote the op orders never had to carry them out, never had to walk that little two and a half inches on the map that turned into a man-killing three thousand two hundred meters on the ground, the 3200 meters on a flat piece of colored paper on a flat table that grew into five thousand meters up hills and down streambeds. And no matter how hard they tried to send out the needed water and C-rations and mail and new socks, if it didn't get off the landing zone and out to the companies in the bush today, well that's okay, the rear pogues still got to sleep on their Stateside mattresses after seeing a movie every night or a live USO show twice a week. But that wasn't all they had back there in the rear. On top of all those bennies they had ice cream and ice-cold beer! Quite naturally the sentiment was: "Them turds in the rear ain't worth a flying fuck, not one of them! If they gotta put down their cold beer for five minutes to cut somebody a hus they won't do it. Shit-worthless pogues!"

Anyway, with this operation order printed and distributed, the staff horses' work was largely finished. Now it was time for the privates first class and the sergeants, the lieutenants and the corporals to take over, to conduct those "aggressive" patrols, to "seek out, close with and destroy the enemy by all available means," which means anything from a Phantom jet to a knuckle sandwich.

After ten days at Cua Viet, Bravo Company was in pretty good shape. Defective weapons, toothaches, broken eyeglasses, jungle rot, and empty stomachs had all been taken care of. And the troops were hung over. About the only remaining need was that for willing women, and there wasn't much anybody could do about that one, not even the general. There had been the boom-boom girls from Cua Viet Village hanging around the perimeter wire, but if anyone ever touched one it was a guaranteed case of the clap. So that craving had to be set aside until R & R or rotation back home. But no matter how suntanned and satisfied the grunts were now they would still have been in pretty fair shape as a combat unit without the rehab, for they had one advantage no NVA company could draw on. Bravo Company had Captain Gerald H. Samson.

In the vocabulary of the grunt there is one word that indicates an individual's worth in the bush, in war. If someone is "gungi," he's all right, it's good to have him on our side, he's afraid of nothing, he never gets tired, he can be counted on to help in any tight situation, and he's probably a little crazy. The gungi individual also likes to kill a little more than is necessary. Most of his troopers honestly believed that if the President would let him, Sam would take his Company into Hanoi, capture the city and take Ho Chi Minh prisoner. That's gungi.

There was no sense in even trying to describe anybody as being gungier than Captain Sam—the person just didn't exist. No one could hump faster, no one knew tactics better, no one had more discipline or deeper respect for the concept of duty, and not very many others liked to kill VC and NVA as much as Sam. There were even rumors that he had killed some prisoners a few months before in a manner less than humane, but what the hell, they were only rumors and they were only "gooks." The story only added confirmation to his reputation. He was paid as a captain, but all knew that Sam held the permanent rank of Gungi Mother Supreme.

Sam was a full-blooded Lumbe Indian, born in the small Indian town of Pembroke, North Carolina. The grunts accepted that as the reason he was so crazy, so quiet, so humorless. "Ah shit, you never can tell what them Indians are thinking." He had been in the Marine Corps fifteen years. It usually takes only thirty months to make the rank of captain, so fifteen years made Sam a "mustang," an enlisted man who was offered a commission because of his demonstrated leadership and military knowledge. Captain Sam was feared and hated, but he was also obeyed and followed. He was the kind of leader who could make the grunts do what they had to do to go home alive. For those who met, worked with, and left Sam in war, it was impossible to imagine him in any other environment. He seemed born to it and for it. War allowed him expression and he performed the master.

Bravo Company had someone else at the start of this new op too, but someone looked on as more a source of entertainment than an asset: a new second lieutenant. Carl Andrews turned out to be one of those faceless individuals of the population the military has a way of bringing out of the shadows and building into something at least a little useful.

Andrews had first come to the attention of the grunts because he was the newest arrival—a "newby"—which meant he couldn't really lead or command anyone without at least hearing some war stories from the PFCs and corporals, without asking the lower rankers, the ones who called themselves "us peons," what to do in this or that situation. But shortly after his arrival at Cua Viet, still before his name was known to all, Andrews was noted for another reason, one which marked him apart from other newby junior officers: not only did he not have to be here in the bush with Bravo, Andrews didn't even have to be in the Marines or any other component of the military.

Before he joined the Corps, Andrews had a completely safe job in the World. He was a teacher and as such, exempt from the draft. But, bored after two years and curious about what war was really like, he volunteered for the only one going at the time. Though many of them had done the same thing, the troops who later got word of Andrews' story found it incredible, and were not notably reluctant to tell him so. "You mean, Sir, you was a teacher in the World looking at all that young ass in them miniskirts all day long, and you quit to join the Green Machine? Excuse me, Sir, but with all due respect, your mother raised a fool!"

One year after his enlistment Andrews was in Vietnam but with a rear-echelon unit as an administrative officer. Following a six month wait that seemed more like six years, he was walking across the white sandy beaches of Cua Viet, looking for the Bravo Company post.

"Bravo? Yeah, they're over that way, second row, fourth tent. You'll see the guidon stuck in the sand."

Andrews found the company pennant, walked up to the tent

behind it and parted the entrance flap. He saw eight men sitting on cots and heard one voice. Captain Samson was lying on his back, a shaving mirror propped on the dark green undershirt covering his chest. He squinted into the glass, thrust his jaw forward, twisted his mouth off to one side and with a pair of huge scissors cut away the hairs that contributed nothing to the striking appearance of his mustache. While he did that he talked out of the free corner of his mouth.

"I distinctly remember telling you people last night I wanted all the ammo policed up and put in boxes and labeled by platoons and squads, and then put it all in an empty tent down across from third platoon. Then I go out and check it this morning and I find out it ain't been done. And I find a squad leader who says he never even heard nothing about policing up no ammo and his squad's all out swimming so it'd be a couple of hours before he could get it done. Now I thought I made it clear it's important we get that ammo all collected in one place under guard so we don't have nobody getting killed by no accidental discharges while they're supposed to be relaxing here, and we don't have nobody getting fragged, and none of that race riot shit."

The Captain was not screaming. His voice was very low-pitched, slow-paced, sonorous. It was a voice more appropriate to tired and bored travelers discussing the weather in a small-town bus terminal. One could almost fall asleep listening to it. But that wasn't quite right really, for Andrews noticed that when this man behind the dark complexion and the laser-beam eyes spoke, the other seven men listened. And most of these men in the tent were large men, men of proven strength and leadership ability. Before today he had expected rifle company commanders to have profane, booming voices. Another misconception brought from the World.

"Now that's the kind of shit, gentlemen, that don't get it in this here Company. When I pass the word and every one of you there says you understand, I expect things to get expedited, and right. Now if you can't expedite things around here like they should, just let me know and I'll tell the Colonel and we'll have somebody else out here doing it right and you can go on back to the rear with the pogues in the club. If that's the way you want it, that is."

The new lieutenant heard that voice two more times on his first day with the Company. The next time was in the late afternoon, just before a pair of leggy and busty Australians teased the troops with mini-skirts, a few kisses, and songs about home at the weekly USO show on the beach. It was a briefing by the Captain on the Company and the character of the platoon Andrews would be assigned to lead. It was all part of Sam's show for newbys and it came off beautifully. He was glad to get another volunteer for the bush but he couldn't show any warmth or humor, couldn't give any indication that the next few months would resemble anything pleasant. The exterior had to be cold and hard to insure that these soft-skinned college kids they were giving commissions to nowadays wouldn't get too uppity in the near future. "Understand you been in the rear for awhile."

"Yessir. Everyone got a platoon as soon as we got over except me."

"You out here cuz you want to be?"

"Oh yes, Sir, I really do want it."

"Well, that's okay but don't look for any skating job out here—we're all pretty tight cuz we have to be. Okay, you're going to third platoon. Get to know your platoon sergeant and squad leaders these next few days, and you can learn a lot from these PFCs we got here too, but don't let them get the idea they're running that show there. Some of them get pretty damn salty after they been here a few months. You got a lot to unlearn and a lot to learn. And I know the crazy fucking ideas some of you hotshots come over here with but you can forget about pulling any crazy crap just to get the big medal. Don't look for any free Bronze and Silver Stars—there's none of that end-of-tour shit here as long as I got this Company. We got more than our share of medals here. You talk around to some of the troops and you'll find every one of them was earned. Okay, go on over to your platoon now. Third tent over."

The last time Andrews heard the voice on that first day with Bravo was that night in the staff and officers' tent. The beer had been flowing freely and Captain Samson was holding forth on one of his favorite topics, the inevitability of the next war. "What do you mean 'if' there's another war? Shit, you know there's gonna be one—just look at history. It averages out to every fifteen years there's a war. And just look at these so-called 'statesmen' we got now. Shit—Russians telling us to get screwed, us telling China to get screwed, all these petty-ass dictators in these new countries always fighting and trying to buy up our planes and tanks and ships, and look at the Arabs and Jews. There's gotta be another war. Just look at history—every fifteen years!" This first day with Captain Sam and Bravo One-Three would be one of those in his life Andrews would never have any trouble remembering.

In the early afternoon of April 29, Captain Sam put his Company back on the Navy river launch and started back up the Cua Viet River to Dong Ha. There the Company boarded trucks and were taken down Route Nine. They spent the night in an open grassy field seventeen miles west of Dong Ha and two miles east of the artillery base at the Rockpile.

Bravo was up and on the move by five the next morning; one hundred forty-seven Americans were moving, in most cases reluctantly, back to the reality of being grunts. The life of a grunt in Vietnam was not noteworthy for its variety of experience. There was heat, thirst, walking, boredom, fear, blood and death; a succession of events only rarely broken by things pleasant—beer and letters. One part of that reality would, in the next few days, be much more conspicuous than the others—the humping over hills and through all kinds of vegetation with anywhere from thirty-five to seventy pounds on one's back.

This first day's hump was to be of moderate length, 6000 meters, or six "clicks," and there was a road most of the way so it should have been easy, a skate. But since it was Bravo's first hump after 108 cases of beer, 750 steaks, and ten days of slack during the rehab on the coast, it turned out to be an "ass-kicker." The Company had to stop twice and send its corpsmen up and down the column to pop the pills—give out salt tablets. By eleven they were at the objective, Fire Support Base Pete. The rehab and the bennies were all sweated and vomited out now, parts of the irretrievable past. FSB Pete had been occupied and abandoned by another unit about a month before, so all that had to be done to prepare the defenses of the hill was clean the C-ration cans and other junk out of the incoming holes on the perimeter. Digging into the earth of Vietnam was rarely this easy.

At one in the afternoon the maddening reality that was the "combat situation in Eye Corps Tactical Zone" began to make itself felt on the grunts of Bravo One-Three when Captain Sam called his platoon commanders up to the top of Pete. "Battalion just called up and changed the word. We gotta move again today. We got three choppers coming in a half hour so break your people down into heli-teams and have them standing by all packed and ready to go. We'll be lifted about eight or nine clicks, then we link up with the ARVN and Two-Three and hump a couple clicks before we set in for the night. I'll call you back when the birds are on the way. Yeah, I thought we was gonna stay here for awhile too, but they say this here stop was just to get us in position for the start of the op."

So the lieutenants went back and told the sergeants, who bitched about the word change, and the sergeants went back and told the corporals, who bitched about the word change, and the corporals went down to the foxholes and told the privates and lance corporals, who bitched about the word change, and then everybody packed up and sat down in the holes and grass around the landing zone to wait for the choppers and bitch some more about the word change. After the word change had circulated around the hill, another circulated in its wake. It was the common reaction among marines to all abrupt direction changes: "Eat the apple, fuck the Corps."

This would be Bravo's first heli-lift in over four months. That fact alone should have provoked some optimism, maybe even a little excitement—the heavies and pogues in the rear were actually doing something to help the grunts out of a nine-click hump, and maybe things would be different from now on, maybe there wouldn't be so much senseless walking all the time and everywhere. Maybe the Corps would start heli-lifting the grunts everywhere—like the Army. "Them Army guys know how to do it—they ride whenever they go someplace—none of this humping shit!" But these were marines on FSB Pete and so they brought the marines' cynicism to the situation: "Don't hold your breath waiting for that, they'll find some way to fuck us over. Just watch."

After the morning's move the rest of the day could hardly be viewed with anything akin to optimism. In the morning the grunts had been reminded what a dull, hot, one-step-at-a-time thing an operation was. Waiting faces showed the deep resignation of "goddam, here we go again—back to the same old shit!" There would have to be at least this one more op before R & R, before rotation back to the World, before—Ha!—the war would end. No one was actually tired from the morning hump, but no unnecessary moves were being made while waiting around the landing zone. Packs are always heavy at the start of an op, and strength would be needed for the afternoon. The hills get steeper farther west and that's where Virginia Ridge was. The squinting grunts sat down and leaned on each other back-to-back, staring off into the green and blue hills, the hills beginning to quiver in the early afternoon heat. Conversation was stripped to the minimum, but there was still room for the black humor produced by every generation going to war: "You know, Lieutenant, if I get wounded on this one it'll be bad enough, you know, Ma crying and the whole bad scene. But if I get killed I'll really be pissed!" And on the other side of the LZ:

> "Nine times, I had it nine times," says one grinning trooper.
>
> "Bull."
>
> "Yeah, you talk to the corpsman, he's got my book. It's all there, clap, nine times!"

The quiet ones were the newbys. They studied the veterans, strained to catch every comment, eager to see what they should be doing now, what they should seem to be thinking on the eve of this big First Time in the Bush Against the Enemy. They were a little elated over the prospect of being soon baptized in fire, but what they heard was not quite what they had expected men on the eve of battle would be saying. "I know I'm gonna get it, Man, it's just a matter of time, you know? But just before it happens I'd like to have that Raquel Welch drop her pants and sit square on my face—just once, Man, just once."

And elsewhere, "You know, Behl, I swear you stink more every day I know you."

"That ain't me, that's my ear."

"Your ear? What do you mean your ear?"

"That's the ear I got off the first gook I killed back on Taylor Common, down south."

"You mean you been carrying that fucking thing since Taylor Common, four months ago? What the hell you trying to prove?"

"Fucking A I still carry it. I ain't trying to prove nothing. I just like it. He was my first gook. I got a picture of his girl, too."

"You're fucking sick, Behl. The Nam's getting to you. And don't expect me to share no foxhole with you long as you keep that rotten ear. You're sick, Behl."

"You think I'm sick, huh? You wait'll you been here eight and a half months. You just wait."

At still another place on the hill, Gunnery Sergeant Herman Randall broke the hot silence surrounding the new and pensive Lieutenant Andrews. "Yeah, Lieutenant, don't worry about that round with your name on it. There's nothing you can do about that one. Just watch out for all those ones marked 'To whom it may concern!' "

Soon three black specks could be made out against the clear blue sky; the telltale whump-whump sound followed. Faces lifted to the west to judge how much longer they could remain seated in their patch of shade. The old familiar rubbery feeling, as before the big game—how many seasons ago?—came to legs and shoulders, senses sharpened. Here and there troops gulped down the last of a can of peaches or pineapple chunks, issued a few "oh shits" to no one in particular, and put on their helmets. The choppers moved into descending circles; the whump-whump became clearer, loud, deafening. One at a time they touched down and lowered their ramps.

Fifteen troops grabbed the pack of the man in front, leaned forward and fought through the stinging tornado of dust and rocks raised by the bird's twin rotors. They kneeled inside the cigar-shaped fuselage, holding onto cargo netting and each other as the bird lifted and leaned to the northeast. Up 500, 1000, 2000 feet and one's outlook on the world and the war underwent a dramatic improvement: the heat was gone. This beautiful, beloved, vibrating chopper had lifted the grunts away from the heat. They looked at each other, gazed out the windows and side-hatches, closed their eyes and smiled as the cool gusts whipped through the chopper's insides, down under pack straps and flak jackets, up pant legs into crotches and armpits and ears. "Shit, this Vietnam place ain't so bad. I could probably hump six, eight more clicks today."

From a time of gnawing thirst and anger at a change in plans, the grunts had been moved into a time and place of something near ecstasy by this beautiful green helicopter. But the grunts were now having one of the larger, more cruel jokes of life and war played on them. Soon the chopper would drop back down into the green and the heat, and they would see how life in the bush could be spectacular one day, stupifying the next. For the next four days it would be mostly the latter. In another day, the rehab at Cua Viet would seem a year-ago thing; in two days it would be a decade ago; in four days it would seem so far in the past there would be little sense in even saying it ever happened.

The choppers circled, one began to fall away from the others and the grunts came alive, got ready to jump off the ramp and run. When the bird was still a few hundred feet over the landing zone the grunts' senses were raised to another level of acuity by a sharp sound, familiar but unwelcome, cutting through the whump-whump and rattle of the big green bird. It was the sharp crack and whine of American and North Vietnamese rifles assaulting each other, answering each other. There was nothing superfluous in the deadly, metallic conversation. There was a second of silence, then a burst of a dozen shots, signifying that helmets and uniforms had been discerned from the green of everything, then an answering burst from the discovered, and the cycle repeated itself. Fear and anxiety ended the coolness of the heli-lift.

The birds dropped fast, jamming stomachs up into lungs, banged down on the lip of a thousand pound bomb crater. The grunts stumbled out, leaned away from the filthy prop-wash and lunged for the nearest green they could find. They felt much too exposed, naked. But as the chopper lifted away, taking its screeching and whumping sound up and back to the southwest, the crack and whine seemed farther away. Too far away to push one flat against the earth.

"Anybody know who's catching it over there?"

"The Lieutenant says it's the ARVN got some NVA trapped over that next ridge."

"Get some, ARVN, get some so we won't have to do it tomorrow, baby."

The birds came back again and again, dropped the rest of the grunts on the bomb crater, lifted and headed back home. At two in the afternoon of April 30, Bravo Company was in position to begin assaulting the string of objectives. The operation was no longer the generals' or the colonels'. It now belonged to the captains and corporals, the PFCs and lieutenants. Virginia Ridge was heating up.

It was easy going at first. There was a long downhill slope and then a stream, which meant a cooling dip and a long drink, authorized or not, before starting up the other side. Most important for the moment, the grunts could see where they were going.

"You mean it's that hill over there, the bald mother?"

"Yeah, the Lieutenant says that's the one. Hell, this ain't been a bad day. Now if them gooks just don't chase them NVA up there tonight we'll be okay."

These were the things that made thirteen months in the Nam bearable—a stream and a drink just ahead, the objective within sight and maybe only a click away, a letter on the way from the girl, R & R only a month away, the bennies strung out along the way, breaking up thirteen months into chunks of weeks and days.

"Yeah, this is going okay. Kind of pretty scenery, too. No 'Get Right With God' or 'See Rock City' signs around here either."

The one hundred forty-seven grunts of Bravo inched down off the first slope of the afternoon in single file, down toward the flat grassy plain with its refreshing wet "blue line" in the middle. As the lead elements reached it, Sam came in on the radio.

"This is Six! Tell your people they can stop at this here blue line, but to fill only two canteens, then move on across, expedite that thing down there. We gotta get up this here objective quick."

So they stopped, scooped helmetsful of the warm brown water over their heads, gulped handsful, filled canteens, and moved on and up. Now a pair of choppers appeared overhead, both small "hueys," not the troop carriers. One swooped in low over the stream area in a back-and-forth pattern, north to south, east to west. The second stayed up higher. It was the Battalion Commander and the Commander of the 37th ARVN Rangers, the unit supposedly doing the firing half an hour before. The heavies didn't come out to offer anybody another rehab. They came to make sure the operation got off to the best possible start.

"This is Six! That's the big man up there and he says he sees too many people bunched up down around that blue line. Get them spread out and down outa sight when they're not moving."

The column inched on up the hill. The remaining grunts were thinned out around the stream but the man in the circling bird still wasn't satisfied.

"This is Six! The big man is still seeing a cluster-screw. I told you to expedite that thing down there. Now get them damn people up off their asses and either moving or spread out. I better not hear any more today about any bunching up!"

Now the Colonel had aroused Sam, touched close to his pride in himself, his pride that his Bravo Company was not just another bunch of ground-pounders who had no discipline, who would bunch it up and just shoot the shit when there was a hump to complete through enemy territory, a firefight to find, a war to be won. Sam was bitching and the heat was rising; it might not turn out to be such a good day after all.

It took an hour to get everybody up that hill. It had been "prepped," prepared by bombardment, an hour before by Navy jets, so there was no tangled vegetation, no "wait-a-minute" vines to hack through with a dull machete, but the air was still heavy with the nauseous fumes of napalm. The only opposition was from the heat, the grade of the slope, and the weight of a pack and ammunition belt. No NVA today. During that hour the heat started to get to Bravo. There were three heat casualties—three dizzy, flushed and dry bodies with arm and leg muscles twitching. One of the three was Gunny Randall. He made an impression on the troops who saw him lying there panting in short gasps much more lasting than that made by his 260 pounds in the dirt of the hillside. Gunny was not "short in the Nam" but he was definitely "short in the machine," having only nineteen more months to go before his twenty-year career as a marine was completed. Then he would go back home to Maine where, as he did not hesitate to tell it, "I'll have my hands full—a fishing pole in my left and my right hand taking that retirement check from the mailman." All the grunts knew he had seen a lot of shit in Korea; they figured anybody who had done almost eighteen years on active duty and had walked out of the Chosin Reservoir—"frozen Chosin"—could take a breather now and then. "How about a swig or a piece of gum, Gunny?" On top at last, the grunts could look down to see the hill now.

"This is Six! Put your people down in the shade and outa sight for awhile, over."

"Interrogative, Six: Is this pause permanent?"

"That's a negative! I'll let you know when we're moving again."

They couldn't stay—this wasn't the last objective of the day—it wasn't over yet. The bennies were melting away in the heat—the sweet, sweet bennies. Bravo hadn't humped enough today to satisfy somebody.

How does a person tell someone over and over that the word has been changed, the word has been changed? "What do you mean we ain't staying here—what are you passing that bum word for?"

"You heard it—they changed the word again."

"Well, just how fucking far we gotta hump today, anyway?"

"I don't know, but you better get some shade now while you got the chance."

Two minutes later the words most hated by the grunts were passed around the hill: "Saddle up, we're moving out. Pass it on."

So the grunts moved on but this time they were without the thing that was essential to sustain a tolerance of the Nam—they didn't know where they were going anymore.

"Hey, how come we couldn't stay on that hill back there, how come we gotta leave?"

"I don't know. I guess the dart didn't land on that hill, that's why."

"What dart?"

"Them fucking heavies back in their air-conditioned bunkers at Quang Tri just sit there drinking beer and throwing darts at the map. That's how they decide where we're going, Studly."

"Oh, yeah? My old man would never believe this shit, never."

Sanity was becoming a thing of degrees. The bigness, the infinity of a wide-open landscape, the sense of utter freedom in moving in this space loosely bounded by blue-white sky and green-red earth was leaving. The farther the grunts humped the smaller it all became. The world was taking on the smallness, the heavy limitations of an asylum. Under the heat the mind started to wander easily, began bouncing freely between fantasy and reality.

If you lived in Arlington you'd be home by now. Nevah hoppen, GI. Here's the church and here's the steeple open the doors and here's the gooks. Spare the rod and spoil the child. Spoil the rod and spare the child. Spoil the spare and rod the child. Step right up and win a nice tall glass of cold . . . If you saw a waiter in half you'll find old menus, broken china, tips, pencil stubs . . . .

"Christ—talk about busting heavies . . . ."

Amelia Earhart lives. Pigs can fly too and through rain with goggles on. Body count wart count who gives a flying fuck count. We must recognize that the grotesque is commonplace and the commonplace grotesque . . . .

"This is Six! I'm hearing too much talking and noise back there—get them quiet and keep them spread out, over."

"Why the fuck don't he tell me something important? Something like, tonight half the stars in the sky will be hung upside-down? Something important for a change. Spread it out—I'll spread it the fuck out, all the way back to the goddam World."

Whatever you do don't be a wallflower at an orgy. In sickness and in health til death do us a job with liberty and defecation for all. Yippy skippy fuck. No wonder then that in a recent poll only fifteen percent of American Indians sampled wanted the U.S. to get out of Vietnam while over eighty percent wanted it to get out of America. Oh, the world's too wonderful for anybody in it to be this tired, this pissed off. What's it like to be drunk for ten years, Swifty? Jesus take my hand and lead me through. Jesus, let go of my hand you slimey puke. Winter uniforms will be worn as of Wednesday at 0600. All personnel are advised to be prepared for the change . . . .

It just went on and on with no regard for logic, with the sun getting low. "Six, this is One. Be informed we gotta heat casualty up here, a real one, over."

"What do you mean heat casualty? Who says he's a heat casualty? You gotta doc up there? Get the guy's temperature."

"We got it. It's one-oh-four plus and he's unconscious and hot and dry, over."

"Well, leave a couple troops back to cool him off and go on ahead, we ain't got much time left, you know."

"Roger that, Six, but the doc says he's in pretty bad shape. I'm right here with him and he's gonna need some help."

"Well goddammit to hell! Okay, bring him back here and all of your people. It's getting kind of dark anyway, but we ain't calling in no medevac bird to tell the little guys and the world where we are, you got it?"

They were stopping for the night, actually ending the endless. Grateful wasn't the word for the general reaction. Captain Sam was alone with his reaction.

> "Goddam heat casualties—they just think they're tired. I don't know where they find these non-hacking bastards they're sending over here lately. They don't learn discipline no more—can't push themselves a little. Then when they get zapped their damn old ladies want to know how I got them killed. That's right, they think I'm the one gets their kids killed!"

First Platoon came back from their point position with the heat casualty and Sam pointed out in the dusk where he wanted the defensive perimeter set for the night. A dozen yards away from Sam, the new Lieutenant Andrews lay back on muscles that had never been so sore, staring at a deep, dark sky. He was thinking how a few weeks before at this time of night he was sitting in a club in the rear, soaking up a cold beer. Back then he would sometimes hear the drone overhead of the old converted Air Force DC-3s—"Puff the Magic Dragon"—and the muffled staccato of their guns answering the call of a unit in trouble somewhere. He would join the handful who ambled out to watch it. "Anybody want to watch them get some?" They would sit on top of a bunker or climb one of the sentry towers around the perimeter and watch and listen through eyes and ears fuzzy with beer.

The scene, though witnessed dozens of times, was never less than incongruous—with a cold beer in hand, transistor radio on a sandbag whispering the latest Stateside tunes, they watched a battle at midnight less than two miles away, watched the area framed by red tracers where men worked and died to the accompaniment of sounds which at that very moment were provoking bodies to the boogaloo back in Frisco and Denver, Philly and Dallas. Andrews had seen the same bizarre quality of this war only once again since leaving the rear—when he joined the Company at Cua Viet. Two miles offshore a cruiser and two destroyers boomed their ordnance into the DMZ while fifty feet in front of him young Americans swam and got drunk in the sun. But there was none of that whacky incongruity left now. It was all hard, steel gray reality. And there was no beer to fuzz over the sensation of it.

Back in the rear, before being sent out to the field, the young troops just in from the States are full of questions about what it's really like out in the bush. "How bad's the humping and the heat?" Now, few questions and no naivete remained. Until this day they had seen adversity and suffering at a safe insulated distance—through the television tube. Now it was all very close, very much in focus. There would be no drinking fountain down the hall, no cool shower followed by liberty call, no warm girl after the ordeal. The many days of longing to return to the World with its empty, acquisitive lifestyle—empty but safe—began. Mercifully, no enemy came out of the night.

3 May Day

Up from a drugging called sleep. The parade resumed before there was any sun to burn off the dew on the elephant grass; fog held the draws and valleys. The day was May first; the Russians were putting on a parade, too. They would show the world their latest tanks and missiles. All Bravo Company would show would be a lot of guts and a lot of heat casualties. At least it was still cool. Forty-five minutes later dawn came across the lush and placid hills and valleys. For a few minutes it was easy to forget that so brutal and unbeautiful a process as war was being played on this same stage.

The grunts pushed on. They rounded corners in the terrain and vegetation, grunted up rises and hills, stumbled, fell and rolled down rises and hills, tearing trousers, slashing arms and legs. They stumbled into occasional clearings after hacking and swearing at the stubborn growth, but still it was there. That sun rode the sky as if it had always been there, on top of everything, as if it had never been night; it resented anyone daring to move when it ruled above.

The grunts were no longer in a geographical place named Vietnam. They were in a box full of adversity and suffering, all the things one could think of to complete the old phrase, "anything but that." But this box had no limits—they would walk but they would never reach the other side, the end. Now, in their exhaustion, the grunts were little men—tiny pieces of life plodding numbly through something that was anti-life, bouncing off each other, too tired to bitch and curse each other anymore, wanting to live a little longer, long enough to reach the other side of the suffering-box they were trapped in. The grunts were no longer young bodies carrying young attitudes. They were now the young newly made old; bodies carrying their own corpses of youth. Each had his very own corpse to carry and his very own Dachau or Buchenwald to endure under his jouncing, clanging, oven of a helmet-hell. There was no alternative to living it through, no alternative to pushing one's body, mind and the nostalgic mix of sunny yesterdays and plans made for bright tomorrows back in the World through this limitless hell, no alternative to watching and feeling this battering and erosion, this early aging.

Because of the previous day, the one hundred forty-seven bodies now carried too little salt, too little water, and too many torn muscles. And they didn't even have an idea where this day's objective was. The day before they had been told which of the hills they faced would be the last until the following day. They had been deceived then, with the word being changed twice, but at least for much of the day there had been something to look at and think, that's it, there's the one. But not this day.

"Hey, Tripper, is that our hill?"

"I don't know, George."

"Which one is it? How the fuck far we going today, anyway?"

"I told you, I don't know. I don't even think nobody—not even Sam—knows. Just keep following that dude in front of you there. We'll make it."

"How in the fuck can nobody know. I mean somebody's gotta know, don't they? I mean there's gotta be at least one dude somewhere that knows, don't there?"

"I don't know, George. I don't know."

A new level of pain would be reached and explored this day. At first only a few noticed it but by noon something physical was felt by all. After several hours in the rising morning heat, the hands and feet were no longer sweating. Some would of course last longer than others, but the thing was becoming undeniable: dehydration was setting into these one hundred forty-seven young bodies. The sweat still came out on the forehead, to run down and sting the eyes, but in a few more hours, thighs, chests, and backs would be drained, wrung dry, and more of the priceless water from near-empty canteens would be needed to keep the body temperatures of the flushed and unconscious below the level of death. The heat casualties started falling much earlier, fantasy wedged into minds much earlier.

I wonder if the gooks we're chasing get combat pay like us or maybe the birds get it . . . Whom the gods would destroy they first make Marines . . . You don't want to shoot me gook cuz if you kill me I'll be pissed off and so will Mom and Dad and all the guys I should be getting drunk with today instead of humping after your ass, gook . . . Oh, we bomb the grass good we sure do . . . Me a deputy of death—ha! I like flowers in the spring and passionate broads in the dunes . . . .

"This is Six! I can see some of your people and they're all bunched up—now keep them the hell spread out, dammit."

Spread it out, spread it out—that's all he can say anymore. Smitty, spread it out . . . I know I'll impersonate an angel then the Captain can't find my ass to chew next time he gets bored . . . Hey, anybody know the death rate from breast cancer among beagles and bald eagles? . . . What size bras do beagles wear? . . . All the bombs and bullets destroying all the bamboo villages and bamboo people . . . They ought to take all the cash they spend on bombs and subsidize poets and painters . . . There'd be no such thing anymore as a poet being a pauper—never—and it'd be a better project than burning up babies . . . And peace under me peaceful over me peaceful before me peaceful after me peaceful . . . .

"This is Six, we'll be coming up on this objective here pretty soon. Have your people follow second platoon on up and take from four to eight on the perimeter, over."

Now there could be the chance for some shade, something resembling a reward for enduring those last thirty hours. It took an hour for Bravo to get situated on the new hill. The main body was settled in less than fifteen minutes but for almost another hour small groups straggled in, carrying and dragging those claimed by the heat. The first priority on this hill was the clearing of a landing zone. A chopper would then be called in to take out the worst of the heat casualties and the man with the badly sprained ankle. Sam couldn't be slowed down anymore, which meant this hill was not a real objective. Bravo would have to move again in a short while. The questions multiplied; they came to sound more like the pleadings of the condemned.

"How long we gonna stay here?"

"Can we put up shade hooches?"

"How much farther we gotta go today?"

"We gotta get some water pretty soon, Sarge—my squad's down to less than half a canteen a man and them two new guys ain't got any left."

After a rest of thirty minutes, first, second, and weapons platoons went on ahead with Sam to the next hill. Battalion was getting itchy—their sacred time schedule was not being met as the pogues in the air-conditioned bunkers had planned, so Sam would have to take a chance and split his Company. After clearing the LZ and sending the "non-hackers" out on the bird, third platoon would saddle up and rejoin the Company.

When the chopper touched down it discharged the last person in the whole division the grunts expected to see—the battalion Chaplain. Only a very few were glad to see him. Chaplains are considered by most marines to be largely useless appendages on the corpus militaris. They're always acting a little too friendly to be for real, and when the bullets start flying what good is some guy babbling about the *Twenty-Third Psalm?* This day, however, the grunts would change their minds about chaplains, for not only had this one bothered to leave his air-conditioned chapel to come out and try to cheer them up a little, but this member of the general's "God Squad" was actually going to hump with them, share the merciless heat with them.

This second hump of the day proved short, only about 1100 meters, but it cost the grunts dearly in terms of water, endurance and morale. Third platoon, with the Chaplain, started out at 1:30, which meant this move would take them right into the hottest part of a hot day. The major part of the distance was covered in less than an hour; it was downhill and the trail had already been cut by Sam and the others. Only two stops had to be made.

Earlier in the morning those who were better disciplined and still clear thinking realized the Company would need a new source of strength, a new source of water. Most of the grunts were down to less than one canteen, and that would not last until the next morning. Finally, American ingenuity had bored through the predicament: why not drink one's sweat instead of wasting it on a bush towel or a sleeve? To those in a "normal" environment, the idea sounds absurd, pathetic, revolting. But to the grunts of Bravo, having their brains baked through on this May Day, the idea of drinking their own bodily secretions was greeted with enthusiasm in most, exhilaration in some. Another trick had been discovered to help them endure the agony of the sun, the agony of a craving which all but a very few Americans need never concern themselves within seven decades of life.

So they wiped their foreheads and licked their fingers. They raised a hand and ran the other up the hairless inside of the forearm, then drank the trickle of sweat that coursed down over the webbing of skin connecting thumb and forefinger. But now, two and three hours after, it didn't seem like such a good idea. The urea, dirty salt and carbon dioxide they took in produced dizziness and nausea in empty stomachs. They had to stop now to vomit, to throw up what could have been eliminated in a more logical manner hours ago. But there was damn little logic left in Bravo Company this afternoon. They kept drinking their sweat, some hoping they could get sick enough to get a medevac bird back to an air-conditioned hospital ward for a couple of days of rest.

After an hour on the move the grunts were at the bottom of the objective hill. They could see the rest of the Company sitting around on top of it. They could also see that it was going to be a bastard to get up—it was steep, at least forty-five degrees, and it was bare of any growth. When those who vomited regained a sense of balance, they stepped out of the shade and started up. A bare dirt path with no jungle to cut through was usually regarded as a benny by the grunts. But on this day the bare hillside acted as a mirror for a garish sun. The earth came to look like a desert, the brightness erasing the reassuring horizon line; thirst and headaches worsened. The grunts leaned into the hill for a step, two, three—and slid back down in the bomb-loosened soil. They tried again and again, clawing, cursing, pleading. If there is a hell, this is what it must be like—scratching up an endless hill bare of life, falling back, scratching and crawling back up a few feet, falling back again. A perpetual exertion with no perception of progress.

> *. . . Sing, vulture, sing your sweet song of death, of relief from all the bullshit of human existence, of muddling on, passing our failure on to each new generation . . . on page four, delete para fifty-six and insert the following in lieu thereof: Fifty units of blood consisting of the following groups and types for the West Pac program . . . PROGRAM! . . . Who the fuck's in charge of the West Pac PROGRAM?? . . . What crooked path of reasoning was followed by what breed of yawning fools to declare an operation to this useless goddam country justifiably necessary . . . I hear the blare of barbaric trumpets, I see bronze rivers lapping marble shores . . . barbaric blaring bronze marbles . . . marble whores on marble shores*

But they made it up the glaring and endless hill, and then they huddled together in clusters of three and four, all trying to crawl under one green bush towel to get out of that sun for a few minutes, seconds. Hands cupped over eyes and ears in disbelief that they were really going through this.

Something about war was becoming very clear now. It was not the drama of one side named Us against the other side, called The Enemy. There was more to it than that. War in the middle of the twentieth century in Vietnam was a constant fight to survive against heat, thirst, poisonous centipedes, endless humps, spreading jungle rot, sunburn, chapped and cracked lips and noses, twisted ankles, dehydration, intricate and constant patterns of pain from joints and muscles, unimagined extremes of boredom and exhaustion, stupid rumors about mad tigers that pounce on inattentive Americans at night, too few letters, too little food and booze and women, too much diarrhea, and too much despair that all this shit would never end, that home would never be seen again. The timeless and varied horrors of war were being freshened up and passed on to the newer, greener generation. "Come on, kid, you can make it."

Even the quiet and strong felt that something should be said and done about these maddening moves that began before there was any light on the day and went on and on with no reward; this humping for what seemed like nothing but the sake of humping. "Sir, I'm not in the habit of bitching or anything, but this crap is kicking my ass."

All but one of the not-so-strong stared blankly at the twitching calf muscles, at the blank, nerveless masks on other faces, at the great green oven that confined them. The one pulled his green undershirt up over his head and babbled to no one and everyone, "I can't go anymore, I can't, I can't—leave me here, go on, go on . . . ."

And now, piling on top of all that, exacerbating all this adversity, came the snap and whine of rifle fire racing through the valleys, across ridgelines and into burning ears. It had a muffled, down-below sound to it. Somebody had caught somebody in a low spot between two hills.

All the platoon commanders rushed up to Captain Sam to see what this latest piece of action was, the one their platoons were now least prepared for. "All right now, loyal lieutenants and staff NCOs, I'm gonna pass these binos around and you look down there to your left front, three fingers to the right of that there light green patch. You'll see dear old dying Delta getting their ass kicked but good!"

The only other rifle fire heard on this new op had been when Americans and ARVN had trapped some NVA between a pair of hills on the first day. Now it was the other way around. One of

Sam's sister companies, Delta, had stumbled into an NVA bunker complex on the ridgeline parallel to Bravo's. The heat had rendered both companies equally unprepared to face enemy fire; something or somebody just decided that on this day it was Delta's turn. Sam provided a tragic running commentary.

"There's three more just went down—three marines that is. Shit, there's whole squads just running around like chickens with their heads cut off . . . don't know where they're going, nobody leading, don't know where the gooks is at. I can't get their captain on the hook . . . must have got him and his radioman both. There's supposed to be fixed wing and artillery on the way but they need something down there to hold them off until it gets here. Nobody's organizing nothin' down there . . . nothing."

Sam took advantage of the scene to make an example: "Take a good look at that crap down there and let it be a lesson to you—That's what happens when a unit loses its head. Look at them taking all them casualties for no damn reason, and only a few on our side shooting back. Can't even hear a friendly machine gun firing at them bunkers, can you?"

"We going down there, Captain?"

"Shit, you know we'll be going down. We're the closest friendly unit."

Sam kept watching the action he longed to join. He studied the terrain between himself and the firefight, turning over in his warrior's mind alternate approaches to the scene and various tactics to use once he got there. But the radio kept its silence through the long minutes. When a call finally came, it proved the greatest possible morale-raiser to the other one hundred forty-six. It was battalion reporting that a re-supply chopper was finally on the way out. While the grunts had waited and huddled under the green bush towels and poncho liners and while they listened to one of their sister companies get shot up, one of the world's few humanitarians in the rear got off his fat ass and loaded up a chopper with not only water but—it shouldn't have been true—mail! There would be relief at last from the sun, and there would be those perfumed pieces of paper called letters—reminders, confirmation that humping and sweating and losing hope were not the only things being done at this time on this planet.

While Sam watched the shooting and the dying, the grunts bent all their attention to their mail. They tore it open and studied over and over the words written by feminine, parental, brotherly, sisterly, or wifely hands. The packages full of Hershey bars and canned hot dogs and peaches and apples and peanuts and homemade cookies and cakes were passed around the hill. The few in each platoon without letters or packages collected and filled all the canteens, first dividing the number of canteens into the number of gallons and quarts in the steel cans, then measuring and pouring the precious liquid as carefully as if it were liquid gold, or radioactive. It came out to one-half canteen per man.

Sam got the call to move about twenty minutes after the water and mail came in, after eight more heat casualties were sent out. The bennies were always temporary. The platoon commanders went up on top for one last look through the binos and to hear the Captain's plan. First platoon would move out first, to act as a reconnaissance element for the rest of the company and to cut a trail. The surprise was not that they were moving but that they were not being sent to link up with and assist Delta Company. Stay on the adjacent ridge, and maintain observation of Delta was the way battalion had put the message.

Lieutenant George Sorenson and his first platoon moved out at ten minutes after three in the afternoon. A meteorologist could prove with his records of hourly and daily temperatures that the sun had now moved west far enough so that the temperature was starting the daily decline that would continue until about three or four the next morning. But exhausted and partially dehydrated grunts could hardly be expected to perceive such changes. To them it was still just plain "hotter than fuck and rising."

Sorenson's people went out "light," which meant they were leaving their new water behind for a couple of hours. The other platoons, never too thrilled about doing the work of others, would bring the five-gallon plastic water bottles onto the new objective later. To psych his men up for this next move, Sorenson told his squad leaders they were being cut a hus by the Captain by being selected to move out first. But as it would turn out, everyone would be equally tired that night, first platoon from hacking a new trail and the others from humping the extra weight of the water bottles. Not only were the bennies always temporary but they were usually exaggerated as well.

Even as first platoon was heading out, few grunts knew there would definitely be another move today. As they read the letters and drank the new water they hoped and begged within their own minds harder than they had ever hoped and begged before that "Yes, we're staying here tonight. He's looking out for us, he'll take care of us. We're staying!" But in no one's mind was there enough hope to crowd out the fear that squad leaders would come around again with the hated "Saddle up!" The uncertainty, the word changes were getting as bad as the thirst.

When it was passed around, the saddle up provoked groans and bitches loud enough to be heard in the next province, and it gave Lance Corporal Bill Finney his first chance to show some initiative; to be heard. Two months before, on his third day in the Company, Finney had written on his helmet something that he hoped would tell the world just who William T. Finney really was; just how gung-ho he was: "Yea, though I walk through the Valley of the Shadow of Death I will fear no evil, cuz I'm the meanest motherfucker in the Valley!"

During the previous two days Finney had wondered about the constant humping and about the incomprehensible mechanism back in the rear that kept producing that one solution to the problem of the war: "Tell Bravo Company to move again." This low-ranking warm body in the hierarchy of the military and of life had reached some conclusions in his thinking and now he wanted to share them with everybody of every nationality within range of his voice.

"Why the fuck we gotta move again? Why the fuck don't we just sit down and let the gooks come to us? You know what them gooks are doing now? Right this fucking minute, Man? Half of them are sitting on a hill watching us and laughing, and the rest of them are blowing fucking Zs in a fucking hammock is what they're doing. That's right. While we bust our ass humping these fucking hills. But that's all right 'cuz we're big tough marines—we can hump all day and fight all night. Then at night when we're tired and blowing Zs they come out and overrun our ass. That's when we find the little bastards—at night—when we ain't ready for them. Not now in the daytime. Real fucking smart. Real unfucking believably smart!"

Oh, how the grunts could swear! The four-letter words came out of the young faces as smoothly as they flowed from a forty-year-old whore's mouth in a Singapore alley. It lost its profanity, even started to sound a little beautiful against the absurdities of the day.

Lance Corporal Finney's brand of analysis was now the norm in the Company. Among the few still capable of building their complaint around logic was the head corpsman of the Company. Doc Sellers intercepted Lieutenant Andrews and issued a reasoned appeal. "Lieutnant, you gotta talk to Six now. These guys can't take this much moving in the heat. Talk to him, will you?"

The Doc could not yet accept the fact that there was no real alternative to the madness of the day, that while there were valid, medically sound reasons to say no to the latest order, the move had to be made. "Well that's it—I'm gonna just tell Six we ain't going anywhere for a couple days. Battalion can go fuck themselves—court-martial me. I give a shit now." Sellers walked up to the top of the hill, stood next to Sam and looked down in the direction of the firefight, the dying, for several long seconds. Without saying a word, he turned and walked back down the hill.

Now it was back to the bush, back to licking sweat off arms, sucking buttons, back to trying to hold onto consciousness.

. . . There's a left-handed banana tree over there Gunny. The Defense Department says thirty-one percent of all military personnel wear glasses, and everybody else would

rather wear bell-bottoms and Afros. How's the West Pac program now? Tell Ma I'm coming home and Judy Jingleboobs . . . .

Now the grunts were just leaning forward, trying to get a leg and foot out in front before they fell. There was no sense in thinking about how one got into this activity and how and when one would get out of it. Time no longer figured in the equation of it all. Every grunt, every man everywhere, was born into this mindless trudging in the heat, and every man everywhere would die still involved in it. Dreams were illusions, one's last day in Vietnam was an illusion, ambitions and plans to pursue back in the World were illusions, so why make up any more? All the grunts really had out here in the hot green maze was a sense of mutual dependence, of belonging to the next few minutes of each other's lives.

The television generation was getting its view of the world smashed today. From the boob tube they had learned that for every problem there is a simple, instant solution. With the right pill you can banish acid indigestion or the aches and pains of fatigue. With the right deodorant, one need never fear social ostracism or unpopularity. And if you're pressed for time, throw in a TV dinner. Here the grunts were, though, faced with a new one that wouldn't go away. They had been gulping water and Kool-Aid and salt tablets, frantic to relieve an agony that defied relief. Slowly the hard reality came through: there was no alternative, no time-out, no falling out from this "field problem." All this would have to be endured—second by second, minute by superheated minute, with no excuses from mother good enough to get one out of it. The grunts were being beaten to a psychological pulp. The dream of returning to the great dreamland America was looking more hopeless every minute.

. . . Please excuse Johnny from dressing for gym today. He has a sore ear and the doctor said . . . Oh Christ, what if the gooks hit us now? Goddam don't let them hit us now! Too quiet here, too quiet, no cheers. The broads in short skirts that ride up their thighs when they jump around are supposed to

be cheering us out here. We're about to score—only a little farther. Nobody to cheer for us out here—nobody to call a foul on the Nam for fouling us like this. The Nam is the biggest goddam foul that ever was. No such place as the World—all a big joke—never going back, it all blew up . . . Think of hearses and milk . . . whores and mist . . . pissed, I'm pissed . . . let us go, Lord, back to driving around to the hamburger joints . . . the Frenchies knew how to fight a war; sent over gallons of wine, clean whores and doctors for them . . . that's the way to do it, but not for us—we're civilized . . . .

The grunts couldn't believe it but two of the five-gallon water bottles second and third platoons were carrying for first sprang leaks during the move. Five gallons of water are heavy, whether one is rested and healthy or exhausted and dehydrated, and so some of the troops had probably helped a sharp branch puncture the plastic bottles. Maybe so, maybe not; anyway the bottles were getting lighter with each step.

. . . Green, green, everywhere green . . . the green of the Nam wears off on humping through the green shit . . . when the green grunts fall down they drop their ketchup bottles and say ouch and get ketchup all over themselves . . . all over the ground and the kitchen floor and the green Nam . . . the redder they get, the redder the ketchup flows and then they don't say ouch any more . . . red on green . . . mothers cry . . . mothers cry . . . fathers ask why . . . fathers ask why . . . .

Bravo came up on the last hill of the day in the final fifteen minutes of daylight. The last two platoons in the column were still moving as dusk turned into darkness and, predictably, contact with them was lost twice. And just as predictably, something else intolerable happened—an accidental discharge. In his exhaustion somebody forgot to put his grenade launcher on "safe." Somebody's finger slipped from trigger guard to trigger, and no pair of ears could miss the deep "thunk" as the grenade left its tube and bored into the dirt an inch away from somebody else's heel. It had not traveled far enough to arm itself so the grenade didn't blow, and the heavies didn't have to try and explain to two more pairs of parents how it was their own sons' stupidity and not a human wave attack by the fanatical NVA that cost them their legs and eyes and sanity. But Sam couldn't be bothered by such elementary screw-ups now. He had to have a meeting before they were too far into the night, before the fog came in to carry their voices farther than they already carried, to plan for tomorrow, for the contact with the enemy his Company would surely face, the combat he longed for, thrived on. The grunts were left to dig in wherever squad leaders thought best.

"I understand the water bottles broke on the way over here. That wasn't too bright, letting them get broke like that. That shit don't go in this Company. First platoon needs their water same as everybody else. They didn't get none from that last bird this afternoon. So, second and third platoons, before you hit the rack tonight you go around to your people and collect some from everybody to give to first. I want that expedited with no noise, and before it gets too dark. And don't let something like this happen again. That should be all I ever have to say on that situation.

"I got a message here for you, second platoon, just come over the battalion net. Some hospital in Mitchell, South Dakota, reports Mrs. Joe Belknap gave birth to a baby boy two days ago. Six pounds, eight ounces, both doing fine. Make sure you tell Belknap tonight right after you go back from here.

"Okay, now I want you to listen to the rest of this good now. I know the troops are tired after these last two days but it might even be worse than that tomorrow. You probably guessed we're going down to where Delta got their ass kicked. I got a call from battalion here a while back telling what their casualties were. They had nine killed down there and eighteen wounded. One of the KIAs was the Company radioman and one of the WIAs was the Company commander. You saw what a cluster-screw that outfit was. It only took ten gooks to fuck that Company up that bad—that's all battalion says there was—ten gooks. That ain't gonna happen to this Company. Tomorrow morning we're gonna sweep that hill and clean out that squad of gooks. Battalion's giving us all day, there won't be anymore of that rush-rush shit for awhile. We're gonna take our time and do it right. This thing's gotta be expedited right so we don't lose nobody for no unnecessary dumbass reason, like Delta did. Now tomorrow morning about seven we'll lead outa here with first platoon, weapons, second and third, down that same finger we just came up. About halfway down . . . ."

So while Captain Sam ended his day by reporting the beginning of life in one country far away and planning the end of life in this one, the platoon sergeants and squad leaders of Bravo ended theirs by crawling around in the night, collecting capfuls of water from everyone to make up for what had been lost on the afternoon hump. First platoon was down to one half canteen for every two men. They would need more than that to be ready for the next day, to do what had to be done, but neither they nor anyone else would get it.

The rest of the grunts ended their day by "lightening" their packs. It was an exercise that had more to do with mental health than weight. They laid out in the darkness everything they carried and picked out what could be left behind. Certain essentials, of course, could not be thrown away—water, food, ammunition. There was something illogical but necessary in all this, for what could be taken out and thrown away weighed only a few ounces while what could not be discarded totaled anywhere between thirty and seventy pounds. Old letters, extra books of matches, odd lengths of rope, pretty stones from the dry streambeds were the things taken out and not re-packed.

Just the act of picking up something and saying to oneself, "I'll never have to carry this again," was a source of considerable relief, something close to exhilaration. It was confirmation that one still retained some say about his future. Sam and the Colonel didn't own every minute of these one hundred twenty-eight lives, not every single last minute. "Do I want to carry these extra bootlaces anymore? Fuck no!" A few grunts held a more liberal interpretation of expendable. Here and there in the darkness a trooper slipped a grenade or a couple of trip flares under a bush or a pile of damp leaves and dirt. His load for tomorrow was now 1.1 pounds lighter. And PFC Behl even got rid of the smelly, shriveled ear of his first victim.

After Sam's meeting, after the water for first platoon had been collected and awarded, one hundred twenty-eight bodies, pushed beyond exhaustion and moved by little more than the inertia of a stubborn pride, lay back on poncho liners on a damp hill. The grunts now had the feeling something had been taken out of them that could not be replaced. Eyes played over the stars and picked out familiar formations, the ones learned in grade school. It was the first time those forms had really been looked at since grade school. There was beauty up there, out there dozens and hundreds of light years away. It was all so clear, so clean—white dots on a blue-black infinity—cleaner than a desert. The mind cleared in the cool night, then embraced peace as fog walked into the draws and valleys, giving the hills ghostly halos.

> . . . Before me peace . . . under me peace . . . over me peace . . . after me, there must be peace . . . do we belong here? . . . we're in harmony with nothing . . . we scar and crater the earth here . . . we enhance nothing . . . in harmony with nothing . . . nothing . . . nothing . . . .

4 The Best Years of His Life

The first thing the grunts noticed about May second was that the sun came up again. To truck driver and scientist alike, "normal" people back in a "normal" world, that development was less than elementary. To brains and perceptual organs that had been folded, spindled, mutilated, and baked for two days it was something to note—this day could easily turn out to be another day of seeing dreams die in the heat waves, of craving what couldn't be had, of putting one foot in front of the other and feeling the squinching shock of tibias crashing against femurs. And added to all of that shit, there would probably be the enemy today. It had all the earmarks of one of those days when the closest thing to local amusement would be watching the attrition of youth.

By seven o'clock Sam had enough daylight to send out his point. The column snaked back down the trail it had cut the night before and made a turn to the right at about two hundred meters. Gradually downhill for three hundred more meters, up a sharp little rise and they were on it, the hill connected with the one where Delta Company had been chewed up the day before. The grunts had a perfect view of the NVA bunker complex, a cluster of a dozen little dirt mounds with eyes; mounds that would have so much to say about the tomorrows of one hundred twenty-eight lives. Sam would leave all his machine guns and mortars here with a reserve force of one platoon to act as a supporting base of fire. It was only nine o'clock in the morning but already the sun and the two previous days were cutting into the one hundred twenty-eight. Eight had to stop and get under some shade before they could go; six finally had to be dragged or carried in by buddies. Two others had slipped on leaves and brush still wet with fog, fallen back down the hill and ripped open arms and thighs on bamboo stalks. But Sam didn't want to hear about heat casualties, sprained ankles and cuts this morning. He sat behind a bush and studied the enemy bunkers through his binos.

> "I don't see no movement down there but that don't mean they're not there still. Then again they might have left last night. I thought I heard some digging a couple times. Anyway, the machine guns will be set up right here where they can see all of them bunkers. We'll lead outa here with first and second platoons. Third'll be the reserve back here around the gun pits. First is gonna go down over that way and on around the back of the hill until they link up with that platoon of Delta's that's waiting there. They'll be the blocking force for second sweeping around the face of the hill and through the bunkers. We want to force them bastards down and out in that clear area right down there. Then the mortars and machine guns will work on them."

It went perfectly, better than an assault staged for the heavies back in the States. Forty minutes after Sam passed the word first platoon was around in position with the platoon from Delta, and second platoon was beginning their sweep. The machine guns rained through the bunker complex. Then the grunts walked through it, rifles on automatic. No enemy appeared. They had left the night before, carrying off their dead and wounded through the draw between the two Marine companies, back to a haven in the north.

Disappointed and angry at the missed chance, Sam called battalion for new orders. Destroy the bunkers and call back when it's done was the new directive. And onto it was added something more obligatory than a direct order, something not to be repeated any more than was necessary. American military units take pride in the tradition that they never leave their own dead and wounded on the field of battle. Yesterday Delta had violated that tradition; six men could not be accounted for after the casualties had been counted and sent back to the rear. Sam and Bravo were told to find the six men, or bodies, before nightfall.

The platoons pulled back, shuffled positions and assignments and waited for Sam's next word. Second and third would blow the bunkers and look for the MIAs. On the fifteen minute move down from the mortar position to join Sam, the third platoon was suddenly hit very hard by the heat, now moving over ninety degrees. Of twenty-three who started out to join the second platoon, only fourteen completed the short move. Several were legitimate heat and exhaustion casualties, doubling over and vomiting salt tablets. But several just doubled over moaning "I can't go on no more, no more . . . ." Their bodies were close enough to dehydration to preclude tears.

Sam had his second and third platoons in position on the north slope of the hill by two in the afternoon. They moved out three minutes later. During an operation like this any one man could hold up the entire formation if he saw something that should be checked out in some detail. Things were bad enough with the heat and the brambly undergrowth, but the stopping, moving and stopping again only compounded the frustration. Each bunker was fired into, then torn apart by hand, then the next and the next.

"Hold it on the right. I said hold it the fuck up dammit, we gotta check one out up here."

"Get down, we're gonna blow it."

"No, don't frag it. You'll hit your own people."

"You gonna blow that thing up there or not?"

"Just kick in the top and sides."

"Well shit, do something dammit, let's get this fucking thing over with."

"Okay, move it out, go ahead. Go on."

Third platoon had fired on and torn up two bunkers and second, farther up the slope, had destroyed three when Carl Andrews stopped the formation. He had come to something at the bottom of the hill in the dry streambed that should be checked out. The glare of a mean sun off white rocks blurred the area until they were only a few feet from it. Scattered over the streambed and up the far slope were eight rifles, two pistols, two corpsmen medical kits, blood-soaked boots, bandages, trousers, shirts, flak jackets, dented and shot-through helmets, and piles of spent cartridge cases. Here was one of the places where the NVA had cleaned up the previous day; one of the places where the Delta grunts had run around like chickens with their heads cut off and paid for it.

Andrews, his radioman, and another grunt walked across the littered area and up another dry streambed. They found and followed a blood trail but it disappeared in the rocks and brush after a few meters. There were no bodies in the area, Vietnamese or American, no sign of any of the shallow graves the NVA dig to confuse the American body counters. Andrews called the information back to Sam and the sweep continued.

The sun slid past three-thirty, three-forty-five, four o'clock and the grunts pushed on. They stumbled and fell ahead through the most maddening mix of "wait-a-minute" vines and elephant grass to be found in all of Southeast Asia. All of it, the worst jungle growth in the Nam was right here on this north slope of this unnamed goddam hill. The whole adverse mass seemed to congeal and produce a swimming-through-water sensation. Another hour and still more heat and it turned the water to oil. Another hour and yet more heat, and the oil became grease—stroking through grease with only fog in view where a destination should have been.

The NVA were right, it was a good place for bunkers and an ambush. This was how Delta had found the enemy the day before. Too tired to lift legs anymore, they had leaned forward and fallen into the tangled vines, stood up and fallen ahead into them again until they were twenty—or maybe only ten feet—away from the barely-visible bunkers. Then the AK-47s came alive, on automatic. They had been close enough for the NVA to watch the young American faces register that ultimate oh-God-no-not-now-not-me surprise, fear, pain, and then the resignation in death. But all of that was yesterday. Today there was everything but the enemy.

Here and there a grunt would fall ahead into the brush and not get up. He just lay there staring and panting into the green viney cage around his head. He would stay down until a buddy came back to lift his arm and remind him he only had 42 or 96 or 173 more days to go and then he would never have to go without a cold drink, never have to walk everywhere he wanted to go. Corporal Randolph J. McAdam, who still had the strength to pick up his buddies and hump on, glanced over at his platoon commander and gave Andrews the most pointed and poignant lesson on The Meaning of War the latter would probably ever get. "Ain't this a hell of a way for a young guy to spend the best years of his life, Lieutenant?"

This day's events now had the effect of confirming in most of the young bodies and minds present that the war was, in fact, a massive intrigue to kill youth, the conspiracy of Things Old and Disappointed to bludgeon the hope and optimism of Earth's newest generation. Corporal McAdam was more right than any statesman in the world today—this was a hell of a way for a guy to spend the best years of his life—a hell of a way. This was not war as it was supposed to be enacted in the twentieth century. These were not scientist-diplomats in white jackets seated in swivel chairs at long consoles of buttons—buttons flashing in different colors, blip-blipping, whining like in the James Bond movies. These were last year's football players, pool-playing dropouts from down the block, drag-racing steelworkers' sons who got their girls in trouble at the drive-in movie on warm summer nights, crew-cut ranchers' sons from Kansas. To stalk the fanatical sons of North Vietnamese rice farmers and brick-makers they had no ICBMs or nerve gas or hydrogen bombs or Distant Early Warning systems; they had a couple of gadgets from the Colt Arms Company of Hartford, Connecticut, and then they had nerve endings and muscles and a few doctrines and reactions learned in training. They had damn little more than George Washington's grunts had.

So now today, May second, nineteen sixty-nine, the Big Day

had finally arrived. Not the day of Armageddon or the Final Judgement but the day young dreams born of young minds—dreams of I-want-to-be-a-cowboy, and success, and not-a-care-in-the-bowl-of-cherries-world—would die. Some monstrous hairy-knuckled hand wielding a knobby club rode down these hot midday rays and battered, bludgeoned into the dirt all the dreams, the ambitions the grunts formulated back at All-American High while they gathered in that high-arching pass and streaked into the end zone to bring the crowd to its feet, while they watched young developing female bodies bounce and sway down the halls, while they heard commencement speakers describe the unlimited opportunities they would face in the next half-dozen decades.

These young bodies were being brutally reminded that they were fallible, they could be made anonymous once again and forever. From now on, cheers would not follow the sweat. Here it was—bam bam whack! Tough shit, kid. Now it looked like one's Freedom Bird would never come. The whole damn planet and all of life looked like a lie now, there would be no end to this shit. The Freedom Bird and the States were all myths. They would never come true. And the myths were the President's gifts to all good grunts in the world; for Christmas, for New Years, for birthdays, for all days. Thanks for signing up anyway, kid. We had no way of knowing it would be all this bad, but thanks anyway—we needed the warm body. Carry on . . . above and beyond the call . . . with complete disregard for his own personal safety . . . carry on, kid.

Then it was over—over for the day that is—and the grunts knew there were no enemy near this hill. "This is Six! Send all your people up on top here to get some shade for awhile, all but a fire team or so, then you and that fire team come back along that streambed once more, see if you can't find them bodies. They gotta be around here somewhere."

So Andrews checked it over again, through the bloody and littered area, up the new trails and dry streambeds, but again there were no bodies to be found. Tomorrow morning six telegrams would have to be sent back to the World telling Mr. and Mrs. Schwartz, Jones, O'Donnell, Camacho, Gianatti, and

Smolinski, that their sons were officially listed as Missing In Action. Six months later more telegrams would be sent out, changing the original message to Missing In Action and Presumed Dead.

The grunts humped onto the hill they had just swept, fell into the small patches of shade under bushes and trees, and got drunk on the idea of resting, of cooling off. Pretty soon Sam called again but it was not the hated saddle up order. Delta Company had given him a couple of cans of water and he wanted to pass it out before they humped the 200 meters back to their hill for the night. As they stood in line waiting for their half canteen cup of hot water a chopper circled in and dropped just the benny everyone dreamed of, craved: an external net full of green five-gallon water cans. The hump back would be easier now.

Sam gave the grunts fifteen minutes to savor the rest and the water before issuing his last saddle up for the day. No one was too tired to give the usual response.

"What the fuck's that saddle up shit? I thought we was staying here tonight. Goddam, how fucking far we gotta hump today?"

"Ah, it ain't so far back to where the mortars is at, only about two, three hundred meters at the most."

"Yeah, but that's two, three hundred too far now."

Already shadows were filling up the valleys and draws. This last hump of the day went slow but no one fell out—there was a guaranteed long drink of clean water at the end of this one. Back on the hill, with Bravo Company together again, Sam called a last meeting before nightfall. If a civilian could have witnessed this conference, he would probably report that these half dozen men in green were either rehearsing the rites of some primitive religion or asking the clouds for rain. Three of the six had temperatures over 102° and all were bending forward every few seconds to counter the now constant dizziness. The Captain reported that battalion had called again. There would be no more of the mindless humping in the heat for awhile. Bravo would be staying on this hill, actually sitting on this hill for at least another day. When this directive had sunk into one hundred twenty-seven skeptical heads there was once again reason to smile, even reason to use a little energy to laugh again. "Did you hear that, Man? We're staying, fucking staying! That's right, we ain't gonna do a fucking thing for at least two days the Lieutenant said. Not a fucking thing!"

Sitting in foxholes that night watching the moon, watching shooting stars and sipping the new clean water, the Freedom Bird and the World didn't look like lies anymore, at least not like the big lies they seemed this afternoon. Each grunt promised himself he would live through whatever this hot, hilly, green, wet land held in the next hour, day, week and ride his Freedom Bird away, away from all this bullshit forever—and not in a body bag but sitting in that soft seat staring at stewardess-bodies.

It was good to wake up after the sun was up, for a change. Damn good. And it was good to stand up and look at the deep green hills and draws all around and know these hills and draws would not have to be humped over today. That is, one "knew" that beautiful fact while the dark possibility of another word change hung in the back of his mind. The obscene scream of "Saddle up!" could still shatter the morning tranquility. But as the sun moved toward the midday point it was accepted that May third really would be a full day of slack; beautiful, skating slack. Very few in the Company even felt like expending the energy of thought and muscle involved in writing letters; raising a full canteen of water to one's mouth was enough.

The real beauty of this formerly small and simple act of drinking water was that it could be done with the realization that one was not limited to a capful, and it would not have to be squirted back into the hot canteen. You could take a whole damn mouthful and then you could either swallow it all at once or you could play with it as long as you wanted. You actually had a choice for a change—gargle it, squirt it around inside your mouth, let each tooth and taste bud savor it. Hell, you could almost have a damn orgasm right there on a mouthful of plain old water! Damn good, for a change. And for another change, the American grunts in Vietnam had something in common with the rest of their generation back in the World, for as they slushed that new water over hot, dry, gums and teeth and tongues, an uncountable number of Americans were walking down a hall, pushing a button and putting their mouths over a clear arching stream of water so cold it stung teeth. Life in the bush made the drinking of water one of the greatest of earthly pleasures, almost on a plane with sex.

A re-supply chopper came out in the late morning and dropped five recovered heat casualties from the day before and fifty cases of C-rations. That broke down to four new meals per man. Now another of the great pleasures of life was available.

While shrunken stomachs began working on the new water and food, the grunts went to work shoring up their attitude against whatever new adversity the next three days held. They tore apart all the gear they had to carry and looked for things to throw away, ways to lighten tomorrow's load. And after they had thrown away all the extra bootlaces and empty cigarette packages and extra matches and the pretty souvenir rocks, most of the grunts took a razor blade to their flak jackets and cut out some of the fiberglass plates. Here again, like the night before last, it was the act of discarding part of what they had to carry that sustained and lifted their now-initiated and hardened spirits. No matter that the plates they were throwing away might save them from a stomach full of razor-sharp, red-hot shrapnel in the near future. Just getting rid of something—anything—made them feel better, made tomorrow look a little more tolerable. It was worth the loss in protection.

With the pack-lightening completed, with nothing but slack to contemplate for the whole day, it was inevitable that reflection on what had been survived in the past three days of their very young lives would come over some of the grunts. The brutal exertion of the humps stretching over the last seventy-two hours was over, the heat was over for awhile, and the unbelievable sixty-five heat casualties and twenty-three medevacs without the aid of one booby trap or one round of enemy fire were over. The most horrendous three days in the histories of most of these one hundred twenty-eight lives were over. Now it was somebody else's turn, somewhere else, some other day.

Grunts are and always have been necessarily preoccupied with the here and now of their particular adversities. Throughout military history, of course, ordeals were endured comparable to that just completed by Bravo One-Three. But the grunts of Bravo would never consider any previous ordeal as worse than their own. The worst hump ever was the one just completed, the one that had lasted over the last day in April and the first two days of May 1969. For the next four or five decades they would remind each other and tell wives, children, grandchildren, and anyone else who would listen about the time "back in '69 in the Nam, or maybe it was '68 . . ." when they thought the humping would never end, and maybe a couple of firefights would be added to liven up the tale, but "We made it. Them old-timers back there might have done some sweating but whatever they went through, it couldn't have been as bad as these last three days, no way, Man."

Yesterday was yesterday and today would have to be hoped for all over again. The potential for a second slack day was as feeble as a newborn infant. It would have to be carefully nurtured, kept alive: don't step too fast, don't breathe too hard. So now, on days like May fourth, the grunt felt a strong need to do something to preserve everything about life as he knew it, from values and assumptions of an everyday familiarity to the most basic fundamental: sanity itself.

A grunt in the field is one of the most superstitious varieties of human life. Before he was sent to Vietnam there was a touch of the rational in him, or at least the desire to be somewhat rational, but during his year on the other side of the world, that rationality was pushed aside by events in which there was little or no reason. Frequent disappointment and disillusion caused by faulty intelligence, continuous word changes, and ubiquitous uncertainty and fear pushed the grunt to erect around himself elaborate defenses consisting of no more than hopes, fears, and ritual acts. This delicate barrier was then positioned against the audial perception of that worst imaginable development—a sergeant screaming "Saddle up!" Aided by little or no prior experience with inductive, deductive, or any other kind of reasoning, the grunts arrived at some weird conclusions.

> "Just watch—I bet if I eat this can of peaches now we'll move before noon. That's the way it's been happening every time after a bitching hump ever since I been here—just watch."

"Don't walk up there past Six's area now—it's too early. You get up and walk around and old Captain America's gonna think you want to hump some more, and he'll find some hill for us to hump to. Just stay down here quiet, get some Zs while you can."

That neither the battalion commander nor operations officer—the real originators of every saddle up—would ever have the time or inclination to study individual troops for evidence of hopes that required destruction never entered thought patterns low in the world's hierarchy.

When the two hated words finally did come at eighty-thirty in the morning the first reaction was not that of having a dread confirmed, but relief that no more time would have to be spent sweating the situation. Just get your shit wired together and hump on out. Carry on—129 more days. Carry on—128 more days.

It wouldn't be a real long hump, but it wouldn't be a real skate either—about six or seven clicks. Platoons and people trailed out into the heat and green, a long line of green domes over squinting eyes. Soon the heat began to sink in again.

"Hey, Red Mountain, which hill is it—where we going?"

"Fuck, I don't know—just keep it spread out there."

"Yeah, well at least ask the Lieutenant can we take a break up here and get in the shade some."

"You know fucking A well you can't ask the man no dumbass question like that—let's go, Man."

In only the first hundred meters of the new move their bodies were reminding the grunts they were not doing something new, they were only resuming the old idiocy.

All the old bullshit was coming back now—spread it out, how far we gotta go, keep them spread out there, Tripper says there's a heat casualty back there. No, forget it, he's okay. Goddamn, listen to me—every step—thigh bone crashing onto ground, dumb ground, takes shock sends it up to knee which hollers I can't last forever you son of a bitch. You better stop and let me blow Zs you son of a . . . . Thigh bone pushes, slams up into diaphragm flattens against lungs and the air rushes back up out past voice box and a desperate sigh-grunt "huh-huh" counts the clicks, ticks off the operations. Those damn heavies ought to make a "huh-huh" grunt count just like they make a damn body count and they ought to give a medal for every couple hundred grunts. Then everybody'd have a chestful and be a hero, even old J.S. Wragman. We're gonna fix them fucking heavies. Parts of this bullshit did not previously appear in The New Yorker. *I think how much I hate it, in a disinterested sort of way, then I come to hate so much I can't distinguish my consciousness as a witness of superficial temporal hatred. I come to embody extreme hatred. I am a hateful perception of my hateful self. I don't direct hatred at the exhaustion, the heat, or the gook I stalk—I become hatred. Something that produces hate and requires it to exist. I ingest it and excrete it, I taste hate of the hills, and of my base animal existence. Even that I have to fight, for I will never again have the luxury of taking anything for granted, as they say on Thanksgiving Day, like the fat Americans do all their lives, all their dullish barren sentences on earth. Stupid man, he warred a millennium ago and he wars now . . . . How much more my toenails and eyelashes hate it. I don't produce motion toward the next hill, I produce hatred; blue, turgid, agitated, surly hatred. Hatred almost beyond the control of anything structured to preserve sanity in a goddamn brain housing group government issue, one each. Of those who have much, much is expected. Who the hell said that? The tendons under kneecaps protest the premature aging I impose, the hump imposes. They scream payback's a medevac motherfucker! I promise, I swear, I will not put them through such again—but tomorrow. How do you apologize to your body? It was made to use and God strikes dead those who fail to realize the potential He gave each. Who the hell said that? There is no goddam God—I rule my destiny! Hey Lieutenant, talk to the Captain will you, talk to him will you . . . .*

Through perceptions of madness and weak protest came the unmistakable sound of metal on metal ringing through the hills and the heat waves. It was a measured bam and a pause of three or four seconds, bam and a pause again. And between each bam was that smooth, darkly beautiful swearing. About fifty-eight men behind the point, the newest sergeant in Bravo, Jerry Buskirk, was practicing his newly recognized leadership ability. It was as big a test as he would ever face—looking for new ways to make humans do what they don't want to do. The technique he had decided on to deal with Private First Class Prentice Lichko was to bang him on the helmet with a machete.

"You worthless shithead, get up there, move it out. You ain't gonna lose contact with that man in front of you again. You will make this hump. BAM! Nobody's coming back after your ass if you fall out again, and quit your goddamn whimpering. Too damn many of you guys think if you sweat a little a Freedom Bird's gonna pop outa the sky just for you. BAM! Well, it ain't gonna happen I keep telling you. We're gonna get up this damn hill before it gets really hot so we can blow some Zs for awhile. Fuck yeah, you'll have water, and Cs too. BAM! Move it there, you're losing contact. I ain't gonna get my ass jumped again today. Gotta save some for the Man to chew on tomorrow—not anymore today. BAM!"

At fifteen minutes before noon the rumors started taking on some substance, and they started traveling up and down the column a little faster. "I think this is the one we're going to. I heard somebody say it up ahead. Yeah, this might be it." Final confirmation came soon after: "Pass it back, the Lieutenant says this is definitely the one, right up there, for sure."

Here was the hill—goddamn, at last here was the hill. It was this slope, the one they were leaning into, sweating over, cussing, not that steep bastard over there everybody was afraid it was. Right here, Baby, we're home.

"This is Six! Put your people around this thing from four to eight and put a fire team on this here knob you'll see to the south when you get up here." Second platoon was in, first platoon, then weapons, two squads of the third and last platoon. The celebration began. "Hey, Chief, Six says we're getting birds in with mail, rats and water, Man, fucking water!"

Lance Corporal Dennis Moy was beyond joining this or any other celebration. A few minutes before, the endless walking and the heat had completed the erosion of his *esprit de corps,* his sense of discipline and survival, enough to make sitting down where he was and refusing to go any farther seem not an act of insubordination, but the natural thing to do. And so he sat and stared, stared miles into the deep tangled green surrounding him and the rest of Bravo. A few of those filing by noticed and tried to encourage him to make it.

"Come on, Moy, let me give you a hand."

"Hey this is the hill, Man, you can make it. You're here already."

"Want a drink, a smoke?"

The encouragement had the tone of first the routine, then the curious, finally a vague fear. "Hey, Moy, let's go, Man—you hear me dammit? Hey, look at him—something's wrong. Go on in and get Doc back down here."

Corporal Manuel Rodriguez decided to stay down the slope with Moy. Rodriguez was a genuine "short-timer," with only fourteen days remaining in the Nam. He sat down next to Moy and started talking. Rodriguez had a real feel for anyone not as short as he. It wasn't really sympathy and he wasn't the kind to hold his experience over a newby's head the way some did. He just felt like doing something to soften the harsh reality faced by those with six, eight, ten months more to do.

Moy gave no indication that he heard anyone talking. As Rodriguez put a hand on his shoulder, Moy's every muscle came alive in an animalistic, ejaculative way. He turned on the corporal with red, violent eyes, screaming a language unrecognizable. He grabbed his M-16, clicked off the safety, aimed it at Rodriguez and sprayed the hill and sky with a full magazine. Every one of the eighteen rounds missed Rodriguez; it was one of those freaks of life and war after which the witness who should have been victim accepts without question the frailty of human existence.

Rodriguez grabbed and sat on Moy until the first help arrived from the new perimeter.

"It's Moy—he's nuts—tried to shoot Wetback. You two take him up to the big CP, we'll get his gear. It's gonna be all right now, Moy. Come on it's all right. Get him in the shade and don't let him near anybody's weapon!" The nineteen-year-old Chinese-American was led, carried, dragged up the remaining few yards to the crest, still screaming, and was put under a poncho liner. Half of his body at least was now out of the sun. Moy stopped screaming after a few minutes but babbled on quietly to himself for hours, staring at nothing and everything. "Must have been the heat got him. You know I bet if he'd known how close he was he wouldn't have done it, you know?"

Rodriguez carried Moy's rifle and empty canteens up the rest of the hill and then he too sat in the dirt and stared, and wondered at the great mystery of this green place that decided who would walk again in familiar places and who would be carried home.

"Did you hear that? He was yelling in Chinese and he never even been to China, but his old man and old lady was there back before the Reds took over."

Helicopters were called but all were too busy for a routine medevac and the situation was not considered serious enough to warrant again giving away the Company's position. So Dennis Moy babbled on through the day, never eating, rarely drinking. The staring, the gibbering at the insanity of this business would go on into the night, the next day, the next night. America, the great insulator of her children from adversity, had cheated another of what was needed to live out this day.

At first, others were assigned to watch Moy on a rotating duty basis, two hours at a time, but soon the bond of common experience and a shared fate worked in over one hundred minds, and the grunts closed round their newest casualty. The feeling of this-could-happen-to-me dominated as they did all they could to relieve Moy of his hell. They gave him their Kool-Aid, their Hershey bars from home, showed him magazines, pictures of girl friends and sisters, they held his hand, cooled his face with a wet handkerchief, loosened his bootlaces and changed his socks, told him how nice he would have it in the rear. "Don't eat too much of that ice cream, Man, have a beer for every one of us." Two days after he fired at Corporal Rodriguez and the hills, a chopper arrived and Lance Corporal Moy was taken from the war.

"Screaming in Chinese and he never even been there, you know? Lucky bastard—now he's skating for a big man's ass."

* * * * *

While Dennis Moy lost his tenuous grip on the reality of heat and an unpleasant mission, other Americans back in the World were dealing with other realities. In Coraele, Georgia, Ernie Reber reached behind the desk in his insurance agency and turned up the air conditioner another notch; Mrs. Melvin Hildebrand of Denton, Texas, tried to remember if she had taken her birth control pill this morning; and Columbus Bowers sat on a john in the Greyhound bus terminal in Grand Island, Nebraska. He took a pen out of his pocket, crossed out a "Who needs niggers" and a "Back to Africa you black bastards" and scrawled his own "All white beasts eat shit—black is beautiful."

And in Beanville, Vermont, Rhonda Schimmel opened the oven door for a peek at her rising bread. Rhonda's husband Frank sells and services snowmobiles and other sports equipment in the Beanville area and, "Frank likes some homemade things to munch on after a hard day in the shop and I like to have some goodies ready."

In between saying hello and goodbye to her husband and caring for Sherry, three, and Dee Anne, twenty months (number three's due soon), Rhonda Schimmel has become something of an expert on yeast breads. "I've been teaching the girls in the neighborhood to make yeast bread and rolls. We also make a lot of sweet baked goods." Fortunately, no one in the Schimmel household needs to think thin, and calories don't count.

Florida natives who met and became high school sweethearts in Lake Worth, the couple married a year after graduation. Rhonda Schimmel began studies in nursing school but took a leave of absence when she got her ring. "We want to have all our children when we're young, and then we can all grow up together," she says. Husband and wife are twenty-three.

Next time you want to fill your kitchen with the aroma of love, try Rhonda Schimmel's bread. "I guarantee this recipe every time," she says. "One package active dry yeast. Beat with a spoon. Knead the dough. Punch out air . . . ."

5 The Third Herd

Now began a long dry time, a time when heat and boredom would dominate the bright days. For more than two weeks there would be no blood. There wouldn't even be the sound of distant gunfire. The humping through the green and heat would continue but it wouldn't have the frantic urgency of before. It was as if the battalion were slowing down its pace of life a little in order to more completely recover from Delta Company's disaster. In such a time a perversity was born, something that could only have a human brain as its source—the desire that anything, even a firefight, would occur to dilute boredom's acid-like eating away of optimism and youth.

Two hours after Moy's outburst, battalion called and told Sam that Bravo would keep their position for the next few days. The word spread fast and brought undreamed of relief. There was once again room for joy in life. "Kind of pretty, this little hill, ain't it?"

The company gunny collected all the explosive compound, C-4, carried by Bravo, took a squad onto the northwest edge of the hill and spent the next two hours blowing a landing zone. When no trees or brush over three feet above ground remained standing, the re-supply chopper was called in. Blowing the LZ was a race against the late afternoon darkness, but it was won. Everything fell from the sky this time—orange juice, socks, new canteens, gallon cans of pickles, tins of foot powder, cigarettes, grape juice, bootlaces, Red Cross kits of stationery, candy bars, toothpaste and brushes, chewing gum, razor blades, and "Oh Christ, that pilot better not drop it," one hundred twenty gallons of clean water in twenty-four marine green cans. It was a beautiful shade of green today. A new lifestyle was now possible and orders reflected it.

"Have your people shaved by noon tomorrow and tell them to eat up all their Cs—we gotta pallet coming in the morning."

The sounds now coming from the hill were more those of kids at Christmas than of men in war, as the grunts joked and joshed each other through the afternoon. Their joy was unbounded as they gorged themselves on rediscovered luxuries: the sharp sensation of toothpaste being brushed around in dry mouths, the ecstasy of taking and savoring a mouthful—a full mouthful—of clean water. Hands and feet could sweat again.

> "Hey, Man, would you like the honor of sitting next to me and watching me smoke this entire cigarette, would you, huh?"
>
> "Right on, Brother, right on your dying ass—I'm gonna have the honor of watching your face tomorrow when the bird brings the word and you read that Jody's come and got your sweet woman, ha! Got her right there while you're over here chasing gooks, oooo-weee!"

Of the dozen ambushes run in the next two days, no more than three or four were strictly ready to react, according to doctrine. On the rest, the grunts simply walked out to the designated ambush site, hid under the grass or brush and wrote letters, slept, or just lay back on the ground with eyes closed to contemplate the beauty of holding a mouthful of water, working it around with the tongue for ten minutes, twenty. At the end of the second day the squads and platoons came back up the hill to find the first sergeant with two long-awaited morale-raisers, mail and pay.

> "Just like I said, Man, a letter for PFC Edward Haskins. Let's see if Jody's been snooping around that stuff. Open it, Man. Well, what she say, Man?"
>
> "You just go fuck yourself, Joe Moore. She says everything is fine and the baby's still coming in about two months, and

we're still getting married when I get home, so you and Jody can go straight to hell, Joe Moore, straight to hell."

"Well now, ain't that nice—she just afraid to tell you this week but wait'll next week, Man. Jody be done come and gone by then, you just wait—ha!"

Part of being a grunt is knowing when to prepare oneself mentally for the worst imaginable reality. Right now, after three full days on what had become known as Bravo Hill, Change 37, the worst reality imaginable was not death, but a resumption of those endless humps in the heat, pursuing an enemy who would not allow himself to be found or even seen. The grunts began to sense it individually and were almost afraid to reveal the common realization.

"Hey, ah, you know how long we been here now? I mean it's kind of unbelievable, ain't it?"

"Yeah, and my hooch is just getting comfortable."

The call from battalion came at about eleven in the morning; the hated frenzy of preparation was taken up again. The Company was caught at a time more awkward than usual: there was too much water and too many C-rations to carry. But a heroic effort was made to consume it all.

"Here, Man, drink the rest of this juice."

"I just drank half a fucking can. I drink anymore and I'll get diarrhea in five minutes instead of two hours from now!"

Every canteen, every plastic water bottle was filled but still there was too much of the precious water. Who among these men-children thought they would ever see too much water? Living the agony of thirst and heatstroke, then gorging themselves on a sudden flood of water in the space of three days produced a mind-bending bewilderment on this morning in May. All knew they were engaging in the grossest sacrilege.

"Look at this shit, throwing away water. If anybody pulled this three days ago we'd have shot his ass!"

Captain Sam called up his platoon commanders, pointed them in the right direction and formulated a plan as he spoke.

"We'll lead outa here with second platoon, then the CP, weapons, and third. First platoon, you stay back to send the water cans out on this bird we just called in, then take off on the same trail we use. We won't get no more than a click ahead, then we'll wait for your lead people to link up. We're going to that hill that's got them two big craters on it. I want to be walking outa here in ten minutes."

In the next ten minutes, Lance Corporal Craig Billings and Private First Class Booker Carver Lincoln added a new twist to the preparations they had gone through so many times before. One of these grunts had, in the last two days, bent his every thought to avoiding a repetition of those first three days in May. By themselves such thoughts were not now uncommon in the Company, but the distance between thought and act was still considerable in all but these two.

"Hey, Lincoln, come here, pal. Hey listen, ah, how about paying me back that hus I cut you on your R & R?"

"Yeah, I'll pay you back, soon as this op is over. I gotta go pack and be moving in a couple of minutes."

"I mean now, Lincoln, right fucking now."

"How in the fuck I gonna pay you back now, out here?"

"Listen, Man, you and me start grab-assing, see, then I act like I get pissed and start throwing hands. Then you grab your E-tool and hit me in the foot, right here real hard, see?"

"Oh, that's real sweet, Billings, real fucking sweet. You get outa the bush, back with the beer in the rear but I'm still humping my ass off. Fuck that shit, Man."

"Ten bucks, Brother Books . . . Twenty bucks, Books . . . Twenty-five . . . ."

The first corpsman to look at Billings' ankle knew what the deal had been. Not only the mastermind of the plan but Lincoln too got out of the next few humps. Both were left to escort the water cans back to the rear and await their courts-martial.

It was real nice going at first, but then the humps were always nice at the beginning since they were always downhill, to get off the old hill. And it was even a nice day; at least as nice a day as you could want for a hump—fairly cool, since the sun was overcast with what looked like rain clouds. But of course they couldn't be real rain clouds, could they? In the Nam? In May?

When one platoon, the company headquarters section, and half of the next platoon were outside the old perimeter, the column came to its first stop. It was dead quiet so there was no contact and there couldn't be any heat casualties after only thirty minutes. "What the hell's going on?" The word filtered back and a few inched forward to see something.

"It's that battalion radio guy—says he can't make it anymore, won't even try. Griswald's up there beating his ass, and he still says he can't go no farther. There—look at him just laying there taking it."

Lance Corporal Jerry Helman wasn't tired yet, but he was more afraid than he had ever been in his young life—afraid the next three days would be like the first three of this May, afraid he could not push himself through such a time again, and in need of escape from his fear. He was so afraid that he was willing to walk back the same trail to the old perimeter and the water cans and Billings and Lincoln; walk past over two-thirds of the Company, each man every two or three meters starting, glaring, a few envious.

"Couldn't hack it, eh? Have a nice time in the rear, Shithead."

"Thanks for leaving us out here."

"Don't forget to tell your girl back home about this. There, don't cry now."

His war stories back home would always be followed by the worst of qualifications: "Yeah, maybe he done all he said he done but let me tell you—I saw him once quit a hump in the Nam! That's right, he just quit, fell down crying and begging to be sent back—even after some of us beat his ass too. He actually quit on us. We wanted to kill his ass right there!"

Captain Sam sat the Company down where they were and called up his lieutenants. "All right now, you three get this word out once we set in on that objective. This Moy shit is spreading and it's gotta be stopped. These guys ain't tired, they just think they are, and it's your job to see that it don't go no farther. So grab your platoon sergeants and light a fire under them squad leaders. You tell them if anybody pulls this shit again I'm gonna rock them in office hours, and they'll never get promoted in this Company. And tell them I'll decide when they can go on R & R, not whenever they damn well want. Now get back and let's get this moving."

Down off the hill into a dry streambed, between thirty and seventy pounds settled onto each of one hundred twenty-four backs. All but first platoon were now off the old hill and still the lead elements of the column were moving into a gradual downgrade. It felt nice now, but all knew that one of the hated "grunt laws" would soon work its way: "He who humps downhill must sooner or later hump uphill, Man." Patches of shade from the clouds above moved across the ground, giving seconds of relief from the heat. It was nearing one in the afternoon of May 8; so far the hump had been too pleasant to believe. "Six on the hook, Sir."

"This is Six! Look for some shade to put your people under. We gotta stop again since some non-hacker broke the column again. I'm gonna find out who it is, so make sure it ain't none of yours. Six out."

Corporal John Jason Rattner was simply "Rat" to all in his family, school, hometown, and all who had known him in the Corps during his eleven months of service. Before he enlisted, his nickname was a simple shortening of the surname, but after he had been in Vietnam for a couple weeks it took on a new meaning. Corporal J.J. had been the Company's premier tunnel rat for the past six months. He was the one who went down in any bunker or tunnel encountered to search for weapons, supplies, or North Vietnamese. No extra pay was offered for the extra danger, so others were glad to see Rat come along and volunteer.

"You know, most guys don't like that part of being a grunt, but I got to like it after I found out I could be good at it. I've only had to kill two guys I found so far—brought thirteen out alive when I was doing it. I think it was cuz I took the fear out of them, I'd just flash my flashlight on my face when I knew there was one there, and I'd smile—real big, like I'd just knocked off a piece, you know—and they'd come right out. I even brought out two at once one time."

In the past two months Rat had been given an extraordinary responsibility by Sam. He was made mortar section leader, a job normally held by an experienced sergeant. Rat soon knew everything about the three squat 60-millimeter mortars and what they could do. He further learned that he was one of those rarities among 20-year-olds, one who could tell belligerent young men of the same age what to do and not be resented for it. His peers did not feel less than masculine in deferring to his lead.

Today Rat was bothered, and he was determined. He was greatly bothered by the scene put on earlier by the radioman, Helman, and he was determined never to show such weakness himself and burden the whole Company, even though he now felt another of those dizzy, shivering spells coming on. Whenever it happened in the two days before, he would just lie down and wait until it stopped. Everything was perfectly normal afterward, so he had not told a corpsman. But now it had started again, just after Helman quit, and it was worse than before. Rat started to stumble, fell forward, and was too weak to get up. One of the mortar crewmen stayed with him, tried to get him going again as the column continued on by. The last thing Rat wanted was to have the Company stop in the middle of a mission because of some failing on his part. But the last man in the column approached and the word had to be passed to hold it up. Rat's temperature was moving over 103° but, "No, dammit, don't tell Six, don't stop them, I can make it. No, I'll carry my own pack, no . . . ."

Sam came back, saw who it was and all knew there would be no office hours following this halt. "Looks like you got malaria. Why the hell didn't you tell somebody about this?"

"I'll be okay, Captain, don't send me back or call in any chopper. I'll make it all right."

Rat was cooled and led to the head of the column, a few men behind the point. If he fell back again there would be plenty of friends to help him along. In the space of only one hour, Bravo Company had seen within their own number the two opposite extremes of reactions to what they were doing this day worlds away from the States, the real World.

Moving again, a few wondered what else could happen this day but most issued the standard: "Back to the same old shit again—I bet this thing turns out to be ten fucking clicks long." Soon a helicopter could be heard. It cautiously touched down on the old position, hesitated, then lifted off with the water cans and those who thought they couldn't make it anymore. The whump-whump of its rotors lingered over the trees and died off as first platoon came off Bravo Hill, Change 37. The Company would soon be whole again, and alone.

"This is Six! Get on the romeo with that other group moving in on your six o'clock and make liaison with them, and make damn sure nobody shoots anybody when you first see each other. We'll be coming to a blue line up here pretty soon and we'll wait for them there."

In the next half-hour something even more unbelievable than Billings, Helman, and Rattner happened—rain! Rain, in the hot part of the day—"never saw this before, no sir." It started, and remained through the rest of the afternoon, as one of those soft spring rains that beats softly on rooftops and puts people to sleep on dry, warm mattresses under dry, warm blankets. It was one of those gentle nostalgic rains one associates with fireplaces and long ago. As the fat drops soaked helmet covers, dripped onto hot salty necks and traced down lean filthy backs, none of the grunts could imagine what they or anyone else had done to deserve such a gift of coolness. Grateful, relieved bodies slumped back, mouths open to the great faucet and drank it all in: "Soak it up, Man, you'll never see this again in the summer!"

First platoon linked up and moved through everyone else to take the point position. Only a football field length ahead the downgrade came to an end at the anticipated blue line. The stream was larger than most encountered, about fifteen feet wide and three feet deep. On its far bank began an upgrade leading to the finger that would take the grunts straight up to Bravo Hill, Change 38. It was a continuous climb of about one mile.

First platoon pushed on and up and found that the rain had made an otter slide of a hill of only routine slope. With a little muscle and considerable verbal accompaniment, a one hundred foot rope was fixed over the steep rise from the streambed, and the grunts spent the rest of the dark afternoon pulling themselves up the muddy slope. Almost the entire column could hear whenever one of their own slipped and slid down ten, twenty, sometimes fifty meters of the incline. For a few minutes there were the sounds that reminded one of the kids sliding down a snow-covered hill, but the laughing and joshing died as soon as the grunts could see the trick of it all. The rain was cooling but the energy a glaring sun would have claimed was spent in making every step sure, and then regaining the lost meters, feet, inches. "The green weenie strikes again, eh, Lieutenant?"

The new hill looked like nothing anyone could anticipate. Usually they're either completely virgin, untouched by either side in the war, or they have been cleared, dug up with incoming holes and then trashed up by former occupants. This one had been thoroughly cleared, was badly cratered and chewed but no humans had walked over it yet. The only things related to man that had been here were the bombs of the B-52s and Phantom jets. It was easy digging into dirt pulverized by the five hundred and one thousand pounders that had rained from 30,000 feet, but here again there was a price exacted for a temporary easing of the task. There were no enemy in this night but almost every man, as he lay waiting for sleep, could feel the rain collecting under and soaking toward him. He could feel it washing away a patch supporting his elbow, hip, foot—changing the mold he had learned to scrape in the ground his first week in the bush, the mold his body had come to like and sleep in. Somebody, or something, was determined to get X amount of sweat out of these men, make them feel and thrash against X intensity of discomfort during each day and night. "That Sky Six ain't cutting no husses this week, Man, not one."

The next morning Sam received word that there would have to be another move. The rain had stopped around three in the morning, so now the sun could bore through a clear sky. Today, May 9, would be a test for one of the three rifle platoons in Bravo, not a test with the North Vietnamese, but a test within the Company, a test concerning reputation. Third platoon, called "Third Herd," had been considered, for several months, the weakest in the Company. A grunt in another platoon described the recent history of the Third Herd: "Third used to be the best, but then on Taylor Common they got hit a couple of times and turned to instant shit."

The Herd was the least cohesive, exercised poor noise discipline on humps and poor light discipline at night. Whenever the column on the move was broken it was usually because someone in Third fell behind. But, in the past six weeks, the Herd had gotten a new platoon sergeant and a new platoon commander. Lieutenant Carl Andrews and Staff Sergeant Jerry Goodman were certain the platoon's reputation was no longer deserved, but they needed a chance to prove it. For the past week or more Captain Sam had been thinking it was time to see what improvements the new platoon leadership had been able to affect. This day looked like a good one to find out, considering the moderate length of the move and the appearance of the terrain on the map. The decision was conveyed on the lip of a bomb crater while two men squinted into binoculars.

"Think your people can handle point today?"

"Yes, Sir, I think it's time they had a chance at it."

"Okay, you see that flat-top thing with the downed chopper on it? The one we want is two fingers to the right of it and a little closer to us, the one with that lone white tree on it. Go down this finger here and then use your own judgement."

The going was fast and easy through the first three clicks. It was downhill and it just happened that a load of bombs from a B-52 raid had strung out along the direction of march and cleared most of the brush. Sam and the other platoons were more than surprised at the progress thus far. The halfway point of the hump was a dry streambed, reached at ten-thirty in the morning. The grunts were not nearly as tired as usual, either at this time of day or at this point in the move. "Christ, Man, we're really moving out. This might even turn out to be a half decent hump, you know—the kind we want to write home about!" Without a pause the Herd moved into the second and uphill half of the six thousand meter distance. Sergeant Goodman made the day's last rotation of the point squad, passed up two dull machetes, and Corporal Ken Worthington's nine-man squad took off.

"This is Six! You going up that thing yet?"

"That's affirm—all of mine are on it now but it's gonna be one of them long, gradual rising jobs."

"Yeah, well don't let them think they're tired. Keep at it."

Two hundred meters later Worthington hit a stand of bamboo, one of the two or three most difficult types of growth to move through. The stand turned out to be about one hundred meters wide; it was hacked and cursed through at the expense of all noise discipline, all patience, and much endurance. Before the objective could be reached, two more bamboo stands would have to be cut through. The heat was getting worse and the calls from Sam were successively more impatient, demanding.

"This is Six! Now what's the trouble up there, we should be there by now. You better light a fire under them people and get us up there before this heat really gets bad."

The crest of the hill was finally reached, but only after there were no more fresh arms to swing machetes and after the bamboo was found to be reinforced with the tough, thick vines the grunts had not seen since their last Tarzan movie. Once again the hump had exacted its tribute. "Shit, Man, that could have been an enjoyable little hump but it turns out to be another ball-buster."

Compounding the frustration of the day for one-third of Bravo was the fact that third platoon would not even get a "well-done" for their three hours of work, for Sam lost himself in the details of planning artillery support, verifying his location, calling a resupply chopper and setting the defenses of "Bravo Hill, Change 39."

"Did the Captain say anything, Sir, I mean about us and all?"

"Fuck no, just the usual get your people tied in with first and second, and dig in, and get them in the shade, and let them eat something, but you and I know how good they were today—we were right with them every step."

"Yes, Sir, they did damn good today, damn good."

After an hour's rest the company gunny collected all the C-4 and began blowing a LZ. The last tree to fall was the tallest—the lone, dead, white and branchless spike, the one on which third platoon had guided for three hours. The grunts were grateful for it, had become attached to it, since its prominent whiteness had led them out of the maddening green maze below. But the minute it was reached and clung to, it became a threat—it was now the best aiming stake a North Vietnamese mortarman could hope to find. It had to go.

Preparations were made, but the tree would not so easily acquiesce to its suddenly reversed value. When the charges placed around its smooth white trunk were detonated, the tree seemed determined to take on a last gasp of life and foil the new security needs that dictated its destruction. It didn't fall in the predicted direction, but right across the middle of the planned helicopter landing zone. The tree now added to the grunts' burden of existence: it had to be moved, somehow pushed or rolled or blasted outside the perimeter and down the slope.

> "Before we start that we gotta get some squads out on local patrols and have a look around. Leave your machine guns back, just take a radio and a corpsman and search out that finger and draw down there. You know, look for trails, signs of visitors, see if you can't find a water point somewhere. Call me when you get down in that dark green patch there and I'll tell you whether to come back or whatever else."

Forty-five minutes later Sam called back. "This is Six! Bring your people back as fast as you can—battalion says we gotta move —yeah I know, but they're sending Alpha Company up on this one so we gotta move."

The predictable reaction was predictably quick. "Christ, here we go again—I'd like to get the Colonel out here and see how he'd like humping just to be humping, and twice in one day. That's real fine—we clear the fucking hill for somebody else—real fucking fine. I don't know why they didn't just wait till we pushed that fucking tree down the hill—that would have made the day complete."

At least two of these one hundred twenty-two were determined to preserve some measure of choice over their pawn-like fate. The heaviest equipment a grunt has to carry is the 60-millimeter mortar and its ammunition. The mortars are carried by their gunners, but the ammunition is spread-loaded throughout the Company, one round per man. In the hurried confusion of re-packing things unpacked only two hours before, no call to pick up mortar rounds ever came. And the grunts, once again seeing the agony of thirst and pain without relief as a real and close possibility, willingly and silently assumed the mortarmen would carry their own.

"Hey, Grub, you notice they ain't said nothing about no mortar rounds yet?"

"Yeah, I notice. Just go on packing, and when we move out, act like nothing is different—and don't ask anybody about it, goddam don't ask about it!"

It was a short move, six hundred meters, and consisted of only one descent and one ascent. Both were steeper than usual, however, since the two hills were not in the same, but parallel ridgelines; the deep cut between had to be crossed. The grunts came up with thigh muscles burning and lungs heaving. But at last here was a surprise, a victory of sorts: the new hill had been occupied recently so no LZ had to be cleared, no holes dug for the night. The feeling of injustice at having to clear a hill for someone else was somewhat softened. What happened after the packs were dropped only underlined again the idiocy of this day's succession of events. Captain Sam summoned Andrews and Goodman: "Sergeant Herr tells me third platoon didn't carry any mortar rounds over here. What the hell, your people looked real good on the point this morning and then they pull something like this. Well, since they claim they forgot, they can remember by going back and getting the damn things—get it straightened out."

An armed work party from third platoon retraced the steep route and brought back some forty rounds, but only after a hot exchange with some mortarmen.

"Why the fuck we gotta get your shit when you forgot to give them to us back there? You want the fucking things, you go get them."

"Knock it off, Grub, just go get them. We gotta bird coming in with plenty of water."

The re-supply bird deposited the usual bennies plus freshly-baked bread and pickles. Ten minutes after the chopper crew headed back to their base for warm showers and cold beer, merciful darkness ended further exposure of Bravo. Another company had lived through another day of the war, but within ten of the day's hours a part of that company had displayed both a high degree of professionalism and discipline, and a base selfishness. Vietnam today had exposed to hot open scrutiny some human frailties normally secreted. Score for May 9: no gain.

6 Ho's Birthday

Bravo was now on the ridgeline they had walked those first three days in May, but their direction was reversed. Each of the next three daily humps was hot, of course, but each was also fast, since there was no tangled growth to hack through. And each hill was a little shorter than the last, since the grunts were now making their way back toward the seacoast, where it had all begun. There was only one incident to break the routine.

On the second morning, about a third of a mile into the move, Bravo walked through the battalion field headquarters. The grunts' resentment of the rear-echelon and staff pogues was renewed as they saw the pallets of beer and Coke, the career officers and sergeants—the hated lifers—lounging in sun glasses and lawn chairs. "Look at that shit, will you, fucking folding chairs, and can you believe it—some hot dog up on a pallet with his shirt off, actually trying to get a fucking suntan, trying to get the rays!" The grunts were in no condition to imagine inviting onto one's body the rays which were to them a source of daily discomfort, sometimes of agony.

Five hundred meters beyond the pogues and their headquarters, Bravo stopped for the night. There was light enough for one chopper. It brought the usual water, C-rats and mail, and nine morale-raisers—one Navy chaplain and eight brand new grunts fresh out of training in the World, wearing shiny new flak jackets, clean helmet covers and black boots.

The Chaplain could give a little good feeling by listening to anything a guy wanted to say, even about the lifers. The new troopers could give the grunts much more. Handled properly, newbys could be sources of laughter and the feeling of being important, knowledgeable and no longer on the bottom of the hierarchy in the bush. The gunny called the platoon sergeants and assigned each of the newcomers. They were taken back to each platoon commander for their first word on what really goes on in the Nam.

> "Now, we don't want to see no John Wayne performances out here. Just do your job and listen to your fire team and squad leaders—they're the ones who'll teach you everything and help you get through the next few months."

The veteran grunts listened hard, small smiles growing across their faces. They couldn't wait to get their hands on one of these scared young bodies; if they could spare the moisture they would probably be drooling. They were hungry to repeat the words each of them had cringed under months or weeks before: "Hey, new guy, let me show you how to do that there," and at night on the lines, "Now you hear that? That ain't a gook, it's probably a rock ape or maybe a tiger, and if you ever think . . . ."

> "Hold it! You mean there's tigers and gorillas over here?"
>
> "Oh, hell yes—see them all the time—sometimes they come right up to the line at night and attack guys, but not every night, not every night."

The next morning battalion called to report that Bravo would stay on their present hill for several days. So patrol routes were planned, foxholes and ammunition bunkers were dug, fields of fire were cleared. Four hours later, battalion called back, this time directing Sam to be ready to move his Company in one hour. Sam didn't like the word change, nor did his grunts but "this looks like real good hunting around here." "Well fuck, here we go again, digging holes for somebody else again—for nothing."

The move was delayed when the chopper coming for the water cans, outgoing mail and the Chaplain drew fire from the next ridgeline to the north. The green tracers didn't come very close to the bird but they were close enough to call an air strike.

Two Phantom jets were circling overhead in ten minutes. The grunts let out a chorus of "oo—get some, Sweetheart!" as each load of bombs exploded against the suspected hillside, but the North Vietnamese answered with new bursts of fire between sorties. The Phantom pilots then switched to napalm, and Sam added artillery to the air attack; the enemy gun was finally silent.

Though the threat was soon ended, the grunts were reminded that there was an enemy out there even though he had not shown himself recently. Once begun, it was a fast move. It proved a shock to the newbys when the heat exhaustion claimed one. Third platoon was on point and saw the chance to work something on the rest of the Company that would kill forever their bad reputation. "They're all the time saying we're the ones that break the column. Well fuck them, this time they can try and keep up with us." So the Third Herd took off, faster than they might have, had they known just where the break in the column would occur. Company commanders don't like to get lost or to have to slow down their platoons on their own account, but the predictable bitch sounded sweet coming from someone else for a change.

> "This is Six! Dammit all, you had better slow that outfit down and send somebody back to link up with my radioman!"

At Sam's meeting with platoon leaders that night, nothing was said of the embarrassing break in the column caused by third platoon's racehorse tactics. There was much heavier news to consider. Sam reported that just after Bravo left its position, Delta Company had moved onto the same hill and immediately received twenty-seven rounds of incoming. "That's what those choppers are for over there, taking out their wounded." It was the third time in five days that Delta had been hit after occupying a position vacated the same day by another company. Both previous times, the departing unit had received no incoming, no enemy contact during its tenure on the positions. The North Vietnamese seemed to prefer certain Americans over others as targets.

Things had been going smoothly for Bravo long enough now—three days. And there was another reason for a few to sense it might be time for another day of idiocy: the day was the thirteenth of the month. At eight in the morning all of third platoon headed out to set up an L-shaped ambush at the junction of two streams, some 300 meters outside the company perimeter. Four hours later first platoon was to move into one of the streambeds leading to the ambush site and push slowly toward third platoon, nudging the North Vietnamese in the area into the ambush ahead. If no enemy were flushed, first platoon was to assume the same ambush site as third returned to the Company base. Third platoon's ambush was conducted with no enemy appearing. On his way back up the hill to the Company area, Lieutenant Andrews stopped to watch first move into the site. Seeing the point squad move on through the stream junction, Andrews called the first platoon commander, George Sorenson.

"One actual, this is Three! Be informed your point is past the promised land, over."

"Roger that, Three. I'm gonna have a look around, see if I can't find a better one, over."

Andrews turned and put third back on the move upward. Twenty minutes later a burst of gunfire from the ambush sight froze the column, turned all eyes back and downward. First platoon had not only moved past the ambush site but without realizing it, outside the battalion area of operation as well. Then, as he rounded a sharp bend in the stream, Sorenson's point man almost bumped into three North Vietnamese loaded down with rice and ammunition. The three NVA scrambled up out of the stream and took off across the flat grassy flood plain for the nearest hill as the first five men in the column opened up. One of the three was hit but all got away. Sam was on the radio while the gunfire was still echoing through the draws, over the grass.

"Is that your people, Three?"

"That's a negative! It's One, over."

"You know where he's at?"

"He's around six or seven hundred meters past my old promised land, over."

"What the hell's he doing out there, that's outa the damn AO! Get off a minute, I want him on the line."

"Six, this is One, go."

"You know where you're at? You got anybody hurt down there? How the hell'd you miss it by five hundred or whatever? Well, you get that outfit together and stay where you are, we got some air coming in."

So first platoon, eager to pursue the three "visitors" and bring something back to Sam to atone for their map-reading error, stayed low against the stream bank and just waited. Within five minutes a "Bronco," a twin engine observation plane, was circling overhead. The aerial observer was eager too, and let loose too soon with a burst of .50 caliber rounds. Huddled against the stream bank below, Lance Corporal Paul Stanton turned to see who had just stepped on his shoulder. Instead of someone standing next to him, he saw the fiberglass plates falling out of the left shoulder of his flak jacket, and then, blood coursing onto the dirt. "Hey, Lieutenant, that fucking cowboy upstairs got Stanton in the shoulder!" The "cowboy" made a few more passes, slamming half a dozen rockets into a hillside before he was called off. A medevac chopper was called and in fifteen minutes Stanton was on his way out of the bush. Now first platoon could start back home.

It had retraced only about 300 meters of the route in the streambed when there was another casualty. Private Garth Corley had felt lousy all night and on the way out to the ambush in the morning. And he felt lousy after yesterday's fast hump; it was his first, since he was one of the newbys. His body was only beginning to acclimatize; he had gone as far as he could and now collapsed in the stream. He was hot, dry and flushed when the corpsman got to him.

Corley was stripped and laid in the water as an intravenous solution was injected into his arm. He was carried a few yards, then put back in the water, carried a distance, then dunked again until they reached the last area suitable for an evacuation by helicopter before the trail wound up the hill—a bomb crater. The chopper pilot could not touch down on the crater's edge without putting the rotors into a tree so he hovered twenty feet above and lowered a cable and harness from a side hatch. With the rotors raising a blinding, stinging cloud of the loose dirt in the crater, three grunts strapped Corley to the cable and signaled the crew chief to take him up. In the swirling chaos in the crater the harness had been placed on Corley upside-down so he now dangled by his legs, still unconscious. Carefully lowered, he was rigged and taken up, finally on his way to an alcohol bath in the air-conditioned wards at Quang Tri. At last, first platoon could begin the long climb home.

The blunders, trials and missed chances of the day were set aside in the exhilaration over what the re-supply chopper had brought—carrots, cucumbers, tomatoes, C-rats, new socks and jungle uniforms, orange juice, grape juice, mail, water, and 300 mortar rounds, many more than the Company could carry. "Hey, B.J., you see them boxes off to the side? Mortar rounds, hundreds of them. That means we stay for awhile, Man!"

As night and the fog came down, the mortar gunners fired one hundred rounds out around the perimeter, half of them in the open area where first platoon had found the three NVA. Every half hour through the night they would fire three or four rounds to discourage any approach to their hill. Alpha, Charlie, and Delta companies were doing the same thing, for all were set for a few days now. At eleven-thirty the 81-millimeter mortar section of battalion headquarters sent two rounds toward a hill they were certain was unoccupied by Americans.

One of the fat green missiles exploded fifty meters outside the machine gun position of Corporal Manuel Rodriguez, the same Rodriguez who had been fired at by Dennis Moy nine days before. The second round landed twenty meters from the sleeping areas of Andrews and Goodman. Except for a temporary hearing loss in the three, there were no injuries. This time, Rodriguez had company as he wondered, "Why?" The next morning George Sorenson wrote his bride of eight months that he had just played a major role in a day that would never make it in the official Defense Department histories.

Captain Sam didn't sleep well that night, not because battalion had fired at him but because the day was so full of missed opportunities. How could an entire platoon wander six hundred meters out of its assigned area—don't they train these kids anymore? And how, when they found three NVA too loaded down to even fire back, could they help but bring back three bodies? The

Company needed to see some bodies, needed to see what all the humping over the endless string of hills was all about. Maybe if battalion would extend the area of operation Bravo could work the area and come up with something? Battalion returned the call at six the next morning: Bravo could work the area but only for one day; they would be moving out the following morning.

May fourteenth dawned bright and clear. Fog was burned out of the draws and streambeds by six-thirty. Today Sam was taking out two of his three platoons, second and third, all of his six machine guns and one of the three mortars. In the training manuals this would be called a Company-minus patrol. First platoon would rest today and take the point tomorrow. By seven-thirty the Company-minus was down off the hill and in yesterday's ambush sight. The two platoons spread out on either side of the stream, up the low foothills and fingers, and slowly swept toward the area of first platoon's encounter.

"This is Six! Send some people up each of these here draws and streambeds as you come to them—that's where the little people hide their goodies. Take your time, we got all day." Everything went smoothly, quietly, until about eight-thirty when Doc Richards told Andrews he had a heat casualty. "What do you mean a heat casualty, it ain't even nine o'clock yet!"

"Temperature of a hundred and four. You better take a look at him, over here in the stream. I noticed he looked real weak after we got off the hill, then a little later he just fell over in the water."

PFC Delmar Stowe was a recruiter's dream—six feet four, two hundred fifteen pounds when he was sent from his home in Philadelphia to boot camp at Parris Island, South Carolina. Most important, Stowe wanted to join, just like his two older brothers had wanted it when they were eighteen. Doc Richards suspected what had overcome Stowe was more serious than the usual heat exhaustion, but he was not at all prepared for the truth. "You're a what? How did you ever get through boot camp? Why did you come in the green machine when you had the perfect deferment?"

"Both my older brothers was in so I wanted to join, and all my friends was in the Marines or Army and I didn't want to stay home when everyone else was over here. First I tried the Army, but they said they don't take anybody who's had diabetes, but the Marines said they'd take me." A three-man security detail was left with Stowe. He would be picked up when the two platoons headed back to the hill for the night.

The grunts slowly worked down the stream some eight or nine hundred meters, examining every fold in the terrain. Only a few footprints, a pair of North Vietnamese tennis shoes and a fuselage section from a shot-down helicopter were found. Sam turned the patrol around and headed for home. No NVA bodies, no blood trails, no rice, no mortar rounds. Half way up the hill the Company experienced its second casualty of a quiet day. With the carrots and clean socks, yesterday's re-supply bird had brought another new guy, this one a new lieutenant fresh from training. Second Lieutenant Tom Henderson, like PFC Stowe, wanted the Marine Corps program and he wanted some time in the Nam with a line company. He was getting a quick introduction. At his arrival Sam told him he would be going on every patrol with every platoon for the next few days, "so you'll know what goes on out here, and to get yourself acclimatized and all." Henderson made it through the patrol all right but the climb back got him. One of the corpsmen had him under a bush beside the main trail. Over half the Company filed by and saw him on his back, pale and gasping. It was not the best way to be introduced to those whose performance and safety he would soon be charged with.

"Hey, you see that new second looey?"

"Yeah, a real humper, eh? I'd like to know where they get some of them non-hackers and then I'd like to know how they ever get through that OCS. Must not be nothing like boot camp, you know?"

"Yeah, must be a real skate."

Attachments to this hill had been formed, most with good reason according to the value system of the grunt. It did not have to be cleared of any tangled growth and someone else had dug all the incoming holes. No one was real excited about leaving the next morning—not because they had to start at five in the morning, not because leaving meant another hump, but because they were leaving a place that had offered some relief from the monotony of walking under the heat and a pack, of digging holes and being tired and pissed off all the time. From this hill the grunts had at least seen some NVA—there really was a live enemy out there somewhere. But even that small regret was soon forgotten as the grunts got down into the valley they had swept the day before. More than a few looked back in relief, a measure of victory. They had made it—the merciless humps were over. Surely nothing in the future could duplicate that exhaustion, that madness of moving just to be moving for fifteen days. Now they were down off the last one, the easternmost hill in Virginia Ridge. Now they would be moving where breezes flow close to the ground, in the flat grassy plain that becomes beach on the South China Sea. "Hey, can you believe this shit? It's flat, Man—like a fucking airport!"

The one-mile move turned out to be the nicest hump of the operation, one even bordering on the enjoyable. A cloud cover shielded Bravo from the sun, and as they walked past the last checkpoint and turned toward the ocean, a small breeze came up. Faces lifted, flak jackets were held open to receive as much of the miracle as possible before it was taken away and the heat came back. "Oh Man, that old Sky Six is really coming through, ain't he?" Both the cloud cover and the breeze held until the objective was reached. And what an objective—so low it could barely be distinguished from the other small undulations on the horizon. At its base the grunts were saying things they could only dream of saying in the previous two weeks, for this "hill" was only 125 meters above sea level, not 289, not 367. "You heard it Man, the Lieutenant says this thing's a hundred twenty-five meters high. This ain't no hill, Man, it's a fucking pimple! I don't know if I can make it, it's gonna be a real ass-kicker—ha!"

The grunts were into the flatlands, determined to skate. Coming out of two weeks of endless humping through superheated hills, they felt justified in their determination. They thus deliberately ignored a law of life in the bush they had all seen proved: the jungle, the hills, the sun, the war exact X amount of patience or sweat or blood from all who live closest to the workings of those forces. For the most part, the grunts got away with their skating. But not one of them could possibly have guessed what a crazy mix of blunders, near-misses and the unnecessary would fill Bravo's time in the flatlands.

For one, there was the night "the Hunter" came over the radio. "This is the Hunter! Bravo Six will die tonight. All yankee devils will die tonight. Don't fall asleep, American." Sam put the Company on full alert before answering the challenge. "Come on out, Hunter, let's have it out tonight."

"Brave Bravo Six will die tonight. Do not sleep tonight."

"Yeah, you sound good on the radio—we'll see you guys in Hanoi next week."

"Americans sleep forever after tonight. Watch for the Hunter tonight."

For forty-five minutes the grunts wondered out loud whether the Hunter was a North Vietnamese who had mastered English or the soldier they had all heard about, the tall blonde American who had defected and was advising the NVA in the field. The Hunter turned out to be neither. He was Gunnery Sergeant Harold Zell and he was calling from an American tank base ten miles to the east. After a few beers in the club, Zell felt the need for a little excitement, so he climbed into one of his tanks and turned the radio dials until he stumbled onto a field unit's frequency. Gunny Zell then spread as much terror as the listening unit could work up in its collective imagination.

And, there was the night Private First Class Paul Jenkins showed more carelessness than usual. Jenkins was known for losing things, misplacing things, forgetting things and for leaving his pistol and grenade launcher on "fire" when they should be on "safe." One night Jenkins fell asleep holding his pistol. Something caused his trigger finger to contract and Jenkins' forty-five sent a bullet whistling through the night air. But before it lifted into the cool breeze off the sea, the bullet disturbed the quiet air two inches above the right ear of Corporal Roger DeHaan, Jenkins' squad leader. Jenkins was later fined twenty-five dollars by his company commander.

Then there was the day Sam conferred his approval on the Third Herd. Andrews' platoon had taken point on one of the daily moves and had done well. After the Company was settled, Sam called a meeting with the Herd's squad leaders. He told them they had made much improvement in the past few weeks and he no longer considered them the weakest platoon in the Company. Those who had been with Sam more than a few weeks now wondered if he had been affected by the heat, for nearly everyone knew he offered compliments about as frequently as he expressed laughter—very rarely. Sam knew he was considered excessively critical, demanding, more like a machine than a human, but he also knew that to preserve every grunt's chances for a safe return to the States he had to constantly push people to produce what they considered impossible or unnecessary. He had to be sparing in his praise to keep his grunts tough. After meeting with their commander, the grunts went back to wondering how much more of the unexpected the operation held.

While Sam was grudgingly admired for several of his abilities, he was detested for others. Those for which he was detested were related to the fact that he intended to make a career of the military—Sam was a lifer. He was also a proud and sensitive combat leader. Sam was proud of the fact that he had never gotten his company lost in the jungle or in the hills, he had never left anything useful to the enemy at a former position or along the trail, and he had the highest body count in the battalion. Now on the latest operation Sam was sensitive of a certain development, one which did nothing to uphold his reputation: the other companies in the battalion had more enemy contacts than Bravo so far. All Bravo had produced lately were heat casualties. Another career-oriented individual in the battalion thought he saw in this situation the chance to engage in the game of one-upmanship that would enhance his own career pattern.

A few hours after Bravo left Hill 125, Alpha Company assumed the position, and the company commander decided he had found some equipment left behind by Bravo. He was only too willing to report his find. The next morning, battalion called Sam on the matter. The operations officer was professionally tactful in passing on the veiled admonition, "See if you can't do something about this kind of thing in the future, cuz you know how hot the Old Man is on hanging onto your gear." No company commander could stand for the implication that his troops were so poorly disciplined as to intentionally discard essential gear. Sam called a meeting of all his staff NCOs and officers and explained the situation. "That fucking Alpha Six—we can't take an accusation like that and do nothing about it!" The discussion of what to do lasted well after sunset.

Finally, wrapped up in what he thought to be the ultimate loyalty, the executive officer volunteered to take a detail back to 125 and check out the allegation. Now the only question was who would accompany the exec on the mission. Sam made it sound like an open question, but he knew his grunts were far too precious to risk on so selfish a mission, so it was to the honor and pride of his career sergeants that he appealed in describing the necessity of the detail. With visions of fitness reports subtly dangled before their eyes, the three staff sergeants "volunteered." The patrol, certainly one of the least sensible ever run by an American force in the entire war, left the perimeter at seven the next morning.

An hour later, Alpha Company called, reporting that there had been some confusion, the man who found the gear was mistaken, the matter wasn't really important and should be dropped. So, halfway to Hill 125 the patrol was called back. On this day the troops saw demonstrated the special vanities of which lifers are capable. There was no longer any room for doubt in young minds now. To the junior officers and grunts who talked about it for days after, the special patrol provided just "another reason why"—another reason not to stay in the Corps beyond the first enlistment.

And then there was the most memorable day of all in the flatlands, the day Bravo Company observed Ho Chi Minh's birthday. On May 19, 1969, the leader of the Vietnamese nationalist movement and of the Democratic Republic of Vietnam would be seventy-nine years old. It was widely known that communist forces had a habit of launching major attacks on national holidays or birthdays of historical figures, so Sam asked for some reinforcement from the eighteenth to the twenty-first. Since Bravo was in an area flat enough to support several roads, the grunts were augmented by two tanks. For the day preceding Ho's birthday, Sam planned a complete perimeter sweep to make sure no NVA would crawl up to an attack position. What he had in mind for second and third platoons was a coordinated patrol, a sweeping-force, blocking-force action like the ambush-turned-fiasco first and third had run a week before. Sam figured it was impossible for either unit to get lost this time, since there were both roads and streams in the area. The plan was simple: the platoons would leave the perimeter in opposite directions; second, and one of the tanks, would ambush a road-stream junction; third would sweep down a streambed toward second. If no enemy were pushed into the ambush, the platoons would go back home by different routes, at different times.

Three hours after it began, the patrol took on the potential for disaster. With no enemy sighted and only 100 meters remaining between the ambush and third platoon in the streambed, the coordinated phase of the patrol was over. Each unit began to change course and move into its assigned route home. The third platoon point man, PFC Ron Tobias, was the first man out of the stream; he looked ahead and froze. He was the first in either platoon to realize the tank crew had not received word about his unit's whereabouts—they were still looking for the NVA to shoot. Tobias watched as the tank's barrel swung toward him, stopped and lowered to his height. He looked down the deep, dark 90-millimeter gun tube seventy-five meters away for about half a second, then dove head-first down the ten-foot embankment. Then came the ear splitting wham and a screaming whoosh as two hundred quarter-inch ball bearings from the tank's anti-personnel round flew a few feet overhead. Andrews grabbed the radio, "Bravo! Bravo! Bravo! This is Three! Get that bull off us, over!" Again the wham and whoosh overhead. And a tree across the stream disappeared. "Bravo! Bravo! This is Three! He's still after us—get him off, get him off!"

The tank was finally reached and silenced, but the driver was sure he saw some NVA instead of friendlies, so second platoon turned around and swept along the west embankment as third sat and waited on the east. No NVA bodies. Ron Tobias and the rest of third platoon decided to take a break. "Fucking tankers can't even tell the difference between us and gooners—guess people get stupid as hell when they ride everywhere they go instead of humping."

Two hours after the American tank fired at the American grunts, the latter were walking into their Company perimeter. They could see a definite improvement in the patrol base—on the landing zone sat a pallet of beer. They could also see that no one seemed to notice their return. There was a crowd around a tank that had moved inside the perimeter to assume a night defensive position. Rolling past the mortar pits, it had set off a mine. The tank had its right tread blown off; Bravo had five mortarmen injured. It was not a fragmentation mine so the injuries were broken legs, rocks and dirt driven under the skin, and temporary deafness instead of punctured lungs and intestines, and severed limbs. All of the five would return. For the next two hours, while the ice around the beer melted and drew a dark red line down the tank trail, the grunts probed with knives at the dry hard earth for more booby traps. Three details of a dozen men each crawled on hands and knees, shoulder to shoulder. Their cautious jabbing uncovered five more of the large flat Russian mines.

In the final hour of daylight the beer was distributed. No one could tell it had once been cold. Far to the north in Hanoi, Uncle Ho would be most pleased to know what his birthday had meant to one American company.

The next morning the futility of tanks in Vietnam was further illustrated. A tank with a towbar arrived and began dragging the disabled tank back to its base. The rescue vehicle got only one hundred meters down the road before losing a tread of its own on yet another mine. The grunts could find no sympathy for the crews of the two crippled tanks.

"Now ain't that too bad—them tankers will have to do a little walking for their showers and beer tonight!"

"Yeah, and carry their own Cokes and all them Cs, tough shit, eh?"

Only one occurrence during the days in the flatlands contributed to the accomplishment of Bravo Company's mission. One afternoon a squad from second platoon found a cache of fifty-two 82-millimeter rounds and fuses for North Vietnamese mortars. The cache was one of thousands like it placed all over South Vietnam. Viet Cong and North Vietnamese attacks are planned around the locations of such deposits of food and ammunition. The mortar rounds were discovered when Lance Corporal Archie Lawson almost tripped the booby trap wire that would have detonated the entire cache and taken his squad with it. Lawson's squad returned the following day and blew the cache with demolition charges.

The rest of Bravo Company's time in the flatlands was filled by just about all the small hour-by-hour activities experienced by all other grunts in all other wars. There were 27 poker games played, 137 weapons cleaned, seven mustaches grown, six night ambushes run, 328 foxholes and 12 mortar pits dug, an uncountable number of bitches uttered, two promotions awarded, 488 malaria pills taken, 1220 C-ration meals eaten, 125 cans of Seven-Up drunk, 389 pieces of mail (which included one birth announcement and three Dear Johns) received, 93 canteens of Kool-Aid mixed, 18 guards caught sleeping on post ("Must be a bad battery in the radio, Captain"), nine cases of diarrhea suffered, 347 letters written, and an infinite number of sexual conquests dreamed.

7 Moaning and Groaning

Operation Virginia Ridge was now twenty days old. It was not only unusual for a rifle company in a combat zone to walk almost three weeks and encounter no ambushes, no firefights, it was unheard of. The quiet had of course been welcome, but by now all the grunts were nervous about it. It couldn't last forever, could it? Uncle Ho up in Hanoi wasn't about to give it all up now, was he? As all knew it would, the word to move out again came. This time it provoked, not the usual bitches, but a slightly ominous quiet. The word was that the grunts would be moving toward the north for the next few days.

The rest of Virginia Ridge turned out to be a steady movement toward the Demilitarized Zone, the five-mile-wide strip that had divided Vietnam since the Geneva Convention of 1954. Throughout its existence, the DMZ has come to mean different things to different people. To the diplomats who drew it, the line represented a face-saving truce to a problem whose solution was too deeply tied up with personal vanity and national honor to be dealt with realistically, a truce which saved but little western face and few Vietnamese lives. To the Vietnamese living south of it, the line meant a flimsy guarantee that rice could be planted and harvested in peace, that a governing group could have its sovereignty recognized the world over. To the Vietnamese living north of it, the line was a constant and humiliating reminder that the reunification of a homeland and a way of life, ravaged by westerners for more than a century, was still unfinished.

To the young grunts who would walk toward it now, the DMZ meant other things still, some things known and some not. In the first place, the Z was the reason the grunts were in Vietnam; if it had never been violated, the grunts could be making decent money, chasing girls, fixing up their cars, getting drunk or going to school back in the World. For now, walking toward the Z meant walking back up on Virginia Ridge and that, of course, meant humping the hills again. It also meant there would be a slight increase in danger, since everyone knew there were NVA north of the line, while south of it there were, between encounters with those same NVA, days of boredom and safety. The rest of what moving to the Z meant was not known by anyone, not Sam, not the general, not the most daring of diviners.

The tanks and grunts both moved out at six in the morning, the former rumbling back home to the east, the latter cursing and farting off to the north. After 800 meters Bravo stopped so Sam could examine the terrain ahead through field glasses and talk on the radio with Charlie Company. The two companies were to meet on Charlie's position of the night before, then Bravo would push on for some 1400 meters and a one-night stand.

At their link-up an hour later, the grunts of Charlie were relieved to see friendly faces again. All they had seen the previous two nights were North Vietnamese faces. A platoon of NVA hit Charlie's lines three times in those two nights, and followed each assault with mortar barrages through the remainder of the night. The score so far was twelve NVA dead to four dead Americans. The scene on top of Charlie's hill was anything but a model of tactical discipline. It was a mob scene, as the latest and friendly visitors crowded around the grunts of Charlie to hear about the last two nights.

"Did they come right up to your lines?"—

"How many was there?"—

"How many confirms you get?"—

"Did they have rockets?"—

"Did they use gas on you?"

Bravo was up and on the move again in fifteen minutes, just as the heat was starting to get up. The map showed a streambed about seven hundred meters ahead, and there Sam expected to find a temporary NVA patrol base. "Second, you take point and pick your point man real careful—there's gotta be something a little ways ahead." Six hundred meters ahead the Company heard two shots. Safety selectors clicked off down the column; against the silence born of fear, they seemed as loud as freight car couplings taking up slack. The column dropped to the ground. "Hey, that don't sound like a 16 or a 47 . . . and only two of them. What the shit?"

The two rounds had come from Lieutenant Herb Marriott's pistol, and they had killed two North Vietnamese regulars. Second platoon had been careful enough to sneak up on a small bunker complex on the stream without being seen or heard. The point man began hearing voices, halted the Company, and signaled for Marriott. The two advanced slowly toward the voices—"They sound like a bunch of damn turkeys, them gooks, you know, gobble, gobble"—the rest of the second platoon inching along behind. The trail went into a small bend, straightened and, "There we were, me and my radioman and two gooks, just staring at each other. They had this dumb look on their faces—I guess we did too—like, how you guys get here, you know?" Marriott was the only one of the four to speak: "Lai dai, lai dai" (come here, come here).

The two NVA looked at each other and ran for the nearest bunker. Marriott fired two shots from about twenty feet and the two enemy fell dead on top of their bunker. Such shooting was not typical of the average marine, but the result was no less final for its luck. Resuming the hump, the grunts filed by the fresh bunkers and saw their first dead NVA in two months. All the newbys acquired by the Company in two months came up with the predictable reaction. "Jeez, I heard they were small but not that small. That one looks like he's about twelve years old. Jeez!"

The last eight hundred meters of the hump produced six more heat casualties. Canteens were filled in the stream and Sam decided enough daylight remained for a break in the shade. Fifteen minutes later first platoon began trailing out toward the objective but had to stop when two more heat casualties developed. Another break in the shade was ordered. For the remainder of the move the grunts walked a hundred meters, laid in the shade for ten minutes, then walked another hundred meters. Even the old salts and short-timers thought it was unusually hot. "Christ, I can't remember it getting this hot, can you?" An unexpected stream, not on the map, was found and fallen into. The grunts poured helmetsful over their heads, down shirts and pants, then moved on, back to another of the humps that had to be completed.

Just before the second stream was found, Lance Corporal Thomas Ecroyd's mind decided it was time to reverse the madness of the hump and the heat. It was time to say screw it, time to survive. Ecroyd tripped on a tree root and rolled downhill into the man ahead. When his buddies tried to help him back up he started moaning and his legs refused to support any weight or take another step. His pack, rifle and canteens were carried by others and he was half pushed, half carried the remaining distance.

> "Six, this is Three. Be informed I got four heat casualties but am not stopped. We'll bring them in but we might break the column."
>
> "This is Six! Leave a squad back with them who think they're so thirsty and keep the other two squads on the column, then when you get up here I want the names of them non-hackers."

Just after the last man in the Company reached the objective, Ecroyd's protest took a violent and directed turn. At the sight of Sam, Ecroyd began running up the hill screaming, "I'm gonna kill you, you bastard! Leave us alone! You want to kill us, all of us —I'm gonna kill you, kill you, kill you . . . ." He fell, clawing the earth, his face reflecting more exhaustion and disillusion than his mind could contain.

Sam's verdict was characteristic. "These non-hacking babies get every damn thing they want growing up back in the States, then they get over here in a war and they think they get a little tired, they just think they're so tired. Hell, he could go another five clicks today at least. He just thought he was through."

Ecroyd was sent out on the next chopper for his psychiatric evaluation. The grunts debated into the next day whether Ecroyd had staged a scene like the Dennis Moy incident of two and a half weeks before just to get out of the bush, or whether he really had, like Moy, cracked in the heat. They decided it probably was the real thing when they learned later they had humped through a 118° afternoon.

On the other side of the hill Herb Marriott debated something else in his mind: how had five hours of practice in firing the pistol on the training range prepared him to shoot with the perfection he had shown today? That night the grunts rested on soil 3500 meters from the DMZ.

The next morning all of Bravo but one platoon moved out to the north. Second would make the move after sending out the water cans. The hump was short and it was over before the heat had a chance to do any damage, but it ended in a climb sharp enough to break a free-running sweat on one hundred twenty-six bodies. It turned out to be one of those rare enjoyable moves. The grunts could smile and laugh as they bargained over the meager treat they deserved.

"If you get a heat tab and the rest of the makings, I'll put in the water for coffee."

"Thought you'd never ask, Miss—do it for us and this time put in four sugars."

The grunts were told in the morning where they were—two thousand meters south of the DMZ—but it didn't mean much to most. Their hump for the day was already over. But being 2000 meters away from the Z meant a lot to Sam and his plans for the safety of Bravo. It meant that Bravo was just within range of the North Vietnamese 61-millimeter, and well within that of enemy 82-millimeter mortars and all sizes of rockets. Later in the afternoon, however, the idea of 2000 meters took on more meaning to each of the other lives here on the new position, Hill 130. Two choppers arrived with two 81-millimeter mortars and their crews.

"Hey, Chief, you see what the birds brought?"

"Yeah, no mail and two 81s."

"Wonder why; think we're gonna stay awhile?"

"That ain't what the Lieutenant said. He says we're gonna keep humping it toward the Z, but shit, who knows? Don't sweat it though, you won't be humping them 81s."

Sam held up sundown until his new and bigger mortars were dug in. Two squads from first platoon and one from second would have the ambushes this first night on 130; third and the rest would have the perimeter watch. One of the ambushes would be on the stream touching the western slope of the new position. The other would be farther down the same stream. Both were set half an hour after sunset. Five hours later the shadows began to move for Lieutenant George Sorenson and his squads on ambush.

A night in the Nam always comes alive to some degree—things are either seen or heard. If something is both seen and heard, it usually turns out to be a tiger, rock ape or North Vietnamese. With a half-moon out tonight Sorenson expected to see bushes move and work on the imagination. This time he and his grunts also began hearing whatever it was out there, and the small noises were coming closer. A few moments later sounds and human forms came together. The suspected NVA re-supply trail turned out to be exactly that. A small shock set in—battalion intelligence was actually right for once. Then a larger shock—there were more than a handful of NVA in this party. One grunt measured the number of enemy as "a whole shitpot full!" Sorenson got on the radio and whispered his discovery back to Sam. "Six, this is One. I think I got some visitors out here."

"This is Six, keep your people alert out there and let me know what happens. Don't let them get excited—it could be some damn rock apes, you know." Sam had received dozens of such calls during his tour and since he knew what the night could do to a tired and scared grunt's perceptions, he greeted all with skepticism.

In as little time as it took him to press the transmission button on his radio, Sorenson was back. "This is One. I can see them now, there's about seven or eight moving right for us, all in a row."

"Okay now, let their point go on by, and hit their middle, then we'll wipe up the ends after."

But this was no small reconnaissance in a local area. "Six, this is One. I'm still counting and twenty-seven have gone past us so far —some are really loaded down looks like. They just keep coming!" Sorenson had never seen anything like it but Sam recognized it as a major re-supply movement. The NVA were going to plant some new ammunition and food caches in the area. Within a month an infantry unit would follow and use the supplies to support operations against the Americans and South Vietnamese here in Quang Tri Province.

Sam put the Company perimeter on 100 percent alert and told the mortar crews to get all the ammo they could find ready by the tubes. Then back to Sorenson. "Can you tell how many of them there is yet?"

"They're still coming—there's thirty-nine, forty, forty-one, forty-two . . . ."

Sensing that he was on the verge of a beautiful body count, his first in months, Sam could barely control himself as he told his lieutenant what would happen next. "Now listen, you're gonna get six rounds of HE right on them, then the illumination will start. You open up as soon as the first six rounds hit them, not before, or you're liable to get yourself overrun in the dark. Then you stay there and move the 60s around on them after they start to split up and scatter—and don't let your men chase anybody, stay there."

Before the privates and corporals took over for the evening Sam had one last message for the mortar crews. "This is Six! Now don't mess it up, it's gonna be six HE, then the illum. Get them rounds right next to you with the safety wires off, One actual's gonna tell you when. When I hear them first rounds splash, I want to hear a lotta fire and a lotta gooks screaming. I better see nothing but heads and arms and legs flying—and don't let any of them get away to tell about it!"

Four seconds later Sorenson whispered "fire" to the gun pits. Over one hundred North Vietnamese ammunition and rice-bearers froze as they heard those six rounds, fat with death and pain, leave their tubes in quick succession—thunk-thunk-thunk. The enemy column did about all it could do—walk a little faster and hope the shells were meant for someone else. But fourteen seconds later, as the rounds quietly whistled back to earth through the cool air, they knew they were to be the victims tonight. The first rounds overshot the column, but they were close enough to stop all thought in North Vietnamese heads about empty stomachs, girl friends, sore feet or reuniting the fatherland.

After Sorenson called back an aiming adjustment, at least half of each volley hit within twenty-five meters of the trail. The North Vietnamese were seeing and hearing explosions in front of them and behind them—blinding white flashes, massive rushes of wind and thousands of white-hot steel fragments were shattering young bodies, shattering myths about what poor matches the imperialistic American aggressors were for the battalions of Uncle Ho and General Giap. Then the crack and rattle of M-16s and machine guns at close range filled the night.

The grunts were only about fifty feet away from the enemy trail—it was difficult to miss, even in the dark. The ambushing rifles and machine guns built their fire to a crescendo, held it for a few seconds, then slowed as each man and crew picked an individual target. Sam just listened and stared at where the red tracer bullets and mortar explosions blipped and streaked through the darkness. He wasn't happy, he was ecstatic. And, at the karump-rump-rump of each volley of mortar rounds splashing, at each burst of rifle fire, the grunts back on the perimeter looked at each other and grinned—"Get some, Man, oh get some! Shit, why can't I be down there!"

Sam interrupted his spectating long enough to call an artillery battery. He wanted to saturate the area around the ambush and pick up any enemy scattering back to the north. In fifteen minutes a twin-engine spotting plane was overhead and the 155-millimeter rounds were whistling in from the Army battery four miles away at Con Thien. With the spotting plane came the large support plane, Puff the Magic Dragon. Through the night Puff droned high overhead in a tight circle, dropping basketball flares and spraying the area with his guns. "Get some, Big Man, get some!"

Sam and the Defense Department's technology were turning

this once lush and life-giving land into a surrealistic stage suggesting the place where one awakes after his funeral. Shadows were pushed across the yellow-orange ground and brush by flares falling slowly on tiny parachutes, swells of red light came out from behind trees and draws as each artillery barrage impacted, and Puff's tracer bullets stitched a gently waving red line earthward. And the sounds, unnatural sounds, anti-life sounds—the sputter and crackle of flares falling into bushes and among the grunts, the once-in-awhile crack of ambushing rifles, the thunk-thunk of Sergeant Herr's mortars, the whine and whump of artillery, and overhead, the droning spotter plane, the extended belch of Puff's guns.

The grunts felt good, reassured, doing this kind of work knowing they were being backed up by Puff and Phantom jets and Navy cruisers and maybe the battleship *New Jersey* lying offshore, and even a battery of the U.S. Army, "those good old worthless fucking doggies." And, if by some fluke something went wrong to reverse one's fortune in the bush, the American grunts could count on a short helicopter ride back to an air-conditioned hospital and the care of real doctors.

For one side tonight there were thousands of people, well trained in specialties of support, willing to leave a television program, a cold beer, a USO show in the clubs in the rear, to jump into planes or choppers or gun turrets and help the grunts in the bush. For the other side, there was none of that support—no ships reaching fifteen miles inland, no all-weather jet fighter-bombers, not even the faintest hope of a big shiny Freedom Bird to take them from the war after a certain number of days. If he got ambushed this night, it would probably be better if the NVA soldier died here in the stream named Song Ngan, for survival meant the agony of several days of crawling back into the DMZ with wounds unattended. And if he made it to an aid station alive he could expect to be operated on by a fanatic better trained in the politics of peoples' liberation than medicine. If there were no ambushes there were the endless humps south, the hunger, the malaria.

George Sorenson, Sergeant Herr, the Army, and Puff kept up

their turkey shoot through the night. For five hours it was nothing but:

"That last bunch was right on them—I could see the helmets and arms flying . . . Now go left five-zero and add two-five, six more . . . ."

"Roger that, One. Six rounds for effect—left five-zero, add two-five . . . ."

Thunk——thunk——thunk——thunk——thunk——thunk.

"Beautiful . . . you're right on . . . I can hear them laying out there just moaning and groaning . . . Give me twelve more there, over . . . ."

"Roger that, One . . . ."

"No, wait, Disregard . . . There's some getting away from the blue line . . . add two-five . . . rounds away . . . rounds away . . . rounds away . . . ."

When dawn came Sam went down to the ambush site with second platoon for an assessment and a piece of whatever action remained. For the next three hours he kept the four squads on line and swept through and around the streambed, flushing the remaining wounded from the draws and folds in the cratered landscape, from behind the few small bushes. The pattern of this mop-up went beyond the pathetic, almost to the ridiculous: none of the remaining NVA able to move offered any resistance to the oncoming grunts. They either cowered in terror as their boyish faces absorbed the point blank rifle fire or they turned and ran up the barren slopes a few steps before having their backs and legs shattered by the bullets. Killing was unbelievably easy this morning—the grunts raced one another to drop each new enemy who tried to raise his hands or run. The next day the full account made its way around the lines.

"Yeah, it was just like practicing up for the range—we'd get some from the prone position, then the sitting, from one knee, standing up. Hell, it was easier than the damn range! No way you could miss them. You should have seen Chief do in this one slope that was trying to give up—he just stared him down, flipped his cigar ashes on the guy and blew his head almost clean off!"

Since this grim business was being carried out by human beings who had been brought up in a society which encourages individualism, there was more than one reaction to it. There were some who just did it, who years later would explain it with the old it-was-him-or-me line. There were some who couldn't get enough of it fast enough; those who wanted to kill and then carve initials on lifeless chests, or rearrange facial features. And, there were a few who were repulsed by this killing that was too easy, a few who wanted it stopped. These last few realized what Marines are supposed to do to an enemy in war, but they also realized that the bounds of reason were being crossed this morning. A valuable chance to take prisoners and possibly save other American lives was being ignored. But Bravo was out in the bush by itself, miles away from witnesses, and Sam was all alone with his victims, miles away from criticism. Only once did the outside world come close to finding out about the one-sided battle. Halfway through the mopping up, Sam received a radio call from Herb Marriott of second platoon. Marriott had just seen a grunt shoot on unarmed and wounded NVA soldier who would have made a good prisoner.

"We ought to get as many of these guys as we can, and send them back for questioning, don't you think?"

Sam was in no mood to debate matters he considered peripheral to the opportunity at hand. "Get off the radio with that kind of talk! We can't have the whole damn world listening in. Get back with your outfit."

By ten o'clock Sam was satisfied that he had found all the NVA there were to find. He turned the four squads around and headed back up his hill to call battalion with the body count: nineteen dead and one wounded, the latter a good intelligence prospect. Then the killers were turned into work parties to collect all the enemy gear worth sending back to division. It came to one rocket launcher with six rockets, fifteen half-pound blocks of demolitions, over twenty packs full of rice and personal possessions, six AK-47 rifles with several hundred rounds of ammunition, and a complete 61-millimeter mortar. Next to the bodies, the mortar was the most valuable prize of all, since it could fire the smaller American rounds and thus augment the company's firepower. It was nicknamed "moaning and groaning," after George Sorenson's comment of a few hours before on the condition of his victims. Sam officially ended the ambush by distributing among first and second platoons and the mortar crewmen the enemy packs, belts, canteens and personal effects of the newest victims in an old war. "Here, Chief, you take the gook's money and letters. I want his belt—you can tell by the buckle he was their lieutenant last night."

The score of the night's action would be a challenge for even a communist propagandist to report and explain. While losing at least twenty soldiers and hundreds of pounds of war supplies, the North Vietnamese Army could exact from the marines no more than a few hours of sleep. No one even twisted an ankle on the way back up the hill with his souvenirs.

The rest of the day was spent in fondling souvenirs and "blowing Zs." Around four o'clock a chopper came out. It took away the wounded prisoner and captured weapons after unloading mortar ammunition, water, C-rations, and a new second lieutenant. Later that night there was another I've-got-movement-over-here plea but no human forms came out of the dark. The Song Ngan continued on its way toward the sea as it had for centuries before this American unit staged an ambush on its banks, but for the next three days its brown water took on a reddish cast it had not shown before.

What had occurred in the first ten hours of May 22 at grid coordinates 055669 was something that should not have happened to the proud young warriors of any nation. But it did, and for the marines there was a beautiful vengeance in it all: the thousands of grunts who had stepped on all the box mines and booby traps and pungi stakes in the past five years had died like this too, without the chance to fight back. The grunts gorged themselves on the good taste of it in the next few hours. Then after lost sleep was recovered, as they looked again at the souvenirs claimed from bodies and packs—the pictures of North Vietnamese girl friends and families, the letters—the grunts of Bravo came to reflect more deeply on what they had done. Things hometownish and emotional, things right and natural in an adolescent sort of way came to mind. "Christ, Tony, did you see the look on that slope's face when he took that last round?" A few realized that at this same time on another hill somewhere, North Vietnamese soldiers were triumphantly sifting through the pictures and letters of new American casualties. An unvoiced question here on Hill 130 was "How can I hide my girl's pictures so no NVA ever puts his dirty commie gook hands on them if I buy the ranch?"

Fewer still reached the bottom level of these reflections and came to see the young Vietnamese they had killed as allies in the bigger war of individual existence, as young men with whom they were united throughout their lives against the big impersonal "thems" of the world who would make the grunts in a few years think they could never make it big. The grunts knew there were things that caused people to lead different lives. From their parents they had heard the nervous excuses, the flashes of resentment when they had first asked why some people lived in bigger houses than others, why some people wore dress-up clothes to work. A few of the grunts now saw their dead enemy as comrades in the struggle against the realities of weakness within themselves too painful to admit, brothers in the struggle against the faceless and nameless forces of circumstance which would send them to the union hall instead of the country club, which would keep them at the gas station, the factory. In killing the grunts of North Vietnam, the grunts of America had killed a part of themselves.

8 Hill 174

The Company mortar section, now four tubes strong with "moaning and groaning," began the morning of the twenty-third by firing over 200 rounds in the direction of the day's move north. The move turned out to be another of the rare enjoyable humps. All 800 meters of it were under a cloud cover. Since they were getting so close to the DMZ, battalion was telling all four company commanders to stay off the more prominent hilltops. Sam set Bravo in on a finger coming off a hill about 170 meters high. There were comments about what a benny it was not to have to climb all the way up, but there were also comments about being fired at or attacked from higher ground in the night. The routines of digging in and cursing everything in sight and mind were altered somewhat by the universal realization of the Company's new position—1200 meters from the Z. The sounds of talk and laughter were less audible; those of digging incoming holes a little deeper, more prominent. But the new diligence was relieved in midafternoon when the great green chopper arrived from Quang Tri. There were bennies for everyone—carrots, orange juice, C-rats, lettuce, tomatoes, oranges, water, grape juice, cucumbers, canned hamburgers, three sacks of mail, one man returning from R & R and four slackers from the rear.

One of the most popular grunts in the Company was Corporal Anthony Stankiewicz, just returned that afternoon from his rest and recreation leave in Singapore. Everyone knew Stanks as the kind of marine and friend who would give some of his water, even his prized can of peaches, to any other grunt who said he needed it, who really needed it to go any farther on a hump. But no one ever asked for it. Just knowing it was there, bouncing up and down on the humps, having its paint chipped off by other C-rat cans, sustained a lot of grunts during their time in the bush. Stanks was glad to get back to his friends in the bush and Bravo was glad to see him again. For the next two days the grunts would tell him about the big ambush and he would tell them about Singapore.

Stanks loved to take pictures and he had promised everyone he would take plenty while he was gone. The anticipation of seeing the album of new polaroid shots made it easy for the grunts to forget where they were, what they were close to.

"Hey, Chief, you seen Stanks' pictures yet?"

"Not yet. Red Mountain's got them. Says our squad gets them after we're done digging in."

"I ain't seen them yet either, but that guy what humps a radio in the first platoon says they're really outa sight."

For those who had not yet been on R & R or in a pornographic movie house, the pictures were a little "outa sight." There were two postcardlike scenes of the city and then dozens of snapshots of the marine and his five-day girl friend in their hotel bedroom. In each successive picture ("Fucking A, Man, turn the page!") there was less and less clothing until Stanks and his girl with the name that would be forgotten in a few weeks were down to doing their basic thing of life and love, down to doing what was the reason a grunt dreams of his R & R, counts the days and hours to it. "Oh Christ, how did that feel after seven months in the bush, Man? Look at him going at it in this one—get some, Stanks! Put it to her, Pal!"

When the study of R & R pictures became difficult in the light of a dying sun, Sam called his platoon commanders and sergeants together for a meeting. The session was approached warily, since for only about the second or third time on the operation Sam was smiling and laughing. "Listen to him—I bet he got permission to take us into North Vietnam, probably all the way to fucking Hanoi!" Sam was wearing the small nervous smile worn by an adolescent asking his favorite girl for his first date. He was sitting next to his incoming hole but he still shifted as if on legs weak with nerves. A trace of a blush came through the dark Indian complexion. "Good old Mustang Six sent us a message here and I want to read it here to you now." It was a message of congratulations for Bravo's ambush two nights before: I therefore commend your Company . . . professionalism . . . maximum use of supporting arms . . . dealt insurgent Communist forces a heavy blow." The proud Captain tried to make his reading of the message sound as officious as the typed words but it didn't quite come across. He pulled his mustache, pinched his lower lip and scratched his cheek a little harder but it was no use—that small smile kept growing, kept betraying the pride in the career, the pride in mastering the doctrines ". . . while at the same time sustaining not one American casualty . . . credit to Corps and country."

"So go on back to your areas now and take this message back to the troops—I want every one of them to know the big people in the rear think they done all right back there. Okay, that's it."

There had been more satisfaction in this day than in a long time, more than anyone had a right to expect. Usually whatever satisfaction one found had only one source—some mail, maybe a beer or Coke. Today, however, there were three sources—Stanks' pictures, the Colonel's congratulations and a quiet night.

May twenty-fourth dawned clear and cool. It looked like today's would be the second tolerable move in as many days. "Two nice humps in a row—that's unreal. Now it'll probably rain for two days straight."

"Maybe, but that's in the future. Take all the bennies you can get right now."

The mortar section fired 225 rounds in the direction of the march and Bravo stepped off to the north. In a few seconds the day's temperature did an about-face, from cool to very hot, as three incoming mortar rounds landed within twenty-five meters of the column. After hugging the earth and finding no wounds, the grunts got back to the hump at as fast a pace as loaded packs would allow. Sam and his Company were no longer alone in the green hills; their every move would now be watched by the unseen adversary to the north.

After sending three rounds at Bravo, the North Vietnamese turned their tubes a few hundred meters to the west and gave Charlie Company a few rounds. This time they were right on target and Charlie had to call in choppers to get four emergency medevacs out.

The new position was different from the last two in a way terribly obvious to the grunts. They were not on an inconspicuous slope coming off a larger hill, but right on top of a peak all too prominent, Hill 174. Bravo was dangling right in front of North Vietnamese binoculars and gun tubes. Walking over the top of 174, one wanted to duck as if moving in front of a movie projector so as not to draw any undue attention. Now the grunts crouched 300 meters from the Z.

Besides its prominence, the thing most obvious about Hill 174 was that it had been home for someone else before. A trenchline zigzagged across the eastern half of the hill, partially overgrown and filled in during the past few months. The trench and the discovery of a red-soled shoe made the previous occupants North Vietnamese. The grunts established a perimeter and sat down to study the terrain to their front for unfriendly movement and listen for enemy mortar pops, the muffled pings that give warning of enemy rounds on the way. Two hours later, with nothing sighted and nothing heard, Bravo dug in. During the afternoon of getting the new position ready for night, there occurred the only semi-humorous incident that would ever happen for this American Company on Hill 174.

Earlier that morning, when telling his platoon commanders where the Company would be going, Sam had pointed out "the hill with the white tree on it." The dead barkless tree had been an essential landmark to the grunts approaching 174, but now its height and color made it just as obvious to enemy gunners as it had been to Bravo earlier. It was probably only a matter of time before it would become an aiming stake for the NVA. Demolitions could not be used to bring down the tall white spire—the noise and smoke would give away Bravo's exact position. There was still a chance the Company had not been detected and that chance must be preserved as long as possible. The tree looked rotten but it exacted much sweat and energy before succumbing. First they tried pulling it over with ropes but it would not come down with five, ten, fifteen grunts pulling and sweating. Then they tried hacking it down, using entrenching tools as axes; only the E-tools broke.

For one of the very rare times in their history the Marines decided to fall back from a mission. They said "screw it," and swung Tarzan-style from the short remains of branches. The tree had become another rare benny, allowing the grunts to forget the DMZ, the NVA, and the war for a few precious minutes. It was once again like climbing trees and racing go-carts back home in the summer. There was no longer any choice about the method of removing the tree. Demolition charges would be used to blow it a few minutes before dark, as the mortars registered their night defensive fires outside the perimeter. The old white tree had shown a tenacity the marines came to admire. It had preserved an existence beyond life through twenty-three years of war and was not about to give it all up without protest. "Fucking thing don't want to come down. Well hell, let's leave it there . . . leave it alone."

An hour later after the escape from war granted by the tree, the grunts were jerked back to it all by their sister Charlie Company and the NVA. Around three in the afternoon mortar pops were heard. The scream went round the perimeter—"Incoming, hit it!"—and one hundred thirty-eight young filthy bodies scrambled for seventy foxholes. The grunts uttered short hopes and fought to stretch steel helmets down over shoulders and knees. Twenty-one seconds later the dominant feeling was relief as they heard the karump-rump-rump hit on somebody else's hill. After the initial impacts the grunts raised heads to see where it was hitting. They watched in awe as the rounds were walked up, on top of, and over the hill Charlie Company occupied to the west, a uniform twenty meters between each burst. Karump-rump-rump from the north side of Charlie's perimeter across to the south, six splashes in a row scattering packs and ponchos and water cans and bodies, then a shift a few meters to the west and six more in a row. It ceased only after some twenty rounds had neatly perforated the hill, leaving a geometric pattern of destruction, death and pain. Fifteen minutes later the medevac birds were hovering over the neighboring hill. Feeling awe for the deadly accuracy of one's enemy is no way to begin a night, or a day, in a combat zone.

The sun was down. The grunts held their breath, held it to listen and stare, breathed again. Talk was low and of the essential —of cars that would be driven back home, schools that would be attended, girls who would be taken. The thoughts were from the television generation, from those to whom death had never been a close possibility. "If I get it I wonder what my last words will be?" The fear now felt was the old one about the neighborhood bully waiting around the next corner to wash your face in the snow. All sounds became those of the enemy.

"Hey, Johnny, what was that?"

"Relax, that's a rock ape."

"My dying ass—that's a gook!"

"You throw a frag out there and the Captain'll have your dying ass."

"Yeah, but we gotta do something or he'll just crawl up here and slit our throats!"

"We are gonna do something, shit-for-brains—we're gonna shut the fuck up and crash before the real stuff starts tonight."

Now the DMZ was felt, really felt. Nowhere else in South Vietnam, nowhere else in the war that had no front, did a line on the ground mean what it meant here. No matter where a bush company stopped and set a defensive perimeter, the grunts knew the enemy might be out there, and then again he might not be out there. The enemy might attack each night, and then again he might not. There was considerable room for uncertainty in one's favor, for hope. But sitting on a hill 300 meters from that pink line dividing one kind of Vietnamese from another kind, one could feel how the spaces normally allotted to hope and luck were now greatly constricted. There was simply no doubt about it here: the NVA were out there and they would never let any American unit sit around so close to the land they drew life and strength from without doing something about it. Never.

By some miracle the NVA granted Bravo a quiet night. Coming out of a light, nervous sleep, the grunts again felt the atmosphere loaded with imminence. Consciousness was back; Hill 174 was back. All was quiet here, as if the grunts had ventured onto a tender place on the earth's body and she was holding her breath at their intentions.

Things happened in fairly quick succession on the morning of May twenty-fifth. At seven-thirty a chopper brought out a pallet loaded with mortar ammunition. Half an hour later a second bird brought out thirty cans of water, two R & R returnees, and took from the hill one man due to rotate back to the States and one for R & R. Around eleven, Sam began sending out his first patrols. Two weeks before, a squad leader from second platoon told Sam that before he rotated back to the World, he wanted to take his squad into the DMZ—it would be something nice to tell the guys back home. For about the same reason, Herb Marriott said he would go with the squad. So Corporal Lonnie Bradley took nine grunts, a machine gun team, a medical corpsman and his lieutenant north.

Since the pink boundary line on the maps was not on the ground, Bradley didn't know exactly when he crossed into the Z, but he soon had a good idea by the new look of things. The squad found trails used less than a day before, maybe only a few hours before. They found small campsites where North Vietnamese had eaten and slept and crapped. They found hastily abandoned fires with ashes still warm and smoking. Marriott called the findings back to Sam, "Yeah, well that's okay. Go on a couple hundred more meters and call back." The trail showed more use the farther the Americans intruded. Almost simultaneously Marriott and Bradley concluded they were on the trail of a mortar crew, and it was very possible they could capture it. An enemy mortar would be a nice trophy for the Company—it couldn't be much farther. So in they went, deeper and deeper, still seeing the campsites with rice scattered around recent fires, still finding footprints, rice bowls, discarded clothing. Finally Marriott's sense of responsibility got the best of him and he called Sam again for advice. As near as he could tell, they were about a click into the Z. For nine rifles, one machine gun and one radio that was deep enough. Nothing smaller than a battalion should go any farther. Bradley and Marriott decided to leave the war trophies to others.

Eight hundred meters later, with Hill 174 in sight and its perimeter only about 500 meters away, the North Vietnamese chose to confirm to Bradley's squad that they had indeed been on the trail of an enemy mortar. The first round was some fifty meters short. The grunts were almost in a full run when the second and third rounds hit. They, too, were short, and the enemy purpose was understood. They just wanted to play with the grunts a little, remind them that a real live enemy was out there, and chase the Americans back onto their hill.

At one in the afternoon Sam went out with his second patrol, to the west. They had been out about two hours when Marriott called a third time, reporting his squad was back on 174. Sam and his grunts were finding nothing to compare with the evidence of enemy activity Bradley had seen. In a few more minutes the difference in findings would be of no consequence.

A mortar increment is a small cloth bag, four inches square, containing an explosive charge. Attached to a fin assembly, a cluster of increments propels a mortar projectile to its target. Desirable firing distances are obtained by both adjusting the angle of the mortar tube and detaching from the round one, two or three increments. When ignited outside a gun tube the increments do not explode but burn, very fast and very hot, and thus present a constant fire hazard around gun pits and ammunition points. Once started, an increment fire is nearly impossible to stop.

Private First Class Vincent Pavone, Jr. was an ammunition-bearer and he was getting impatient. His can of hot dogs and beans was taking longer to heat than he was willing to wait, so he decided to add a couple increments to the trioxane ration heating bar under his can of lunch. The irritation Vince felt rose dramatically when he saw the increments melt the can, and dump his boiling lunch in the dirt. He then saw the fire run across the floor of the gun pit from one increment bag to the next until it settled in a pile of empty ammunition boxes and more loose increments. The junk pile flashed into flame and now posed a new and larger danger. The pallet of mortar rounds brought by chopper five hours before, not yet stored underground, rested only a foot away from the fire. If the fire spread to it, Sam would have much explaining to do and many letters of condolence to write. The mortar section leader hollered to the company executive officer, Mike Lancaster, that he had a fire in one of the pits, and several grunts ran up to help put it out.

The rising smoke on Hill 174 was as obvious to the North Vietnamese a few hundred meters away as it was to the grunts fighting it; the former recognized it as a rare opportunity. Now, on the warm afternoon of May 25, 1969, there came to the North Vietnamese within range of Hill 174 a pay-off for the uncounted months of endless marches through roadless jungles, dragging thousands of pounds of food and equipment on aching, bleeding backs and shoulders; the months of eating cold, clammy rice day in and day out with only a little rotten fish and a few drops of *nuoc-mam* sauce to add some taste; of suffering from the dysentery and malaria without proper rest or drugs; of dying on nameless hills, in unrecorded valleys and streambeds; of cowering in terror and hatred as the B-52s and Phantoms roared overhead at will, dropping an array of weapons designed to do nothing else but snuff out their small quiet lives. Now would come a reward no mortar crew in any nation's army had a right to hope for. At two in the afternoon a North Vietnamese Army assistant gunner let one of the heavy red rounds he had carried for weeks slide down the long tube on his Russian-made mortar. With a brain-jarring wham, the round shot into the hot clean air, lifted over the wounded land about 3180 feet, pointed its nose southward and began a long whistling descent.

The mortar pop was easily heard by all the grunts in Lancaster's firefighting force, and caused fear and conflicting orders to replace discipline and organization.

"Incoming! Back to your holes."

"No, we gotta get that fire in the pits out first."

"Get down, get down!"

"Get your ass up here on this fire."

"Fuck the fire, it ain't going nowhere—get in the holes, get down . . . ." Twenty-nine grunts raced for their foxholes; thirteen stayed to fight the fire.

The speed of descent of the enemy mortar round and the earth's rotation were such that after twenty-one seconds in the air the round would not land in the dirt of Hill 174; instead, it crashed into the top of the pallet of ammunition next to Vince Pavone's gun pit. An explosive chain was initiated as the round smashed through the top row of ammo boxes, and one-thousandth of a second later the main charge went, setting off the whole pallet, over 2500 pounds of high explosive. Hill 174 shook as in a death rattle and then for Bravo Company the world turned into a dark chaos of noise, dirt, hot metal and blood. The hill lifted, then fell back down in a rain of dirt, helmets, hot shrapnel and human limbs, dragging the chaos through longer and longer minutes. Even before the thunder of that massive explosion reached the ears of astonished North Vietnamese gunners, the dying was over. Whoever was in charge of such things back in the World would now have to send thirteen recruiters to thirteen pairs of parents with the news of Hill 174, thus causing thirteen ministers or priests to conduct thirteen memorial services, and thirteen undertakers to arrange thirteen more funerals.

But the North Vietnamese were not through with this American Company. The hill with the dark brown cloud hanging over it was now a target hard to pass up, difficult to miss. Twelve more rounds crashed into Bravo, adding to the day's wounded-in-action total. There could easily have been more, and without effective retaliation for some time, since Bravo's mortars were wiped out. But for an unknown reason the NVA decided they had done enough for one day.

Sam and his two squads had started running back to the perimeter when they heard the ammunition explode; they reached it just as the NVA mortars quit pounding the hill. Now they ran around to find corpsmen, platoon sergeants and squad leaders and get them functioning again to find and treat the wounded and get things ready for the medevac birds the radioman was calling. It was soon obvious the day's action was over, and survivors began crawling out of holes half-filled by the giant explosion. The grunts looked around trying to recognize the hill whose face had been so drastically altered. They saw chunks of flesh and boots and packs and rifles scattered indiscriminately. Walking down off the crest they began to find the dead and the wounded, dazed and moaning in the grass below. Some had been blown a hundred meters off the hill. All who had stayed to fight the increment fire were dead. Of those thirteen bodies, ten were found.

With death and pain all around, the living fell into a variety of roles and exhibited a variety of reactions to this day. As they looked for and recovered the wounded, some fell back on a religious discipline, some just fell apart and reverted to a dazed and preadolescent disbelief; they felt a superficial joy in refuting the obvious. A few held a stoic dignity, then joined the most serious of games in war, deciding who should have the privilege of giving his poncho to wrap the bodies of friends for their final chopper ride. And there were the ever-present emotional athletes—always ready with a mawkish sentiment at the drop of a helmet.

Four choppers ferried between Hill 174 and the Third Medical Battalion hospital at Quang Tri for the next hour and a half. Those untouched by the blast searched the grass and brush for victims, then carried the limp forms up to where the birds would touch down. Up the hill with a body, turn around and back down for another, up again.

> "That's all I remember that day after I came to—carrying guys I knew up that hill in a poncho. Up and down, up and down, all day long. I was in a daze all day, I didn't know what was happening—I started thinking like the whole world was like this and I was doing normal things."

Only after the last medevac bird took off was the final casualty count known. It came out to thirteen dead and twenty-eight wounded. The dead included two short-timers. One was Lance Corporal Alan Owens, a Kentuckian due to leave in eight days. In her last letter, his fiancee had reported that the wedding and reception were all set. The other short-timer was Corporal Stankiewicz of recent R & R fame. He was scheduled to leave in five weeks. Most of Stanks' body was found but nothing remained of the treasured album of R & R photographs. By the way he went, Stanks provided Bravo Company with one of the saddest war stories any grunt ever heard, or experienced, in seven years of war in Vietnam. He got the wound the grunts dread the most, the one they had occasional nightmares about. Stanks' abdomen, groin, and legs had been peppered with white-hot shrapnel; he would certainly lose one leg, maybe both. But the larger fact here was that Stanks would never again participate in the ecstasy he knew on his R & R, the celebration that involved every cell and voiced every dream—two sweating bodies climbing to a mind-blowing orgasm. His R & R would always be the last time—at twenty years old, the last time.

Stanks had regained consciousness only a few minutes after the incoming ended. "That's okay, Stanks, no sweat. You're gonna make it just fine—no problem, Pal." The excessive encouragement made no sense to him; they continued to answer his questions with evasion. "Gonna be all right, Stanks—don't worry about it now . . . no sweat, Pal." When he saw where on his body the corpsman was working, Stanks knew what it was.

"What's it look like, Doc? Tell me, goddammit, I gotta know!"

"Lay back there, Stankiewicz—we'll take care of you, you're gonna be okay."

"Tell me, Doc—goddammit, you gotta tell me—I gotta right to know!"

"Take it easy, dammit, you're gonna be all right. You're going back to Third Med and they're gonna fix you right up fine."

Corporal Anthony Stankiewicz died on the chopper, in the air somewhere between Hill 174 and Quang Tri City. The thought of "never again" was too big for Stanks' young mind—he died because he didn't want to live, and the rest of the Company understood. "Fuck it—can you blame him? When the gooks blow away your balls there ain't no reason to live anymore. I wouldn't want to live like that, would you?"

Lieutenant Mike Lancaster also died on the chopper ride back to Third Med, but those who saw him said it was better that way. His body from the waist up had been turned into a lump of carbon.

The luckiest among the medevacs were those whose bodies

were missed by the shrapnel but whose brains were temporarily rearranged by the noise and shock of the massive blast. They were brought into the emergency room, stripped, examined and carried to the shower room for a wash-down. While awaiting ward and bed assignments they were placed on stretchers in the corridors. There on the cool cement they babbled and moaned at the ceiling through the night in their nakedness.

Those who yesterday morning had tried to interpret this new place and the atmosphere of Hill 174 had their answer now. This was the place where all things sacred for their familiarity would be disrupted forever in short horrible moments none were prepared for. Now the grunts of Bravo Company 1969 had seen Yorktown and Chickamauga and Belleau Wood and Tarawa and Pork Chop Hill. All of those other battles and Hill 174 came to look alike on this warm afternoon in May. The new generation was blooded.

Today the veterans were reminded and the newbys knew at last—this is where body counts come from. They didn't all come from a last glorious charge to take the hill and plant the flag. The relentless formula was still at work. It was the adding together of six or ten or two dozen Hill 174s each day that had for five years allowed the young voice in Saigon to tell the world: "The U.S. Command in Saigon announced today that scattered actions with enemy forces accounted for three hundred fifty-eight Communist dead. American losses were described as light."

The grunts have a favorite warning among themselves, used mostly in jest, sometimes not. "Payback's a medevac" is another way of saying that any deserved retaliation will be serious enough to put the victim in need of a medical evacuation to a hospital. The promoters of this red-on-green, America-in-Vietnam spectacle had decided that nineteen dead and one known wounded North Vietnamese from the ambush of four nights before would cost the Americans thirteen dead and twenty-eight wounded. Payback really was a medevac.

In seasons past, the coming of June had been a time of joy for the grunts. Only a short while ago—only last year for most—June meant the end of school, the beginning of a new freedom in the sun; no more bitchy teachers, no more dull assignments; just climbing trees or drinking in the back seat of a buddy's car or spending your own money and not telling the old man where you're going. In this June there would be a new order. From the interminable routine of patrols, C-rats, humps and dreams, all overhung with the corrosive uncertainty about when the next firefight would happen and who would get zapped in it, the men and men-children of Bravo moved into a time when they could taste relief. Now it was known who would get mangled and killed. That earlier wondering had drained off a little energy from each man in the last few weeks, in addition to the humps and the heat. Now the mystery was over—after the big blow the grunts had more dead, a measure of relief, and faces which looked twenty years older.

In the next few days the uncertainty that has always been a part of every grunt's thinking came back. This time, however, the wondering was not about who would get hurt and who would go untouched. This time those who had survived were trying to figure out what meaning, what lesson should be taken from the freak disaster on Hill 174. Only one answer was readily apparent—pallets of ammunition must be broken down and placed in bunkers immediately after they are received. Beyond that there was nothing—nothing to be learned from a lucky shot by the enemy and no way to defend against another. Some days our side makes a lucky shot and some days their side makes one—is that all it meant? No matter how many minds thought about it, what happened on Hill 174 didn't seem to mean anything, and that was the most maddening aspect about it. No meaning could be derived from thirteen deaths, twenty-eight injuries and an extensive rearrangement of the landscape. How could anyone be expected to retain his sanity in an environment producing that kind of event?

Only one survivor in Bravo ever voiced his assessment of Hill 174. Two weeks after the lucky shot the second platoon sergeant, Staff Sergeant Melvin Rabbers, was sitting in the Battalion Staff Club at Quang Tri. Rabbers, scheduled to fly out the next day on his R & R, leaned across the pool table and whispered in a loud beery voice to his first sergeant that there was "At least one good thing come outa that pallet blowing up back there—at least that worthless, chickenshit sweater of an XO, that panicky bastard Lancaster is dead, too. Fucking panicky turds like that always get some good troops killed, always happens . . . always happens . . . ."

At Sam's meeting that night there was little more than hope. "Christ, we better not get hit with any more lucky shit shots like that. Another one could knock everything outa the Company for quite awhile. The troops're scared now, talking about the way the gooks did it. All right now, go on back to your people and talk to them . . . calm them down. Don't let them get the idea the gooks can't do nothing wrong, or some stupid idea like that. Remind them about the ambush."

War is as big and horrible an event as man has yet devised to touch a massive number of lives at the same approximate time in an unforgettable way. But no matter how large any particular war has been, there have always been thousands or millions of individuals able to preserve an existence untouched by the chaos and carnage. The number of people not in Vietnam, but directly touched by the deaths and injuries sustained by Bravo on Hill 174, was only about one hundred twenty-five, making generous allowance for the size of immediate families. Thus on May 25, 1969, over 200 million other Americans were wrapped up in experiences other than war or the mourning of its victims.

* * * * *

While the grunts of Bravo Company struggled with a freakish but deadly happening, millions of other people were doing millions of other things back in Uncle Sam's Empire of Average Men. In Glastonbury, Connecticut, Roxanne Madden was trying, and failing, to kill herself by gulping oven cleaner: she had decided her life was a failure because it was becoming more obvious every day she would never get married. In Malta, Illinois, Ora Rugg was sitting on the floor next to a grocery store magazine rack, absorbed in a *Police Gazette* story about a 1934 axe murder in a Texas border town. In Sweetwater, Oklahoma, Grace Boomer deviated from her diet; it was the forty-seventh time in the last two months she had gone over by one thousand calories or more. And in Tiffin, Ohio, Lester Plant rocked back on his bar stool in Isola's Tavern and hollered at the country and western band ("all the way from Toledo, the Blooo Notes, featuring Wanda and Hubie!") that he wanted them to play his all-time favorite, *I've Got Everything I Need to Drive Me Crazy.* As he crumpled onto the floor and the beer splashed over his face he bellowed, "or if you don't know that one, how about *Kiss An Angel G'Morning?*" And the rest of the world plodded through another work day, gave birth or awaited the final sleep, read their newspaper and cursed their neighbor.

9 Hill of the Angels

Finally, away from Hill 174. This time not one man bitched at the word to saddle up. The grunts humped out under unusual circumstances. Everyone knew where they were going and everyone knew how long it would take to get there: Con Thien and five days. That was a slow pace, an average of only a mile a day if they went in a nearly straight line. It either meant a lot of patrolling on the way or a lot of slack. But right now nobody seemed to care which of the two possibilities they would have to carry out. It was enough just to savor the fact that they were leaving, putting Hill 174 in the past.

Sam took his time and followed a meandering route that tended to the northeast. There was none of the frantic idiocy of humping to nowhere that there had been on the first few days of the operation. There were no heat casualties either. When Hill 174 was two days into the past, some outward signs of life began to return to the Company.

The grunts resumed their bitching at the heat, the hills, and the lack of cold beer and hot broads. Once in awhile a laugh could be heard and Sam had to start passing the word back down the column to "hold the goddam noise down; you're not home yet." The patrols weren't too bad either. They were always short, especially if they were to the north: the DMZ was still only 600 meters away. And since they were moving toward the sea, the hills got lower each day. It was at the end of each patrol and each hump that a new spirit could be seen growing in Bravo One-Three. Each man felt it in himself and watched it in the actions and faces of his buddies. Earlier they were hurt and afraid, individually and collectively, but out of that hurt there now grew something new. It was the bare determination, not to take this hill or that one, but to survive this hell, to outlast that little slant-eyed, rice-powered bastard they chased no matter how many hills had to be humped or how many monsoons or 118° days had to be endured.

Captain Sam's traveling road show walked into the south gate of Con Thien late in the afternoon of June first. June, June—another name for another bunch of days, a little closer to the Freedom Bird. A small convoy of trucks rumbled past the column of troops. Each truck was full of artillery ammo and each pulled a water tank. The grunts had seen all of this before, but what struck them now was the water splashing out the top hatches of each trailer. It was just splashing out onto the Nam dirt, with nobody screaming about wasting the precious liquid! If there was enough water to splash all over the damn road, there might be enough for showers. No, wait—no sense getting hopes up about the bennies without being sure.

Bravo joined the rats that afternoon in the ring of perimeter bunkers. The grunts, the transients, and the rats—the permanent personnel—eyed each other warily, as established residents eye newcomers. Once again the rats lost. They can tell when the marines move out for good, when flak jackets and packs are picked up for the last time, not for another patrol. They must think, hopefully, at last, this bunker and the garbage dumps will be ours with no more traps laid, no more pot shots taken—ours at last. But a few minutes later here come the next occupants.

Tired bodies, exhausted minds slept through the next dawn. With the earth starting to heat up again, Corporal Denny Sayre of Avondale, Arizona, stumbled out of his stinking, sandbag-lined bunker number 18, squinted into the big orange ball moving up over the barbed wire and radio antennas, stretched his arms over his head and screamed as loud as he could, "Good morning, Vietnam!" Thus began the war's next day.

The name Con Thien translates as "Hill of the Angels." Considering the variety of small pleasures and the relatively low number of losses the grunts would experience in their four weeks at this forward outpost, it did seem as if the place were being watched over by divine beings.

In the next few days the grunts settled into quiet routines with plenty of room for the bennies—steaks on a charcoal grill every night, mail with an occasional bottle of booze from home, plenty of Z time and showers and ice cream and cold Coke and movies, and only a couple of rockets every few days from the NVA. One of the best bennies turned out to be the details sent back to Third Med at Quang Tri for dental appointments. While some grunts had their teeth fixed on such details, others found the dentist too busy and, "the dental tech said we'd have to come back again tomorrow or some time. Gunny, I know that sounds like bullshit but it's the truth, Gunny, honest!" The rest of the day was spent in finding a boom-boom girl—"Hey, Chief, let's go in the vill and get the old pipes cleaned out, eh?"—and a bottle of whisky and maybe some grass for the rest of the squad.

The bennies at Con Thien were so good and the occasional rockets from the north of the Ben Hai River so poorly aimed that the change coming over Bravo at Con Thien was barely perceptible. Much more than the morale and combat efficiency of the Company was changing. The unit once called "Bloody Bravo" was taking on a new character and a new identity. Three and a half weeks at a base near division headquarters was enough time to receive thirty-one new bodies. A few weeks before, the blooded veterans, the old-timers of the war and the Company, had been those who were "down south on Taylor Common back around Christmas." Now those who had survived the explosion of Hill 174 were the real veterans. A bare thirty days ago was suddenly "way back before we ever had any of this shit here like steaks and ice cream and movies and fucking showers." Then would come the final attention-getter for the newbys: "And don't get the idea it's gonna be like this all the time—you ain't even barely seen the bush yet!"

After a few days, after the newness of the Stateside bennies wore off, there wasn't too much excitement for the grunts in their weeks at Con Thien. One source of entertainment was "firing up the rats." Traps were improvised in the garbage dump at night, the rats collected the next morning and held through the day. At sundown they were doused with diesel fuel or gasoline, set afire and turned loose. "Looks real cool at night, them old rats screeching and running around in circles. Don't know where the fuck they're at. Then they just stop dead, roll over on their backs and just crackle and simmer—ha!" After the last few weeks, the grunts had grown numb to suffering and death.

Other breaks in the routine were provided by the occasional NVA rockets 500 meters off target between eight and eight-thirty in the morning, the NVA skeleton first platoon found draped over the outer perimeter wire one morning, and that shoving match one night in the chow line that never really turned into a fight before the lifers stepped in. It wasn't over who would get what steaks—there were enough for each man to have three in each meal if he wanted that much. The real issue turned out to be an argument about whether Two-Four had saved Three-Three's ass at the battle of Jones Creek the previous spring or whether Three-Three had saved Two-Four's ass. It was important to get your war stories straight before they were taken home and told to girl friends, children and eventually, grandchildren.

Those incidents weren't much considering they were all that was produced in thirty days by over one hundred and sixty grunts virtually locked behind barbed wire—with no broads, either. But that was just fine with everybody. There had been more than enough excitement for Bravo in the month before they got to Con Thien.

Rounding out the routine bennies were the patrols. They averaged out to just one every other day. Most days they reminded one more of a high school class trip to some historic shrine than a search for the enemy. Patrol routes were keyed to debris left over from the hot summers of '67 and '68—days when Leatherneck Square was filled with battles between, not snipers and ambush squads, but battalions supported by tanks and artillery on both sides. Battles for Con Thien were among the few, in the five years of the American involvement, during which the North Vietnamese Army felt it necessary to stand and fight, not only in the night, but during the day when the Phantom jets with their

250 and 500-pound bombs and their napalm could be called in from Phu Bai and the Seventh Fleet carriers in the Gulf of Tonkin. Sam would simply say, "Take your squad out the south gate over to the west to that there tree-line, then check things out around that burned-out chopper. Then go over by that shot-down jet . . . ."

Only one patrol during Bravo's entire stay at Con Thien was remembered as a real bummer. The morning after they arrived at the fire base, Sam took three of the four platoons on a sweep completely around the perimeter. The hump turned out to be fourteen clicks long and took nine hours, which made it the worst since those of the first three days in May. The Company had found several tank trails and the debris from earlier battles, but no NVA and none of their rice and ammo caches.

The first sign of enemy activity was found by Staff Sergeant Jerry Goodman of third platoon and his radioman, PFC Herman L. Hopper. Three days before, Goodman had the dubious honor of being named acting platoon commander while his lieutenant was on R & R. Acting leader is not a sought-after position among the grunts, since they, along with radiomen and corpsmen, are much preferred as targets over riflemen by the enemy. What Goodman and Hopper found was an old mine. They found it in a manner not recommended in the field manuals: they stepped on it—without ever seeing the little green plastic trigger sticking up among the blades of grass. About half a dozen bodies were lifted from the earth and scrambled around. The only two who died were Goodman and Hopper. The NVA weren't even around but they still got the right people.

The mine accomplished just about what the Russians who made it and the North Vietnamese who planted it had in mind. The only things left inviolate on those two human bodies and their clothing was the propriety of boots on feet, though the feet were ripped from their legs. The mine mixed trousers with calf muscles and tendons with genitals with intestines with bladders with shit with livers and spleens and kidneys and stomachs, and jammed the oozy mass up into lungs and throats. Then it burned hands and arms and chests and faces to the texture and appearance of dried prunes. Just like it was supposed to do.

There was no longer any doubt about what warfare in the modern, industrial era had come to mean. The grunts—newbys, short-timers, and lifers alike—could see now that what happens to human beings in mechanized warfare has absolutely no poetic or theatrical possibilities. Fuck you, John Wayne!

Lance Corporal Roland Epps and the rest of his mortar crew were there when Bravo Company walked into Con Thien back on June first. Troops from different units usually don't mix very fast, since all are taught that theirs is the best battalion or company, and "if you hang around with them other horseshit outfits, anything's liable to rub off on you." But here was something of a special situation. Only a few days before, it was announced that Epps' unit, Second Battalion, Ninth Marines, would be taken from Vietnam as part of the President's withdrawal policy. So, very quickly, Epps of Two-Nine met the grunts of One-Three. Almost every day the grunts ambled over to Epps' mortar pit, ate Cs with him and helped him get things ready to go, as if by thus associating with and helping these short-timers, some of their shortness would rub off and help them get home sooner. They shot the shit with these mortarmen from another unit, shot it all day long. And at night they got together behind the perimeter wire and sang their favorite song, the one about getting out of this place if it's the last thing we ever do.

At first there were questions like "Bet you're glad to be leaving this fucking place, huh?" That one turned into "What you gonna do soon as you get home?" and "Smile if you're gonna bang your girl—ha!" which led to, as do all conversations between marines, "How did you ever get in this green mother anyway?" Roland Epps of Austell, Georgia, had quite a story to tell, for his family and the Marines had been together a long time. It was a story the grunts long remembered.

Elton Epps, Senior, was the first in his family to enlist in the Corps, back in 1888. The high point in his twenty-year career was his service in the Spanish-American War. He later tried to go back on active duty against the Hun in World War I; he was lauded for his patriotism and graciously turned down. Next was Elton, Junior, who enlisted in 1920. A promising career, and one he loved, was cut short when his first wife made him leave the service after only eight years. But his younger brother Elbert stayed in for twenty-five years, retiring in 1947. It was Uncle Elbert's endless stream of war stories of the Pacific campaigns that first planted, and then kept alive and burning, young Roland's ambition to join the Marines the first chance he got.

The third generation of Epps marines was represented by Elton III, who joined in June 1950. Four months later he was in the newest American war, the Korean "police action," and two weeks before Christmas of that same year, he was killed in the freezing withdrawal from the Chosin Reservoir. On May 31, 1950, Elton, Junior's fourth wife gave birth to his fifth child and second son. He was named Roland and on his eighteenth birthday he became the fourth in his family's direct line to join the Marines. He had wanted to enlist the day after his seventeenth birthday but his mother made him promise years before that he, unlike any of the other Epps marines, would graduate from high school.

Four months later he was in Vietnam and assigned to the 81 mm mortar section of Two-Nine. On June 25, 1969, he was at Con Thien along the DMZ with his mortar crew. The day before they had been told they would be re-deployed to Okinawa with the entire Ninth Marine Regiment. There had been rumors, but here it was at last ". . . the fucking President was gonna let us skate right on outa the Nam, forever! I couldn't believe it, Man. I didn't know whether to shit or go blind, so I started packing!"

The jeep and trailer had come out in the morning from Quang Tri for the mortar, ammunition, and the seven crewmen. They had planned to be back to Quang Tri for lunch in the mess hall with its cold milk, so Epps and the rest of the crew threw their C-rations into the grass behind the gun pit as a way of underlining and celebrating the fact that they would never again have to eat the meals that come in green cans, the crap that tasted lousy and gave one as much diarrhea as nourishment. But packing the trailer took longer than expected, so they decided to have that one last meal out in the bush.

Everyone at Con Thien, including Roland Epps, knew there were mine fields both around the outer perimeter and inside the wire in the fenced-in grassy areas. But those mines had been there over three years and probably didn't work anymore, and besides, they were going home—the President and all the heavies said so. So Roland Epps walked out into the grassy area behind his bunker with nothing more on his mind than finding the can of beans and franks he had thrown away two hours before.

The "Bouncing Betty" anti-personnel mine is one of the more brutal products of American military technology. When triggered, it doesn't explode in the ground and take feet off legs. It springs up four feet before it goes off, and separates heads and arms from bodies and perforates lungs, stomachs, and intestines. Lance Corporal Epps' Bouncing Betty picked him up and, while he flew through the air, ripped off his clothes, legs, hands, and all of his head but the lower jaw, then dumped him on his back—stumps of thighs and arms raised in supplication to a garish sun. The first man on the scene told a corpsman that he thought he saw a pink mist hanging over the corpse for a few seconds. In the last possible hour of the last possible day in the least sensible of all way to do it, Roland Epps had won his plastic body bag with the big long zipper. About one hundred twenty of their son's one hundred seventy-two pounds were sent home to Mr. and Mrs. Epps.

* * * * *

While at Con Thien there were people like Roland Epps, Jr., elsewhere and doing other things were people like Frank Parks. While the former's last and violent noon was ending, the latter was spending his as he had every other noon for the last three years. He was standing at the corner of LaSalle and Adams streets in Chicago, waiting for "Don't Walk" to change to "Walk."

When he wasn't waiting for lights to change, Frank was working in a bank. And when he wasn't working in a bank, Frank was engaged in what he considered the important things in life—picking up secretaries at his favorite bar, furnishing his apartment, driving his new Corvette, and keeping himself in the latest clothing styles.

Like Roland Epps, Jr., Frank Parks thought about Vietnam, but much less frequently and in completely different terms. To Frank, the war was an annoyance, an unpleasantry. And if not handled correctly, the war could also be a threat to his social life. He learned very quickly that those who injected the sordid subject of war into parties soon found themselves beating the bars alone. After about ten seconds of analysis, Frank decided to leave the war to others and to concentrate on more important things, the activities centering on that mad race of the unmarried, the swingles circuit.

Frank Parks was pleased that after analyzing his life to date, he could conclude he was generally in step with the procession of his generation: his feet were in motion and his brains were at rest. He fit the mold of the partly-educated hedonist, the image he consciously admired. Frank was "on his way," as they've said the last few generations, but on his way to what, he didn't know.

* * * * *

In the early afternoon of June 25, Sam had a meeting with all of his platoon commanders and sergeants. After the death of Roland Epps and C-rations and beer and dental appointments and test-firing of weapons and the rumors about the next operation had been discussed, Sam added one more piece of information. "Oh, and tell your people Operation Virginia Ridge officially ended at midnight last night. I don't know what the next op's gonna be called or where it'll be, but we'll probably be walking outa here in a few days, so tell them to be ready."

part two
The World

To those who fight for it, life has a flavor the protected never know.

anonymous, written on a C-ration case at Khe Sanh, 1968

During the twenty-three days at Con Thien, six grunts reached the end of their tour in war. For these six there were new joys in this next summer of the war. There was the first sergeant's gruff "You're leaving tomorrow—be at the CP ready to go at zero-nine." There was the beer—and maybe pot—party the night before; there were good-byes and address changes; the last chopper ride, the last overhead view of the emerald and pock-marked Vietnamese countryside; a real shower in the rear; another drunk; a C-130 flight to a larger terminal. And then the most fantastic sight of all—a big shiny 707, one's own Freedom Bird, walking down the runway, nose bulging through heat waves, swinging around, doors opening. "All officers and civilians of equivalent rank followed by E-6 and above form a line over here, E-5 and below this side . . . Good afternoon, gentlemen, welcome to Continental Air Lines government contract flight . . . I'm Shirley from . . . will demonstrate the life jackets to be found over . . . ." As the bird raced down the runway, one hundred eighty-five pairs of hands and feet tensed against plastic and carpet, straining to feel every pebble and indentation in the strip, straining to feel the exact second of lift-off, the exact moment they could put Vietnam and whatever it meant to them in the past.

At the instant of separation between Freedom Bird and Vietnam, a cheer rose throughout the cabin. The new ex-grunts felt the same mix of relief and exhilaration they had felt dozens of times before in the past year when they received a letter, began their R & R, and ended each of the dozens of patrols and humps they had made. But this was the biggest hump of all, so the exhilaration was raised to a higher power than ever before.

Within a few minutes voices died away as the new veterans leaned back to savor the sweet fact of leaving, really leaving.

Shortly after they reached home, the six new veterans and many parents and girl friends of those still at Con Thien, began writing letters about some special news coverage the grunts were getting. It was like no attention they had ever before been paid. The editors of Life *magazine thought it important to give an impression of the Vietnam War that would go beyond the usual shrill protest or caustic editorial. They wanted to report, not only the number of dead for the week, but exactly who did the dying on those days. So in its June 27, 1969, issue the magazine staff printed individual photographs of 217 of the 242 American servicemen killed during the week of May 28-June 3, 1969. The pictures and names filled thirteen pages in addition to the cover. Six of the 217 pictures were of Bravo Company marines killed on Hill 174 the afternoon of May 25.* Life *called the article "A Record and a Tribute."*

The grunts called it something else. They were hurt by the article, openly resentful about the way Life *treated their dead of that week. They were probably more bitter than other units represented in the pictures, for they had not yet found the chance to avenge their loss. After things were evened up the grunts would be glad to show America and the world pictures not only of their own dead but those of the enemy who would be riddled and blown apart, posed with and perhaps mutilated. But until that day, death would remain to these grunts a private thing, something to be faced and shared with only the closest of friends. Death was not to be displayed or advertised in any way, for any motive.*

"What the fuck's going on back there? They think we actually groove on this kind of shit? They don't do nothing for a guy till after he buys the ranch. Then all the pictures get put in the papers and magazines. Really nice, eh? They ought to send every one of them mother-fuckers over here—put them right in the middle of a firefight—see how they like it! Fucking civilians back in the World don't know what it's like over here—don't want to know—don't care. Just so that they get their new car every year and their cold beer and a hot piece of ass every night!"

10 Our World and The World

Just as the Vietnam War was different from any previously fought by Americans, so was the experience of returning from that war different from any other. Soon after they had settled back into families and neighborhoods, the newest veterans could see that all the Hill 174s and Khe Sanhs and Hamburger Hills could not be left completely behind.

Virtually all the veterans expected that their settling back into familiar places and routines would be one of the most pleasurable experiences they would ever know. But most found the process to be a succession of painful adjustments to a way of life which contrasted sharply with the one they had just left behind in Vietnam.

Consider only the larger contrasts between the war and the home society: where the veteran once could afford to be concerned with only the next few moments or days, he now had to formulate plans that would affect him for years or decades. Where he once had to make only one or a very few decisions to survive, he now had to make many decisions about many different subjects—and those sometimes in the same day. Where there was once the ultimate penalty for mistakes—death, there was now only a casually administered system of rewards and punishments. And where the veteran once had only a few very close friends he could always count on, he now moved in a much larger society of short-term acquaintances, almost none of whom were willing to make any deep commitments. Thus, coming home amounted to living through an experiential blowup.

The last of these contrasts was for most the first felt. The impact of the loss of close friends is well illustrated by only a brief statistical analysis. During the entire period of direct American military involvement, about 2.5 million troops served in Vietnam. Once back in America, those 2.5 million were dispersed within a population of over 200 million. Thus, the veterans had only about a one percent chance of meeting each other. Back in the World the veterans were surrounded by persons unable to understand their thoughts, their actions, or even their words.

The veterans' first few steps back into the world of things relatively peaceful and conventional might have been taken at a transient center on Okinawa, where they found billboards offering "Thanks from a grateful nation for a job well done." It might have begun at airports in El Toro or Fairfield, California, where they found Red Cross ladies serving cookies and coffee, and VFW volunteers passing out handshakes, congratulations and key chain charms stamped "Welcome Home, Your Country Is Grateful." Or it might have begun at reception centers in Oakland or Seattle where they were required to listen to welcoming bands and speeches. Wherever such introductions to their postwar America occurred, the ex-grunts noticed a common feature about them: they were contrived events, not spontaneous. They happened because base commanders ordered them to happen. That was something of a tip-off, a signal that it might be a good thing to be a little wary of America, to put off for a few days embracing the things they had missed and expected to be the same when they got back.

From their first few impressions on returning home, some veterans concluded America was as beautiful as ever. Some found it indifferent; others found it hostile and ruthless toward itself and its newest veterans. The latter two of these three groups deserve considerable attention for, having stepped outside and then reentered American society, they are among the few able to provide some commentary on how the war affected the idealized view of themselves Americans have long held.

Contributing to the impression that America was full of hostility, was the fact that in the latter years of the American involvement a large number of veterans, perhaps over half of the returnees, came back hating something or someone: the Vietnamese for being so unfathomable, so generally "fucked up"; American politicians for lying to them about why they had to go to Vietnam; hippies for "stabbing us in the back"; and the Joe Blows and their housewives who went about life as usual while the grunts had been counting off their hours and days in the paddies and hills. Along with the hatred were mixed generous amounts of fear and suspicion. Was it true that hippies were going around shooting every Vietnam veteran they could find? Was it true all the girls thought the veterans were baby-killers and would have nothing to do with them? When the veteran learned those rumors were not true, his suspicion still remained; and it was, he felt, justified.

Back in the States, he felt alone, naked, exposed to the dumb peering and probing of those afraid to get involved with things outside their own life-cocoons. He wanted to be left alone to heal his wound, to "get his thing together," so he could somehow face tomorrows that looked too bright, too hard. But they—the newest adversaries, those who hadn't gone—wouldn't let him. They kept boring in, sticking him in the private parts of his experience.

No matter how sincere the concern of family and friends might be for the veteran's smooth adjustment to a peaceful environment, it was usually received as an assault, an aggression on his peace of mind. The best thing most could do in the face of such assaults was to anticipate and try to head off the dreaded questions. Many of the veterans adopted a new method of judging others. The test was simply, were you there? If the answer was no, the barriers went up.

"What was it like?"

"It was a bitch most of the time—sometimes okay. Hey, I heard you got a new car while I was gone."

But while almost every veteran devised some defenses against probing hometowners, he also ran into one or two friends who wouldn't be put off, who really wanted to listen and understand what it was like. Genuinely interested listeners were a welcome change to most veterans, but after hearing about the war in the bush, most were left with a squinched up face and in a mood which momentarily precluded eye contact or sound.

"You really want to know what the Nam was like? Well, okay, I'll try to tell you. It was like a big-ass greasy machine with plenty of parts but it don't do nothing. You been to a big discotheque, haven't you? Well, throw in a lotta that psychedelic crap and people doing stuff they don't know why they're doing it and they wouldn't do it anywhere else, and then throw in a big bummer trip on LSD with no up, down, right, wrong, yes, no, left or right, new or old, no noise, no silence, and then add a seventy-five year old VFW jerkoff standing in a graveyard full of twenty-year-olds giving a lecture on the proper display of the flag, and that's about it—a lotta motion, noise, color and smoke but no progress, no meaning."

The superficial commercial and trivial aspects of America were the parts of their beloved culture that hit the young veterans early, and hit them hard: . . . *Dear Ann, your reply to Cheated On who wanted to phone her friend 2000 miles away and tell her that hubby just confessed they had slept together thirteen years ago stank—Will Congress wake up now?—God loves you and has a wonderful plan for your life, call 334-0467 (a recording)—Medical costs top GNP rise—I was troubled thirty-five years with red patches, scaly skin of dreaded psoriasis—gum chewing now legal—Ruth Cobb and Cliff Madden were named today as December bowlers of the month—Why singles are swinging to the suburbs—Austria tries two ex-SS officers for war crimes—Cigarette smoking might not interfere with the development of an unborn child as is widely suspected.*

When Vietnam did make the news it was reported as something far away, of little consequence; it didn't sound like the same event that had almost taken the veteran's life during the past year: *Pentagon is silent on second massacre—Long-locked GI goes on trial in Viet—United States and the Viet Cong clashed today on the third anniversary of the dead-locked Vietnam peace conference . . . Each accused the other side of sabotaging the meetings—Draft dodging Eskimo caught.*

The veterans could easily see the great variety of games and deceptions America plays upon herself daily, all the while thinking she is enhancing her glory, moving closer to the dream realized. Back Stateside the synthetic had resoundingly triumphed over the real. America was on a trip, an endless fantasy journey, careening onward under a garish sun to brighter, odorless, unstained tomorrows.

A view of any nation or culture which dwells on things marginal is of course neither complete nor objective. But such a view says much about the psychological condition of returning Vietnam veterans. What they had done in the year before their return had not prepared them to be objective or generous to a people and country who, most veterans believed, had either ignored or helped make more difficult their trials in the war.

After all that ennui had been waded through and the new veteran had turned off the radio and television, and wadded up the paper and thrown it at the world, there were other things to be contended with, other things a little too big for the mechanisms of toleration and assimilation. An ex-marine from Chicago who left an arm in Quang Tri Province said it for all the veterans.

> "Things are more screwed up in the World now than they ever was. Christ, I get back and people are more bananas now than ever. My girl's pissed at me now cuz I don't want to get married for awhile and then I gotta write this paper about the war I don't want to write and—ah shit—it's back to normal. Nothing is like it was supposed to be when I planned it out back there. Seems like they're all coming home now, you know? All the same crazy fuckers we had over there are back now and screwing up the World.
>
> "Yeah, this instructor I got wants me to write themes and essays about my experiences in the war. He asked me if I ever saw a gook up close or shot one I could see, and I says hell, yeah, I did. So he says write about it. He says I should write about what I was thinking when I was doing some of the crazy shit we did over there. I can't think of any reason—

not one—why I shot the guy—nothing—except maybe to stay alive but no, shit I don't know . . . .

"But I think the worst change was the broads. You know how we used to think about them and talk about them back there? Well, I knew they'd be different, but, Man, I didn't think they'd be that different. About half of them didn't even recognize me at first and then they say stuff like 'Oh, you were on the basketball team weren't you; no, the football team wasn't it?' Then it's crap like 'Gee, I bet you're glad to be out now,' and 'When do you think it'll be over anyway,' and when you're about halfway through answering them they kind of half turn and start to drift off and then if you try and talk with them again or ask them out they get real snooty, like, anybody's had any connection with the Nam, they don't want nothing to do with them.

"It's like when a guy decided he wanted to go to the Nam, he dropped outa life or something. But then they feel free to flash their ass in your face, and when you make the natural, normal reaction and try to get some of it, they act surprised, like you're trying to do something civilized people don't do. Snooty fucking bitches. I'm even thinking of going back to Hong Kong where I had my R & R and finding the girl I had —I know right where to find her. She's got these bitches around here beat all to hell, all to hell."

From life and death to snooty bitches and a pile of rubber, steel, grease and vinyl from Detroit called "Something To Believe In" was too great a distance for the veterans to cover in sixteen hours, or even sixteen days. It could be done physically but not mentally. Few could quickly assimilate that stark dichotomy, few could quickly move away from it and formulate those things their parents call career goals.

The veteran took the mountain of ennui he found in America as evidence that the hometowners didn't really care what he had gone through in the previous year, didn't care about the buddies he lost or those still there when he came home. Such extreme apathy was inexcusable to him. And if he asked people why they weren't stirring from their routine he heard an answer that compounded his bewilderment: "Vietnam's been going on ten, twenty years—how can I afford to worry about it all the time? I got too many other things to worry about, and if I did think about it all the time, what could I do about it? I can't change the world by myself. Marching and writing letters to senators don't do no good at all—it don't change nothing."

The veteran's bewilderment at the civilian reaction to the war revealed a large flaw in his observation of those who did not go, and in what he did with that observation. The hometowners were no more interested in Vietnam when the veteran they knew left home than they were when he came back. The civilians were thus consistent and logical in their own minds. It was the veteran's sense of commitment, his definitions of logical and rational that had changed by his participation in the war and so, on his return from it, he criticized civilian attitudes he had not even noticed before he went. If that inconsistency struck him at all, it was usually passed off with the comment that his lack of prewar criticism for civilian America was "before the Nam showed me what things was all about." But whether or not there was a flaw in the veteran's thinking, his analysis of civilian America was no less real to him: apathy about the war was still inexcusable.

After seeing his buddies blown apart, his country refuse to unite behind his war, and hearing many at home say his buddies died for nothing, the veteran badly needed psychological anchors on which he could build some kind of adjustment to his recent past, and on which he could base a value system that would serve him in the future. In their postwar America most veterans found none of the anchors they so desperately needed.

Most of the veterans then fell into a period of condemnation of the "fucked-up civilians getting their ass every night and rodding their hot cars around." Many found themselves going out of their way to insult homebound civilians. For many, the period of condemnation turned into one of wandering. There was a strong revulsion against staying in one place too long, seeing and hearing the same people too long, watching the same deodorant commercials and hearing the same sports announcers mouthing about the "life and death" importance of this game and how many hundred thousand dollars so-and-so is holding out for.

Staying in one place too long built up a rage that could not be contained for the sake of courtesy or any other arbitrary value; a rage that drove the vet to move on, to gulp down the next experience . . . and the next . . . and the next. The rage pushed them into an accelerating succession of friends, parties, girls to conquer, places to see . . . more and more . . . faster and faster . . . according to no plan and with no visible end. Some had to leave the country to get away from the land of contradictions, warped values and hypocrisies, away from the America they no longer recognized, that barely showed any awareness of and no interest in what they had done for their own vision of America the Beautiful and Pure. For many there seemed nothing left in America for "our kind." It looked absolutely insane and hopeless to try and make any sense out of this place and its "fucked-up civilians" who didn't care what their country was doing to another people ten thousand miles away.

Why couldn't they just say, "I don't give a damn about what you did, about your friends who got zapped," instead of faking their concern and asking their questions while their real concerns were elsewhere. The civilians just couldn't do it, they had to go on asking their shallow questions—Is it really hot over there? Are the people really as small as they look in the papers? Is it true the Vietnamese don't value life like we do? What's the monsoon like anyway? When are we going to win? Do the people eat anything besides rice?

The veteran's desire to condemn and escape America revealed another flaw in his thinking. He assumed that all the fault, all the inability to understand what he went through, lay with the civilians, with anyone who did not go. The veteran, however, must share some of the blame for the resultant misunderstanding. He assumed that Vietnam, or war, was the only really enlightening experience in life, because Vietnam was that kind of experience for him. Unless one had been there, he was automatically an incomplete individual in several ways. The personal frustration the veteran felt when attempting to explain the experience of war to others confirmed that belief. The veteran forgot, or discounted the fact, that before he went to Vietnam he was equally inexperienced at interpreting and describing events. As big as that flaw in his thinking was, it remained functional and led to certain decisions by the veteran about how he would exist with his postwar America.

These flaws in the new veteran's thinking illustrate the difference of the returning grunt's orientation toward the war compared to the attitude of those who did not go to Vietnam. Both veteran and hometowner were looking for something when the former came home, but neither was able to satisfy the other's need. What most veterans did not see on their return was the deep frustration Americans felt over the course of the war. The richest and strongest nation in the world was not bringing a "small" war against a small and underdeveloped country to a decisive conclusion, and those who had not seen the war wanted to know why.

The veteran, however, could give no satisfying explanation. He was unqualified by experience to explain how decisions had been made in the White House or in State and Defense Department policy planning sessions over a period of nearly two decades. He was also unqualified by temperament to ease the frustration he found—he returned looking for consolation, for understanding. Instead of offering what the veteran needed, the stay-at-homes asked about the failure of national policy: "When is it going to end? How did we ever get involved in that thing anyway?" When the veteran talked about the only thing he was qualified to talk about—what his war in the rice paddies or the hills had been like—the frustration of the hometowners was only compounded. What followed then was a mutual withholding of what each side needed. Since the hometowners found in the veteran no relief for their frustration, they withheld their consolation and understanding. And since the veteran found no empathy in the hometowners, he withheld any attempt to understand their views.

Vietnam gave most grunts a clearer view of themselves and America. Life in the bush had lain them bare for themselves and everyone else to inspect, and moving outside of America had given them a chance to see what most of those who would never leave would never see. On his return the new veteran could see several stark contradictions about America he had missed before.

He also noticed new contrasts between himself and other Americans. For one, there was a big difference between his and others' ideas of what is important in life. In the shopping center, Mrs. Schmitz might feel free to make it known to the clerk, an ex-grunt, that she must have a light blue sweater just like that gray one for her husband's birthday or, "my Roscoe will simply be beside himself." Answering the obligations of his job, the veteran will push through his mouth the words, "Yes, Mrs. Schmitz, I understand completely—here, let me help you find it." But in his mind he formulates and holds his true sentiments on the matter: "The world ain't gonna blow up if you don't find the fucking thing, Mrs. Schmitz. Why don't you tell old Roscoe to go screw himself for his birthday?"

Much larger contrasts and hypocrisies become visible. Americans pay most of their professional athletes more than their cancer researchers, marine biologists or ecologists. In some parts of the country Americans seem unable to decide if teachers or garbage collectors are more valuable members of society. And no matter how much the politicians babbled on about equal protection under the law, those with money always got more equal protection. More painful to the new veteran was the discovery that there were millions of Americans protesting bitterly the loss of 55,000 American lives in Vietnam over a period of ten years while those same protestors, and millions more, quietly accepted the same death toll in one year—every year—on American highways. It didn't make much sense to the veteran for people to reject 55,000 deaths but accept 550,000 when the elimination of both was well within the realm of possibility. And Americans are great ones to holler about the need to eradicate organized crime, but when it comes to acting against it they come with all kinds of excuses and dodges such as "leave well enough alone, don't trouble trouble," and "I can't take on the whole mafia by myself . . . besides, I'm too busy raising a family." To the untrained and longing eye, absent for one long year, it appeared that America the land of a better life had become America the land of "if you don't see it, it doesn't exist."

Considering the rapid change during the 1960s in black Americans' views of themselves and their rightful position in American society, it cannot be surprising that the black grunt on his return found even bigger hypocrisies. The American dream and its documentary accompaniment about all men being created equal and entitled to equal protection under the law seemed more a joke than ever before suspected. It takes little effort on the part of any member of any race to imagine the deep rage and bitterness a black grunt on patrol in a nameless jungle or sitting in a foxhole must have felt on hearing that thirty-two of his brothers and sisters had been gunned down in the streets of Detroit in 1967, or that in 1968 his most effective leader in the fight against a second class existence in white, "who-needs-niggers" America —Martin Luther King, Jr.,—had been assassinated. At some point in their tours, most blacks came to feel that in Vietnam they were being used to fight "whitey's war." Their resolve, understandably, was to return to the States, where the real struggle awaited settlement, and help settle it. The veterans, black and white, could see they would have to adopt attitudes somewhat schizophrenic in order to tolerate things intolerable but inescapable, in order to get along in America and the world for four or five more decades.

Except for those who didn't notice the world beyond their own families, the veterans had to make some kind of accommodation with the indifference and hypocrisy they found in their postwar America. Many just went along with it and returned to the niche they left before they went to war. These veterans succeeded in suppressing their revulsion for people who feel powerless and accept massive contradictions. Others could neither go back to their old niche nor find a new one. In their wanderings away from the business-as-usual world of those who did not go and could not understand, they withdrew to memories of the deep friendship they found in the environment of war; the friendship that recognized no differences of background, race, education or belief. They withdrew to the time and place in which Whites, Blacks and other ethnic group members could call each other "chuck dudes," "splibs," "bean bandits," or "wops" without a trace of racism intended or detected. These veterans were more than a little surprised to find that the war was taking on the aura of the good old days, for while it was being experienced it seemed to have absolutely no potential for nostalgia. But in one respect it *was* the good old days. It was a time when humans cared and helped each other with no questions asked, for no reason other than the grunts were all human beings facing the same adversity in the same time and place.

After a few weeks and months back in the World most of the new veterans found that their best friend was time—big fat, indefinable, irresistible, all-around-them time. It kept moving on, over times of peace and war, joy, indifference and sorrow, rounding off the jagged edges of terror and blood, keeping the future a realm of possibility and victory over things petty and wrong. Time didn't erase Vietnam from memories, but it granted more room to the things each veteran wanted to remember about this war, and it pushed into smaller and smaller corners those things painful to recall. Time made easier an accommodation with whatever America presented her newest veterans.

For a few, even the passage of time was not enough to make America tolerable. They rejected their home society and its definitions of acceptable behavior. Recounts one veteran, "I was back from the Nam only two days and my sister started screaming at me for the same petty crap she did before I went. 'Pick up your clothes, be back by twelve, don't drink so much, don't hang around with that Perez kid.' So I threw an iron at her and split her forehead open. I was sorry after but I thought she deserved it. No—hell I don't know." Most of the actions stemming from a rejection of things familiar in America were confined to the circle of family and friends, but some such acts could not be so contained.

There are some grounds for the conclusion that whatever difficulties the veterans had in adjusting to civilian life were the result of their own imaginations. Many civilians made exactly that criticism after observing what they believed were no more than the rantings and whinings of a bunch of spoiled kids who had run into the hard world for the first time. As has been shown, the grunts were capable of some surprisingly faulty reasoning on occasion, thinking that produced surprisingly ineffectual, even pathetic, actions. But the "rantings and whinings" judgement suffers from being superficial; there were sources of veteran discontent and disillusion other than the imaginary, sources far more concrete.

Virtually all the grunts returned from the war anxious to resume or begin jobs and careers, but economic conditions were not notably accommodating to that desire. The rates of unemployment among all American workers in the years 1969, 1970 and 1971 were 3.5 percent, 4.9 percent, and 5.9 percent respectively. As the withdrawal of American troops from Southeast Asia began and continued, unemployment rates among Vietnam veterans increased sharply and remained far ahead of the rates for non-veterans. The 1969 unemployment rate for veterans aged 20–29 was 4.5 percent; the rate rose to 6.9 percent in 1970 and 8.8 percent in 1971. It was not until the last quarter of 1972 that the Vietnam veteran unemployment rate fell back down to the rate for nonveterans.

Compounding young veterans' bitterness on the issue of jobs after Vietnam service was the attitude of expectation brought home by most. The ex-grunts came home, not expecting ticker-tape parades, but half expecting the country with an international reputation for generosity to offer them a job, an activity that would help them put the Nam in the distant past. When they remembered what they went through in the war, the veterans didn't think they were asking too much. The employment situation they found on their return seemed to stand as confirmation that America really had turned indifferent and hostile in their absence.

11 Preparation

The story of the Vietnam grunts cannot end with the close of another search and destroy operation or with the first few experiences back in the World. The environment in which they grew up before they went to Vietnam must be examined if the grunts are to be understood for what they were in a foreign culture and in the war. The people in that environment did not comprise anything very close to a cross-section of the American population, for America's wars are fought only by the sons of a certain segment of American society. America's wars are fought by the sons of bricklayers, truck drivers, policemen, steelworkers, farmers and telephone linemen. With few exceptions, the sons of working class Americans did the soldiering and the dying in Vietnam.

It has long been noted that particular social classes exhibit particular values. Since the grunts by and large were raised by one socioeconomic group, they were exposed to a set of values unusual for its uniformity. Several features of that value system are easily identified. Working Americans live with much economic uncertainty, most probably because they were much more deeply impressed and hurt by the economic depression of the 1930s than other groups. They generally feel that hard work, not welfare, will keep such uncertainty at an acceptable distance. Success in the battle against that uncertainty is indicated by the continued acquisition of material things. Working Americans firmly believe their country and what they call "the American way of life" are the greatest in the world, especially in the areas of economic and military power. They believe just as strongly that other ways of life—especially communism—deserve their contempt. Working Americans generally view social changes as threats to their own tenuous position. They are suspicious of superficial differences in people, particularly those of race, for racial and life-style differences imply changes and threats.

The Vietnam grunts and the rest of those Americans born between 1940 and 1954 were affected by a series of experiences and developments originating both within and without their home environments. Those experiences did not complete the maturation of those who would go to Vietnam, but they did contribute to an attitudinal framework from which reactions to subsequent experiences, like the Vietnam War, would be formed.

The first experience was being raised by their parents. Those who had been touched rather heavily by depression and war in the 1930s and '40s resolved to spare their children as much of such suffering and want as possible. Most parents succeeded a little too well. In their zeal to relieve their offspring of the painful parts of life, the grunts' parents created a generation shielded from much of what has steeled every previous generation—the realization that a certain amount of adversity not necessarily deserved will be encountered in the course of one's life. Two events of the 1960s illustrate this particular lack in the preparation of young Americans. The more politically active members of the postwar generation were actually surprised when they got their heads cracked at the Democratic National Convention of 1968 for demanding that the political heavies of the country simply give up their hard-stolen grip on one of the major political machines of the modern world and retreat to retirement. The kids ignored, or never found in their casual studies, one of the bigger lessons of history—right rarely wins without might. And, many young Americans could go to the Vietnam War with the incredibly infantile notion that they had a *right* to return from the industrialized carnage alive or in the same condition in which they went. For most of their offspring, the parents of the postwar generation had perverted the American Dream to mean 24-hour protection from reality and other unpleasantries.

The timing of the younger generation's lifetime played a part in their preparation for life: they grew up during a period of high tension between the world's super powers. The Cold War made it easy for the grunts' parents to pass on to their children a hatred of communism. Through the late 1940s and 1950s communism appeared to most distant observers to be a united international conspiracy bent on the quick conquest of western civilization. For convenient proof, Moscow poured forth a steady stream of threats about catching and surpassing, even burying, the West. But the Cold War also made easy the questioning of the older generation's virulent anti-communism. For one thing, the younger generation was not trying to defend an idea they had held for over thirty years—it was simply less painful to question. Second, no one could fail to notice that no matter how many threats and deadlines came out of communist capitals, no Russian bombers or ICBMs ever came over American territory or that of a western ally and no invasion fleet ever left a Russian or Chinese port.

The postwar generation was the first to grow up with television, a medium of communication whose profound effects are still not fully understood. In the fifteen years before American ground troops were sent to Southeast Asia, television gave illustration and emphasis to several values and habits of mind that were not helpful to people who would have to adjust to a rapidly changing and increasingly complex world. Television glorified violence and at the same time kept it at a safe distance. The viewer was encouraged to accept the idea that swift and violent action usually yielded positive results. He could also see that he didn't really have to get involved in the problems of others if he didn't want to, he could let somebody else do it. Thus some of the incentive to develop the requisite amount of discipline to face and solve one's own problems was missing from the environment in which most young viewers were growing. The evasion of problems seemed a viable alternative.

Television helped many Americans, young and old, to adopt an escapist mentality. With the aid of television one could leave far behind him the numbing repetition of his own existence. Things unpleasant could be made to seem far away, for other people; things fantastic could feel close and credible. The "boob tube" encouraged both superficial and black and white thinking. Viewers quickly learned they didn't have to exert any effort at analyzing people and events—the tube did it all for them. Nor was much effort needed to distinguish between good and evil. The "good" guy always wore a white hat and rode a white or golden horse; the "bad" guys, dark brown and black. And of course no problem, no evil could withstand the determined attack of the former. Television did much to give the postwar generation a "great-man" interpretation of the world and its events, and by so doing made them vulnerable to the disillusion they found in Vietnam; for one of the notable characteristics of that war was its lack of heroes. All the above negative features of television in its formative years combined to help deprive the post-World War II generation of the kind of experience they needed to deal with either the Vietnam War or the consequences of protesting it—they had been insulated from too much reality.

Three personalities greatly affected the postwar generation in the 1950s and early '60s—James Dean, Martin Luther King, Jr. and John F. Kennedy. All three were, in varying degrees, challengers of convention and all three were assisted in their rise to prominence by the special character of their particular time. The period 1945–1965 was a time in which relations between men were shot-through with insecurity, the result largely of machines taking a larger place than ever before in human communities. During the same period, relations between nations were overhung with the Damoclean sword of nuclear destruction. It was a time of quiet, but building, tension. Since there are limits to the human capacity for tolerating dissatisfaction and frustration, it was inevitable that rebellions small and large against the extended anxiety would be occasionally manifested.

In the young actor of the mid-1950s, James Dean, a new American made his appearance, the personified antithesis of traditional American values. The new hero was the antihero; it was perfectly appropriate that the movie crowning Dean with instant celebrity was entitled *Rebel Without a Cause.* Dean's doctrine was quickly lapped up by young America: throw out the "tried and true," tell off the old man and old lady, drink in every pleasure in life you can find, don't give a damn about anything, and get your kicks now because you might be dead in a little while. Dozens of other celebrities in the Dean mold soon followed, and millions imitated the image of the black leather-jacketed greaser rebel.

White rebels were bad enough for many witnesses but along with James Dean conventional America had to watch a black man assert himself in protest against the lowly place maintained for his race. In December 1955, Martin Luther King led a bus boycott in Montgomery, Alabama, which culminated a year later with the elimination of segregation on Montgomery's public conveyances. Millions of minority Americans were encouraged to a new view of life. One didn't have to wait in quiet resignation for the sympathy and fawning benevolence of those in power to end injustices: they could be ended by direct action.

John F. Kennedy offered living affirmation to the belief of young generations everywhere in every age, the belief that a better world is possible. With his rise, power had finally passed from white-haired, seemingly unimaginative men born in the 19th century, men associated with depression, discrimination and war. In word and act the young President gave strong suggestion that he and those who followed him could answer a universal desire: the aching need to do something meaningful in one's time on the planet and leave some mark as proof for eyes unborn to see that earlier lives had been full of purpose and worth remembering and building upon.

But the accession of Kennedy revealed a weakness in youth of the 50s and 60s. Raised as they were on television, young Americans, and many of their elders as well, had come to be as impressed by imagery as by performance. Young Americans embraced their heroes more dearly than would those who understand how terribly fragile heroes and hopes really are. They thereby opened themselves to deep hurt, disillusion, and cynicism if by some intervention of tragedy, their dreams should not come as true as they did on television or in the movies.

That of course is exactly what happened—all three heroes

were taken in early and violent death. The passing of Dean, Kennedy and King left in many young Americans, the feeling that they had been cheated of the brighter future that was rightfully theirs. Other violent deaths of heroes—Malcolm X and Robert Kennedy—underlined the reaction. Many assumed, with little real justification, that the world was reverting to gray older men of shorter vision and smaller purpose, and that injustices would live on.

The adoption of Dean, Kennedy and King as heroes pointed out a fundamental difference of perspective, of philosophy, between youth and their parents. The latter had several decades of experience in living with extra-moral and extra-legal practices such as lying politicians and racial injustice. They had learned to accept such as part of life, they had learned to exist around it. But the postwar generation did not come to the same easy acceptance of the deceptive in life. They resolved to end it. To them, more things moral and just seemed possible. It was the same difference of outlook that characterized almost every other generation, only in the 1960s it was carried still farther.

There were other larger developments witnessed by the postwar generation, experiences so broad of later effect yet so imperceptible in their earlier stages that they almost escaped notice or label. During the 1950s and '60s there was a great expansion of educational opportunity. In 1950 there were six million persons enrolled in American colleges and universities, and vocational schools. By 1960 the total post-high school enrollment had risen to seven million, and by 1970 to 15.7 million. The education explosion indicated that more people every year were determined to translate into reality the legacy of the postwar generation's heroes—improvement really is possible, one is not programmed to repeat in dumb imitation his parents' lives and frustrations.

Permeating the environment in which all heroes emerged and all developments ran their course, and determining much of the individual and public reaction to each, was the collection of values which came under the label existentialism. While they were first stated in the early nineteenth century, existentialist doctrines did not come into prominence until after World War I. The generation born after 1940 has been more deeply affected by existentialism than any other—the philosophy both created the environment conducive to the emergence of individuals like Dean, King and the Kennedys and was in turn given new expression by them. Existentialist doctrines reflect the disordered and tragic character of the past one hundred years, a time of world war and world revolution. The philosophy constitutes a revolt against recent absolutisms—Nazism, communism and corporate statism—which have overrun individual freedom.

According to existentialism there are no universally binding moral laws, no absolute moral values—man creates moral values. Man is considered a finite but contingent being, existing in a world devoid of purpose. Man is also free and responsible, but he is responsible only to himself. Existentialism encourages the individual to believe he can exercise rational control over his own existence, and it offers legitimacy to the questioning of authority figures and groups—parental, religious, social, industrial and governmental—considered unjustifiably arbitrary and absolute. By the 1960s strong currents of escapism and hedonism had been injected into the existentialist spirit and were reinforced by developments such as the birth control pill. The slogans of the youth revolution merely gave word and voice to ideas and activities that had been in practice for several years: *God is dead, Off the pigs, Revolution for the hell of it,* and *If it feels good, do it.*

The experiences of the grunts' early lives held the potential to revolutionize relations with their parents. The values they were taught by their parents were retained, altered or rejected under the influence of different events and personalities than those experienced by their parents. At the risk of misrepresenting the views of some individuals, a risk inherent in all generalizations, certain attitudinal differences and likenesses between the grunts and their parents can be described. Most of the grunts retained their parents' anti-intellectualism and their narrow range of tolerance for differences in others. Both generations are almost equally responsive to peer pressure. Also retained were the views that most changes of routine or thought were too painful to be beneficial and that success was properly defined in materialistic terms. The grunts significantly altered their parents' anti-communism, racism, patriotism and work ethic. Rejected almost completely were the older generation's social morality, particularly their ideas of proper sexual conduct, and the view that the United States alone among nations speaks with the voice of high morality and pure truth.

The events and experiences of the grunts' impressionable years determined how they would react to and perform in the Vietnam War. Since a cataclysmic event like war is so thoroughly unpredictable and uncontrollable, no one is ever really prepared for its occurrence. War always makes extraordinary demands on those it touches. The Vietnam War, however, placed demands unprecedented as well as unusual on those Americans directly involved in it. At certain times the grunts were stalking and fighting an enemy nearly impossible to identify, and that was the task for which they were trained. At other times they were supposed to be understanding and making friends with a people thoroughly foreign, an assignment for which they were not trained. And it was not always clear when either one of those activities was more appropriate than the other. Combat alone would have presented the grunts with the toughest experience of their lives; on top of that was a baffling and maddening culture clash. It is doubtful whether any military force ever faced a more difficult, perhaps impossible, task.

Considering the events and experiences of their lives, most of the grunts were poorly prepared for what was asked of them in Vietnam. There had not been enough hardening experiences which could have tempered them for the most demanding event of their young lives. A surprising number (to this observer) seemed shocked to find that after they filled sandbags for five hours they had dirt under their fingernails; or, when they walked through streams and paddies, leeches sometimes attached themselves to their legs, or when a malarial mosquito bit them they got malaria, or when they were shot at they felt about nine times the fear they ever felt before, or that when human beings get shot they bleed and scream and turn blue and sometimes die.

As a result of the grunts' poor experiential preparation, combined with the absence of a clearly-understood objective in the war, the conduct of the two and one-half million who went was marred by actions—drug abuse, atrocities against Vietnamese civilians, and fraggings among American servicemen—which precluded even a partial accomplishment of their official purpose in going to Vietnam. Even if such incidents occurred only a few times, they would warrant detailed analysis but in Vietnam they occurred on an unprecedented scale.

12 Atrocities—Why?

Every generation has grown up with heroes to worship and big events to live under. Considering the particular mix of people, values, and events which influenced them during their formative years, the grunts, as the corresponding group in every generation, developed both positive and negative capabilities. In the environment of war those capabilities were projected to extraordinary dimensions of both beauty and depravity. The grunts could commit acts of love and acts of hate.

Vietnam presented young Americans with an unprecedented amount and variety of adversity. Besides the blood and death, there were the endless humps under a merciless sun and daily contact with perhaps the most baffling culture to which America has ever sent its troops. There was not enough water, food, booze, women, pay, or sleep; and there was no Honda 350 to jump on and leave it all behind. Every grunt reached a certain point in his tour when the ubiquitous adversity made him aware of two things, the effects of which were almost as sobering as his first experience with hostile fire. He realized, first, that he was fast approaching the limit of his toleration; the anti-adversity armor he had acquired in boot camp was wearing thin. At the same time, he also realized he had no really satisfactory alternatives to the mounting irritations of his existence. He felt he was losing the control of his destiny to people and forces who did not value highly his own well-being. Suppressing his anger and frustration and somehow plodding on was no longer considered a viable alternative. That had been tried before and was seen as no more than an alternative to itself, another deception; it thus became just another facet of adversity. "The Nam and all its bullshit" always came back after each renewal of discipline, each resolve to finish the tour with no bad incidents to stain the record, the memory. That realization was unprecedented for most of the grunts, for television had given their generation the idea that there was an alternative to every adversity, every boredom: change channels or walk away. Such an attitude had no validity in Vietnam. For some of the fed-up, booze was enough to make tolerable the remaining hours and days; for others, it was pot; for others, heroin provided the needed sanctuary. But still others found no relief in those alternatives—they moved on to atrocities against Vietnamese civilians or fraggings of their own unit leaders.

When dealing with a subject as serious as atrocities, it is important not to add to the emotion with which the issue is charged. Such incidents must be put in a proper perspective. It is simply not known how many atrocities occurred in the war, but personal observation and interviews lead me to believe that between one-third and one-half of all Americans who served in Vietnam committed one or more of the atrocities cited below. It should be kept in mind that most of those who served in the war quietly did their jobs without calling any undue attention to themselves, either of praise or censure.

Of the more than two million men who served in Vietnam many gave unselfishly of their money and time to ease some measure of the pain and burden of a standard of living which to an American looks only slightly more advanced than the Bronze Age. Both specialists and non-specialists offered their services to a wide variety of projects in all areas of South Vietnam. Thousands of doctors, dentists, nurses, and medical technicians spent hundreds of thousands of hours administering modern medicine and teaching basic standards of hygiene, in both large cities and tiny villages, under the Medical Civic Action Program (MEDCAP) of the U.S. Command. Hundreds of clinics, hospitals, and schools were built and thousands of Vietnamese trained to staff them. On their own initiative, thousands of American servicemen spent much of their off-duty time working in orphanages and schools. Thousands with agricultural experience in civilian life volunteered their services to improve and increase grain and livestock production. Thousands with construction or engineering experience planned and helped construct wells, roads, irrigation and plumbing systems, bridges and all types of buildings. And nearly every unit assigned to the war conducted fund drives for the repair of homes, schools, and hospitals following their destruction by one or both sides in the conflict.

When the bullets flew, the grunts were the greatest people in the world to have around. But, between firefights, probably half of the grunts, in their dealings with the people of an ancient and very different culture, were at least counterproductive and often just plain disastrous.

When Americans now think of atrocities, the My Lai massacre comes to mind. But murder was not the only type of atrocity, and My Lai was certainly not the first, only the most widely publicized. There were literally tens of thousands of incidents of malicious intent and atrocious result. Most did not involve murder and only a handful were ever followed by any attempt at redress.

In addition to murder, rape and robbery were common types of atrocities carried out by American troops. Americans on patrols and sweeps often had ample opportunity to pacify a sex drive and engage in souvenir-hunting in private homes. And in every unit were a few individuals, dubbed the "zippo squad," who liked to burn villages to the ground whether or not the combat situation dictated such. In heavily-populated areas there were many who enjoyed riding around in jeeps and forcing Vietnamese on motorcycles or in three-wheeled buses off the road. Others got their kicks by driving close to pedestrians and kicking them into roadside ditches. Still others got a laugh out of teaching hungry young orphans living on the streets how to swear in English, without explaining what the new words meant. Older concepts of entertainment and relieving boredom received new definitions in the context of the war in Asia.

The grisly details of atrocities have been amply documented elsewhere. Here the concern is with the particular values and prejudices which Americans carried to Vietnam and which produced atrocities. There are probably as many different reasons for the occurrence of atrocities as there are individuals who committed such incidents, but four major groups of characteristics and interpretations of the grunts, the Vietnamese, and the war answer most questions of causation.

There were several physical and cultural characteristics about the Vietnamese which set the foundation for an environment in which atrocities could occur. The first thing any westerner notices about the Vietnamese is their small physical size. Half the adult population appears to be under five feet tall and weigh less than 120 pounds. Also obvious to the armed American was the fact that the Vietnamese were unarmed. Those two observations together invited the impression that the Vietnamese were unable to effectively answer injustices done them. Once that impression was reached the grunts fell to the temptation of taking on the attitudes and swagger of the Great Western Conqueror. Abuse has always come easier from those who consider themselves conquerors than from those who consider themselves invited guests.

The language difference between Vietnamese civilians and American troops did much to increase the probability of atrocities. Effective communication between the two groups was prevented for all but the few willing to learn a foreign language in a short time. The two groups thus remained for the most part unintelligible to each other; neither was able to ask the other for explanations of superficial traits that may have provoked wonder, irritation or outright anger. Instead, misunderstanding compounded misunderstanding until the general reaction of each to the other was at least a constant suspicion and at worst a deep anger and hatred. When an American on patrol walked into a village and saw two Vietnamese talking, he assumed they were discussing the best time to shoot him in the back or trigger the booby trap that lay just ahead, not the best time to plant the next crop or the chances of rain during the next week.

The American was confirmed in his belief that Orientals have always been a sly and cunning race, "just like the Japs showed at Pearl Harbor." When Americans expressed their frustration or anger aganst the Vietnamese, the language difference worked to the benefit of the former. No matter how loudly the Vietnamese might protest, the grunts couldn't understand; according to the perverted logic of which the latter were sometimes capable, the complaint then wasn't a complaint. Thus, whatever feelings of guilt that might follow an atrocity were either considerably lessened or completely precluded.

On casual inspection, the Vietnamese don't seem to have any definitions for terms like right and wrong, moral and immoral. That erroneous view is reinforced by a number of practices which in America would be punished promptly by social pressure or the courts, but which in Vietnam do not even draw a passing glance. Three practices or attitudes in particular earned the revulsion of Americans in Vietnam: people of all ages defecating in public areas, a monstrous black market operation, and an attitude toward love and sex that is, to those raised in a society which generally values Christian ethics, unbelievably casual.

There were several characteristics about the grunts which helped to bring atrocities to reality. Going to Vietnam represented the most radical departure from the routine of their lives, the greatest possible break with familiarity. Just seeing an underdeveloped Asian country was that much of a change; on top of it was combat. Vietnam hit the grunts hard, for it made them exercise their limited capacity for toleration of things strange more than anything they had encountered before. For many, Vietnam simply presented too many things that could not be assimilated. In such a situation most grunts fell back on a trait of their parents—a quick condemnation of identified differences.

The Americans with the least inclination to be patient or tolerant, and those with virtually no education about a very foreign culture, were exactly the people placed in the position which demanded maximum amounts of those traits and preparations—a daily contact with the Vietnamese people.

The grunts' habit of defining success in materialistic terms, also learned from their parents, contributed to atrocities. Over three-quarters of all Vietnamese live in flimsy-looking huts with no air conditioners, television or stereos inside and no swimming pools or fast cars outside. With so few material things attached to their lives, things the grunts believed added importance and meaning to life, it didn't look like the Vietnamese would be losing much if they were robbed, belted around a little or killed.

Many troops harbored and were capable of expressing varying degrees of racism against non-whites, and nationalistic chauvinism against foreigners. This capability was brought close to manifestation by one of the few historical facts of the war known by a large number of troops: the South Vietnamese government requested American assistance against the Viet Cong and North Vietnamese in 1965. That request was taken by most troops, and many Americans, as proof of Vietnamese inferiority, as an admission of weakness. A related fact, the result of simple observation, underlined that judgement—the Vietnamese did not even seem capable of establishing the prerequisites of national development and greatness: social order and political unity.

The susceptibility of most grunts to peer pressure did much to allow atrocities to continue. On one level there was the unwritten but very strong law that buddies in war do not turn each other in to authority figures—they don't "rat" on each other for anything, least of all for the sake of a few "worthless gooks." On a second level was the fear that one would be considered less than a man if he didn't participate in atrocities with his buddies. Murder, rape, or any form of harassment of unarmed civilians somehow constituted an expression of masculinity to some grunts.

Overlaying all their other traits was the focus of the grunts' minds during their year in the war—they were glued on the day they were scheduled to go home. After 365 days it would be all over—if they didn't get killed or wounded before then. If they kept their date with the Freedom Bird they could forget everything they ever saw or did in the Nam. The grunts became willing to do anything to stay alive until their last day in the war. Nothing within their view or contemplation—taking any unnecessary chances or the lives of Vietnamese—was important enough to delay in any way their return home. At that point the grunts allowed the "Mere Gook Rule" to enter their value system: a crime wasn't a crime if it was committed against a Vietnamese, a Mere Gook. When individuals holding such attitudes were placed in an environment where pre-modern attitudes and practices dominated, the atrocities which could result did result.

Once in Vietnam, with the particular values they brought to the experience, the grunts found several specific tendencies about the Vietnamese which they felt deserved their hatred. They made the predictable mistake of all subjective observers—they judged the Vietnamese against American standards of conduct. Complaints varied with individuals, but among the most frequently cited were: the Vietnamese appeared to have none of the team spirit, long-range planning or can-do determination so admired by Americans; it was every man for himself among them, the only disgrace was to be found out; they expected too much from westerners and were not inclined to take responsibility themselves; they showed no reluctance to break their word unless there was a strong advantage in keeping it.

In addition, there was still another characteristic about the Vietnamese which completely repulsed the grunts. Asian peoples are much less inhibited than westerners about displaying their affection for friends of the same sex. Among Asians, holding hands or walking arm in arm in public does not arouse suspicions of homosexuality. The grunts, however, were shocked at such behavior. They needed to believe their allies and those whose freedom they were supposedly defending were better than "a bunch of queers."

Many troops witnessed incidents which added painful verification to the alleged Vietnamese propensity to lie. Everyone had heard about the patrol that came to a village and was greeted by smiling elders and children. On the way out the other end of the village the patrol ran into a Viet Cong ambush. "Why didn't the villagers tell us about the ambush? I lost two buddies there. Fucking gooks never tell you the truth . . . worthless fucking gooks."

With the loss of friends dominating their thinking, the grunts were in no mood to try to understand the two conditions—one cultural, one military—accounting for such behavior. The Vietnamese do not feel they lie to westerners, since they and most Asians respond to feelings of shame more than guilt. One of the many sources of shame is giving bad news to recent acquaintances and persons not in one's own family. Since one of the criteria of successful (harmonious) relations with others is the avoidance of situations giving shame to either party, the Vietnamese make every effort to give others good news. If that effort involves doctoring or ignoring the western definition of the truth, and if all other alternatives (only slightly lesser deceptions to the westerner) are closed, then the western definition of a lie is given.

A condition imposed on villagers by the war goes farther to explain alleged civilian deception. The Vietnamese populace found itself in an impossible position in the conflict—caught between the war's adversaries, unable to give complete loyalty to either side. With no front line in the war, opposing units might sweep through the same village only hours apart. For the sake of survival, civilians could not afford to give either side any more than minimal assistance or toleration—to help one side too much meant punishment at the hands of the other. Life in most villages was a succession of extortions—for information, food and young recruits by the VC, and for information and suspected VC by the Americans. The villagers thus considered Americans and Viet Cong equally deceiving and exploitive—neither was willing to stay in the villages and offer a lasting protection from the other. But in one respect the VC were less painful to have around—they had no artillery or air force with which to bombard villages by mistake.

Those who came into frequent contact with the Vietnamese had to work around an expression they found on almost every Asian face and one they found very maddening—the perpetual smile that soon became known as the "shit-eating grin." The more frustrating Vietnam became, the less sincere the smile appeared; after a few days or weeks of seeing it, the smile came to look like a sneer especially designed to anger Americans. "I tried for six months to get this guy I was supposed to be advising to level with me on something, anything, but he never did. No matter what question I asked—which way did the VC go, are there any booby traps down that trail, is the village chief on our side or theirs, is your sister a whore?—all I ever got was that shit-eating grin. And one time I even told him one of my squads lost three men in an ambush, and the guy just stood there grinning. I wanted to smash his filthy little slope head and spray his brains all over his fucked-up country. These fucking gooks are sick, Man, sick."

The action by the Vietnamese that angered the grunts even more than the perpetual grin and the deception was the performance, or more accurately the lack of same, of their ally's army in the field. The grunts believed, with strong justification through most of the war, that they were doing more than their share of fighting and dying in a war that was not theirs. To the American grunts, those for whom the war was being fought were doing more running away from it than fighting. There were too many accounts verified by disinterested observers to call that impression the result of emotionalism or imagination. And raising the grunts' resentment to an even higher intensity was his belief, again verified, that the crooked politicans and political generals were spending more time partying in Saigon nightclubs and manipulating the black market to their advantage than they were training the ARVN and instilling it with the determination that might have shortened the war.

Every war has presented certain environmental factors that allow some actions to occur which do not contribute to the accomplishment of any official mission. The Vietnam War was no exception. In war, troops are placed in an environment which suggests they can do almost anything they want and there will be no punishment. Whatever method they choose to express anything from a temporal frustration to a deeply-held racism will, they believe, be absorbed without reaction by the local populace, the country, and the war. The physically and militarily weak appearance of the Vietnamese reinforced such a conclusion. Not only in war but also in peace the strong and partially-educated have never shown much respect for the weak. The discovery that one could get away with abusing Vietnamese civilians removed most of what prevented that abuse. The only other restraint on abusive behavior—a moral standard that reserves no room for it —was either suppressed or not felt by many of the grunts.

In spite of the legends and movies, war never has been one bloody scene after another. There has always been plenty of room for boredom as well. Their past experience with the American standard of living caused the grunts to develop more boredom than they had ever had to deal with before. Back in the World there were girls, fast cars and bikes, and all the music, pot, and booze a guy could want to relieve boredom. And perhaps most important of all, there was freedom of movement. If one wanted a change of scenery he could always jump in his car and head for Florida or California or any place he wanted. But in Vietnam most of those avenues of expression or escape were closed. For some, committing an atrocity offered welcome relief from the boredom.

War and peace give prominence to different people in any society; the former condition seems to bring out all the less reputable types from whatever their peacetime hiding places. For many grunts, the type of Vietnamese they met in the context of the war made a positive impression of the first foreign people they ever encountered nearly impossible. The only civilians many Americans met were pimps, whores, draft-dodgers, black marketeers, informers for the VC or starving street urchins trying to steal the watches off their arms. For many, the logical conclusion was that since Vietnam was full of such types, the "gooks" really were worthless, deserving of hatred and abuse.

At some time in his tour practically every grunt developed a soporific fatalism about the war and his tiny place in it. The first symptoms usually became manifest by about the third month of the tour and helped bring atrocities to reality. "Hell, we figure we might be dead the next minute or day anyhow so what the fuck difference does it make what we do? What difference does it make if we shoot at farmers in their paddies or screw village girls or jerk an elder's beard or beat up a cowboy trying to steal the watches right off our arms? Who would give a shit? And even if they caught us what could they do that was any worse than shaving our heads and sending us to Nam? Ha, we're already here!"

Several special characteristics of the war helped increase the grunts' frustration and thus increased the probability of atrocities. Many believed they were sent to Vietnam to do nothing but kill communists. They were therefore not at all receptive to official directives about treating civilians as equals or "winning the hearts and minds" of the people. "What the hell kind of deal is this anyway? I came over here to fight, not to pass out candy and bandaids to ignorant slopes who don't even talk my language!" In addition, Viet Cong policies of avoiding prolonged battles with American units often made impossible the avenging of a buddy's death. Kept alive long after the VC melted into the jungle, the desire for revenge frequently caused grunts to turn on the first Vietnamese they could find. In many instances, the victims turned out to be children and the elderly. The rationale for such action usually ran something like, "Most of them are communist anyway—the kids and old ones set up booby traps and hide rice for the VC all the time—and they tell them where we are, too. They always know when we're coming and then they get their ambushes ready."

Many of the grunts never could accept the fact that they were not greeted in Vietnam as their fathers and uncles had been received in Europe and Korea—as liberators. The grunt was not, he believed, being appreciated by the very people he was sent to help. Thus, concluding that he was sweating, humping the hills, going without his girl, and bleeding for nothing, the grunt then could commit atrocities more easily.

Finally, no American fighting man ever faced a more confusing enemy than the Vietnam grunts faced in the Viet Cong. Unlike members of the North Vietnamese Army, the VC wore no uniform. VC looked like civilians, and civilians looked like VC. Many grunts then considered all Vietnamese active Viet Cong, "just to make sure." The difference between suspected and confirmed VC was consistently obscured, often with fatal results for the suspected.

The best one can do to explain atrocities is to come back to one of the general conditions accompanying all wars—the absence of any sociolegal system other than might is right. The lack of a mechanism of redress for the weak gives a psychological justification for abuse by the strong—if a soldier thinks he can get away with abusing others in some way, there is a high probability that he will try.

13 "Take Care of Your Men"

Some of the grunts showed themselves capable of still another negative act—the fragging of commissioned and noncommissioned officers. The deliberate throwing or planting of fragmentation hand grenades by American troops against their own unit leaders was a side of the Vietnam War just as hideous as the atrocities against civilians. It could be said that the misunderstanding, resentment and outright hatred which was manifested in fragging incidents originated in the different socioeconomic background of officers and their men, but such a judgement would ignore the many officers who were once enlisted men as well as the fact that many victims of fraggings were middle and high-ranking enlisted men. The more immediate and telling differences between small unit leaders and troops had their origin in the different training given each.

Junior officers and noncommissioned officers in training are constantly urged to "take care of your men," to "think of the troops first." But troops and leaders settled on different definitions of that concept. To the latter it meant keeping each man functional in a combat sense. To the troops, however, taking care of them meant sparing no effort to soften the adversities with which combat presented them. The platoon sergeant and the lieutenant were somehow supposed to make the tour in combat go as easy as possible. In pursuing their own understanding of the *take care* concept, small unit leaders issued a constant stream of orders that seemed to the troops to make even less tolerable the adversities of life in the bush. Examples of the two *take care* definitions clashing are innumerable, but three were likely to recur daily, and for over a year in the cases of many troops.

The best time of year for conducting search and destroy operations or patrols was also the hottest part of the year in Vietnam. The troops always wanted to leave helmets and flak jackets behind, since they only made a hot day hotter. But with few exceptions small unit leaders always directed that the two items be worn, since they lessened the seriousness of wounds incurred.

A second clash of interest centered on the approved Defense Department methods of combatting malaria and heat casualties —the infamous yellow malaria pills and pink salt tablets. By ordering the pills' consumption, small unit leaders were helping keep their units combat efficient, they were taking care of their men. As far as the troops were concerned however, both pills only made life in the bush more miserable—the former caused diarrhea and the latter nausea, and besides, everybody had a buddy who took both but still became a heat casualty one day and was medevaced with malaria the next.

The third example centered on the occurrence most frequent and frustrating to junior enlisted men both in and out of combat —the word change. In the bush the word change could take forms nearly fatal to morale. A unit might reach an objective hill in the late afternoon and be told by a higher headquarters to spend the night there. The troops would then be told to "dig-in" —to dig foxholes for shelter in case of attack. Digging a hole three or more feet deep was a project costly in strength and patience, but at its completion the distant headquarters might call back and direct still another move before nightfall.

Whatever explanation offered the troops was insufficient— they considered the dig-in directive no more than unnecessary harassment, a make-work project whose only purpose was to prevent their taking a much-deserved rest while the lieutenant or company commander leisurely shot the breeze with the faraway battalion headquarters. The result in the troops' minds was, at least, lingering questions about the sanity of their leaders, and at worst, a growing resentment for which there was no vent. The two unit leaders, however, had ample justification for their dig-in order in the uncertainty inherent in combat—one never knows when "the shit will hit the fan," when the enemy will open fire. They were thus taking care of their troops' lives. And if that wasn't convincing enough, they could always redirect upward the question of the sanity of leaders—the colonel and the general didn't know what was really going on outside their air-conditioned bunkers.

The two different interpretations of the *take care* concept point out a fundamental difference in the outlook of leaders and troops. The former were concerned with the performance of a group; the latter, with one individual. The differences which grew out of such opposite perspectives were virtually irreconcilable and led to a long train of misunderstandings. The leader-trooper relationship was simply not at all conducive to the exercise by either of an empathy for the other which perhaps could have prevented both misunderstandings and fraggings.

Every soldier, marine, sailor or airman who fragged a unit leader believed at the time of the incident that he acted with more than ample justification. Such a view may sound incredible now, but anyone who has seen combat and perceived what it does to one's thinking processes can appreciate the extreme difficulty, perhaps even the folly, of making value judgements on the thoughts and actions of men in a combat environment from a haven now made safe by both time and distance. The assignment of guilt borders on the immoral when made across such differences of perspective. Being within a few weeks or days of a safe exit from so dangerous and unpredictable an environment as the Vietnam War caused one to formulate definitions of terms like "reasonable" and "justified" which he would not make in any other situation.

Explanations offered for the fragging of unit leaders indicated a belief that one's survival was threatened. Two specific and one general type of incident provoked nearly all such assumptions. First, two dates were always in the minds of Americans in Vietnam: R & R and Tour Rotation, one's last day in the Nam. The last thing a trooper wanted to hear was that either of those dates had been changed. In his anxiety to leave the war, he could see no real justification for either of those two dates being "messed with by some paper-shuffling lifer in the rear." Yet these important dates were sometimes changed, often with no explanation to the grunts.

The occurrence of a fragging is even more understandable, though no more justifiable, in the light of a second incident. Normal, though unofficial, practice among field units was to relieve men of patrol responsibilities within a few days of their rotation. Both troops and leaders were aware of the practice and the former naturally looked forward to the few days they could pass out water, C-rations and mail instead of stalking VC or NVA. Occasionally, however, the combat situation dictated that such a policy be set aside. In such cases the troops affected were convinced there was someone around who "didn't like me and wanted to screw me out of some slack time and maybe even get me zapped."

The general variety of incident can be labeled "unnecessary harassment." With their different training, duties and outlook, leaders and troops held as completely different interpretations of unnecessary harassment as they held of the *take care* concept. Examples of unnecessary harassment are nearly infinite in number, but the most frequently and loudly bitched about included making troops: cut their hair, salute and shine their boots in rear-echelon areas; collect and bury all refuse from C-ration meals in the field; carry more weight in the field than the troops felt necessary; improve defensive positions constantly when "any fucking idiot can see the damn hole's good enough—I mean how perfect can you make a damn hole in the ground anyway?"; clean their rifles when they much preferred sleeping, eating or bull-shitting with buddies; plus the standard three mind-blowers in the bush, malaria and salt pills, flak jackets and helmets, and the constant word changes. And behind all these things was the fear that they would get stuck with a lieutenant or platoon sergeant who would want to carry out all kinds of crazy John Wayne tactics, who would use their lives in an effort to end the war single-handedly, win the big medal, and get his picture in the hometown paper. In the troops' view, by increasing the unnecessary harassment or by merely allowing it to continue, unit leaders were "pushing too hard where they didn't have to"; they were keeping the troops' lives full of "petty bullshit" which understandably provoked deep anger and resentment in the latter. Some could not deal with such heavy emotions.

The abuse of authority did much to provoke fraggings, and developments far away from Vietnam contributed much to the abuse of authority. Preparations for any war necessitate a rapid increase in the size of an armed force. To meet personnel requirements, standards of recruitment are lowered, and training cycles accelerated. Inevitably the quality of both leaders and troops declines. In addition to the usual wartime attrition by combat casualties, there were two features of the Vietnam War which further accelerated the personnel turnover and thus the decline in quality.

First, by official policy, officers and most NCOs were rarely allowed to keep their combat assignments for more than six months, approximately half the tour of duty in Vietnam. A leader could barely learn his job or get to know his troops before he would be transferred. Field units were thus led by a succession of the inexperienced. Second, anti-war sentiment in the United States grew steadily after the 1965 introduction of American ground forces in the war. With fewer volunteers available, there were far fewer highly-motivated leaders and troops to be recruited in 1968 or 1969 than in 1965. In the fourth and fifth years of the war incidents of abuse of authority became more frequent. There were simply too many leaders who, to cover deficiencies in their own ability, settled on the most Machiavellian methods of leadership in pursuit of their visions of battlefield glory. And there were too many leaders who hid behind smug sentiments like, "they don't have to like what you say—they just have to do it."

Perhaps the most perverse manifestation of the lower quality of small unit leadership was the use of the combat environment as a punishment. Standard practice among field units was to rotate each day the dangerous point, or lead, position on patrols or unit moves; each man could thus project which day he would have point. On occasion, however, certain men were kept on point several days in a row. Such selectees were not kept on point because they possessed any special ability for the duty, but because they had been identified as "troublemakers" by their platoon sergeant or platoon commander. They had probably bitched too much, or were a little slow or lacking in enthusiasm while carrying out an earlier directive. In some cases the abuse was carried even further—a man was kept on point up to the day before he was to leave Vietnam. So malicious and twisted a practice could always, however, be buried under a flood of words about the "situation imposed by the enemy."

In at least one sense, lower ranking enlisted personnel not oriented toward a military career contributed more than their leaders to the tragic reality of fraggings—they were the ones who threw or planted the grenades. The overwhelming majority of the troops were not prepared by background, temperament, or intellect for the amount of thinking which would have developed even some understanding of the priorities involved in their leaders' decision-making. They were only prepared to be highly suspicious and resentful of authority figures and those who had been to college, since in the view of most, such people were only "snobs and pricks out to screw a guy." And most troops were prepared to be very selfish in the smallest sense of the term: "It's just like my old man said—a guy's gotta look out for old number one first and all the other turds in the world last."

Bringing the probability of fraggings even closer to reality was a change in the character of the troops' basically self-oriented outlook occurring in the course of a twelve or thirteen-month tour in the combat zone. During the first half of the tour troops were concerned with their own combat efficiency; in the latter half they worried about their own survival first and their combat functioning second. They then had no trouble putting their own well-being above that of the rest of the unit. Therein lay the danger of an attack on another American, for any perceived threat to one's survival of his "year in Hell" was likely to cause him to consider fragging as his only effective recourse. Deep anger and frustration often demand an outlet more satisfying than mere profanity can offer. Those who needed someone to blame for general adversity or for a specific irritation or threat quickly settled on the nearest, the most visible authority figures: "That's it, Man—I'm gonna frag me a lifer some night!"

American servicemen have always bitched about the situation imposed by the enemy as well as the situation imposed by the Pentagon; malaria pills and more word changes were merely new issues to which an old practice was extended. New developments in war appeared in Vietnam and go much farther in explaining fraggings. The percentage of ethnic minorities in the armed forces in the late 1960s was higher than ever before, and reporters suffered less censorship than their predecessors in any previous war.

The Vietnam War was fought by troops coming from a society undergoing rapid changes. Most notable was the improved living standard and social position being won by minorities. Troops, white and not, could see the many gains that had been secured by the long train of dramatic acts of protest, and often of violence, which occurred in the 1960s. This is not to imply that minority group members were responsible for the fraggings that occurred in Vietnam; only that the socioeconomic groups from which troops come were more aware than ever before of the lines between classes and the actual power and rights enjoyed by people on different sides of those lines. They were more sensitive than ever before to such ideas as equality, justice and oppression. The psychological condition of some individuals in Vietnam was not at all conducive to their making a rational interpretation of such terms.

Considering the number of troops involved in actual combat operations, an unusually high number of reporters and VIPs were allowed access to the war. In addition to the more professional journalists, there were many young and inexperienced observers overly susceptible to the sensational. With the war largely devoid of big, decisive battles, other kinds of drama had to be looked for. Fraggings, drug abuse and atrocities answered the need; with censorship more relaxed than in previous conflicts, such incidents could be reported immediately to America and the world. What such circumstances meant to the individual trooper—worried most about surviving the war and sensitive about justice and oppression, real or imagined—was that he had available to him the means of projecting himself and his complaint over both his adversity and the entire military hierarchy. By fragging a lifer he could take his case directly to his people over the heads of all the "snobs and pricks out to screw a guy."

There was one major feature of the Vietnam War that was absent from all other wars in which America has been involved. It was a characteristic that explains why the adversity and harassment that have always filled the lives of soldiers were much less tolerable to the Vietnam grunts; it thus explains fraggings more completely than any individual complaint. In spite of hundreds of explanations, exhortations and pleadings from the White House, the objectives of the war were never clearly understood by the grunts who fought it. There was no easily-identified evil to be defeated, as Hitler, Tojo, and Mussolini had personified for an earlier generation.

The lack of a clearly-understood objective helped make the Vietnam grunts the least docile that America has ever put in uniform. The war seemed meaningless to many, especially after the massive Tet offensive by the NVA in 1968, so why should one endure adversity for nothing? Since the troops answered that question in the negative, they refused to tolerate any more than the minimum amount of adversity—and the troops reserved the right to define "minimum." In an environment in which too much of their lives seemed to be in the hands and arbitrary minds of others, deciding when they could tolerate no more adversity—whether or not they would frag a lifer—was the one decision troops reserved for themselves—for dear life, for dear sanity.

Though anger or blame directed at a specific individual might be justified, fraggings never were. It is true that built into the system of the military hierarchy and the different duties it dictated was the means for provoking much resentment and misunderstanding between leaders and troops. But there was not built into that system the means for either making understandable to troops the priorities that caused leaders to make the decisions they made, or for making understandable to leaders the basically different outlook of troops. This lack of proper orientation caused the troops to consider supposedly sound directives merely unnecessary harassment. Whenever such priorities or orientations were understood, it was only the result of a few individuals, leaders and troops, making an extra effort. In most units, more autocratic attitudes prevailed.

During a decade in which authority came under increasingly heavy attack in all fields of activity, a high potential for confrontation between leaders and followers was nurtured. The refusal or inability to lessen that potential in the military, combined with the absence of an easily understood objective in the war, increased the possibility of fraggings. It will never be known exactly how many times the potential became a reality, but one fact will always stand out—such incidents between Americans never occurred with such frequency before the Vietnam War.

14 Reactions

In the months and years since the final American ground patrol was completed in July 1972, the Vietnam veterans have registered a wide variety of reactions to what they saw and did in the war. There were actually as many reactions to the war as there were Americans in it—about two and one-half million. Little understanding results from dividing the two and one-half million into hawk and dove stereotypes or variations of either to describe the war's effects, for even within such arbitrary subdivisions one soon runs into so baffling a variety of reactions that the categories themselves are rendered largely meaningless. The most accurate and realistic thing one can do now is list the reactions to the war that have been manifested thus far. Such a listing may well give some indication of future reactions now only latent.

Many of the ex-grunts returned home proud of what they and their country had done in Vietnam. Many others returned ashamed of their own and their country's connection with Southeast Asian affairs. And still others returned with a wide variety of reactions between pride and shame. Making easier an understanding of the proud is the fact that so many of them have been among the most vocal veterans. The proud veterans freely express the same sentiments they used to put in their letters home; the hope that North Vietnam would be blanketed with atomic bombs or at least invaded and occupied so the people there could be "straightened out." And though they hoped for their own safe return from the war, they could also write that they were willing to stay in the war "as long as there's a VC or NVA that's trying to kill me and my friends and the flag I stand for."

The pride many veterans feel had three major sources. First, they are unshakably convinced that the United States is the greatest country in the world, and they feel privileged to have been given the chance in Vietnam to help keep America the greatest. These veterans believe that one of the best contributions to American greatness is a military contribution.

A second source of pride for many veterans is their admiration for group unity, probably derived from a fear of peer ostracism learned from their parents and schoolmates. They are acutely aware of the fact that they gave their President unquestioned loyalty; they did their part to preserve unity in the execution of America's mission in Vietnam. These veterans consider the willingness to give loyalty to authority figures one of the few valid tests of one's worth to his nation.

Like their parents, the proud veterans hold a deep intolerance for those not sharing their views on the values of giving loyalty and preserving unity. Some back in the States who did not share those values kept their differing views to themselves. Others felt their dissent should be expressed in a voice loud enough for all to hear. To the proud grunts, the loudmouth hippies back in the World were the most obvious of adversaries—they were guilty of two unforgivable acts. First, by their constant demonstrating they had poisoned the minds of many civilians, thereby preventing the latter from uniting behind the President so the war could be won or at least ended as fast as possible. Second, by their draft card burning and constant screaming, "Ho, Ho, Ho Chi Minh, Viet Cong are gonna win," the hippies had encouraged the North Vietnamese and Viet Cong to fight instead of seeing the light and surrendering. They had thus made the grunts' job of fighting those enemies infinitely more difficult; they had stabbed the grunts in the back. While the grunts had been humping the hills and getting caught in ambushes, the hippies were sitting around with a reefer in one hand and the other on their girl's body, discoursing on the evils of American society and the illusory point at which loyalty ends and treason begins. Small wonder the proud grunts came home aching to "get my hands on one of them fucking hippy-bastards who was hiding behind his college deferment and waving a VC flag while my buddies was getting blowed all to hell, all to hell!"

The third source of pride is the grunts' prewar experiences. A particular combination of experiences allowed the military to take on a deeply personal significance. There are and always have been many for whom the military and war offered the first real opportunity for meaningful association and expression in life. They had rarely had the right answer in class, they had never been invited to parties, they had always been cut from the team, and all that their teachers had been able to come up with was, "George, you must apply yourself more, just apply yourself." Many of these found that when they got to boot camp there were things they could do about which others would say "Wow!" or "Nice going, Georgie." The praise was welcome, intoxicating. In Vietnam it continued, but for much different acts. Expertise in the application of brutality or even killing won the same praise in the war as had 100 pushups in training.

For others the war offered a nice continuation of a kind of expression and recognition they had grown used to. Those who had made the football team back at All-American High School found the same exhilaration from combat exploits—carrying a buddy out of enemy fire or killing Vietnamese—as they had previously found in scoring touchdowns and winning the big game. For them the war offered the chance to live certain illusions they had formulated themselves or had been taught, principally the one that says there is glory in war just like there is in football. They were not at all prepared to hear anyone even hint that in following such an idea they had been chasing a ghost.

Another large number of veterans came home full of shame over what they had seen and done in the war. Some are ashamed of themselves for being part of a group, the Military Assistance Command, Vietnam, that produced so much bitterness and blood, so much disillusion and death, but so little progress and peace. They are surprised and disappointed that they were so easily and thoroughly deceived by the politicians into joining such an enterprise. Others are ashamed in an impersonal way.

They are ashamed of what they saw their country doing to another people involved in their own version of the American Revolution.

Like the proud, the ashamed veterans carry some intolerance but it differs from that of the proud in two respects. First, it is directed at those who stood up like robots at the presidential call to arms and those who said anything goes—atrocities, nuclear weapons—in the fight against communism, and second, in it is mixed an element of pity for those they believed misled by the super-patriots. To the ashamed, the protesters were heroes, the gifted vanguard who could see more clearly than the masses the true character of events.

The ashamed have done different things with their reaction. Some want so badly to erase the war from their memories that they don't admit to anyone they were once there. A few of these have enough will power to suppress their shame; they are using whatever routine they adopted on their return to push Vietnam into the distant and fuzzy past of other people. "I'm a different person now—I was never there," says a veteran now helping an uncle manage a resort in Canada. Others who want to erase the memory don't have the will. Whatever they do they can still feel their war experiences hanging swollen in their conscience. They are doing the only thing they can—waiting for time to obscure the sharper corners, the brighter colors of the memory.

Still other veterans who reacted with shame have decided they can do things worthwhile with their shame. For these the war occasioned a new application of the attitude exemplified by James Dean, Martin Luther King, Jr. and the Kennedys—a more just world can be built. War, like segregation and cancer, not only should be eliminated but can be. These veterans have decided to organize and try to explain to the country their revulsion to the war. Though there may be some basis for criticizing some of their methods, the impact on the American news media and public of Vietnam Veterans Against the War is not to be overlooked in any consideration of veterans' activities. VVAW has shown that veterans who prefer peace to war are not spoiled kids throwing tantrums nor are they communist dupes. The activist veterans are concerned young Americans who have identified and are committed to changing certain widespread attitudes that make more possible the occurrence of war; attitudes such as: the President is always right because he is the President, communism is worth crusading against, and there is glory in war. The activist veterans have succeeded in making many in the working class aware of the inequalities in war and the terrible price of their patriotism—it is their sons who do the dying in wars declared by politicians and acquiesced to by the majority of the population.

One group of veterans is noteworthy for their complete lack of adjustment problems. Their attitudes have been personified as long as there have been big events to batter people around. They are the uncommitted, the uninvolved, and they feel that big events only hurt those who think about them. These veterans figure the Vietnam War was just another of those big and sometimes bloody events that happen to people in the course of life. If such events can be avoided, then fine; but, if not, then one just has to go along with them because "there's not a hell of a lot one guy can do about them things anyway. Hell, Man, war's been happening for thousands of years and they're gonna happen for thousands more. No use fighting it . . . just go and get back as quick as you can, that's about all you can do, right?"

Many more of the ex-grunts could not take the war in stride. They were simply and thoroughly horrified by it, by its bigness and by the mindless way it ran over individuals, feeding on bodies and dreams with no regard for friendship or promises made. Some were horrified because the massive and uncontrolled event that was the war did to them what they would allow no individual or event to do—strip away the veneer of pretense from their own particular weakness and deficiencies. They have carefully selected the memories and interpretations they will allow to survive and be recounted, discarding that which does not reinforce the myth they now cling to in a death grip—the view that they knew exactly what they were doing every step of the way.

These veterans will not let themselves do anything that might convey the slightest hint that they were taken advantage of and used, that they were not astute enough to see through an event of shallow justification, that they were exposed as the character no one wants to be, just another "dumbass peon." Never again will they allow themselves to be lured close to the glare and heat of events in the making, naked of the cushion of time and space such events always wore in high school history classes. As soon as they touched back down on American territory and their discharge was processed, they raced back to the womb-niche from which they had been pried loose either by the draft or visions of glory. Once back in that niche they resolved never to leave it again: "The whole country, the whole fucking world could blow up and I wouldn't lift a finger for them again. I did a good job over there—I know I did—but my thing's right here and I ain't never gonna leave it again, never."

Others were horrified for another reason. They may or may not have been strong in the face of adversity when they went, but they came back broken, for they were presented with a bigger dose of shock than they could assimilate. They are terribly and perhaps permanently confused about the war. They long to understand it so they can build a future above and beyond it, but it took something from them that cannot be quickly or easily replaced—the frame of reference needed to distinguish between the logical and the illogical. Except possibly for the quadriplegics, these veterans are the most tragic victims of the war.

To them, logic looks absurd, absurdity looks logical. They can't make realistic decisions about the future because they are no longer sure what reality is. The war was madness in motion; it was a surrealistic landscape brought to life and yet it was a real historical event, real enough to wrench once solid values out of all recognizable and useful shape. Now for the confused veterans the mad play of life on the planet Earth goes on, bouncing back and forth between reality and illusion, and they feel strapped to a seat before that stage. Action is okay, passivity is okay, brutality is okay, love is okay—they're all okay, they're all worthless, "who gives a shit?"

One final major reaction is probably held by more veterans than any other. Those who hold it are not a group apart from those who hold other reactions to the war—they are for the most part veterans who have reacted with anything but pride. After they had been home for awhile, or during the latter months of their Vietnam tour in some cases, a considerable number of the veterans came to feel they had been lied to and used for a purpose not worth their sweat and blood. Though that number is impossible to determine, I put it at between fifty and seventy-five percent of all the younger generation veterans.

The origin of this fourth reaction probably lies in an attitude widespread among infantrymen in Vietnam after 1968: the grunts of the latter years of the war did not feel they were part of a crusade to save Vietnam from communism. But they did think they were going to do something important, something that would help a less fortunate people, and something that would answer their own human need to find meaning in life. Most believed their national leaders when they said there was a good reason to go, and most understood the implication in the call—the project might not be exactly pleasant. Once in Vietnam, however, that sense of importance began to dissipate. No matter how many patrols they went on, how many air strikes they called, how many rounds they fired at sounds in the night, and no matter how much money they gave to build schools and hospitals, nothing ever got any better. Vietnam stayed as backward and screwed up as it was at the beginning of everyone's tour. The war then became an apolitical and personal project—the struggle to survive it. The only thing the grunts found to win in Vietnam was 365 consecutive days of life.

The politicians had lied, and worse still, they could either never see the war as the grunts saw it or they refused to listen to those who tried to tell them why it could never be won. So most of the smiling, glad-handing public officials continued to deceive the grunts, the grunts' parents, the whole country and worst of all, themselves. To these grunts phrases such as, "honoring our commitments to the South East Asia Treaty Organization," and "Turning back the tide of communist aggression," or "buying time for the South Vietnamese," and fighting on until we can achieve "peace with honor," were all bullshit. The name of the game was survival.

It is obvious not only from this account but the publicized actions of the veterans themselves that the war had a massive effect on the grunts' lives. In many cases it had an even larger effect than that worked by their parents. We don't have to wait decades to judge that the war was the hardest experience the grunts have faced in their lives. For most it will remain the hardest thing they will ever face. The war taught them what they either did not know at all or only suspected before they went—life is full of adversity and it is rarely deserved. There are many ways of learning that lesson, but none of the other ways can teach the lesson as fast and in so direct a manner as war. The Vietnam War invested many young minds with some very old attitudes.

No one can now tell what lasting influences the Vietnam veterans will have on the rest of their generation or what effect the war will have on American society and history, but a few indications already can be discerned. An event as big as war always touches many more than those who wear uniforms and carry arms in it. It occasionally happens that a war provokes a common resolve in those who saw it close up and those who witnessed it from a great distance. The Vietnam War in particular provoked a unity of sorts between the minority of the young generation who went and the majority who did not. Those who were bloodied in the hundreds of demonstrations against the war were also lied to and deceived, and tasted disillusion. They and the veterans have resolved to tolerate less abuse of authority and deception in life than previous generations. They have advanced new answers to old questions: what is the proper role of America and its military machine in international affairs? What is the proper role of force in human relations?

Those born between 1940 and 1954 saw the same gaping contradictions in life every other maturing generation saw, and many of them made the same complaint against official deception and brutality other generations made. But, reformers in the Vietnam generation enjoyed an advantage over their predecessors. They were assisted in making their anti-war/anti-violence case by television—the very instrument that had kept so many of them naive—and a large army of reporters. Thus the peace message received wider dissemination than ever before. And while it also provoked a passionate and sometimes violent opposition, it is now a firmly-established tenet in the lifestyle of millions of Americans.

The Vietnam War was the event which blooded another American generation. It was for them what Bunker Hill, Gettysburg, Belleau Wood, and Guadalcanal were to earlier generations; and like those earlier generations, after the event they too are taking another small degree of inhumanity out of our way of life.

Epilogue

By now most of the Vietnam grunts have found what they consider an acceptable postwar existence. Most have stopped wandering and have either gotten their thing together or made enough progress toward that end that it will soon be reached. They are doing the same things the grunts of other wars have done when they became veterans. They are selling insurance, pumping gas, attending law school, tending bar, raising beef cattle, putting up telephone poles, sorting mail, photographing babies, driving trucks, piloting airplanes, wearing police badges, leaning on air hammers, teaching analytical geometry, laying bricks, polishing caskets, fixing car engines, coaching football, cutting hair, programming computers, growing corn and repairing television sets. And they are doing something else their predecessors did. They are slowly deciding how to answer the question their children will ask in five, ten, fifteen years—what did you do in Vietnam, Dad?

The colors of First Battalion, Third Marine Regiment now wave in the warm Pacific breezes over Pearl Harbor. In the battalion and regimental commanders' offices another campaign streamer hangs from the unit battle standards. The battalion operations staff now issues plans to "advance the state of training" instead of orders to "seek out, close with and destroy the enemy." Advancing the state of training now includes scheduling unit beer parties, classes on drug abuse and venereal disease, practicing for inter-command golf, rifle, and boxing matches, and selecting a command nominee for Military Wife of the Year.

Bravo Company has a new generation of grunts. They have never heard of Captain Sam, Virginia Ridge or Hill 174, and they don't spend their precious liberty time poring through the official histories for such details. They are now doing the same things marines and soldiers have always done after the shooting stops: practicing battlefield tactics they will probably never use, manicuring lawns, polishing everything in sight for the next inspection.

Though the postwar troops are probably not aware of it, links do exist between themselves and the Vietnam grunts. On the walls of all the company recreation rooms hang portraits of those who won the Medal of Honor in Vietnam. The newest grunts, those who will never see the Nam, watch television, shoot pool or check out for weekend home visits and parties under the cold gaze of boyish faces, under the officious descriptions of legendary feats now largely forgotten. "With complete disregard for his own personal safety . . . crossing the fire-swept terrain . . . refused medical attention . . . skillfully maneuvered his squad through dense undergrowth and withering enemy fire . . . silenced the enemy machine guns before succumbing to his own wounds . . . brought credit to himself and his Service . . . in the finest traditions . . . the finest traditions . . . the finest traditions . . . ."

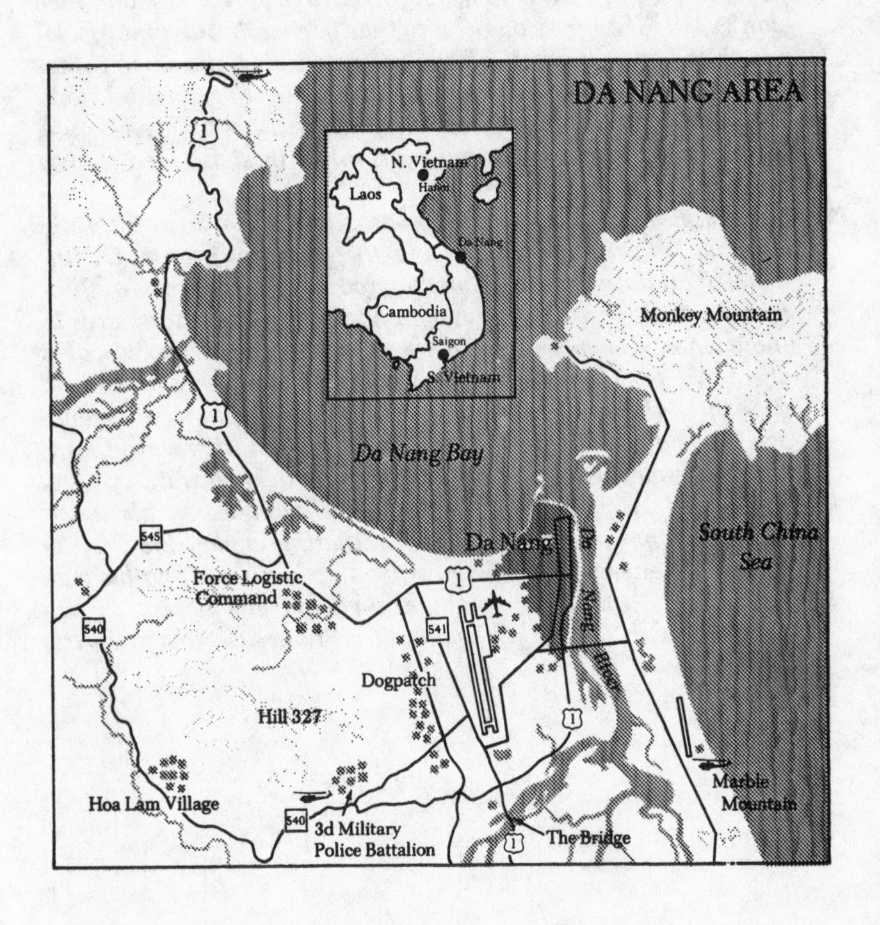

DA NANG AREA
N. Vietnam
Hanoi
Laos
Da Nang
Cambodia
Saigon
S. Vietnam
Monkey Mountain
Da Nang Bay
South China Sea
Da Nang
Da Nang River
Force Logistic Command
Dogpatch
Hill 327
Hoa Lam Village
3d Military Police Battalion
The Bridge
Marble Mountain
1
545
540
541

VIETNAM:
The Other War

Contents

1 The World of the Rear

Most people have very definite images of what the Vietnam War was like, images formed by television, movies, newspapers, and accounts of relatives. Those images almost exclusively center on bloody battles and the headlines and news films that report them. Young men scrambling across grassy fields toward a tree line, helicopters hovering over bomb-cratered hilltops, sleek jets strafing bamboo villages, and endless lines of refugees streaming away from burning cities are among the most widely held images of the Vietnam War. Repeated thousands of times in news broadcasts and movies during and after the war, these fragmentary views contributed to the impression that Vietnam was continuous action and combat for all involved. This image persists in spite of developments that make such a view obsolete. There was another side of Vietnam, the side behind the battles and the headlines.

Twentieth-century developments in warfare have resulted in the creation of huge staffs for the service and support of combat units. By the time of the Vietnam War this trend had continued to the point that for every young man who charged an enemy position under fire and for every pilot who strafed a village, there were six or eight others far away supporting in some way those infantry assaults and air strikes. The huge staff of those engaged in combat support was referred to in military officialese as "Service and Support." Both the staff and its location were referred to in troopers' slang as "the rear." Service and support included such diverse and seemingly unmilitary occupational classifications as baker and typewriter repairman, stationary engineer and water supply specialist, computer programmer and helicopter mechanic, food service or refrigeration specialist, even radio and television programmer and announcer. In the rear there were also all the comforts of twentieth-century life the troops in the field were denied. In the rear were most of the accessories and conveniences of life back in the States, the real world: security, movies, free time, dry beds with clean sheets, mail and showers every day, radios and stereos, and plenty to eat and drink. Far behind the battles and the headlines was a different world, the world of the rear.

As the war escalated, huge urban concentrations of Americans grew up around air bases and ports along the coast, cities of ten thousand, twenty-five thousand, fifty thousand Americans. These rear-echelon base cities were placed all along the eight-hundred-mile coastline of South Vietnam. From the DMZ in the north to the delta in the south the largest bases were: Quang Tri, Dong Ha, Phu Bai, Da Nang, Chu Lai, Qui Nhon, Nha Trang, Cam Ranh, Phan Rang, and, biggest of all, the Tan Son Nhut–Bien Hoa complex on the outskirts of Saigon.

The physical appearance of the base cities was much the same in every locale. From the air they looked like three concentric circles with the sea limiting expansion on one side. In the middle was the old Vietnamese city with its legacies of the French colonial period: French-named streets, wide tree-lined boulevard along the beach, and whitewashed administrative buildings and homes with louvered windows. In the second circle were the service and support facilities of the American Military Assistance Command, Vietnam (MACV): sprawling supply sheds, ammunition dumps, repair shops, motor pools, tank parks, barracks, and mess halls. Few buildings were more than one story high, all were painted green, and all had sandbags on the roof to hold the sheet metal in place during typhoons. Sandbagged trench lines zigzagged around and between buildings and neighboring units. The third circle of the base city complex consisted of shantytown settlements built by refugees from the war in the field. Though there was some variation from area to area, the rear-echelon base complexes followed the same pattern: a temporary American military community sandwiched by two Vietnamese communities, one permanent, the other temporary.

In the temporary Vietnamese communities around the American bases were tens of thousands of refugees who eked out an existence on what the well-supplied Americans threw away. The war in the field was destructive of the rural economy, and as a result millions of peasants fled burning villages and streamed into the cities for whatever measure of security could be found. Urban populations doubled and tripled in many areas. In the cities the refugees no longer had to worry about being made the target of gunfire by either or both sides in the war, but they found no jobs, no housing, and rampant inflation. The most telling commentary one can make on the living standard of these underfed, illiterate, barely clothed, hardworking, displaced but determined people from the countryside was that the things we Americans considered useless were at least useful and in some cases luxuries for the refugees. Discarded soft drink and beer cases and pallets were salvaged and reappeared as the walls of shacks giving only the barest protection from weather. Scraps of sheet metal became roofs. Worn tires became playpens. Used aircraft fuel tanks became water tanks. No city in South Vietnam was without its wide outer ring of refugee shantytowns. Because of the dilapidated appearance of these areas, they were called "Dogpatch" by American GIs.

The resourcefulness of the Dogpatch residents, people who had nothing but a proud spirit, never ceased to amaze us Americans, raised as we were to consider television and a full stomach our God-given rights. Not only did they construct passable "homes" from things we threw away, but they managed to find ways to earn some money as well. Refugees who found themselves near a water source went into the laundry and jeep- and truck-washing business for both South Vietnamese and American GIs. Others collected brass shell casings from artillery positions and beat them into beautiful bowls, trays, even statuary. Some pieces were so well made that a customer could not tell what the original use of the metal had been until he turned it over and saw the dented primer. Others chipped blocks off the numerous marble peaks jutting up from the sandy coast and carved desk nameplates. But since most of the refugees hated the Americans, whom they blamed for their having been forced from their villages, Dogpatch was also a breeding ground for Viet Cong. Occasionally a GI who entered the nearest maze of cardboard and sheet metal shacks never came out alive.

As resourceful and hardworking as the refugees were, they were still hungry and, therefore, desperate. They would sell almost anything they could get their hands on to get a few grains of rice. Every Dogpatch was a thriving black market in which one could buy just about anything but a tank. One of the easiest things to buy was marijuana or drugs, and so Dogpatch was a popular place with young GIs who needed an occasional escape from the war and wanted to keep in step with the stateside drug scene. There was still another manifestation of desperation in Dogpatch. The refugees had daughters, and never very far away were lonely young men with more money than they needed in a combat zone. Those factors have always added up to only one thing—prostitution.

The focus of the ring of American service and support facilities was an airstrip. Along the sides of the airstrip were the repair shops, hangars, and ammunition bunkers, the whole length compartmentalized by jet-exhaust baffles and steel bomb-shields. At the corners were observation towers manned by troops with searchlights and machine guns. At the end of the strip was the most vulnerable part of the entire complex, the "fuel farm," a broad expanse divided into tennis-court-size rectangles by sandbag berms. In each rectangle lay the big black rubber bladders full of diesel, gasoline, and jet fuel. The fuel farm was a terrorist's dream and a security force's nightmare—it was impossible to camouflage, difficult to guard, and easy to hit with almost any kind of weapon. Protecting a fuel farm was a never-ending job requiring constant patrolling within a radius of several miles by at least a battalion—1,500 men. But a battalion could not always be spared for the duty, and fuel farms were occasionally hit by enemy rockets. The resulting fires and secondary explosions would last for days, and the smoke would make it difficult for the all-weather fighter-bombers to take off and support combat operations in the field.

In addition to all the sprawling facilities built and manned in realization of the mission of the rear-echelon bases—combat support—there also was established a range of facilities to support the combat support units. Vietnam was a nine-to-five war, and from five in the afternoon until curfew tens of thousands of Americans in Vietnam were looking for something to do. Thus, recreation became an official concern of MACV, and hundreds of facilities were built to answer the social needs of Americans. The main social centers in every base compound were the clubs, at least two for every sizable unit: the Enlisted Men's Club for lower-ranking men and the Staff Non-Commissioned Officers' and Officers' Club for the high-rankers, the "heavies," as they were called by the troops. In the clubs the troops in the rear could find all the diversions and atmosphere-conversion devices necessary to take their minds off the war, the boredom, the heat, or almost anything else that was bothering them. The first thing one noticed on entering a club was the air conditioning. After a day of sweating under the fierce Vietnam sun and breathing the hot, dust-laden air, there was no greater pleasure than gulping in the cool air of the club and feeling the pores of one's skin slam shut. With the cool air accepted as reality, not a dream or some new trickery, one could step up to the bar and order beer, a mixed drink, or something soft—all teeth-stinging cold. For those who wanted to do more than sit and soak up the cool drinks and air, there was a modest variety of activites and diversions to choose from. Almost every club had a jukebox, a pool table, a set of dice, and a couple of pinball machines. Larger clubs had slot machines and a dining room where one could order hamburgers and French fries, fried chicken, or a steak. Some even stocked wine.

Other forms of entertainment offered included movies two or three times a week and strip shows once a month, usually featuring a tall blond Australian. If the strippers were booked elsewhere, a Filipino band could usually be found to bang and moan its way through copies of stateside songs, and send everyone to his hooch with an emotional rendition of "God Bless America" or something similar. For the more active, the clubs organized several kinds of teams—volleyball, boxing, touch football. Those who liked to build things could go to their unit hobby shop and put together model airplanes or build furniture.

The largest noncombat facility in the rear was the PX, the GI's link with his prewar normal life in what he longingly referred to as "the World"—the U.S.A. In the local PX the GI could find all the baubles and goodies to help take his mind off Vietnam and its war, the unreal environment he wanted so badly to leave that he knew exactly how many more days and hours he had to endure before his "Freedom Bird" would swoop down and take him away from it all. The larger PXs were almost as complete as stateside department and grocery stores. In Uncle Sam's overseas treasure troves there was food and drink, clothing, and entertainment goods—just about everything except toys and furniture. In deference to the hot, wet climate of Vietnam and the scarcity of refrigerators, most of the food could be consumed quickly—candy, cookies, potato chips, peanut butter and jelly, cheese dips. Soft drinks were sold by the case to anyone, beer and liquor were rationed. The PXs stocked a surprising array of luxuries, considering that they were located in a combat zone—pearl necklaces, opal pendants, ruby earrings, even diamond rings. And I don't know who needed perfume or after-shave lotion in a war, but it was there. Except for the Vietnamese clerks behind the counters it all might have been back in the World.

Cameras were one of the best-selling items in any PX, and GIs could spend from fifteen dollars to more than three hundred. With the development of sizes small enough to fit in a pocket, a camera came to be considered almost essential equipment by Americans, even in the field, and no PX was without its photographic developing service. There was also a stereo corner where GIs could choose from all the newest Japanese and American audio equipment. In the record and cassette files were all the latest tunes on the stateside charts—pop, soul, country and western, blues, jazz, golden oldies. On the magazine rack was everything from *Time* to *Car and Driver* and *Playboy.* A prominent part of every big PX was a car dealership, complete with a smooth-talking salesman ("Defense Department Approved") who sat on a folding chair under huge glossy color posters of new cars racing through the countryside or parked in front of mansions, and always with a blond in a low-cut evening dress seated on the passenger side. The man smiled a lot, called everyone "sir" and promised that anyone making a down payment today would see the car of his choice parked in the driveway the day he got home. "Yessir, I'll take care of everything but the girl!"

Next to the PX there was often a drive-in, just like a Dairy Queen or an A & W stand back in everybody's Hometown, USA. But in "the Nam" no one pulled his modified Chevy or Corvette up to the curb. Instead, the vehicles were jeeps, trucks, even forty-ton tank retrievers. But the orders were just like back home. "Two hot dogs and Cokes, to go." All of these comforts and services made the world of the rear a warm, insulated, womb-capsule into which the sweaty, grimy, screaming, bleeding, writhing-in-the-hot-dust thing that was the war rarely intruded.

2 Third MPs

I

Unlike ninety-five percent of all new infantry officers during the Vietnam War, I spent the first half of my thirteen-month tour in the world of the rear. Standard practice was to send personnel trained in the "grunts," the infantry, to the combat units in the field, the "bush," as soon as they arrived in the country. I guess the government's intention was to get a quick return on the investment in training before anyone lost any of the "Gung-ho, kill VC!" motivation they were so recently encouraged to develop. Then, after six or seven months in hell, grunt officers were supposed to be reassigned to a rear-echelon unit for the remainder of their tours, as a kind of reward I guess, or maybe to make room for the next planeload of "Gung-ho, kill VC!" grunts. For some reason known only to the Marine Corps personnel bureaucracy the standard policy was reversed in my case: I got the reward before I served my time in hell.

As a result, I had some difficulty appreciating life in the rear. I kept thinking of my friends from stateside training enduring life in the bush against the fanatical Viet Cong and North Vietnamese, as well as a myriad of lesser adversities. I should be out there with them, sharing it all with them, I told myself. My reaction to my rear-echelon assignment, in short, was one of much disappointment and some guilt, and it interfered with my enjoyment of the fat "bennies," the benefits, available in the rear. But, I consoled myself, I was not the first who lost a round against the military bureaucracy. There were many others who had fared worse. I acquiesced.

The Third Military Police Battalion compound was located five miles southwest of Da Nang, the second largest city in South Vietnam. Third MPs was one of two MP battalions in Force Logistic Command, the service and support unit for the III Marine Amphibious Force, the parent command of all marine units in General Westmoreland's Military Assistance Command, Vietnam. The other MP battalion, 1st MPs, was based in the center of Da Nang, in an old European-style building left over from the French colonial period. Da Nang and 3d MPs were located in what came to be called "Eye" Corps. MACV Headquarters in Saigon had divided South Vietnam into four corps areas, the numbers for which were printed on the maps in Roman numerals. At some unknown time in the recent past, someone had read Roman numeral one as the English capital letter *I* it looked like, and the mistake had stuck.

The 3d MPs was what is known as a "bastard battalion"—a unit of uncertain parentage and purpose. Only two of its four companies were true military police companies. One of them, C Company, was permanently attached to the 1st MPs downtown. The other, A Company, staffed the only marine brig in Vietnam. The other two companies in the compound, B and D, were engaged in completely unrelated duties. Bravo Company operated a small prison for some North Vietnamese the U.S. Navy had captured about a year before I arrived. Delta Company a staffed scout and sentry-dog compound. Most of its members had been trained in the States with German shepherds and were attached to infantry companies in the 1st and 3d Marine Divisions for one- or two-month periods to discover and check out enemy trails, caches, and caves. No more than half of Delta Company was in the battalion compound at any one time. Thus, within the 3d MPs concertina wire and trench-lines were a headquarters staff and two and a half companies, which together numbered about three hundred men. The brig and prison populations brought the total compound population to about five hundred.

The first person I talked to who outranked me was the battalion executive officer, or second-in-command. The major filled neither his swivel chair nor his uniform. He stood about five-foot seven and displaced about one hundred eighty-five pounds. From under a brush crew cut, the major presented me and the rest of the world a rodent-like face. His expression suggested he ate nails for breakfast, and that is where he got his nickname: Major Nails. His sweat-stained uniform sagged and drooped on his frame, as if in despair that it would ever be worn by the six-foot three, two-hundred-twenty-five pounder it was made for. And when Major Nails sat down behind his executive-size desk he looked even smaller. The major was not exactly recruiting-poster material. But he was sitting there behind that big desk and under those gold oak-leaf clusters on his collar tabs, and so I listened.

What the XO lacked in size he more than made up for in voice. He was talking to me, but I'm sure several dozen other people also heard. "Welcome aboard, Lieutenant!" Marine commanders always say that, as if you've just climbed the gangway of some great gray warship, even though you're standing on dusty dirt or scuffed linoleum: an old and hallowed custom from the days when most marines really were on warships.

The XO proceeded to tell me what company I was being assigned to, who the company commander was, where I could find the mess hall and supply shed, and generally what life in the rear was like. "Sometimes it's pretty quiet around here, but don't get the idea it's always like that. Something could happen at any time, and it usually does, it usually does." The major concluded with an exhortation I would soon learn was a standard part of his introductory briefing to new arrivals. "And don't get the idea you're not doing nothing important around here—you and every other man in this battalion is doing a useful and productive service for all concerned!"

In the next few weeks a more complete picture of Major Nails emerged. The XO filled his number two role in the battalion quite well. He was the assistant, the accessory, the appendage, the underliner of whatever the colonel posed or proposed. There was nothing very striking about him, nothing that hinted of any stirring leadership potential lying just below the surface, waiting for a challenging event to allow it expression. In the picture of the 3d MPs in Vietnam, he was off to the side; he could not be ignored but one's eyes saw other things before moving to him. There was no chance he would ever upstage the colonel in anything. He probably received an excellent-to-outstanding fitness report.

Major Nails was memorable for only one characteristic—his habit of repeating with maddening frequency the most banal instructions in typically ungrammatical Pentagonese. His favorite for all of us below his rank was "I expect all you gents to take a careful inspection of your outfits and eliminate all the superfluous bullshit." His favorite for the only member of the battalion above his rank, the colonel, was the assurance that the latter's every wish was being implemented even before immediately: "I took care of that last week." That statement was true not less than fifty percent of the time. And in between those pronouncements, Major Nails could be heard reminding young lieutenants and NCOs that in 3d MPs they were performing "a useful and productive service" for Vietnam, the Commandant, and the president.

The commanding officer of 3d MPs had an Italian name which I don't remember but which rhymed with "Palooka," so that is how we younger members of the battalion referred to him—out of his presence, that is. The CO granted me an audience lasting about one and a half minutes. It happened the day after I met Major Nails and was of the same introductory character as that earlier meeting. After that I only saw him in the mess hall or the club. The colonel didn't come on as hard as the major. No scowl, no booming voice, no machine-gun issue of directions. He just looked around me, through me, and said nothing I remember.

Lieutenant Colonel Palooka was at least a decade older, four inches taller, and about fifty pounds heavier than his XO. He smoked more cigars and appeared in the club less frequently than any other member of the battalion. the colonel took his drink in quarters.

The colonel still had his crusty military exterior, but it wasn't as thick as Major Nails'. Every night, six days a week, that exterior was dissolved in whiskey by eight o'clock. On Sundays, I was told, the exterior was dissolved in whiskey by mid-afternoon. In another decade the exterior would be dissolved by the natural aging process and the colonel would emerge as another example of the grandfather stereotype—graying, round, almost jolly on occasion.

Neither the colonel nor the major had a shining intellect or any other particularly outstanding talent. Both knew they would never wear the stars of a general, and assignment to a rifle battalion in the field or to Marine Corps Headquarters or the Pentagon would probably have exceeded their abilities. They had the usual abilities of those in the vast middle ranges of the world's many hierarchies—they could look very busy and deeply concerned when they were perfectly idle and thoroughly apathetic. They could generate enthusiasm about anything that originated from a higher headquarters, and they could see proof of success in evidence which suggested otherwise. Under an officious military exterior they were both rather plain, likable people. Had they never had dreams of battlefield glory (or, perhaps, domineering fathers), they would have been insurance salesmen or high school football coaches or small-business managers.

No one in 3d MPs took the colonel or the major as living proof of any structural defect in the American military establishment. They were just taken as confirmation of the human frailty one finds in any field—business, government, academia, and whatever counter-communities a society provokes. They were much less mean and petty than any other commanders I would know later. They didn't go out of their way to bother anyone, as long as he did his job. If anyone wanted to leave 3d MPs, they understood. If anyone wanted to join 3d MPs, they tried to make room.

The CO and his XO came close to being dangerous in only one respect—both carried in their ordinary brains a not-very-dormant racism. I first saw that racism expressed during my second week in the battalion. At one of the weekly staff meetings someone suggested there might be a more efficient way to utilize an old Vietnamese allowed to work inside the compound than having him walk around picking up gum wrappers and cigarette butts all day. Major Nails killed the suggestion with "Naw, I don't think so. I like the old gook—he sort of adds some class to the compound." The colonel grunted his assent from around his cigar and the Vietnamese was kept in his place.

Colonel Palooka and Major Nails did not seriously detract from the official reputation of men in their positions—"an officer and a gentleman"—but neither did they add to it. They did their jobs in a generally acceptable manner. Both would complete twenty- or twenty-five-year careers with no letters of reprimand or any other blemishes in their record books, both would be retired honorably, and both would be quickly forgotten.

Like all other ordinary persons in positions of responsibility, the colonel and the major depended rather heavily on talented subordinates. The most talented of their many subordinates was the adjutant and administrative officer, 1st Lt. Ralph J. McLucas. The adjutant's title, rank, and name were shortened to "Luke"—out of his presence.

Luke owed his rank and title to the rapid personnel buildup necessitated by the American involvement in Vietnam: more officers were needed to lead and manage more troops. Officer Candidate School didn't produce officers fast enough. To fill the need, experienced sergeants who could pass an intelligence test and an interview were given commissions. Luke had been a staff sergeant with twelve years in the Corps before he was offered a commission.

As with any policy applied to large numbers of people, results do not always reflect intent. Many former enlisted officers, about half, if my experience was representative, used their rapid promotion to display their inflated egos to more people. In too many cases the "administrative action" commission did little more than facilitate the magnification of personality and leadership defects. Small abuses of authority sometimes became quite large.

But Luke lived up to the best intentions of the "instant officer" program, especially in the area of personnel administration. He had a fantastic memory for numbers, names, and policy directives, and for which cards had already been played in the lunch-hour and late-night poker games he hosted in his hooch. I once heard him give a personnel briefing about 3d MPs to the commanding general of our parent unit, Force Logistic Command.

Out from under his well-trimmed mustache came sentences like "We are currently six percent understrength in Category III occupational specialties and eleven percent overstrength in Category II." He had memorized entire chapters of the *Marine Corps Personnel Manual* and the Uniform Code of Military Justice and could recite passages correct to the letter when the need arose.

Luke wielded much more authority than his rank would suggest. He decided which company new arrivals would join, and by doing that, he decided much about the character of each man's year in the Nam. He decided when each man could take a vacation from the war—the five-day Rest and Recreation leave all were entitled to. Luke also was in charge of each man's most important number—his "twelve and twenty," the twelve months and twenty days each man had to serve before becoming eligible for a seat on a "Freedom Bird," a jet airliner going back to the World. Luke decided when each man's twelve and twenty began, he counted the days, and he decided when to submit each man's name for a Freedom Bird seat.

Luke also decided whose names would appear on the numerous extra-duty rosters he had to compile to get various tasks done the colonel considered necessary. And when anyone bitched about his name being included or excluded on some roster, or about his R & R being earlier or later than he wanted, it was Luke's job to explain things to the complainant. On such occasions Luke's memory for detail was turned lose—the man would be subjected to verbatim recitations of current directives authored by everyone from the colonel on up to the Commandant. Luke was not particularly liked for his ability with this technique but his competence was highly respected. Few tried to have the last word in a conversation with him and only one man, the colonel, ever succeeded.

Lieutenant McLucas assigned me to Alpha Company, the brig company. My title was Company Executive Officer, which gives a good indication of the imbalance of rank in 3d MPs. No second lieutenant fresh out of stateside training is qualified to be a company executive officer. Nor is any second looey only one month out of stateside training qualified to be a company commander, though mine was. But those conditions were the rule in 3d MPs, as in most rear-echelon units. Among the officers there were too many on the bottom of the rank list and too few in the middle. Among the enlisted men the situation was the reverse: too many sergeants and not enough PFCs.

On my second day in Vietnam and 3d MPs, a young sergeant escorted me into the brig to meet the Alpha Company CO. I was saluted, searched, and offered coffee, then shown to a small office. The room was paneled in what I would soon be told was GI pine: plywood whose grain lines had been brought to a dark prominence by a blowtorch.

I was about to meet my first combat zone commanding officer, the experienced, hardened individual whose every directive my training instructors had told me I must carry out without hesitation, the being who would, with the full approval of Congress, exercise such complete authority over the next year of my life. Questions and hopes raced through my mind—is my tie on straight? No, stupid, you're not wearing a tie—you're dressed for *war,* remember? Is my pistol on "safe"? No, stupid, the sergeant checked your pistol at the door. . . . Please don't ask me about company tactics, oh great commander—that was my lowest test score in training.

The awesome personage squinted up at me from an altitude eight inches below mine. "Mornin'—welcome aboard! My name's Mullens, as you can see right there on the door—just call me 'Moon'—everybody else does!"

How could things possibly work out so that my first leader in a life-and-death experience—a real war—would call himself after, and even look like, a comic strip character I had read about so many times while delivering papers in my safe, quiet, hometown neighborhood years ago?

Before my coffee was half gone, Moon had me outside his office and was giving me my first inside view of a prison. We walked past small groups of sweaty young men with shaved heads swinging picks and shovels or filling sandbags under the gaze of armed guards in towers at the four corners of the brig compound.

"Most of these prisoners are good men, damn good men. They

just got pissed-off or drunked-up one night and told their CO to get fucked . . . something like that, you know. Our job is to build up their discipline, their pride in being marines, and get them back to their units where they can do some good. But a few of these turds are bad, real bad—I got twelve in solitary right now —on drugs, most of them, before we got them, and we even got one who killed his squad leader with an ax. I'd like to shoot his ass instead of feeding him every day but the chaplain says we can save him . . . but I fucking doubt it . . . I fucking doubt it."

About halfway through our walking tour, Lieutenant Mullens noticed I was less than ecstatic at my first unit assignment and changed the subject to the benefits of life in 3d MPs. "This place might not look like much, but we got it pretty good here, pretty damn good. Just relax and enjoy it."

In the next few days I saw much more of the prisoners than of Moon. My primary job was to maintain records and investigate any offenses committed while prisoners were serving their sentences. Most of the offenses I investigated involved fighting or smoking the marijuana smuggled into the brig by prisoners returning from outside work assignments. My secondary job was to conduct an educational program after working hours so prisoners could earn the high school diploma they had missed or rejected back in the States. The educational program wasn't much of a success, however. In six months only one man received his high school equivalency certificate, and most enrollees quit the program. The main problem was that after eight or nine hours of swinging a pick or shovel under the Vietnam sun, few prisoners were in any condition or frame of mind to enter a high school classroom.

II

Within the 3d MP barbed wire and trench line boundaries was a collection of people so varied in background and motivation that no reasonable person who saw those five or six hundred could continue to believe the robots-in-green stereotype of military men held by most civilians. Beneath differences of rank, the most prominent cleavages in the microsociety of 3d MPs were those caused by different orientations toward the military as a career and toward the 3d MPs as a combat zone assignment, and those stemming from race, nationality, and relative ability to adjust to the privation inherent in war.

The most influential, though not the most numerous, of the identifiable groups within the battalion compound was that comprised of those who were staying in the Corps for a career—twenty years or more. Included in their number were all enlisted men of the rank staff sergeant and above, and almost all officers above the rank of lieutenant. For their career orientation they were called "lifers" by those outside their group—out of their presence, that is.

Their complete lack of reluctance to hide any of their views made the lifers the easiest group to identify. In blustery voices they made known their version of truth on any and all subjects, whether one wanted to listen or not: "America is the greatest country in the history of the world; the duty of every American citizen is to do all in his or her power to keep America the greatest; the best way to help keep America the greatest and to show one's love of country is to serve in the military; the line between dissent and treason is so vague that it can safely be ignored; communists and hippies are the most despicable forms of life on earth and should be locked up forever if they can't be killed on sight; and, this Vietnam War is a great patriotic crusade that got off to a good start but recently turned into a chickenshit no-win thing because the pinko socialistic professors and politicians back in Washington won't get their hands off it and let us invade North Vietnam and atom-bomb Hanoi, Peking, and Moscow so we could end the war right and straighten out the world."

The lifers were at once admirable and pathetic. They were admirable, almost lovable, for the clear and pure, even humane, virtues they could display so easily—the unqualified loyalty to the ideal of America, combining political, economic, military, and moral leadership; the quick offer of counsel to anyone in need; the strength of leadership under any adversity. They were pathetic for the way they misled themselves by oversimplifying every issue they considered, for their either-or, good-bad categorization of everything, and for the speed with which they labeled things different as "bad."

At the opposite end of the attitudinal spectrum were those who were not going to "re-up"—sign up for a second term of enlistment. They were the largest group in terms of numbers but the smallest in terms of influence—they were on the bottom of the rank scale and they were the quietest. Included in their number were almost all enlisted men below staff sergeant and almost all lieutenants. The lifers referred to them, either in or out of their presence, as "kids." With time-in-grade and time-in-service such firmly established tenets of military life, the difference in rank meant at the same time a difference in age; between kids and lifers in Vietnam there was reflected the generation gap then opening in society back in the States.

Beyond their differing opinions on a military career, the most striking differences between the lifers and the kids were to be found in their views of war (lifers: "It's manly and shows a nation's strength"; kids: "It's the easy way out and indicates weakness") and the Vietnamese (lifers: "worthless, hopelessly fucked-up"; kids: "real fine, decent, tough people . . . amazing how they have survived over twenty years of continuous war"). However, not all of the views of the kids were direct opposites of those of the lifers. More often the differences were of intensity. Like the lifers, the kids hated communism, but unlike the lifers, the kids were willing to accede that communists and persons following other ideologies could live together on the same planet. Nor were the kids so quick to find communist infiltration behind every dissenting voice. There was also much more variety in the views of the kids. There were some who hated the war but liked the military, and some who hated the military but liked the war.

On their lunch hours and at night, while the lifers were playing poker, listening to country and western music, drinking whiskey, or sleeping, the kids would collect in little groups in their hooches or outside around a bunker. There, with a transistor radio playing the latest acid rock, the kids would discuss the things younger men in a war far from home have always discussed—what the girls back home are doing, why wars happen, why some wars are short and others are long, why the Vietnamese are so small, what kind of car they will buy when they get back to the World, why the Vietnamese can work in the sun longer on less water than Americans, the current price of cigarettes on the black market, and what could possibly make any guy in his right mind want to become a lifer. Fortunately for the entire battalion, there was considerable toleration by the kids for the lifers, probably because most of whatever humor was produced in 3d MPs came from the lifers.

The third and fourth identifiable groups counted both lifers and kids in their memberships. Most of those who wanted to be in 3d MPs were making a career of the military. Most had served a previous tour in Vietnam in a field unit—infantry, armor, or artillery. A few had served two previous tours. They had walked through rice paddies and over hills under the ferocious Vietnam sun, drunk filthy water, eaten insufficient amounts of tasteless food, and seen friends maimed and killed. Most had collected a few injuries themselves. They had returned to the World determined to collect the benefits they felt they deserved for serving their year in hell—a slack stateside duty assignment, cold American beer, warm American steak, and hot American women. But things didn't quite work out that way. They found the cold beer and the warm steak but not the more important things. Instead of a slack duty assignment, they ran into volumes and volumes of regulations, which after a life-or-death experience seemed like nothing more than pure petty bullshit—get a haircut, get it cut again, that's not short enough; no mustaches on this base; buy new uniforms; stand in line at the PX; shine your shoes; stand in line at the laundry; shine your brass; stand in line at the commissary; pick up cigarette butts; stand in line at the mess hall; look straight ahead; stand in line at the movie; clean your rifle; stand in line at the disbursing counter. And as for the women, well, they were there but most of the ones who were available were the usual half-whores hanging around the bases. The nice ones weren't too anxious to go out with guys they thought were injuring babies and napalming villages on the six o'clock news.

So, after six months or a year they began firing request-for-transfer forms at Headquarters in Washington. Everyone knew, of course, that Vietnam was definitely dangerous to a guy's health, and everyone had sworn there was nothing that could ever make him go back, but that was before the petty bullshit began to eat away at his toleration, at his sanity. The only thing a guy had to worry about was being sent back out to the bush with the tank jockeys or the cannon-cockers or the anything-but-that infantry. But that could be taken care of with a few well-placed bottles of whiskey or other favors as soon as one arrived in Vietnam . . . that could all be taken care of. So, back to Vietnam they had come, carrying the same determination to find some kind of reward for surviving their earlier tour in the war. And that is how 3d MPs had come to have too many sergeants.

The fourth identifiable group was the smallest. Those who did not want to be in 3d MPs included all but two lieutenants and about a fourth of the younger enlisted men. If there had been no war going on at the time, the number of those dissatisfied with assignment to 3d MPs would have been much smaller. It was the war—not the military itself—that was the source of their personal motivation to join the Marine Corps: to test oneself, to fight for one's country, to answer the challenge of a war-veteran relative or friend. Throughout their training they had expected, they had looked forward to, a combat assignment in Vietnam, while they were marching across sun-baked parking lots and running through freezing streams yelling "Kill! Kill!" Filling a soft and safe stateside-style place in the rear held no attraction for them; the soft and safe stuff was for the postwar years. To them, 3d MPs was a luxurious disgrace to both the Marine Corps and the American effort in Vietnam.

To be one of the dissatisfied was to go through every day with a measure of guilt. While others who had gone through the same combat training were in Vietnam dealing with extremes of thirst, hunger, exhaustion, and danger, those who had been sidetracked into 3d MPs were dealing with a completely different category of "problem"—should I have two steaks tonight at chow, or three? Should I go back for another helping of ice cream? Should I bet five dollars or ten on this next pool shot? Should I drink two beers tonight in the Staff Club, or ten? The feeling of guilt was brought to a peak of embarrassment when one happened to meet a friend from stateside training in one of the large joint-service PXs around Da Nang, a friend in from the field for a couple of days. The contrast in appearance was too obvious for either to miss. Mr. 3d MPs stood there like a recruiting poster—short hair, no stubble-beard, pressed uniform, shiny brass, and polished boots. Mr. Field Marine stood there displaying the exact opposites of all those details. Explanations were futile.

Since I was one of the dissatisfied, I can testify as to how we had come to 3d MPs. None of us in the group had ever heard of 3d MPs until the day we arrived in Vietnam, and after we had been in the battalion a few days we understood why we had never heard of it. The Marine Corps did not have a military police occupational specialty until after the Vietnam War. During that war and before, MPs were selected from those trained for the infantry. Whatever knowledge one gained about how to be an MP came through OJT—on-the-job-training. By waiting until the day we arrived in Vietnam to tell us we could not yet join the infantry, the occupational specialty we wanted and trained for, the Marine Corps saved itself all the time and paper it would have taken to read, endorse, reject, and forward to the next higher headquarters the series of request-for-transfer forms we would have launched had we known about our MP assignment earlier. Now we were caught under an unwritten but absolute rule of Marine Corps personnel administration which the adjutant conveyed to us in a triumphant voice: "No new man transfers out until he's put in at least six months here." So, for the first six months of my tour the Marine Corps got its way. There I was: in the rear with the beer.

Inside the only marine brig in Vietnam were between 150 and 250 prisoners. After I had worked at my job of keeping the record books of our inmates up to date, I gained a fairly complete picture of the 3d MP brig prisoner. The average educational level was 9½ years. About thirty percent were functionally illiterate. They came from almost every American ethnic group, although groups more recently arrived in the U.S., or more sharply discriminated against, were overrepresented—blacks, Mexican-Americans, and Puerto Ricans. There was one experience they all had in common: some kind of failure. About half had served short terms in civilian jails before joining the marines. The prisoners' most recent failures involved breaking some article of the Uniform Code of Military Justice, in most cases during the first six months of their tours in Vietnam. The most common offenses were smoking marijuana, refusing to get a haircut, or refusing to go out on a second combat operation after surviving the hell of their first.

In the 3d MP brig the Marine Corps was trying to restore what was diagnosed as a breakdown of discipline. They were trying to restore discipline by recreating the environment of marine boot camp, which means the prisoners were treated as subhumans. All prisoners shared the same sentence: hard labor. Only the length of the sentence varied: from six months to a year in most cases. From seven in the morning to five in the afternoon, six days a week, the prisoners filled sandbags for defensive positions, dug garbage pits, built bunkers, and erected lookout towers. Every day between ten and twenty percent of the brig population was taken outside the compound for work assignments at other units in the Da Nang area.

The prisoners illustrated very well what happens to the character of personnel recruited either when a nation pursues an unpopular war, or a war continues longer than the policy planners expect. As opposition to the war increased, the number of highly motivated volunteers decreased. Recruitment standards were lowered and recruiters began signing up men they would never have considered accepting in peacetime or in the first two years of the war.

In addition, the American judicial system at the local level helped alleviate the need for manpower. At least a quarter of the brig prisoners had in the past year come before a city or county court judge for the second or third time. Instead of repeating his previous sentence, the judge had suggested that the man consider joining the marines. The defendant had been more than happy to get out of a jail term and onto the government payroll, and the local recruiter had been only too glad to receive another warm body to help fill his monthly quota.

Two years before I arrived, there was no need for a prison for Americans. But in the fourth year of the war there were two—

our 3d MP brig and the Army Stockade at Long Binh—and the population of each was steadily increasing.

In most prisoners the Corps failed to restore any discipline. The boot camp regimen only increased the already considerable resentment the prisoners felt toward a hard and distant bureaucracy. Most prisoners went through the hours and days of their sentences playing the ancient game of prisoners and disparaged minorities—how to appear to be conforming to the dictates of one's captors while at the same time disrupting as much as possible the captors' system. Since guards and counselors assigned to the brig staff were motivated more by commands than by qualifications in psychology or interest in criminology, our brig prisoners were considerably more successful in that effort than were civilian prisoners back in the States.

The most notorious of our brig prisoners was a group of eight marines who had once comprised a squad in an infantry company. About five months before I met them they had been out in the field on a routine night patrol. Before dusk became darkness they spotted a hamlet that was not on their map. The cluster of grass and bamboo structures looked more interesting than their list of patrol checkpoints, so no objection was raised when one of the eight suggested they check it out. The first person in the hamlet who saw the intruding Americans was a seventeen-year-old girl who was walking between her father's and her uncle's homes. At the sight of the big armed foreigners, she began running, and it was the sight of the young girl running that made the Americans forget why they were away from the rest of their company. The lonely young men were immediately reminded of what it was they missed most in Vietnam, and the minds of a few recognized the ease with which they could make up for that lack in the isolated and unprotected hamlet. Four marines half-walked, half-ran to the home the girl had run into. The first man to reach her grabbed her by the arm and pushed her protesting mother against the wall.

As he pulled the terrified girl out of her home, the leader of the unofficial raid, who according to the rank distribution of the group was second, not first, in command of the squad, formulated a plan that would allow everyone in the group to satisfy his desire and still complete the patrol with a minimum loss of time. With two marines preventing any opposition from the girl's parents or neighbors, all but two of the squad members took turns going behind the girl's home and raping her. The two who refused to participate in the atrocity were told that they could either keep their mouths shut about the evening's activities back in the patrol base or face retaliation in the form of death.

After finishing with the girl's body, the squad faced the problem of what to do with her. No one had considered the question before she had been used. But now, with passion no longer blocking reason, the question demanded consideration. Only an hour before, the girl was seen as an object of pleasure, but now she was viewed as a threat. Anything the other Vietnamese from the hamlet might report could easily be denied, but if the girl talked that was another matter entirely. After a frantic discussion dominated by a mix of guilt and fear, the unofficial squad leader decided the girl would have to be killed. A quick poll of the squad made it clear that he would have to be the one to do the job. With the leader of the evening dragging the dazed girl away and the others holding off protesting parents, the squad quickly departed the hamlet. About fifty meters down the trail, the self-appointed leader pulled the girl into a stand of bushes and trees and strangled her. He and three others then scraped a shallow grave in the dirt, placed the girl's body in it, and covered the corpse with a few inches of dirt, grass, and leaves. Then they walked around the bottom of the hill on which their patrol base was located to the point at which they were supposed to reenter, and sat down in the grass. At twenty-minute intervals they reported to their company commander on the hill above that they had reached their second, third, and fourth checkpoints without seeing any Vietnamese, hostile or friendly. An hour and fifteen minutes after they had committed, assisted, or witnessed rape and murder, the eight young men walked back inside their company perimeter, confident, or at least hopeful, that their failure to carry out an assigned combat mission would never be detected.

But the people from the hamlet talked. One week after the rape/murder a legal officer took a helicopter to the patrol base and began asking the eight squad members about the patrol they had run a few nights before. The legal officer skillfully exploited the glaring inconsistencies in the marines' accounts of their recent patrol until one of the two who had not raped the girl agreed to tell the real story. That same day the eight squad members were arrested and confined to quarters.

In the next few days a team of investigators was assigned to the case. Every step of the squad on the night of the murder was retraced. The hamlet residents were interviewed, and the murder site, corpse, and grave were photographed. The eight were, of course, allowed to prepare their defense and had written their parents about their arrest. By the time the trial began, the court had received dozens of letters from former teachers, employers, and clergymen recounting incidents from the defendants' early years to illustrate their upstanding character. The court, however, had overwhelming evidence of a different kind of character and sentenced the eight to prison terms ranging from three to twenty years. In the 3d MP brig the eight were awaiting an armed escort back to a military prison in the States.

If you applied the criteria of political ideology to the more than five hundred people who spent their days inside the 3d MP boundaries, twelve men stood out from the rest of the compound population. Those twelve comprised the crew of a North Vietnamese coastal patrol boat that had been captured by the U.S. Navy about a year before I joined the battalion. That made those twelve, of course, communists. But they were best known for characteristics other than their ideological leanings. They displayed the strictest sense of discipline, the most unwavering loyalty, of anyone in the battalion compound except the most recently arrived PFCs fresh from stateside training. So impressive were their discipline and loyalty that they were occasionally referred to by some of our sergeants and officers trying to restore those qualities in American troops who had grown slack in the security of the rear: "If you screw up anymore, Smith, I'm gonna turn you over to them North Vietnamese and they'll square you away, but fast!"

Inside the prisoners' compound were twelve tiny hooches, each no larger than what would pass for a weekend gardener's toolshed in the States. In each hooch was one bed, one footlocker which doubled as a desk, one washbasin, one mirror, and one light bulb overhead. Every day the twelve North Vietnamese followed a schedule which Westerners would consider mind-numbing in its precision and repetition. At exactly 6:00 A.M. they arose, came out of their hooches dressed only in loincloths, and stood at attention awaiting the next command from their captain. Then for thirty minutes they went through a set routine of exercises, calling out the numbers in unison for each movement.

Calisthenics finished, they returned to their hooches and for another thirty minutes swept out the tiny plywood boxes in which they slept and carefully made their beds. At exactly 7:00 A.M. they formed two columns and marched to the battalion mess hall escorted by two armed marine guards. They returned with two large insulated canisters full of breakfast. At noon and at 5:00 P.M. they again marched to and from the mess hall. In between meals they washed their clothes, wrote letters, played volleyball, and held classes on whatever our censors would approve: written Chinese, the Geneva Convention Regarding Prisoners of War, and so on. At exactly 10:00 P.M. they went to bed.

During most of the activities of their daily schedule, the North Vietnamese wore the same clothes and expressions. Their uniforms were the khaki shirts and trousers in which they had been captured. Only when they played volleyball did their clothing vary—they stripped down to loincloths. But no activity in which they engaged caused a change in their common expression. In their eyes was a look of certainty, and in their bearing an air of confidence, which we Americans found unnerving. Most of us who observed the enemy prisoners for any length of time walked away from their compound asking ourselves the same question: "What the hell do they know that we don't?"

3 Time to Kill . . .

I

In my first month in 3d MPs there were plenty of new people to meet, plenty of new things to learn. Life in 3d MPs was almost interesting during that first month. And I could see that for those in the last two months of their 3d MP tours life was interesting. Those who were approaching their last day in Vietnam, the short-timers, were living on expectations of how great it would be to get back to the peaceful, pleasurable routines of life in the real world. The problem with life in the rear was the ten months between the first month and the last two. The hard fact of life in 3d MPs was that very few people had jobs that kept them busy more than three or four hours a day. Most members of the battalion went through half of each day in torpor.

Some of the most popular boredom-countering activities were those centering on the Staff Non-Commissioned Officers' and Officers' Club, the local bar. There one could drink, listen to stateside music from a stateside jukebox, play cards, gamble over a game of pool, or just sit in the air conditioning and forget for a while the wilting heat of Vietnam. Of those activities, the first was by far the most indulged. The club also provided stateside movies once a week and live shows once every two or three weeks, complete with Filipino bands and, sometimes, Australian girls.

From the club one could also witness something not scheduled by the manager. One could occasionally occupy a front-row seat in the theater of the war, and in so doing sample the incongruity of life in the rear. About once a week someone in the club who was not yet half-paralyzed on a combination of beer or whiskey and thoughts of willing women or home would perceive through loud beery voices and the jukebox the drone overhead of an old converted Air Force DC-3—"Puff the Magic Dragon"—and the muffled staccato of its guns answering the call of a nearby unit in trouble. He would holler out, "Anybody want to watch them get some?" and then lead six or eight others outside. The group would sit on a bunker or climb one of the sentry towers around the brig and watch and listen through eyes and ears fuzzy with beer a battle less than two miles away. With a cold beer in hand they could watch the area framed by red tracer bullets, the area where frantic men, Vietnamese and American, were fighting and trying to survive and dying, while from behind the spectators, from the open door of the club, came the stateside sounds which at the same time were provoking bodies to the boogaloo back in the World. After a guy had been in 3d MPs a few months, that activity came to seem like entertainment.

Other inside-the-compound activities included sports—tag football, volleyball, jogging, and weight lifting—rereading letters or listening again to taped messages, and trying to communicate by a mix of gestures, unintelligible sounds, and pictures with the Vietnamese allowed to work inside the compound during the day.

If one wanted to remind himself that there were other kinds of problems in the world besides war and boredom, he could take a walk over to sick bay, the battalion doctor's office. There a guy could stare as long as he wanted at the Marine Corps' graphic warning about the results of patronizing the local ladies of the evening. Nailed to a supporting post in the middle of the examination room was a series of color photos of swollen, distorted, and seeping genitalia in advanced stages of venereal disease. After they had seen the pictures the first time, most members of the battalion made a point of staying away from sick bay one hour before and after meals.

At least one man found relief in a routine from the stateside military which most of the rest of us hated with a passion—spit-shining boots, polishing brass belt buckles, and starching caps, or "covers" as the marines always called them. If there was a Best-Dressed contest in the marines, Gun. Sgt. Herman Blake would certainly have been in the top ten. The gunny spent more time on keeping his huge image spotless, starched, and shining than anyone else in the battalion, so he was more often called Gunny Spitshine than Gunny Blake. Once a week, come rain, shine, or the best strip show in Eye Corps, the gunny would shine his boots—all six pairs of them. For three hours or more he would spit and polish in tight circles, muscles bulging, beads of sweat forming on his forehead, until he had brought each pair to an onyx-like finish. And when he finished, he would get down on his knees and stretch a string between two of the legs on his bed. He would then line up each boot on the string line, center all six pairs between the two bed-legs, and carefully remove the string so as not to scratch in the least any of the brilliant black toes.

Once we decided to play a trick on the gunny, to give both him and ourselves another break from the routine of life in the rear. We put an extra pair of boots under his bed next to his own. Gunny Spitshine didn't hesitate one second. He shined them as if they were his own and then lined up all seven pairs on the string.

To his own mind the gunny was probably bringing order and acceptable appearance to an event, the war, which looked completely disordered, dirty, scuffed, and scratched. To the rest of us he was a welcome diversion from the 3d MPs routine, and we appreciated greatly his remarkable attention to detail.

There were also things to be done outside the battalion compound. A guy could get a jeep and driver and go around the other side of Hill 327 to the Freedom Hill PX, and do a little shopping at one of the largest PXs in the Da Nang area. A guy could also do a lot of inspecting of young Vietnamese womanhood, since the Freedom Hill PX had one of the largest staffs in the area.

Going to the PX was a valid reason to get out of the battalion compound but there was a rather severe schedule attached to it—it was good only once every two weeks. An excuse that was valid more frequently was that one had to go to the unit with the titillating name and look for parts for a generator, typewriter, rifle, or whatever. "Force Logistic Support Group Bravo" was a unit composed of more than a thousand mechanics whose job it was to keep every machine and weapon in the marine units in Vietnam operating. The name of the unit was far too long to use anywhere except on the sign at the main gate of the unit compound, and the first letters of those words were too awkward to say with ease. At some unknown time in the recent past a nameless lifer somewhere in Eye Corps had rolled those letters around in his mouth and mind, mixing them up with what he missed most, and come out with "Floozy Bravo." There was also a "Floozy Alpha," but she was up north somewhere servicing 3d Marine Division. Once inside Floozy Bravo, a guy had only to make a show of looking for some parts, make friends with some idle corporal or lieutenant, and before he knew it he was bullshitting the afternoon away over coffee or Coke.

Going to the PX or to Floozy Bravo were usually good enough reasons to get away from 3d MPs for an afternoon, but there was another excuse that was even better. The airtight, guaranteed-to-get-permission excuse was to say you had to go to the MARS station to send a message back to the States. The letters M-A-R-S stood for Military Affiliate Radio System, which was a communications unit that could make a direct connection with any home phone in the U.S.

No commander would dare say no to that reason because to do so might cause the offended man to fire off some privileged correspondence to his congressman which would provoke a request-for-clarification from the congressman's office. Letters of complaint from members of Congress were considered definite threats to one's career, especially to one who had designs on wearing the eagles of a colonel or the stars of a general someday, since such correspondence would have to go through several echelons of command between Washington and 3d MPs, and the whole incident would likely be remembered when those commanders sat down to consider who should be promoted and who should not. The answer was automatic. "Of course you can go to the MARS station tonight, but be careful on the road, the VC might be out."

The nice thing about going to MARS was that a guy had to go at night, due to differences in time between Vietnam and the U.S. Being outside the compound at night was more dangerous than being out during the day, but there was also in the former condition more opportunity to make up excuses for not returning directly to 3d MPs. After making his call, that is, if a guy really did go to the MARS station, he could "hear rifle fire" on the way back and be forced to go to the nearest American unit to find out about the security situation around Da Nang for that night. The best place to get that information, of course, was in that unit's club, so the man and his driver could get in a couple of hours of serious drinking before the roads were declared safe again. For that reason the MARS station excuse was one of the most widely used by anyone stationed around Da Nang and probably by everyone stationed around large rear-echelon bases elsewhere. If everyone who said he had to go to the MARS station really went, MARS would still be operating.

The nights one went to the MARS station were the unusual nights. Most nights, of course, had to be spent inside the compound. If a guy wasn't drinking or playing cards in the club, he was most likely doing something to make his tiny living space more luxurious. All of us in 3d MPs lived in what we called "hooches," one-story wooden frame structures with sheet metal roofs. Each was about fifty feet long and fifteen feet wide. The hooch was placed off the ground on four-by-four piles as a defense against the rainy season. The plywood sides of the building reached only halfway up to the roofline, the top half of the sides being screened, in hopes of relieving some of the heat at night. However, the screening neither let in much of a breeze nor kept out many mosquitoes. By American standards, the hooches were low-quality temporary houses. By Vietnamese standards they were luxurious mansions.

There were several things that could be done with a hooch. For one, a guy could panel his area. In Vietnam, the term "panel" didn't describe the same operation it did in the States. In Vietnam it meant waving the flame of a blowtorch back and forth on the plywood wall until the grain lines turned a dark brown. The result of that operation was to make the walls look like they were covered with the skin of a mutant zebra—the stripes had come out brown instead of black. Back in the States such "paneling" would probably be called trash but in Vietnam it was high class, strictly high class.

Other things one could do to "improve" his living space and kill time included painting in fancy Old English letters beside the front door the names of the inhabitants of the hooch, covering the hooch floor with linoleum stolen from the Air Force, installing a "ceiling" by hanging brightly colored sections of parachute silk from the roof beams, covering a wall with nude centerfold pictures from *Playboy* or any other skin magazine, and partitioning the area around the bed by hanging camouflage-patterned ponch liners. The surrealistic effect one received from sitting or lying in such a space, enclosed by brown zebra stripes, with centerfold nudes and dark green jungle patterns on the sides and bright orange or lavender parachute sections overhead, was wholly in keeping with the whacky atmosphere of life in the rear.

Throughout the continuous process of making one's surroundings more luxurious, none of the men involved seemed at all aware of the great contrast between their actions and their own images of themselves in the military and in their home society. During many evenings and most Sunday afternoons men who considered themselves the finest examples of manhood their country had raised, and the guardians of the American way of life, could be seen doing things that only a few months before they had considered far beneath their dignity. Senior sergeants in the middle or second half of a military career could be seen doing many of the same things their civilian peers back in the States—those undisciplined softies they despised so deeply—were doing: laying linoleum floor tiles and fixing shower plumbing just like any weekend do-it-yourselfer, or drinking too much too early in front of a television set. The story was very similar on the other side of the generation fault. Young officers and sergeants who a bare two or three months before were hiding very little of their determination to kill Viet Cong and win the war, as they ran through war games back on Okinawa or in the States, were reduced to sanding and varnishing tabletops, painting chairs, or building model airplanes.

At an imprecise point in this work, the process of merely making one's surroundings more comfortable became a process of insulation from a war with new rules and from the baffling culture that was its backdrop. In this effort the Post Exchanges around Da Nang and MACV Headquarters in Saigon helped greatly. In the well-stocked PXs the men of 3d MPs and every other rear-echelon base in the war bought an array of gadgets and luxuries never before associated with a military mission—transistor radios, Instamatic cameras, television sets, tape recorders, stereo record players, after-shave lotion, books and skin magazines, jewelry, and nearly every alcoholic beverage and snack food available in the States. And from MACV, American-style radio and television programming reached into every headquarters and nearly every hooch from Cua Viet in the north to Vung Tau in the south.

Variations on the same theme included a hooch known as "the library" whose occupants used the Book-of-the Month Club to further their insulation from the war, another called the "jockhouse" whose members converted their quarters into a weight-lifting gym every night, and several others designated "boozers' heaven."

The men in the rear of the Vietnam War came from a country that defines success in terms materialistic and they searched for meaning in the war in actions materialistic. In pursuing their desire, their need for insulation from Vietnam and the war, most members of 3d MPs unknowingly derived a new definition of victory. After a few months it became nearly impossible for these men to see a direct relation between their safe job and the official reason for going to Vietnam. The president who sent them to Vietnam was far away. Even the Viet Cong and the North Vietnamese were far away. To answer their psychological need for a raison d'être, they made their own definition of victory, a definition far different from that carried by the troops in the field or the policy planners in Washington. Victory to the rear-echelon-unit member was not measured in terms of dead bodies or captured weapons and rice or secure hamlets and villages. Victory was measured in terms of completeness of isolation from the war. To push away as far as possible a frustrating no-progress war and the incomprehensible cultural environment in which it was taking place was to secure the objective, to win back some of the 385-day segment of the war defined by each man's orders.

Complete victory was defined as the perfect reproduction in Vietnam of all conditions and luxuries of life in the States, the real world. No rear-echelon unit achieved complete victory, but many came very close to it, so close that inside the plush premises of some units the only reminder that one was not in an expensive restaurant or attending a general's reception in the States was the green field uniform on everyone present.

The handful of men at the top of the military hierarchy enjoyed access to additional means of pushing the war away. American colonels and generals, when not directly involved in the supervision of combat operations, could take a break from the war and repair to the solitude of a private cabana on the cool Vietnamese coast. Local Vietnamese authorities were usually more than willing to add to the luxury of the unauthorized beach cabanas. As a way of showing their cynical officials' brand of gratitude for the way the Americans were fighting Saigon's war for Saigon, South Vietnamese commanders and province chiefs were quick to offer American generals steak and whiskey (stolen from the American supply system) and, occasionally, Vietnamese women.

Most of the things we did to counter boredom were of our own choosing. Only rarely was the routine broken by things unwanted. The first such occurrence was the rainy season, which for about six weeks forced everyone to spend a couple of hours a day either wiping green mold off everything or stringing communications wire back and forth across the inside of the hooches so everything from paper money to undershirts could be hung up to become a little less wet.

There were also two inspection visits by generals, which forced everyone to paint, polish, or spit-shine everything that was or was not capable of independent movement. We succeeded in satisfying one of the generals.

Then there was the surprise announcement that we were to turn in our special Vietnam-type American greenbacks, called Military Payment Certificates or MPCs, for a new series in order to disrupt the black market. That order forced most members of 3d MPs, and probably every other unit in the rear, to suspend for most of the day whatever contribution they were making to the war effort and stand in lines at the company offices in order to surrender the old MPC and receive, count, and sign for the new.

All of those activities and events might seem like a lot now, in the retelling, but they weren't. All of them, whether done inside or outside the compound, whether of our own choosing or not, were only of temporary value. As each occurred a second, third, or fourth time, its novelty value decreased until what was once a break from the routine became a part of the routine itself. The 3d MPs routine always came back and had to be dealt with. The only thing a guy could do was take the simplest daily tasks and work them up into elaborate rituals. The successful performance of one of those tasks was considered a victory of sorts in two respects: both the planning for the task and its execution killed time.

Even the act of refilling a coffee cup, if properly done, could consume as much as half an hour. First, you had to let out a loud sigh and a sentence indicating some degree of fatigue with Vietnam or the job, something like "Jesus Christ, it's hot today," or "Well, think I'll get me another cup of rotgut." That was a signal to everyone else in the hooch that the ritual was about to begin.

Then you had to stand up, move out from behind the desk, and walk across the room to get a cup. But more was involved here than simply reaching out and picking up your own cup. Not that a man would use anyone else's cup—never. To do that would be to defile a souvenir from another man's career, to break one of those unwritten hallowed traditions of the Marines, like hollering "Welcome aboard" to the newest arrival on the dry, never-rolling, landlocked base. It just wasn't done.

Before picking up your own cup you were expected to turn all the other cups around and read the messages painted on them, to keep up to date on recent creations in military graffiti: "3d MPs—

We Serve To Keep The Peace," "Death Before Dishonor—USMC—Silent Swift Deadly," "When I die bury me face-down, So the whole world can kiss my ass," "Marines never die, they just go to hell and regroup."

With that study completed, you pulled the tap on the big green urn and let about a quarter-inch of hot coffee run into the cup. You then swirled it around to melt off the bottom the dried sugar from the previous cup, walked over to the door to throw the contents outside, and returned to the urn for a full cup. The preferred amounts of sugar and powdered cream were then added, and an excessive amount of attention was put into stirring the mess. On the way back to your own desk, you were expected to stop off at the desks of others and engage them in bullshit conversation for no less than five minutes each. And you quickly learned that you should never offer to fill anyone else's cup—that would deny the other man the chance to kill his own time. After the ritual of filling the coffee cup was over, you were half an hour closer to dinner or the club or whatever it was you were looking forward to.

There came a time every evening, of course, when the company offices closed. One then entered the most difficult period. The block of time from the end of the evening meal until midnight was the longest continuous span of time in the day. It was also the period when one's choice of time-consuming activities was the most limited. As each man walked away from his office with the big green coffee urn, he knew he was not walking away from the problem of what to do with too much time. The problem was just moved to a different place.

For one large group, mostly the career-oriented members of the battalion, the place was the club, with its beer and whiskey, gambling and gossip, and the look-but-don't-touch floor shows. For another large group, mostly those who were not interested in a military career, the place was inside a hooch, where there were letters to be re-read or written, books to be read, or plans and dreams to be traded and revised, plans and dreams prefaced with "After I get out of this marine green machine. . . ." Both of those groups were just trying to kill that big fat evening block of time, and they were for the most part successful. Life in 3d MPs presented them with nothing threatening; they would end their tours substantially the same people they had begun.

But there was another group identifiable during the evening block of time, a group trying to do more. Members of the third group were trying to not only kill time but also prevent or at least soften the effects of developments they were being forced to deal with, developments charged with threat. In the lives of these men unwanted changes were taking place. To one who had never served much time in the rear echelon of a war, saying some men were being changed by that kind of service might not sound like much. Most people justifiably assume that anyone who has been to war in any capacity has seen and done some horrible things and has in the process been changed by it all. But to those who have served in the rear, such an observation is quite surprising, almost shocking. They, or rather we, know how easy it was to serve in the rear and preserve almost perfectly one's prewar self. I estimate that about eighty percent of those who served in the rear returned to the States with no visible or psychological marks from their "war" experiences. But for the remaining twenty percent, service in the rear was a different kind of experience. Within the 3d MP compound there were sixty or seventy men who were not only trying to kill time but who were also wracking their brains to find ways of combating transformations they could feel happening within themselves day by day, undesirable and unwanted transformations fueled by the torpor of the rear, or the incomprehensible ways of the Vietnamese, or any one of a dozen other phenomena. For these sixty or seventy men the evening block of time in 3d MPs was a huge leaky vat of acid drip-dripping through the shiny surface of their prewar selves, their marriages, their health, or whatever resolve they brought to their tours in 3d MPs.

There was a young sergeant who watched helplessly as his new wife's letters became cooler and cooler until finally the one came that said being twenty-one and married and alone made no sense at all and there would have to be a divorce. He knew that a phrase like "rescue of dying marriage" was not good enough to get a few days' leave. I asked the adjutant if there was some way the sergeant could be allowed to go back to the States for a few days to straighten things out. The adjutant replied that if the colonel let that sergeant go, he would have to let everyone else in the same situation go and there was no way he could let that many men leave the battalion at the same time without getting himself relieved by the general.

There were a few older sergeants and temporary officers whose disillusion and hurt had taken a much longer time to build up. One of our gunnery sergeants, who was such a hard taskmaster that he was called Gunny Hard, was as representative of this scattered group as anyone else in it. All his life Gunny Hard had looked forward to, had prepared for, the time when he could prove his love of country, his willingness to lay his life on the line for what he believed in the innermost parts of his being. When he was a young boy growing up in rural Indiana he had heard many times the stories from his uncles who had fought in Europe and the Pacific. Long before his friends in school, he had decided on a career—he would join the marines the minute he was old enough. Then he would train hard and go off somewhere, anywhere, to fight for the bright ideals of the country he loved.

When he was in high school the Korean War broke out. He hoped it would last until his seventeenth birthday so he could quit school and go to war, but he missed it by a few months. Then the day finally came when he took the oath of enlistment before his local recruiter. The young man was ready but world conditions were not. There was plenty of international tension in the years following the Korean Armistice but nothing big enough broke out to give him the chance he was waiting for.

The eager young marine waited and trained and waited and filled a series of dull assignments mostly in the States, and then he waited some more. For twelve years he waited. Then finally, when he was well into the second half of his career, his chance came in a place he had never heard of before—Vietnam. So now here he was in the hot little country with the strange name and a war. But it was neither what he expected nor what he wanted. All those years of preparing and waiting had come down to this—instead of spending his days in the field looking for the enemy, he was sitting behind a desk, and instead of holding a rifle in his hands and occasionally pulling a trigger, he was holding a pile of papers and pushing a pen.

Every day Gunny Hard's rage at the twists and turns of events in his life built up to the danger point. And every night he had to let out a measure of that rage. Whiskey made that venting process go a little easier: at first a few shots a night, and later more than half a bottle. The more he sipped, the louder his complaints about his country's current war policies became: "The strongest, the greatest country in the history of the world is letting a half-assed, backward, worthless little country push it around while the whole world looks on and cheers the wrong side. And instead of doing something about that situation, instead of ending it right, the president and Congress back in Washington are helping it continue—they're actually helping the enemy with all the peacenik talk and the bombing halts. Instead of winning the war quick by giving North Vietnam a real shot of American power, the politicians and their pinko professor advisors are putting more and more restrictions and rules on their own American fighting men—don't shoot at women and kids even though they throw hand grenades at you, don't shoot at rubber trees even though the VC fire at you from behind them, don't enter Buddhist temples even though the VC and NVA hide rice and weapons in them: don't do this, don't do that. Things are so bad now that a guy almost has to get a petition signed by all members of Congress and approved by the president before he can return fire when the VC take a shot at him!"

The meaning of Gunny Hard's soliloquy was clear to all in the several hooches within listening range of him: America was squandering the patriotism and loyalty of its finest citizens, and the longer that squandering continued the more serious would be the result. America's own leaders were compromising the power of their own country and nobody was doing anything about it. The day might even come when America would no longer be the leader of the world, and everybody knew what would happen then—we would have the Dark Ages all over again.

Gunny Hard's rage reached its climax when he grabbed anything movable within arm's reach—helmet, aerosol shaving bomb, or the whiskey bottle in front of him—and threw it at the light bulb overhead. The shower of broken glass that followed seemed to remind the gunny that he was acting contrary to the regulations of the institution to whose continued glory he had dedicated his life. As if to compensate for his destructive impulse, he would pull himself to his feet and execute in the darkness what he thought was a perfect recruiting-poster salute. But putting one's heels together after drinking as much whiskey as the gunny consumed almost every night meant only one thing as far as the laws of physics were concerned: the standing position could not be maintained for long. Before he could lower himself back down into his chair or onto his bed, the combination of whiskey, tear-provoking pride in service and country, and mounting disillusion would push the gunny's mind beyond the boundaries of consciousness. On some nights his large soft body would simply crumple into a heap on the floor. On other nights he happened to hit a bed. On a few nights he would crash through the screening above the plywood wall and pass the night in a stupor, his legs still inside but the upper half of him hanging outside his hooch under the clear deep of a starlit night.

The stupefying boredom of life in the 3d MPs with its endless evening block of time was taking another kind of toll, one just as heavy as that being exacted from Gunny Hard, on those who at the beginning of their tours did not want to be in the rear. The 3d MPs worked some strange transformations on the desires that had brought these men to the military and to Vietnam. They had come to Vietnam determined to be in the front of this war. They were gung-ho and they were going to kick some VC ass and they were going to prove themselves to everybody back home. So as soon as they arrived in 3d MPs they asked, "How long do I have to stay here before I can go out to the bush?" But not long after their arrival, the motivation and spirit of about thirty or forty of these men began to erode slowly and irresistibly. They were looking for ways of stopping that erosion but they were not finding any.

For a few weeks they fought the erosion of their spirit. They fought it by doing all they could to stay in top shape for the day they could transfer out to the bush and test their physical and mental conditioning—joining as many battalion sports teams as they had time for, lifting weights, and jogging around the compound every night. They also fought the erosion by buying the adjutant drinks in the club in hopes that he would shorten their sentence in the numbing and overheated routine of the rear. But after they had been around a few months they got to like the warm mess hall food three times a day and the cold beer and ice cream and the showers every night and the clean beds up off the ground and the USO floor shows and the security. After four or five months in the rear these men had put back on most of the excess weight their drill instructors had run off them only a few months before, and the steely, purposeful look had gone from their eyes. The once lean and bright-eyed believers in happy endings to all unpleasantries became sloppy, overweight, moody introverts.

After a little more time passed they began to feel something happening within themselves—their will to resist the erosion of their resolve to get out of the rear at the first opportunity was dying. After a few months they stopped trying to oppose it. They began letting it happen. Then one night they just stood off to the side in resignation and watched as the structure of their former selves, including all the beams and supports and braces of values, self-respect, and ambitions carefully erected and preserved over many years, began to sway and crack and come crashing down right before their consciences. What was going on in the hooches of these men was not very pretty.

The final stage in the erosion of spirit came when these thirty or forty men began seriously asking themselves the question whose contemplation they had only a few months before considered disgraceful—"With only a few months to go, why should I take a chance on losing everything?" They began breaking promises they made to themselves in training a few months ago, promises that they would use their training and make the best contribution to whatever their country meant to them. But all those promises were made back in the World, ten thousand miles away and ten thousand maturing experiences ago, before they got used to the benefits of the rear, and before they heard the rumors floating around the PXs about friends they met in training who were permanenty injured or killed.

Therein lay the real pain and challenge of staying in the safe, soft rear for someone who did not seek it—how to explain to himself and to others his acceptance of the security he had, only a few months before, told himself and everyone within earshot he would never accept.

They still asked about being transferred out to a field unit, but now behind the words was the tone of voice which pleaded for another negative answer. And when they filled out their request-for-transfer forms they used the curt, defeatist wording they knew would bring another rejection. Months before, back in the States and far from the war, they hadn't realized the emptiness of their resolve. Now, close to the war, they saw their weakness and were desperate to shield it from the view of others. They coudn't face either themselves or the war, and so they spent that evening block of time avoiding those mirrors and digging up excuses that had never occurred to them before. "My girl and I want to get married as soon as I get back. . . . I don't want to do anything that might wreck the plans. . . . My parents aren't getting any younger; if anything should happen to me they might not be able to take it." And the rock-bottom excuse: "Looks to me like the damn war will be over in another six or eight months anyway. . . . Hell, it'll take almost that long to get the transfer papers through the mill!"

That's what some of the young warriors did behind the barriers of parachute silk and nude centerfolds and transistorized gadgets.

For those who, after their return to the States, felt the need to present themselves as something they were not, there was a real advantage to serving in units like 3d MPs. There was built into each man's assignment to the rear the means of covering up not ony that assignment but also all the embarrassing reordering of values and the frantic searching for excuses it had provoked. At the end of their tours these warriors far from the war could go back to the States and say they were in Vietnam during the war. That statement would, of course, be technically true, but not completely true. No civilian listener would think to ask if the veteran had been in the field or the rear, since those who served in either area wore the same uniform and in most cases the same campaign ribbons. The veteran would be assumed to have faced and survived an extraordinarily demanding experience. Veterans of this type could, in effect, carry out a cover-up of a cover-up. By declining to explain certain facts about their Vietnam experiences, they could conceal their earlier concealment of their loss of resolve to face danger head-on.

Such veterans could thereafter claim to be tested combat veterans without ever having faced the test of combat they once sought, and they could then receive as much attention, respect, or even awe, as their unknowing listeners were willing to pay them. They were then forever protected from anyone questioning their courage or their manhood or whatever it was they valued so highly as to put themselves through that whole elaborate charade.

II

Not all the breaks in our boring routine were of our own making or the result of seasonal change. Several accidents occurred during my time in 3d MPs, most of which could have happened to any unit, two of which could have happened only to an MP battalion. Unlike most battalions, ours had its own mess hall and kitchen, doubtless because we were so far away from any larger unit. One day one of the stoves in the kitchen blew up. Unfortunately a cook was standing in front of it at the time. The blast burned through his white cook's jacket, his undershirt, and several layers of skin, which put him into immediate shock and earned him a place on a medevac, medical evacuation, flight back to the World and a discharge. The incident earned the cook's supervising sergeant an embarrassing investigation which certainly had an inhibiting effect on his chances for promotion.

Another accident took place during a routine firing range exercise. Marine policy was to train every man as a rifleman before allowing him to specialize in anything. Then, after each man was assigned a specialty, he was still required to maintain proficiency in several small unit weapons, such as the M-16 rifle, grenade launcher and mortars. The idea behind the policy was that if a major attack occurred, every man should be able to take part in the defense of his unit. Once a month one company in the battalion was taken to a firing range and every man, whether he was a truck driver or cook, mechanic or typist, fired infantry weapons. The biggest worry on a firing range is misfires, rounds that do not fire when the weapon is triggered. Misfires are rare but they can occur with any weapon. When they do occur, a set procedure is followed to insure the safety of all near the weapon.

While firing the 60-mm mortar on the range one day, one of our admin clerks followed the range supervisor's instructions perfectly. He planted his feet carefully beside the mortar, held the round in both hands over the mouth of the tube, let it slide down the tube when the sergeant told him to, and then bent low, holding hands and head below muzzle level. Nothing happened. Then the clerk made his mistake. He stood up straight and looked down the tube. He never heard the sergeant scream at him to "Get away from that thing!" because just then the round came out, splattering his ears and eyes and brains and teeth all over the range. That is one explanation for the category "Noncombat Death."

Our routine, and the routine of everyone else in the Da Nang area, was also interrupted by one of the biggest explosions to occur during the entire war. One night the Viet Cong found the largest American ammunition dump in the area and blew it up. The VC were just as surprised as the Americans at their discovery, for they found it with a lucky shot. For more than three years they had been firing rockets at every American unit in and around Da Nang almost every night and rarely doing any damage. Then one night it looked like the whole world was blowing up. The night sky lit up orange, the earth shook, and a thunderous roar rolled across the city and into the distant hills.

And that was only the beginning. For three days the chain of explosions continued. Each blast sent hundreds of shells into the air, and when they descended, other blasts were touched off which sent hundreds more into the air to set off more blasts, in an uncontrollable cycle. Stopping the cycle of explosions was out of the question. With the air full of unexploded ordnance, there was little to do but take cover and wait until it ran its course. Offensive operations on both sides of the war in the Da Nang area came to a halt. When it finally ended, every compound in the area was a shambles. In ours, every roof looked like a sieve and many hooches had been partially or completely burned.

Besides our own inconvenience which the destruction represented, we had the problem of several hundred brig prisoners and our North Vietnamese sailors. They had to be housed elsewhere while we rebuilt. The Americans were a much bigger problem than the North Vietnamese, for the former, despite the criminal behavior that had brought them to the brig, still enjoyed the privilege of congressional correspondence. We were vulnerable to the charge of not protecting them during enemy attack, and they could make huge waves by writing their congressmen about it. Which they did, of course. But for the moment we let the paperwork pile up. We had to prevent a mass escape and rebuild our compound. The first problem we solved by putting the prisoners in tents inside the large FLC compound and surrounding them with rolls of barbed wire and dozens of armed guards. To get our compound back in shape we called in the Navy Seabees. When we came back to our rebuilt base, we learned how expensive our new hooches really were. Before they began building, the Seabees thoroughly looted our old quarters.

Boredom accounted for another accidental break from our routine. Third MPs certainly had no corner on boredom in the rear of the Vietnam War, but some of the more bizarre incidents it provoked could have happened only in our battalion. The brig was surrounded by towers, and guards were on duty in them twenty-four hours a day. Standing atop a tower thirty feet high and looking down at labor parties of prisoners for four hours could hardly be called stimulating work. After a few days of it, each guard was looking for a way to counter the boredom. Some of the attempts included reading pornographic novels, writing letters, drinking whiskey, and smoking marijuana cigarettes, only the first two of which were legal. One young guard, fresh from stateside training, found a way to not only kill his boredom but cause immense consternation throughout the brig and all the way up the chain of command as well.

In his guard tower the private found a dark green box the size of a small suitcase. There was no writing on it to indicate what it might be. No one had told him what it was and no one had told him to keep his hands off it. So he started fiddling around with it. Suddenly the box went "Pop!" and "Whoosh!" and something flew out of it. The private was so shocked he just about fell out of his tower.

Picking himself up, he saw that the projectile from the green box had arched into the brig compound and exploded among a group of prisoners digging a garbage pit. But it didn't explode with shrapnel and cut down people. Instead, it sent out a cloud of smoke which sent the working prisoners and their guard running. When the private saw the duty warden run out of his office with an arm-load of gas masks he understood he had just fired a gas grenade. The green box in the guard tower was a gas grenade launcher and it was to be used in case of a riot in the brig. Once again we received a flood of correspondence from congressmen asking us to look into prisoners' allegations of "gas torture." Once again an investigation was conducted and another career sergeant had his next promotion delayed for "insufficient attention to supervisory responsibility."

The last accident to disrupt our quiet routine was the second worst thing that could have happened. The worst, of course, was an enemy attack. The second worst was a riot in the brig and the escape of some prisoners. We had some idea a riot would occur from our prisoner population. One riot had occurred in the brig before I arrived and a major cause of it was believed to be overcrowding. Our brig was built for 200 prisoners. When the count went over that number we began to get nervous. Our riot began the day the count went over 280.

One hot, humid night, just before one group of guards was to be relieved, when they were thinking more about getting some hot food and cold beer than about guarding the brig, five prisoners grabbed three guards, took their weapons, and held them hostage. As soon as the rest of the prisoners heard what had happened, most joined the uprising, tearing down their hooches and setting mattresses afire with lighters stolen from guards. The prisoners were much better prepared than we were. By the time we put our Standing Operating Procedure for a brig riot into effect they were in complete control inside the brig. Their hostages included not only the three inattentive guards but all other prisoners who refused to join their uprising. Fires were spreading at various places inside the compound. Most rioting prisoners not holding hostages were throwing anything they could pick up at the guard force assembling outside the gate. The planning of the riot soon became evident. Teams of prisoners tore fencing off posts and lay siding from hooches across the coils of barbed wire encircling the compound to make a bridge over the barrier and into the night. By the time our reaction force had surrounded the compound an unknown number of prisoners had escaped.

The commander of the brig company opened contact with the rioters immediately. As they hollered their denunciations and demands, they revealed their identity. Four of the five were black; the fifth, a Mexican-American. Three of them had come to the brig under charges serious enough that they would probably get long sentences in stateside military prisons: things like assault with a deadly weapon and attempted murder. All made known in the most obvious terms their hatred of all whites and all minority persons cooperating with whites in any capacity. Their demands were just as futile as their resort to violence. We could look into things like work party assignments and the availability of reading matter, but as for getting out of Vietnam and reforming what they saw as "inherently racist American society," that was a little beyond the brig commander's jurisdiction.

After two days of nonstop negotiating and no food or sleep, the prisoners were too worn out to put up much resistance when the guard force rushed them. Our control reestablished, we took a prisoner count which revealed that twelve had escaped in the first few minutes of the riot. There weren't many places they could hide—Americans, either black or white, are too big and too different-looking to melt into a Vietnamese crowd—and we found them in the first place we looked. They were in a deserters' colony in the huge Dogpatch refugee slum that ringed Da Nang. The deserters didn't see their surroundings as a slum, though. To them it was heaven, for they were spaced out almost all the time on the full range of stimulants, depressants, marijuana, and pure heroin from the Da Nang branch of the Vietnam drug industry, one of the largest illegal businesses in the world. There were over one hundred deserters from all branches of the American military in the jam of shelters made of Coca-Cola and Budweiser cartons and broken pallets. They were living with about twenty prostitutes, blank-faced girls who dyed their hair orange and smoothed business relations between their American boyfriends and Vietnamese drug pushers. The blacks, who accounted for about eighty percent of its population, ran the deserters' colony. They tolerated Mexicans, Puerto Ricans and whites only if they had demonstrated, preferably with violence, sufficient hatred of what they considered "Whitey's war" and "Whitey's racist American society."

Our commanding officer was quite embarrassed to discover so many deserters only two miles from the brig, and he promised the FLC general he would clean it out immediately. This he did with no regard for adverse side effects. An interservice raiding party numbering about one hundred surrounded the deserters' colony before dawn one morning. We MPs donned gas masks and blasted our way in with a barrage of tear gas. Drug pushers and prostitutes scurried out of the shacks and through the maze of alleys, like rats escaping a fire. Several hundred Vietnamese refugees living in Dogpatch also ran out, trying to get away from the expanding cloud of gas, and we made some new enemies among the people we were trying to help by coming to Vietnam in the first place. But we got the deserters, and our colonel triumphantly reported the haul to the general: one hundred twenty-three Americans. After taking that number into custody, our already overcrowded brig was even more crowded and, of course, vulnerable to another riot. But a series of quickie summary trials and transfers got the prisoner count back down to a manageable level, and we settled back into our somnolent routine.

4 Time to Reflect

But even after all of those things were done or happened, there was still plenty of time to kill. For most of us younger members of the battalion the time became long hours of wondering about the forces that had brought us to this faraway place and its baffling war. What triggered the reflection was often a scene that struck us as unusually incongruous—exactly the kind of thing Vietnam was full of. It might be the sight of a wiry brown-skinned woman under a conical hat walking rhythmically on splayed feet under the weight of two heavy water cans suspended from the ends of a shoulder pole. Or it might be the sight of a ten-year-old boy sitting on the broad back of a water buffalo rolling and snorting in a mud hole. Whatever it was, the question that slammed into the brain was the same: How had it happened that I, a product of the most technologically advanced culture in the history of the world, the culture that was sending rockets into space and transplanting human organs, had been sent to a place stuck back in the Bronze Age, a place where the very concepts of space and organ transplants would not be understood even if they could be translated?

The more I thought about that question the more I saw interests and incidents in my own past that could be interpreted as pointing, though somewhat vaguely, toward a military experience. Fifteen years before I got to Vietnam I was playing war games with my friends after school among the foundations and piles of dirt on construction sites. That was less than ten years after the end of World War II and the fathers of most of us had told us many experiences we were eager to act out. We debated with great care who among us would be the good guys—American GIs—and the bad guys—Jerries or Japs. At about the same time, I took much interest in making wooden models of battleships, tanks, and cannons, then reenacting scenes from war movies. In the early 1950s one of the television networks put together a serialized documentary of naval actions in World War II featuring actual combat movie footage and a Rogers and Hammerstein soundtrack. Entitled "Victory At Sea," it was my favorite program. So strongly did I insist on watching it that my parents finally surrendered and allowed me to stay up past my usual bedtime.

Seeing my interest aroused by television, my father brought the war even closer to home. One day he went up into the attic and returned with a cylindrical object about four feet long and eighteen inches in diameter. When I asked him what it was he taught me my first official military term. "It's a seabag," he said. He set it on end in the living room, untied the rope at the top, and pulled open the flaps. Out came musty air suggesting things adventurous and dangerous in faraway places, and I knew I was in for something special. From the rough canvas seabag he pulled out uniforms and sourvenirs from his World War II navy days. There were manuals about how to tie all kinds of strange knots, send messages by flags, and identify enemy ships by silhouette. There were some coins and bills from the Philippines and newspapers announcing the attack on Pearl Harbor and the surrender of Germany and Japan. There were pictures of buddies in uniform and a list of their addresses.

While I tried on one of my father's sailor hats, my mother added her family's experiences to the record. Her father had gained American citizenship and free passage from Denmark by volunteering for the U.S. Army during the Spanish-American War. More recently, one of her brothers had been wounded and a brother-in-law killed in World War II.

When I was about ten I became sufficiently aware of my national identity to plant a small flag in a flower bed on the Fourth of July. The day before I planted it I saw large flags hung outside most of the other houses in our neighborhood. Most of the flags were about two by three feet but one guy had one so big he needed another house to hang it properly. It measured at least ten by fifteen feet and hung from a rope strung between the second floor windows of the two houses. I thought it was strange that we didn't display a flag, even a small one. I asked my parents about the lack, took an advance on my allowance, and went to the neighborhood dime store and bought the biggest flag I could afford. It measured only twelve by fifteen inches and when I stuck it in the ground it barely stood above the tulips, but I felt it would do until we got a bigger one. It was outside where everyone could see it, and so it put our house among the publicly patriotic. I walked across the street, turned around and looked at it, and felt we were doing our part. The next year a supermarket had a Fourth of July sale and we bought enough groceries to qualify for the discount offered on a bigger flag.

When I entered that weird stage of life called adolescence, things pointing toward a military experience suddenly stopped happening. Other interests came along, chiefly sports and girls. By the time I was in high school a military experience was the farthest thing from my mind. There was simply too much life to enjoy, too many parties to attend, too much glory to be won on the basketball court, to imagine it being circumscribed by uniforms and regulations that ignored all individuality and ended freedom. Only once was I reminded that my idyllic existence might not last forever. During the week I turned eighteen I registered for the draft. I stared with no small amazement at the result: the government had in a matter of minutes succeeded in reducing my whole existence to a big number on a small card. Instead of patriotic, I felt assaulted. What had I done to deserve this, I asked the world.

But the government never called again, and I went back to collecting the benefits of the American way of life. Next came four years of insulation in college. Those were the years of Camelot and the Great Society, when two presidents called my generation to new crusades against segregation, poverty, and communism. After the 1950s, which to me seemed soft and dull, that kind of talk sounded exciting. I considered civil rights work in Mississippi in the summer of 1964 but was overruled by economics. I had to supplement my father's tile-setting wages if I wanted to return to school the following fall.

During my senior year the events leading to the expansion of the Vietnam War occurred: the Gulf of Tonkin incident, attacks on American barracks, air strikes against North Vietnam, and the introduction of American ground forces. But Vietnam still seemed too small, too far away, to pose any threat to me, and I went ahead with my plan to be a junior high school teacher and coach. Others, however, saw considerable menace in those events, as many men on campus suddenly applied to graduate school or changed their fields of study from business administration to education. The reason for the scramble was obvious to them: teachers and graduate students were exempt from the draft while corporation management trainees were not. As naive as it sounds now, I did not connect my own teaching plans with the side benefit of draft exemption. I just liked the idea of teaching young people things I enjoyed: history and basketball. Idealism soon gave way to disillusion, however, when I found out how little teaching actually occurs in a junior high school. After two years I had had enough of being either a babysitter or a policeman for dull and/or destructive teenagers.

On a wintry Saturday morning I went to the post office in Rockford, Illinois and collected glossy brochures from the Army, Navy, and Marines. The Air Force was the only branch I ruled out from the start. The prospect of seeing action at an electronically sanitized distance, either from a cockpit of a panel of buttons and blipping lights, held no interest for me. As for the others, I talked to three recruiters but only to make a show of impartial consideration. I had already decided which one I was going to try: the service known as the toughest, the service whose reputation posed the greatest challenge to what I thought I might become with the right experiences, the Marine Corps. Could I make it? Would I flop and be sent home the first week? Questions and doubts loomed large, but I signed up for the tests. For the last several months of the school year I told no one but my parents about my plans, and, I felt, with good reason. Others my age were talking about down payments on houses, having babies, or avoiding the draft, and I felt it was perfectly futile to explain why I was voluntarily trading security for danger.

The time to make my irrevocable move came before I figured out how I would tell anyone about it. On a sunny Sunday in May 1967, I went to Glenview Naval Air Station near Chicago and recited the oath of allegiance before a marine captain. The only surprise came when the recruiting officer said I couldn't start training for another five months. "Why?" I asked. "I'm all ready to go now." He explained that Officer Candidate School was overloaded at the time. There was actually a waiting list for what I was doing! At least I wasn't alone in my willingness to leave behind excessive security.

On the way back to my teaching job I stopped off at my parents' home in Elgin, a few miles away. I told them in the kitchen. My father puffed hard on a cigarette and said, "Well, you picked a hell of an outfit." My mother said nothing and went back to making a tossed salad. There, I had said it. I stood there feeling some satisfaction that I had successfully pronounced the words, but knowing I wasn't finished yet. For my audience of two, the people who had given me life, there had to be more than an announcement. More than anything else, they deserved an explanation. My speech didn't come out very smoothly but I succeeded in voicing the various motives I felt: the desire to be part of a project bigger than myself, a willingness to serve the country that had raised me in freedom and security, the search for adventure and challenge in strange and insecure places. Of those needs and interests, the strongest, as far as I could tell, was that for adventure. For one like me who was young, more activist than contemplative, and not yet interested in taking on domestic responsibilities, life in the safe, soft States could be immensely boring at times.

I spent the summer moving furniture and painting my parents' home. A couple of months before training was to begin, the Commandant of the Marine Corps sent me a form letter advising me to be in good shape when I arrived, giving particular attention to the feet and upper arms. Accordingly, I began a crash training program, weight lifting for the arms and long walks for the feet. I gradually lengthened distances and built up to a hike of thirty-five miles, which gave me plenty of blisters and pushed my legs into previously unexplored realms of pain. One week before I was to leave I was still walking with a pronounced limp and wondering if I would have to request a delay in training on medical grounds. But my legs and feet recovered and on October 23, 1967, I drove into Marine Corps Base, Quantico, Virginia. I had never been on a marine base before and I was surprised at the scenery. On one side of the road were the rolling green hills of a golf course, on the other a clear stream burbled its way to the Potomac between mossy rocks. And everywhere stately trees turned spectacular colors in the autumn sun. It seemed far too lovely a place to be home for the fighting force that considered itself the world's best.

Once training began I didn't notice the scenery of the Virginia countryside anymore. All my senses were too busy accommodating pain. If the purpose of the OCS planners was to tear down the bodies and attitudes that civilian America had given us, they succeeded magnificently. Two career sergeants were assigned to transform us from civilians into marine officers. For ten weeks they commanded our every move, and we never thought to question their qualifications for being our dictators. Neither was a mountain of a man but both were highly visible and highly respected. Both had been to Vietnam, both had been decorated, and one had been wounded five times.

Our two sergeants taught us to do everything the Marine Corps way: make a bed, mop the floor, dress ourselves, even speak. According to the Marine Corps vocabulary, a floor is a deck, a wall a bulkhead, a ceiling an overhead, a door a hatch, and so on. There were also new terms of address for us. We were no longer Mr. Smith or Mr. Jones but simply "numb nuts," "dumb shit," or "shit-for-brains."

After ten weeks I was reduced to a gaunt shadow of my former self. I had lost fifteen pounds, and my physique had never exhibited the slightest suggestion of unnecessary weight. My ribs showed, my cheeks were hollow, and I carried a case of flu through the last week. I looked in the mirror and wondered where the recruiting slogan had come from: "The Marine Corps builds men." It wasn't exactly true of me, at least physically. But in terms of mental construction I was a good illustration of the claim, for I believed I could do just about anything. I never thought the human body was capable of running twelve miles over hills and through gullies and streams with thirty pounds strapped to the back—until I did it. To the untried, a jaunt like that seems a physical test, but it is really a mental exercise, a test of confidence. If you think you can do it, you can. If not, you can't. I did, and I've never been the same because of it. On the first day of OCS there were fifty-three men in my platoon. At our graduation ceremony there were thirty-four.

After a one-week leave at Christmas the next and last phase of training began. The place was called The Basic School, or TBS, a collection of dormitories, lecture halls, a field house, and administrative buildings, miles away fom the OCS area. The purpose of TBS was to teach us infantry tactics, so those interested in flying jets or helicopters were sent to Navy Flight School at Pensacola, Florida. That left our company with about 240 men, and at the end of five months of training we would be assigned to a ground specialty: infantry, artillery, armor, or supply. At any one time during the Vietnam War there were twelve companies at TBS for a total enrollment of around three thousand.

We had been at TBS barely one month when we got a sobering reminder of what lay in the near future of all of us. In the early hours of January 30, 1968, the Viet Cong and North Vietnamese launched the ferocious attacks throughout South Vietnam that came to be known as the Tet Offensive. For the next ten weeks we read news stories about the increase in American combat deaths from around 200 per week to over 500, and saw gory pictures of the fighting in South Vietnamese cities and around Khe Sanh. Grimly aware that we were not so very far away from our own blooding, we took our TBS lectures more seriously than we would have in peacetime. We also took our weekend partying more seriously, for we had only twenty weekends and they were being counted down with alarming speed. For the unmarried majority of us most weekends were spent chasing girls, either at a women's college near Quantico or in the singles bars of Washington, D.C. After a few weeks the social lions among us became known and party invitations materialized.

One of the most memorable, and humorous, was held in a D.C. apartment building where most tenants were government secretaries. As in almost any social gathering there are persons of varying degrees of attractiveness. Some have more than others. One of the less endowed on our side was Harry, a tall gangler to whom social grace was the unreachable ideal. Fortunately there was a female counterpart to Harry. Marge was her name and large was her frame, so of course she was known as Large Marge. As the drinks flowed, a glow came over all. Couples formed and drifted off to bedrooms and darkened corners.

By the time Harry and Large Marge found each other the only available room was the kitchen which, of course, had no lock on the door and no bed or sofa. The only available stage for their pleasure was the dining table. But that didn't bother Large Marge, for soon she was offering herself on the Formica, oblivious to the possibility that others might walk through the unlocked door in search of another drink. In no time at all Harry and Large Marge were sharing what they had come to the party looking for. As Large Marge was climbing the heights of ecstasy she suddenly got a flashback to a previous partner and said in a not very quiet voice, "Bill, I love you." Not one to let a lady labor under a misunderstanding, Harry rushed to correct her. "My name is Harry, not Bill." Large Marge never missed a stroke as she assured Harry he was a member of her gallery of memorable males: "I love you too, Harry!"

When the snow and ice melted we knew our time at TBS was ending and our time in Vietnam was drawing near. The green and bird song of spring came over our campuslike training area, and like millions of students across the country, we turned to preparations for graduation. We were part of the class of '68 but for us there would be no cap and gown procession amid the strains of "Pomp and Circumstance," no alumni office keeping track of us, no homecoming weekends or reunions in years to come. And instead of a senior prom, we had the tradition of Mess Night. Borrowed from the British a couple of centuries ago, Mess Night is a formal dinner attended by male officers only. Dignitaries are invited, toasts pronounced, brief speeches made, and plenty of booze drunk, the idea being not only to salute the chain of command but improve esprit de corps.

During our preparations for Mess Night the finality of what we were doing became clear to us. As we discussed the protocol of seating arrangements and the wording of toasts, we realized how close we had become in seven brief months. We also realized how little time we had left together. It was not TBS itself that made us such a tight band but the war that lay just beyond. Vietnam was next, and we knew all of us would be changed in unknown ways by it. We also knew some of us would not come back from it.

Our Mess Night began with the stilted formality that nearly paralyzed most of us. Guests of honor arrived and each was met by the lieutenant assigned to take his coat, get his drink, and make sure he was never left alone during the evening. Among the guests were half a dozen military attachés from foreign embassies, and, of course, our own TBS commander. The main speaker was a marine major general. To our surprise, the dinner and toasts went almost as smoothly as planned. We settled back in our seats as the last item on the program began, a brief address by the general. He told us that if we stayed in the Marine Corps for a career we could expect memorable experiences like his, such as dinner with the Queen of England. To which most of us thought, "If I come back from Vietnam in one piece, I'll be glad to dine with the queen."

With the departure of the guests, the relaxed phase of our Mess Night could begin, the phase we had been looking forward to. Formality went out the window, the booze flowed freely, and about half our company ended up commode-hugging drunk. All scored the evening a roaring success.

Mess Night was the last stateside event that all 240 members of our company shared. Although our company was an unusually tight group after training together, each sixty-man platoon was even tighter, primarily because of the TBS billeting policy. Each platoon had its own wing of the building, so we were together not only for classes and field problems but during liberty as well. After Mess Night, one weekend remained and we thought it only natural that we spend it on a platoon party. For our farewell bash we dispensed with Mess Night formality and invited women. As things turned out, it might have been better if we had retained some formality, for the owner of the motel conference room we reserved didn't think much of our wrecking his furniture. Though the businessman's claim for damages was certainly justified in a legal sense, we had the greatest difficulty taking it seriously, no doubt due to the vastly different futures we faced. While the motel owner could look forward to years of continued good business in a secure environment, we faced Vietnam and its terrible potential for changing, and ending, lives. Our sentiment seemed more than justified to us: "Who gives a shit about a few tables and chairs—we might be dead in a couple of months!"

On a bright warm Tuesday in May our orders came through. As our captain read our names and announced assignments before the platoon, everything that had happened in OCS and TBS suddenly seemed long ago and far away. Each of us held our pile of orders—fifteen copies of each page—and read and reread the officious directive: "Subject-named member is authorized 30 days leave . . . will then report without delay to the Commanding General Fleet Marine Force, Pacific for further assignment in the Western Pacific. . . ." I felt some surprise that the Headquarters maze up in D.C. actually remembered me after seven months of training. In the next two days we compared assignments, exchanged addresses, cleaned out our rooms and got drunk again. We spent our last morning filling out administrative forms to confirm such things as the names and addresses of our next of kin. Then we drove off in 240 directions into the warming spring. We were in a pipeline leading straight to Vietnam.

5 Sparrowhawk!

Third MPs was touched by the fighting and dying side of the war twice during the time I was in the battalion. Although over half the men in 3d MPs were trained in the infantry, there was only one platoon that was used as an infantry platoon. The thirty-five men in that platoon spent most of their time executing their primary mission of manning the bunkers around the compound and conducting short patrols a few hundred meters outside the compound every night. The security platoon's secondary mission was to be a "Sparrowhawk" platoon, a unit that could be taken out of its own compound and used to help man the defense perimeter around all of Da Nang and its rear-echelon bases. All units in the rear had Sparrowhawk platoons or companies. The Sparrowhawk mission of our platoon was to help the South Vietnamese Army hold a bridge over a small river on the south side of the Da Nang airstrip. The area south of the river was considered insecure or "Indian territory." If any VC succeeded in crossing the bridge they would be only a short walk away from the flight line, where they could blow up just about anything they wanted —Phantom jets, a barracks, or even the control tower—during the fifteen or twenty minutes it would take to organize a friendly force against them. Thus the Sparrowhawk orders contained the sentence, "This bridge must be held at all costs."

On a warm clear August night an unusually alert South Vietnamese soldier guarding the bridge pylons noticed a large object floating toward him. The thing was not moving as the current would have carried it. It ran with the current for a few meters and then something would splash to the side and push it across the current. The soldier correctly guessed the thing was being guided toward his pylon by a paddling hand. He let the thing float closer, closer. When it was only about twenty feet away he fired at it, as he was free to do anytime of the day or night without his commander's permission, and got the surprise of his young life. The thing blew up with a tremendous explosion that just about took the soldier and the bridge with it. The young soldier was too dazed to analyze what he had just done, but those who ran to his aid immediately knew he had blown up a Viet Cong in the process of floating about twenty-five pounds of explosive toward the bridge. The other South Vietnamese troops also knew the swimming sapper was not alone—his attempt to blow up the bridge would probably be coordinated with a ground attack that would most likely come from the south. With the geyser from the explosion still falling back down onto the river, the bridge garrison frantically prepared for the attack they knew would come.

After the explosion in the water, everyone was awake. With more than enough yelling and noise to give their positions and plan away, the South Vietnamese broke out extra bandoleers for machine guns, extra rounds for their 60-mm mortar; everyone else slapped a full magazine in his rifle and chambered a round. Everyone lay low in the grass around the south entrance of the bridge or in fighting holes along the road. They stared down the road into the darkness, wrapped in the silence of anticipation, certain they were ready. But the VC were more ready. They didn't attack the bridge garrison head-on from the road, as expected. Instead, they crawled along the riverbank east and west of the bridge and attacked from the sides. Thoroughly panicked by the unexpected direction of attack, most of the defenders fired a few unaimed rounds into the night and ran across the bridge. The machine gun and mortar crews greatly improved the firepower of their attackers by abandoning their American-made weapons. In the space of about one minute the VC had gained not only their objective, the bridge, but two priceless weapons as well. Retaking the bridge, if the VC did not decide to blow it up, would now be much more difficult.

Since they had failed to carry out their mission, the South Vietnamese fell back on their favorite contingency: call the Americans. The airstrip was put on alert. The largest ground unit in the area, 1st Marine Division, was notified and began preparing its Sparrowhawk unit, a company. But 3d MPs was much closer to the bridge than 1st Division, so our Sparrowhawk platoon got the call first. The security platoon was fully armed, in trucks and on the way out the gate in even less time than their best rehearsal record: one minute fifty-one seconds. Ten minutes later they were close enough to the bridge to see the South Vietnamese defenders in full retreat and dropping their American-made rifles and hand grenades, which the VC would shortly be using against both our platoon and any South Vietnamese our people would force to stay and fight. The only good thing we found was that the whole battle scene was well lit. As soon as the airstrip had been alerted, the Air Force had sent "Puff the Magic Dragon" into the sky. Puff was a converted DC-3 used to drop basketball flares to light up firefights at night.

Our Sparrowhawk platoon jumped off the trucks about two hundred meters from the bridge, formed a column on each side of the road, and ran toward the source of the firing. On our way to the bridge we passed more than a few South Vietnamese running away from the fight. The realization that our official ally could not be counted on was a sobering preparation for battle. It meant that we faced not one but two enemies in this night: the cowardice of friends and the guns of the Viet Cong. Setting aside the first of those problems for the moment, we formed a line facing the north entrance of the bridge as best we could in the chaos, and the Battle of the Bridge was on. The crack and rattle of rifle and machine gun fire filled the night as red tracer bullets streaked through the humid air. Our two grenade men fired toward the bridgehead and along the riverbanks as fast as they could reload their launchers—thunk-*boom,* thunk-*boom,* thunk-*boom.* From somewhere far behind us a battery of 81-mm mortars fired across the river in front of the south entrance to the bridge to prevent both the reinforcement and escape of the VC. Puff the Magic

Dragon droned in a tight circle far above the battle while its basketball flares sputtered and hissed their way earthward, turning everything a nauseating yellow. Shadows ran across the disputed bridgehead. Most fell in the intense cross fire but a few miraculously made it between the bullets.

The battle raged for twenty minutes. Both sides fired thousands of rounds and threw dozens of hand grenades at each other. We couldn't know yet what effect we were having on the VC, but too much of their fire was finding its mark among our number. The Battle of the Bridge ended when someone on our side noticed that no more fire was coming from the direction of the bridge. As they had so many times before after engaging many other American units in many other places, the VC had slipped back across the river and disappeared into the night. Somehow they got through the curtain of mortar fire that was supposedly preventing their escape.

When the firing stopped it was time for a body count. Everyone got up, formed on line, and moved toward the bridge. Most of what was found was pieces—of weapons, of uniforms, of people. One of the newest members of the platoon stepped on something that felt hard and soft at the same time. Puzzled, he bent down for a closer look. As his eyes focused on the object, his stomach roiled and he vomited immediately. It was a severed hand.

The sweep continued across the bridge and a hundred meters into VC country. Only four enemy bodies were found. Others were dragged off by survivors. The many wounded no doubt had crawled upstream or downstream away from the bridge and were probably still close enough to hear us. We then went back to our side and counted our losses. The bridge was held but the cost was high: two dead and fourteen wounded. Sparrowhawk guarded the bridge the rest of the night while our higher-ups informed the South Vietnamese command that most of their bridge garrison had deserted in the face of the enemy and they had better put together a new force fast. The next morning we returned bridge security to the South Vietnamese, and a bone-tired and emotionally drained Sparrowhawk platoon boarded trucks for the short ride back to our compound.

Three days later a memorial service for our dead was held in a field next to the battalion chapel. Skeleton staffs were left in offices and each company was marched to the chapel. The sound of senior sergeants marching columns of troops through the compound provoked in many of us a flashback to simpler and more secure days, for it was the first time we had heard the bark and song of cadence since stateside training. One group did not arrive in formation: the colonel's staff ambled over in groups of two and three. Finally, the colonel, in sunglasses and starched uniform. The battalion was called to attention and the ceremony began. The chaplain had a thin boyish face; he couldn't have been more than five years out of divinity school. A long purple vestment collar covered his rank insignia, and he carried a small black book. Through the rising heat of the morning he intoned the brief memorial: "There is a time to live and a time to die . . . laid down their lives in the cause of freedom . . . grant Your eternal blessing on these Your servants . . . in the name of the Father, the Son, and the Holy Ghost." The Battle of the Bridge sobered up 3d MPs faster than anything I saw during my tour. Two weeks went by before anyone got openly drunk in the club again.

A month later there was another ceremony. This time the American Marine and South Vietnamese Eye Corps commanding generals were passing out awards. All survivors of the Sparrowhawk section were ordered to shine their boots and put on a starched uniform. After a long truck ride to III MAF Headquarters, all uniforms were well wrinkled and sweat-stained and all boots were scuffed and covered with dust. The South Vietnamese general was easily the most noticeable of all present. He arrived in a limousine preceded by a jeep with flashing red lights. Two crisp and shining aides opened every door and indicated every move. The general wore so many rings, pendants, precious stones, star clusters, and medals, and so much gold and braid that he could have been mistaken for a walking jewelry exhibit. He also wore the obligatory symbol of success in South Vietnam: an oversize belly. A purple silk scarf covered two of his three chins. He stood wrapped in a strong scent of cologne.

In officious tones the American general talked about professionalism and sacrifice. In broken and nasal English the South Vietnamese talked about our going far from America and fighting for his country. The day's haul: five Bronze Stars, fourteen Purple Hearts, and thirty-five Vietnamese Crosses of Gallantry.

The only other time we were touched by the war was the night two sappers tried to blast their way into our little sanctuary. A sapper was a mostly nude fanatic who strapped about thirty pounds of high explosive to himself and then tried to enter American barracks or clubs. The reason he was mostly nude was because he was using his skin to feel and wriggle his way under the barbed wire in front of our lines. The reason he was a fanatic was probably known only to his mother and Ho Chi Minh.

The sapper's plan was to run around inside an American compound, throwing blocks of explosive into barracks and clubs in order to destroy as many buildings and Americans as possible, and then escape back out the hole in the wire through which he had entered. What usually happened, however, was that the sapper was discovered and cornered before he had thrown all of his explosives. In that case he would almost always hold to his chest and detonate whatever explosives he had left, thereby killing himself and, he hoped, the Americans closing in on him.

Our sappers were stopped about ten meters in front of our lines by rifle and machine gun fire so concentrated that it blew up one of the sappers and increased the weight of the other by at least twenty-five percent with the accumulation of lead. The sappers must have been surprised to find such stiff resistance, since they knew very well how notoriously lax the security of rear-echelon units was. They would have understood our determination had they known that the first building they would have reached was our beloved air-conditioned, full-of-cold-beer club. The thought of facing even one day without our club was too horrible to contemplate.

After our losses at the Battle of the Bridge, our complete victory over the sappers frankly tasted good. What was left of the sappers was displayed for all to see in the warm sunlight of the next morning.

6 Hearts and Minds

Whether in wartime or peacetime, the arrival of new men in a battalion hardly provokes notice among those already "cranked into" the unit and its routines. Cursory greetings and pro forma offers are made—". . . just call me Jack . . . let me know if you need anything"—and jobs are resumed. That's why I was surprised to get so much attention from one of the established staff officers. I first ran into him on the road between the supply shed and the brig.

"Hi. I'm Bill Thomas. You just report in?"

"That's right. My name's Anderson. What's your job?"

"I'm the S-5."

"What's that?" I asked.

"Come on over to my office and I'll show you."

So I went, but on the way I couldn't help but steal a few sideward glances at Thomas. He was a stark contrast to the image of the marine officer I had gotten used to seeing in stateside training, the image I had been ordered to emulate. When the PR boys in Headquarters Marine Corps look for a model for their recruiting posters and brochures, they quickly pass by officers like Bill Thomas. He had a concave chest and an oversize stomach, and his head never did support a marine cover the way the Uniform Recommendation Committee in Washington intended. But Thomas knew much more about 3d MPs and Vietnam, and so I listened.

"Yeah, this battalion's got a little different organization than outfits back in the World. We've got the standard four sections, you know, S-1 Personnel, S-2 Intelligence, S-3 Operations, and S-4 Logistics. Over here we've got another one: S-5 Civil Affairs. That's me."

Once in Thomas's office I forgot all about public relations imagery. He had the same blowtorch plywood paneling I had seen in every other office in 3d MPs, but most of his was covered with maps and charts. Thomas led me to a large white board overlaid with plastic. On the board was a grid pattern. Down the left side were printed the names of five villages in the vicinity of our compound. Across the top of the board were written the dates for the next two weeks. In about one-third of the date squares there were written project commitments: "17 JUL–MEDCAP, 19 JUL–Begin Well Const., 24 JUL–Deliver Plywood," and so on.

Thomas said nothing to the two men playing blackjack on a desk in the corner and launched right into his briefing.

"Recently we've been running three missions a week to these first three villages. The other two are controlled by Charlie most of the time but we'll be getting back in there pretty soon. The chiefs of the first two vills are rotten corrupt but usually on our side. The third one tries to be honest most of the time and is with us for the most part. The other two chiefs are rotten corrupt and on Charlie's side but they'll take anything they can get out of us."

"What kind of things do you give them?" I asked.

"We've dug a few wells, built a few storage sheds and school classrooms; sometimes we give out food, clothes, and toys for the kids when we can get them. . . ."

"Where do you get the stuff?"

"Some of it comes from Flick, things like cement and grain. Some comes from charities and churches back in the States. But most comes from our own compound here, like used wood. Some of our best stuff comes from the mess hall. Know what it is?"

"No," I said.

"Garbage."

"Is that right?"

"That's right. Just plain old American garbage. Last week I took five hundred pounds of it out to this vill here. Farmers use it for their pigs. Fattens up those porkers faster than anything they got. Unless the hogs got tapeworms, which about half of them do. And the chickens they got . . . you ever seen a Vietnamese chicken?"

"Not yet," I said.

"I laughed my ass off first time I saw one! Look like they're naked—no feathers, real skinny, and they hardly ever give any eggs. But I got a line on some decent feed. We're making progress but it comes slow in this country, it comes slow."

"That's what I hear," I said, looking at the board. "What's a MEDCAP? . . . up there after July 17," I asked.

"That's Medical Civic Action Program. Once a week we take a corpsman out to a vill and give free treatment for whatever we find. There's a lot of skin infections, simple things like that. Villagers can't figure out why they don't heal up but they keep taking baths in the same streams they piss and shit in. We teach them how to use soap but the next time we go back we see the same new bars we gave them. If they got some serious illness or need an operation, we bring them into a hospital in Da Nang. Flick is building a children's hospital over in their compound. Maybe you saw it when you checked in."

"I saw a sign about it," I said.

"Well, you gotta be an optimist to do this job. Most guys around here think the Vietnamese are worthless but I think all they need from us is a little technology and help in setting things up and they'll be on their own in no time. The Vietnamese are hard-working people, I'll tell you. Why, do you know these people can work all day on only two small bowls of rice?"

"No, I didn't know that," I said.

"That's right. Yeah, I think they'll be on their own in no time . . . if we can get the VC off their back and give them a little help setting things up . . . it's just a matter of time."

"Well, I hope so," I said. "Is everything you've just explained what they call the Civic Action Program?"

"Oh, then you've heard of this back in the World?"

"Yes, I read something about it somewhere," I said.

"This is it. At least that's what III MAF and I call it. Other people call it other things. The reporters call it 'the other war.'

The embassy calls it 'pacification.' And the politicians call it 'winning hearts and minds.' "

The Civic Action Program answered the crying need in South Vietnam for effective communication and cooperation between Americans and Vietnamese on the local level. CAP was administered by III MAF, the headquarters of all marine units in Vietnam. In its formative period, CAP enjoyed the support of the III MAF commander, General Lew Walt, a semilegendary figure in the Marine Corps at the time and one of the few American field commanders to realize the need for unconventional programs in an unconventional war. The American Embassy and the army used other programs to address the need for assistance at the local level. The basic unit of the Civic Action Program was the CAP team, consisting of fourteen enlisted marines and one navy medical corpsman. CAP team members had the expertise and motivation for working with Vietnamese civilians that regular infantrymen lacked. They were volunteers, which eliminated the chances of atrocities resulting from the frustration other Americans frequently felt when working with Vietnamese. At least one man in each CAP team was fluent in the language, and everyone could speak a few necessary words and phrases. All team members had civilian work experience that could be applied directly to the agricultural economy of the rural Vietnamese village, things like farming, livestock breeding, construction, and small engine repair.

As soon as Vietnamese villagers realized the value of CAP Marines—the teams had to convince many that they were not just another gang of plundering foreigners—the teams were successful. CAP projects were there for all to see—schools, clinics, roads, wells, pumps, and generators. Better strains of rice were planted and larger yields were harvested. Better breeds of pigs and chickens gave more pork and eggs. Farmers were taught how to form cooperatives, and bought more grain and livestock. Villagers had more to eat than at any time since the war in the villages began back in the late 1940s. Most welcome of all to the villagers on a day-to-day basis was the security provided by the marines. CAP team members were armed, of course, and had been trained as infantrymen. Most importantly, the marines stayed in their assigned villages twenty-four hours a day, unlike both the Viet Cong and the Americans/South Vietnamese. After working with the villagers during the day, they guarded roads and trails and patrolled around their village at night.

The most striking measure of the success of the Civic Action Program was its effect on the marines' enemy, the Viet Cong. CAP was applied in villages to the west and south of Da Nang, an area which had a population of about 260 thousand. In the same area an estimated 30 thousand Viet Cong were active; yet during the one year 1967–68 the VC managed to recruit only 170 men, not nearly enough to replace losses. Villagers also began withholding rice from the Viet Cong and telling their CAP teams when to expect VC attacks. On the American side, III MAF staff officers proudly pointed to the efficiency of CAP, and with more than enough justification. The entire Combined Action Program consisted of 15 officers and 1,200 enlisted men. The cost of maintaining CAP was only one-fifth the cost of the same number of American infantrymen engaged in search and destroy or support duties, and only one-third the cost of the South Vietnamese Rural Development Program. The Civic Action Program was also less expensive and much more effective than the U.S. Agency for International Development's pacification program with its generous budget and staff of thousands of experts.

In spite of its obvious success and value to the war effort, CAP labored amid a continuing storm of controversy. Opposition came not only from the Viet Cong but all other directions as well: the South Vietnamese, the American Embassy, even General Westmoreland's headquarters. There was no objection to the idea of helping Vietnamese villagers while at the same time fighting the VC and North Vietnamese. All Americans in Vietnam agreed on the need for that. The objection to CAP was based on the way the marines went about their mission: CAP was an all-marine show: it did not employ any South Vietnamese officials. According to U.S. Embassy policy, the pacification program was supposed to work like this. U.S. Agency for International Development (USAID) personnel, in consultation with U.S. Army advisors in the field, determined what was needed for South Vietnamese development. Most needs were in the areas of food, grain, medicines, and construction materials and equipment. After being ordered through the U.S. Embassy, the goods were sent to Vietnam by plane or ship. The needed food and equipment were to be received at Vietnamese ports and airfields by Vietnamese, then distributed through the Vietnamese bureaucracy, down the organization chart from province chief to district chief to village chief and finally to the hamlet chief, who would see that the people who needed the goods got them.

That was the prescribed, on-paper system. The idea behind it was that while the South Vietnamese, with, of course, massive assistance from the Americans, were countering the Viet Cong in the field, they would at the same time be developing a modern, efficient governmental administration capable of reaching all corners of the country. In practice, however, the advisory/USAID concept did not work, though few officials and advisors would admit it. By sending USAID food and equipment through the thoroughly corrupt bureaucracy of our official ally, USAID presented South Vietnamese administrators and generals with what proved an irresistible temptation. They stole USAID shipments from docks and warehouses, sold it to the black market in South Vietnam (or even Hong Kong), and put the profits in foreign banks. Despite the gross corruption, which everyone knew had a crippling effect on the war effort, the American Embassy and the army refused to bypass the crooked South Vietnamese administration. To do so, went the official argument, would be to indicate mistrust of our ally and that would amount to bad public relations in the host country!

Allowing the whole scandal to continue was the complicity of most U.S. Army advisors. Few ever blew the whistle on the corrupt South Vietnamese. To do so would provoke a complaint from the South Vietnamese command to General Westmoreland's headquarters that the advisor was not "cooperating." The complaint would usually lead to a quick reassignment with a bad fitness report, which would ruin the advisor's career. So, for the sake of good public relations with one of the least competent governments of the twentieth century, billions of dollars' worth of American food and equipment was turned over to a gang of corrupt leaders who became rich by selling it on the black market, where much of it was bought by our enemies, the Viet Cong, and North Vietnamese, who, of course, used it in the field against American forces. And that was verified by the discovery of much American medicine and equipment in Viet Cong and North Vietnamese positions overrun by American units in the field.

Fortunately the marines were never as concerned as the embassy/USAID people about public relations. Early in the war the marines decided that if CAP was to succeed, it would have to bypass the South Vietnamese bureaucracy. The result was a lot of bureaucratic infighting in headquarters offices, but one of the few successes of the American effort in the field. Throughout its brief existence CAP was subjected to continuing criticism. CAP was accused of working outside established channels and thereby undermining the U.S.–South Vietnam alliance. CAP leaders were accused of being con-men who juggled statistics to make themselves look good. And anyone who didn't like the marines' program but couldn't think of a specific charge simply said CAP was "counter-productive." But the success of CAP could not be denied, and many an embassy, USAID, and army spokesman had to endure the same embarrassing question from visiting congressmen and reporters: "Why can't you guys conduct your pacification as well as the marines with their Civic Action Program?"

Third MPs was not, of course, a CAP unit. But III MAF policy directed that every marine unit, whatever its primary mission, conduct CAP projects according to its capabilities. Since we had our own compound, and mounting search and destroy operations was not our mission, we were expected to conduct continuing Civic Action projects in five villages. Our S-5 was directed to give special attention to construction projects and agricultural production. To help modernize the five villages, S-5 was allotted one lieutenant, one lance corporal, one Vietnamese interpreter, one medical corpsman for only one afternoon a week, no money, and the oldest jeep in the motor pool. Anyone capable of believing that was an adequate allocation of manpower and resources was also capable of believing in Santa Claus.

Fortunately for our battalion's Civic Action effort, the S-5 officer, Lt. Bill Thomas, wore his commission better than most who carried one. He personified very faithfully an admonition from training: "Do your best in every assignment, whether you like it or not." Thomas had not looked for his job as S-5 officer when he came to Vietnam. Like most officers in 3d MPs, he was trained for the infantry. On his way to the war, he had expected and looked forward to joining a company in the bush. But like many other junior officers in 3d MPs, he was sidetracked into the rear upon his arrival in Da Nang. When he learned he would have to spend six months in the rear before he could transfer out, he asked for the S-5 job. He soon became seriously interested in the Vietnamese people and forgot about going to the bush.

Thomas's full-time assistant, Lance Corporal Farquar, was at first indifferent to his S-5 assignment. He had been sent to Thomas after he had questioned once too often the wisdom of his first sergeant's orders. Assignment to S-5 for him was punishment, and that's the way most of the other junior enlisted men viewed the job, which involved working close to a culture vastly different from their own.

Bill Thomas faithfully personified another admonition from training, "Take care of your men before yourself." Others in the battalion soon noticed that characteristic of Thomas, and our S-5 was more effective than it might otherwise have been but for its considerate officer-in-charge.

One advantage of Thomas's character was that it attracted unofficial help from a few corners of the battalion normally unrelated to S-5. As soon as word got around that Thomas was not Machiavelli reincarnate and was intent on doing more than pleasing the CO, a few junior enlisted men began hanging around the office and volunteering to go along on the weekly trips to villages in the area, "just to see what was happening," as they explained when discovered. Usually after a few such visits, lieutenants or first sergeants from the companies would notice their missing men and drop into S-5 for a surprise visit to pull stray men back to primary duties. But two kept coming around to help Thomas, and their interest served to pull Lance Corporal Farquar out of most of his indifference. One of the part-timers even learned enough Vietnamese to make himself understood by villagers on a few subjects.

There was another advantage to Thomas's attitude, one that helped make up for the lack of supplies given S-5. With neither budget nor requisition forms signed by the colonel, Thomas and Farquar could do no more than beg and barter to get the most basic supplies for their projects—a few bags of cement, a few sheets of plywood, or a trailer to carry it in. For several reasons, most of which were based on a disdain of the Vietnamese, most senior sergeants and officers who had access to any supplies were reluctant to give any of it to Thomas for S-5 projects.

Thomas and Farquar quickly devised a method of bypassing the brick wall they so often encountered, a method which drew heavily on the goodwill Thomas had built up among the junior enlisted men. He would visit the targeted sergeant or officer a few minutes before lunch or dinner and make his pro forma appeal for supplies. When the opposition began his own pro forma recitation of the reasons he couldn't simply give away the precious government property with which he was entrusted by the president, the Congress, and Colonel Palooka, Thomas would glance at his watch, notice it was time to go to the mess hall, and usher his victim out the door. Lance Corporal Farquar, who had been watching from behind a nearby hooch for the opportune moment, would then breeze into the office or supply shed so recently vacated by the authority figure and receive, from a fellow junior enlisted functionary who liked Thomas, whatever it was S-5 needed.

That system worked, but Thomas never stopped hoping for the day when he wouldn't have to use a method so devious, the day when the rest of the battalion would come to see the value of S-5 and give it the support he knew it deserved.

With the necessary supplies safely hidden in the back seat of the jeep or under a tent in the trailer, Thomas and Farquar were ready for the villages. Our villages varied in size, distance from the 3d MP compound, and degree of sympathy to what our S-5 was trying to do. The largest village was home for 2,500 farmers and fishermen; the smallest, for 700. The farthest was eight miles away; the nearest, two miles.

Inhabitants of the friendliest village greeted every S-5 visit by offering Thomas and Farquar the cutest village girls and a private hooch equipped with two thatch mattresses so the great round-eyed bearers of modern ways and gadgets might enjoy an afternoon's respite from their heavy duties of enlightening the darker corners of the planet. Thomas always declined such offers, but only with the greatest reluctance, he later confessed in the club. Farquar cursed his boss's declinations with mumbled expletives the rest of the afternoon.

Inhabitants of the least friendly village greeted every S-5 visit by running inside their hooches, holding doors shut, and making gestures which our interpreter told us meant "Don't talk to us—go away." But even in the two unfriendly villages on his itinerary Thomas usually succeeded in getting the villagers to accept something from his trailer, probably because he had learned early in his tour which brands of American cigarettes and whiskey could melt the resistance of each village chief.

The most disturbing phenomenon Thomas discovered about the reactions of villagers to our efforts was that a considerable number were sympathetic to what we Americans were trying to do, but at the same time they hated the Saigon government and its rapacious army. Since peasants were usually extremely reluctant to complain to foreigners about oppressive authority figures, due to fear of reprisals, the willingness of the villagers to report such feelings to our interpreters indicated not only a serious situation in their lives, but the presence of a definite threat to one of the most basic strategic assumptions of the American presence in Vietnam, the assumption that the Americans should remain allied to Saigon throughout the conflict.

Thomas felt the divided feelings of many villagers were important enough to be reported to commanders and policy planners all the way to the White House. But such facts did not fit anyone's neatly constructed model of what was believed to be really happening in the Vietnam of 1968, so no one listened very closely to what he reported. The few commanders and advisors who did hear what Thomas had to say declined to pass the information up the line. From that time on, the gap between village Vietnam and Saigon, the gap which would eventually prove fatal to the efforts of our S-5 in the Da Nang area, would continue to widen until the time when it could be closed was gone forever.

Subsequent events have shown that not only was the same gap present and widening in other parts of South Vietnam, but a second was operative as well—that between Saigon and Washington. The relentless widening of those two gaps would, only a few years after Bill Thomas and his interpreters identified them, prove fatal to the entire American effort in Vietnam.

Bill Thomas and his tiny section worked under a pervasive atmosphere of opposition to everything the Civic Action Program stood for, and that is why he had gone out of his way to explain his job when I arrived—he was looking for allies in his uphill struggle. The most chauvinistic in the battalion considered it a criminal waste of American manpower and resources to try and help "backward" and "ungrateful" people like the Vietnamese. The most charitable considered Thomas and his staff a collection of naive do-gooders who were only kidding themselves if they thought they were doing anything worthwhile.

In between those extremes were views on cultural distance ("The Vietnamese have their ways and we have ours and they'll never mix them together . . . who was it said 'East is East and West is West and the two will never get together'?") and the unseemly appearance of some S-5 projects ("It ain't manly to pass out soap and candy to women and kids—I was trained to fight!").

Those whose minds were untroubled by more traditional views of cultural identity, race, and masculinity had what they felt were more practical reasons for withholding support for S-5. Depending on their attitude about a military career, members of the battalion considered S-5 either ineffective or dangerous. Those who would not remain in the military thought S-5 was simply not reaching the Vietnamese. Since the Vietnamese did not understand what the Americans were trying to do through S-5, these men reasoned, the success of CAP was a good deal less certain than that of other projects. Other assignments were more interesting than one destined for failure, they felt. Those who would remain in the military considered S-5 a dead-end assignment. It was a threat to one's future promotions because it didn't do anything military—it was for civilians. Far better to have an "action" S-2 or S-3 assignment entered in one's record book. But those in S-5 labored on, determined to show the Vietnamese that America was trying to do things other than burning and killing.

About every two months Bill Thomas would give a briefing to all officers and staff NCOs in the battalion on recent S-5 activities and Vietnamese-American cultural differences. The "suggestion" for such briefings came from the highest Marine Corps authority in the country, III Marine Amphibious Force. A "suggestion" from a higher headquarters is always received as an order, and so the briefings occurred. Our colonel very professionally covered his true feeling about the "suggestion" with his official approval, and his dead silence at the briefings. At the first briefing I saw, Thomas began by showing his S-5 calendar and an area map, and explaining what projects were scheduled, where the recipient villages were located, and what the village chiefs' attitudes toward his efforts were. With that completed he then began an explanation of the different concepts of time held by Americans and Vietnamese, and how their concept affected the actions of the latter. Thomas's audience accepted the first part of his presentation as they had accepted countless other military briefings with visual aids before it—with less than their full attention and with frequent glances at watches to wonder when the preachy college kid before them would finish so they could get on to more important things at the club.

But when Thomas turned his briefing from a mechanical presentation of numbers and dates to an explanation of one facet of Vietnamese culture, the mood of his audience changed from somnolent acceptance to hostile attention. Slouching bodies sat up straight, arms were folded rigidly across chests, mouths turned downward into frowns, creases came across foreheads. Those in the audience came to look more like bricks in a wall than people in a row. Their posture of resistance was a perfectly faithful manifestation of their attitude of resistance to what their S-5 was telling them.

The staff NCOs and officers in Thomas's audience had very definite ideas about what the words "civilization" and "culture" meant, and about who had those things and who did not. Civilization and culture to these men meant a combination of faith in the latest technology, a desire for material goods, acceptance of

Christian moral standards, and a belief in the superiority of white-skinned peoples over yelow-, brown-, and black-skinned peoples. The Vietnamese were found deficient in all categories and were therefore dismissed as lesser beings who did not deserve anyone's tolerance, understanding or sympathy. The cultural attitude of most members of 3d MPs was more appropriate to sixteenth-century builders of colonial empires than twentieth-century warrior-technologists involved in bridging cultural gaps.

The men in the audience believed there was really only one civilization worthy of the title, and it was their own American civilization. Any people who failed to see the superiority of American culture, and declined to emulate it immediately and completely, thereby admitted their own lack of culture and forfeited the privilege of associating with Americans. Any suggestion that the Vietnamese had any culture at all was taken as not only a lie but an insult to one's own American culture as well. That was exactly what Thomas was doing and his audience began firing questions right away. "Why can't these damn people even use a bar of soap?" "Why are the men always holding hands—are they all queer?" "Why the hell don't they stand and fight the VC instead of running away?"

This was not the first time Thomas had faced this same hostile audience. He had learned several months before that the questioners were not interested in understanding the Vietnamese, so they had no desire to really explore such issues. They were only interested in reinforcing their hurried conclusions based on incomplete observation, and in making it clear to their S-5 that no amount of logic or reasoning on his part would shake those conclusions. Thomas didn't even try to answer their charges; he simply deflected them and moved into his conclusion.

There was considerable irony in the situation between S-5 and the battalion of which it was a part, as there so often is in the records of failed projects. Career military members, those who held positions of responsibility in the 3d MPs and every other unit in Vietnam, were among the most virulent and emotional communist-haters. The Civic Action Program was designed to separate the Viet Cong from the civilian population on which it so heavily depended. The communist-haters never saw that in denying CAP their support they were giving passive support to their communist enemy, the Viet Cong.

The organization of the S-5 Section was one of the most ironic features of the entire concept of the Civic Action Program. Considering the many activities implicit in the mission given S-5, and the great importance attached to that mission by commanders at the highest levels and by policy planners, secretaries of state and presidents, S-5 should have been one of the three largest sections, along with S-1 and S-4, on the staff of every rear-echelon battalion and regiment in Vietnam. Instead, it was always the smallest. Because of their mission of service or support, rear-echelon units had no need for large S-2 and S-3 sections. Units charged with finding and fighting the enemy—the infantry units in the field—needed, and had, large combat intelligence and operations sections. But most S-2 and S-3 sections in the rear were just as large as those in the field. The reason for this situation was to be found in the fact of excess manpower in the rear—nonessential men were frequently "dumped" into S-2 or S-3.

From the point of view of the rear-echelon unit commander, the presence of inflated S-2 and S-3 staffs was desirable. The local commander's first responsibility, of course, was to maintain the security and effectiveness of his unit. In a war without a front, commanders everywhere had to be ready at all times. One never knew when or where the VC would strike. In such an environment, serving the needs of civilians in the area was a secondary consideration. However, from the point of view of senior commanders in Vietnam and Washington and American policy planners, such priorities and headquarters structures were not only undesirable but represented a serious compromise of stated policy. In the structure of rear-echelon unit staffs, the spirit of the Civic Action Program was effectively nullified.

Perhaps the most shocking irony of all is that no one, except Thomas, ever thought to ask any Vietnamese what they thought of the program designed to assist the Vietnamese. The very people for whom the Civic Action Program was conducted were completely closed out of the planning and evaluation of the program. Every day three translator/interpreters, all of course fluent in English, came into the compound and one of them went along on the weekly MEDCAP missions to villages in the area, but no one except Thomas ever asked for their views on the effectiveness of such missions. Thus, no one outside the S-5 staff ever knew how far off the mark the Vietnamese considered many of the CAP projects. Thomas never succeeded in having Vietnamese responses to his questions included in the monthly CAP reports battalion sent to III MAF headquarters. If he had succeeded, I'm sure General Walt would have recognized the potential for subversion of his policies in giving Vietnamese children toys that had no relevance to their culture—ghoulish Frankenstein dolls—or in giving adults food that had been judged unfit for use in American mess halls. But the battalion command was more interested in reporting numbers today than in building understanding and trust tomorrow. They did only what was necessary to fulfil an on-paper commitment from a higher headquarters.

In that entire battalion you could count the people who believed in and were willing to work for CAP on one hand that was missing two fingers. And that situation was not restricted to 3d MPs. Unhappily, it was the norm among American units in Vietnam. All but a few, in 3d MPs and in almost every other American unit in the war, failed to see the tremendous potential of an effective Civic Action Program. It definitely could have increased understanding between Americans and Vietnamese, and thereby reduced the number of atrocities so many American troops committed against Vietnamese civilians, and it possibly could have shortened the war. Both Americans and Vietnamese suffered longer than they otherwise would have.

All S-5 officers in Vietnam, like Bill Thomas, badly needed support to make the Civic Action Program justify the humanitarian phrases in which its mission was described. But they rarely got it, and so in most corners of the war CAP was too little and too late. Most Vietnamese continued to believe that Americans were nothing more than greedy, pushy, loud-mouthed, sex maniacs. And most Americans continued to believe the Vietnamese were nothing more than uncivilized, subhuman beggars. What began in the early years of the war as cross-cultural meetings, which both Vietnamese and Americans looked forward to, quickly deteriorated into awkward pro forma gatherings attended out of duty, and, finally, cultural collisions in which there was progressively less interest in creating understanding.

7 Thanh

The first time I saw her I thought I was dreaming. She was walking toward me on the opposite side of a dirt road in the compound in the hot early afternoon. I slowed my walk as she approached and then I just stood there and stared. She was alone. She carried a lavender parasol in one hand, a purse in the other. She wore a brilliant yellow *ao-dai*, the traditional Vietnamese dress that more than makes up for any defects in the figure of the wearer. White trousers set off the loose silk front and back flaps of the *ao-dai*. Her straight black hair hung down in back, almost to her waist. The long flaps of the *ao-dai* danced on a slight breeze. I knew she was subject to gravity, but in that moment she seemed exempt from the physical laws that limit the rest of us. She didn't walk. She kind of glided above everything—the dirt road, the heat, even the war that had brought me to her country so I could see the vision of her movement. When she was almost even with me a cloud of dust came up and I thought the whole scene would be ruined. But that dust just parted right around her and she emerged fresh and brilliant. "You've just seen magic," I told myself.

When she passed she revealed still another type of movement—shiny black hair swishing across her back. She was cool and sensuous then, and unaware of the scene she was producing, which made her even more stunning. As she receded into the distance, bobbing parasol, swishing hair, and dancing silk came together in the shimmering heat waves. I seriously wondered if such a scene had ever been created before or would ever be created again. I stumbled off to the mess hall and didn't taste anything I ate.

A few hours later, after the day and I cooled off a little, I dismissed the whole experience to the fact that I was not used to the heat yet, since I had been in Vietnam only a few days. But I saw the same thing again the next day and asked someone about it.

"She's a translator. There's three of them. And the colonel says anybody who touches them will be in the brig most ricky-tick." So much for inside-the-compound socializing.

That ruled out most of the methods of meeting someone that were valid outside a combat zone. There could be no stolen glances across a dance floor followed by a suave self-introduction. There couldn't even be a chaperoned date in full view of the public. Another way would have to be found. But I didn't think that would be too difficult, and I even felt justified, almost righteous, about trying to meet her. After all, I had no intention of touching her, so the colonel shouldn't mind. I just wanted to talk to her. And if anybody asked what I was up to, I could always say I was new in the country and wanted to find out about Vietnam, and what better source than a real live Vietnamese? To avoid the charge of ignoring my duties, I would have to approach her on my liberty time. And when did that begin? That was another of the million and one details I didn't yet know because I was still too new. As the adjutant had said when I reported in, "If you got any questions, just let me know."

So I did. "What time does liberty start?" I asked the next day.

The adjutant looked at me as if I had just asked where Ho Chi Minh's office was located. He must have been having a bad day before I made it even worse, because he took many long seconds to answer. "We don't have any around here." The voice conveyed barely controlled exasperation. Then he reached for a pile of papers and handed me one. "Here, read this," he commanded.

It was the "Officer of the Day Duty Roster for July 1968," the list of junior officers who would answer the phone and check the security of the compound after working hours. I would soon learn why some called it the "Queen for a Day list," or simply the "shit list." I was listed for duty that night. That killed all thought of meeting the slim girl in dancing *ao-dai.* I walked out of the adjutant's office in a daze. It would be hard to imagine a quicker and more complete reversal of purpose than I had just experienced. What began as a perfectly legitimate search for professional knowledge, not to mention female companionship, ended in my being drafted for a thankless job.

But as things turned out, the duty roster did put me a little closer to the girl in the *ao-dai.* The officer of the day the previous night was the S-5, Lt. Bill Thomas. Since this would be my first night as O.D. I was dependent on his advice about what to do in this or that situation. I walked across the dusty main road of our compound and into the green plywood box with sandbags on the roof and a red and yellow sign beside the door: "S-5." Thomas was hollering into a field phone, trying to make someone at FLC headquarters understand that the VC had blown up a well in a nearby village the week before and he needed four bags of cement to rebuild it. His assistant was playing blackjack with a buddy on the other side of the room. I turned a quick glance at the only remaining corner of the stale dusty room and almost fell over. There she was! The girl I had seen gliding through the heat waves two days before! I couldn't believe it and I couldn't stop staring. I felt a deep blush coming over my face. She was bent over a pile of papers and did not look up when I walked in.

Without dancing *ao-dai,* swishing hair, bobbing parasol, and heat waves she didn't look the same. The magic was gone and she was reduced to mere humanity. Now that she was sitting still I could see the details that were blurred in that magical vision on the hot dusty road a few days before. Her hair was black silk, absolute silk. Her skin was a soft light brown. The cheekbones were high and prominent, the eyes like almonds, the nose tiny and flat. She had long fingernails, longer than any I had ever seen, and they grew out of long delicate fingers. And under the deep purple *ao-dai* she wore today she looked so thin. But she won't stay that way, I figured, after I start sneaking steaks out of the mess hall for her.

"Well, here he is—the newest new guy in the war!" Thomas bellowed, breaking my concentration on the girl in the corner.

"Did you get your cement?" I asked.

"Not yet, but I will. Shit, I know these damn phone lines are bad around here but that turd over there at Flick, every time I ask for something he doesn't want to give me, he pretends the goddam line goes dead." Thomas turned quickly to the girl in the corner. "Ah, sorry about that, Thanh. Please pardon my French, eh?"

"I know that no French. If you no stop, I tell you mother," said the woman. She still didn't look up from her paperwork.

"If you do that, I'll fire you and then you'll have to go work for the VC," Thomas teased. "How do you like that?"

"I no like. I hate VC!" At last she looked up at Thomas. Her face was delicate and warm, and she spoke through a half-smile. "I do this to VC!" She extended a hand toward her boss and made a gouging motion with her very long fingernails.

"Okay, okay,—you can stay, you can stay! We don't want the VC to lose it all in one day! Hey, Thanh, I want you to meet the newest brown-bar in the war. He's so new he doesn't even have a nameplate yet. Chuck, this is Nguyen Thi Thanh, the best translator/interpreter in Eye Corps."

"Hello, Lieutenan'. How you like Vietnam hot weather?"

"Hello, Miss Thanh. Yes, it is pretty hot here, but I'll get used to it soon enough." Conversation wasn't as good as contact but it was a start. Thomas broke my gaze at his interpreter.

"By the way, what brings you to my modest domain?"

"What? Oh . . . I got this duty roster from the adjutant and I'm the O.D. tonight. He said you could tell me what to do."

"Oh yeah, yeah. I was the sheriff last night. Well, I'll tell you what. It's almost five-thirty anyway, so why don't we grab some chow and I'll fill you in. There isn't much to it." As Thomas walked out from behind his desk, Miss Thanh gave her boss his last piece of advice for the day.

"Lieutenan' Thomas, don' eat too much garbage from mess hall or you get fat like pigs in village and I don' know you anymore!" Thomas walked back to his interpreter's desk and gave her a light poke in the side as he answered.

"And if you get any skinnier from all that VC food you eat, you're gonna blow right away in the next typhoon!" Thomas left his interpreter laughing and rejoined me on the road. "I tease her all the time about the VC but she's a damn good interpreter, damn good."

"Doesn't she eat in our mess hall?" I asked.

"Only at noon. My driver takes her home at six every day."

"Oh," I said. Thwarted again! Meeting that interpreter anywhere but in her office was obviously not going to be a snap. The colonel was making it as difficult as possible. I consoled myself with the thought that time, at least, was on my side: I was still in my first week in Vietnam.

The orders relating to officer of the day made the job sound impressive. I was directed to "represent and exercise" the command of the colonel himself. I was to wear a .45-caliber pistol and I was issued one round, which I should be prepared to use to maintain order. I had access to every building in the compound and the power to open, close, or search anything. I could admit anyone to the compound or expel anyone from it. I could even put people in the brig if I deemed it necessary. And if the worst came to pass—an attack on the compound—I was charged with mobilizing the entire battalion for defense. That's pretty heady stuff for a lowly second lieutenant, and I strapped on my .45 with a heavy awareness of my responsibilities.

It soon became apparent, however, that the letter and the reality of my duties were two different things. Should I actually attempt to exercise my colonel's authority, I would quickly be countermanded and criticized, if not punished, for my precocity. If I fired the one bullet I carried, I had better have something to show for it, something like a dead VC, or I would be court-martialed. And if I received warning of an imminent enemy attack I had to hand-deliver the message to the colonel and stand aside. Every two hours I toured the compound to make sure noise levels from the clubs didn't get too outrageous, and then made log entries to that effect: "0200—Toured compound: all secure." Between rounds I dozed in the musty command bunker while two radiomen studied pornographic magazines against a backdrop of hissing receivers. As the humid night wore on, it became obvious that being O.D. was more irritating than demanding. By the time dawn turned the compound pink I felt very clearly the result of my tour as sheriff: lost sleep and nothing else.

After a morning snooze, I resumed my search for a way to meet the girl in the *ao-dai.* I intercepted Thomas on his way to the mess hall. "How did it go last night?" he asked.

"Too quiet to believe," I said. "Doesn't anything happen around here?"

"Sometimes it does . . . sometimes it does. Just wait awhile. Going to chow?"

Over a Spam and potato salad lunch I tried to maneuver the conversation around to Thomas's interpreter, who was sitting at a table across the dining hall with the other two interpreters. "Don't you sit with Miss Thanh?"

He turned a surprised look on me. "Hell no!"

"Why not?" I asked.

"If anybody shows any interest in any of the women, he gets a message from the colonel by way of the adjutant, namely, to forget the women and do your job. That don't bother me much, though, since I see her all day."

"How does anybody else talk to her?" I asked.

"They don't, unless they got business with S-5, and then they go through me. Why, you wanna talk to her?"

"Hell, yeah," I said. "The first time I saw her I just about fell over."

Thomas looked at me and gave a sarcastic little laugh. "Heh, heh—don't get any ideas, Chuck. She's not that kind of girl. Maybe some of the hooch-maids will go behind the supply shed with you, but not my interpreter, I'll guarantee you that."

"Well, I didn't say that. I just wanna talk to her . . . find out about her country and herself," I explained.

"Ha, ha, that's what they all say. . . . Well, maybe you're right; you haven't been here long enough to get horny. You can always come over to my office. She's there most of the time, and the colonel never comes around."

"Thanks. I'll do that first chance I get."

"By the way, her name's not 'Miss Thanh,' like you said the

other day. The Vietnamese say their last name first and their first name last, so it's actually 'Miss Nguyen.' Sounds backwards to us, but that's the way they do it."

"I didn't know that."

"Yeah, and a lotta other things are backwards in this country, too, you'll soon learn."

On the way back to his office Thomas got another idea. "Oh, there's another way you can talk to Thanh. Why don't you go out with us on a MEDCAP next Thursday? We'll be going to a vill about five miles down the road. You can see what we do."

"Great. I'd like to see it."

"Make sure you check with your CO first. And bring your camera if you want."

Our MEDCAP convoy formed up at eleven in the morning on the scheduled day: one jeep and the only ambulance truck in the battalion. Seven people were jammed into the two small vehicles: Thomas, his assistant, his interpreter, a navy medical corpsman, two riflemen, and I. As we began to move out the gate, Thomas turned to me from the front seat of his jeep. "We're going to one of our friendly vills today so we got only two riflemen. When we go to one of our bad ones we take ten or twelve," he explained.

"Did you ever get ambushed in one of the vills?" I asked.

"No, not yet. But we can't take a chance. The VC would love to get ahold of that ambulance and the medicine inside. And the corpsman, of course." Without thinking, I moved a hand to the .45 on my right hip. The handle felt comforting but I felt unprepared when I remembered that I had not been on a firing range for over two months. I'd much rather shoot with my camera today than my pistol.

It was hard to think of the possibility of danger during the five-mile ride. We breezed down the American-built two-lane blacktop just as if we were going down a quiet country road back in the States. We met few other trucks or jeeps. We passed a few Vietnamese farmers pulling carts or carrying loads on shoulder poles along the side of the road. The sun glinted off wet rice paddies, dark green hills rose amid light green bamboo stands, and in the distance the dark blue ranges of the Annamese Cordillera stood immovable. The sun shone bright from a cloudless sky and it seemed a perfect day for a picnic. Thanh the interpreter sat next to me and all I needed was a bottle of wine, a blanket and . . .

BRRRRAAAMMM! I leaned out my side of the jeep and tried to grab everything at once—my helmet, my pistol, the jeep. No small-arms fire followed so I allowed myself the cautious hope that we might not be getting ambushed. "What the hell was that?" I yelled, as Thomas turned around, smiling. Thanh was actually laughing.

"Relax! That was one of ours. There's a one-seven-five battery back across the road. They fire for the grunts in the hills at the end of this valley."

I looked back and saw the long barrel of a 175-mm cannon swing below a low hill a couple of hundred meters off the road. "They got any earplugs in supply?" I asked.

"You'll get used to it," Thomas said with a laugh.

My nerves were still jumping when we slowed and turned off the road onto a one-lane dirt path overgrown with weeds up past the hubcaps. The farther we went, the closer the bamboo and bushes moved to the path. After we had gone about a hundred meters the branches were slapping against the sides of the vehicles and I was thinking about an ambush again. It was a perfect place. We would have no warning at all since we could barely see ten feet into the thick growth all around. But once again my thoughts were the exaggerated fears of a new guy. We drove into a broad clearing and stopped. "We leave the vehicles here and walk a ways," Thomas explained.

We set out across the clearing in patrol formation: riflemen front and rear, the rest of us in between. We took a narrow path into another thickly wooded area. The tangled growth was deep, dark, and cool, and I considered reviving my fear of ambush. But no one else shared my concern—they were talking as if on a school outing. After following the winding trail for about fifty meters we could see we were coming to another clear area.

We rounded the last bend in the trail and . . . stepped back into the Bronze Age. A small stream meandered across the clearing. We began to cross it on a small footbridge. "Me and my assistant laid this bridge a couple months ago," said Thomas with a note of pride. On the far side of the clearing, nestled among bamboo and broadleaf banana trees, were several buildings. They were the first Vietnamese-made structures I had ever seen. The walls were made of crisscrossed bamboo and wide leaves. Thatch on the roofs hung low over corners and doorways. Three of the structures appeared to be homes. A fourth, off by itself, seemed to be the Vietnamese version of a barn. Standing in it, and obviously capable of knocking it over, was a huge water buffalo lazily chewing, and swishing a thick tail at the flies on its flanks.

We walked the rest of the way across the clearing to the tree line, the buffalo staring at us all the way. I approached the nearest house and saw my first villager of the day, an ancient woman with lips stained red from the betel she was chewing. She gazed through me with a resigned look, as if I were just another being her fate had brought before her. I stepped up to a door frame and looked in. Instead of a concrete or linoleum floor there was hard-packed earth. In the middle of the room was a crude wooden table and three stools. A sheet of loosely woven split bamboo partitioned off a sleeping platform from the rest of the house. The whole structure was smaller than a one-car garage. There was no sofa, no lounge chairs, no thick carpeting, no television, no air conditioner, no telephone, no shining porcelain bathroom, no car in the driveway, no driveway, no running water, no electricity, and very little glass or metal. There was also none of the noise one associates with civilization—no honking horns, no blaring loudspeakers, no Muzak, no how's-business chatter.

The whole scene was, it was . . . the right word did not come quickly. It was like something out of a Walt Disney production on primitive life. Primeval seemed the most appropriate term. The only thing missing was the tense music Hollywood throws in when the hero stumbles onto the last thing he is ready for. "It's a different world, isn't it?" Thomas said from behind me.

"Completely different, completely."

The corpsman went into one of the other houses and set up a makeshift clinic on the family's only table. The word filtered down dark trails and into more bamboo houses, and by some signal that I missed completely, mothers appeared, bringing their babies to the Western doctor. Most of the ailments resulted from ignorance of basic hygiene and could be treated in a few minutes: things like open sores and fevers. The nineteen-year-old "doctor" cleaned and bandaged the sores, gave a few shots, and passed out water purification tablets and bars of soap. Thanh explained to each mother how to use whatever the corpsman had given, and Thomas summarized his experience to date. "These women always say they understand but they keep coming back with the same problems. Sometimes I think soap and water tablets are against their religion, or something. Or else they're giving the stuff to the VC. Who knows?"

One woman did not bring a baby to the doctor. When her turn came, she opened her blouse, held a flaccid breast in his face, and said something in a complaining tone. Surprised and amused, the corpsman turned to Thanh for a translation. Surprised and blushing deeply, Thanh translated. The woman said she didn't have enough milk for her babies. "Tell her to drink more milk and stop chewing betel," said the corpsman.

"She say she has no milk to drink."

Thomas overheard and intervened. "Okay, tell her we'll bring some out next week. Corporal Farquar, make a note of that—powdered milk for Hoa Lam Two."

When the corpsman had worked his way through the line of patients Thomas gave the word. "Okay, let's go."

"Are we going back already?" I asked, hoping to see more of this premodern village surviving in the twentieth century.

"No, not yet. To the next hamlet. We gotta walk across some paddy to get to it," said Thomas. Villages in Vietnam are obviously not the same as villages in the U.S. Though the population was usually the same—less than five thousand in most cases—the layout of the Vietnamese village is much different from its Western counterpart. In Vietnam one village consists of several hamlets separated by expanses of paddy fields. While the residents of each hamlet know each other well, they are not as familiar with those in other hamlets, though they might be less than a mile apart. Adults in each hamlet choose a chief, and the hamlet chiefs meet periodically to select a village council and a village chief, and deal with local issues. In traditional Vietnam the village was the smallest administrative unit the emperor and his advisors dealt with, not the family or individual.

There were four hamlets in this village of Hoa Lam, distinguished by the numbers one through four. "Next is Hoa Lam Three," said Thomas. We walked single file on a narrow dike. Wet paddies, recently harvested, stretched half a mile or more away on each side. After walking a few hundred meters we passed a small wooded rise standing alone in the sea of paddy. The sounds of chanting, drums, and bells came from the thickly grown hill. No people or buildings were visible. "There's a temple over in those trees," said Thomas.

"Maybe funeral today," said Thanh.

In Hoa Lam Three I saw my first Vietnamese livestock. The pigs were skinny, hairless, and their distended bellies nearly dragged on the ground. "Some people call them pigs but I call them walking bags of tapeworms," said Thomas. The chickens were also skinny and had very few feathers. "The people here claim these chickens give eggs but I don't see how. Pulling eggs out of those chickens looks about as easy as pulling a grapefruit through a garden hose," said Thomas.

The corpsman set up and the mothers brought their babies out of the woods again. The people here looked worse than those back in Hoa Lam Two. They were skinnier and the children were sallow-faced and had distended bellies. "What you're seeing here," said Thomas, "is what I call the Hoa Lam equation in action. Chickens suffering from malnutrition plus pigs full of tapeworms equals people suffering from malnutrition and tapeworms."

I had seen enough to think of several questions. "What did these people do when they got sick years ago, before there were any Americans or MEDCAPs here?"

"Just died, I guess," said Thomas.

"But didn't they go into Da Nang to a hospital?"

"Oh no, definitely not. These farmers never went into Da Nang. Still don't if they can help it."

"But it's only about ten miles and if they're really sick . . ." I persisted in what was to me a logical line of reasoning.

"They don't want to go into Da Nang for any reason, even if they're dying. They figure if they leave the village they lose contact with their ancestors and the spirits of the land, and they believe that's worse than being sick. They want to spend their whole life right in their hamlet, just this little area here and the paddies you see there. This is it. This is their entire world. Hard to believe, isn't it?"

I stood there staring. The idea of spending one's entire lifetime—anywhere from five to eight decades—in an area of less than one square mile struck me speechless.

Thanh changed the subject by asking me to come over to the side of one of the houses. Walking under a curtain of broad banana leaves we saw a woman squatting between a pot full of rice and a pile of large green leaves. She lay a leaf on the ground before her, put a handful of rice in the middle of it, then rolled the leaf into a cylinder and tied the loose ends with long blades of grass. "Is she making our lunch?" I asked.

"Don't you wish!" said Thomas. "This isn't just an ordinary lunch she's making. It's something special."

"She cook rice slowly in ground," said Thanh.

"Sorta like a luau," said Thomas. "Must be some big feast tonight. Maybe there's a wedding or a funeral," Thomas paused, "or a VC convention, eh Thanh?"

"Don't say!" said Thanh in a loud whisper.

"A VC convention?" I asked in surprise. "How do you know?"

"I don't," admitted Thomas, a sardonic smile on his face.

"You said this is a friendly vill, didn't you?" I reminded him.

"Right. We rate a vill friendly if they don't shoot at us and if they talk to us."

"Oh," I said. My face didn't register any profound understanding, so Thomas continued.

"You see, the point is that they've got plenty of rice, as you can see right there, but they've got people starving, the ones back with the doc now."

"Then we've got another Hoa Lam equation," I said. "Starving peasants plus plenty of rice equals a VC supply operation."

"Very possible . . . very possible," said Thomas. "Well, the doc must be about finished. Let's head back."

Throughout the time we were watching her and talking, the woman rolling rice in leaves never looked up at us.

Back at the makeshift clinic the doc was trying to communicate with an hysterical Vietnamese woman. The American was pointing toward Da Nang and saying "Only a few days, lady," and the woman was pacing back and forth in front of him waving both arms and wailing through a toothless mouth.

"Thanh, find out what's going on, would you, please?" asked Thomas. On seeing our interpreter, the woman turned away from the uncomprehending corpsman and poured out her story with even more gesticulating. The woman's teenage daughter had a high fever and the corpsman recommended she go to a navy hospital for the necessary tests and treatment. To the corpsman it was the professional and humanitarian thing to do, but the girl's mother would have none of it. "See? Just like I was telling you. They don't wanna leave their home village for anything," said Thomas to me.

"Lieutenant Thomas, that girl's in bad shape. Her temp's over 101 and she's damn near dehydrated. She needs some transfusions bad, and if she don't get 'em, she'll be dead in a few days, maybe tomorrow," said the corspman.

"Okay, here's what we'll do," said Thomas. "We'll go back to Hoa Lam Two and find the chief. He'll be able to get the girl out of her house."

Back at Hoa Lam Two Thanh asked a betel-chewing, baby-suckling mother to get the village chief. Once again the word went down dark trails and the chief appeared in a few minutes. He was the first Vietnamese man of working age we had seen all day, another fact that called into question the loyalty of the village. He was dressed in the South Vietnamese Army uniform and wore an American .38-caliber revolver on his hip. After the gun, the first thing I noticed was the nails on his little fingers: they were over an inch long. On other fingers he had half a dozen rings. He smiled broadly and shook hands with Thomas, who then asked Thanh to explain our problem with the feverish girl's mother. While she did, Thomas turned to me. "This is Major Long. He's actually the assistant village chief. The elected chief is an old farmer, about seventy-five years old. He's more a figurehead. Major Long here is the real power."

As soon as he had heard the situation, Major Long called a young boy out of a nearby house and sent him running down a trail. Thanh explained that the chief had sent the boy to get the sick girl with orders to the mother not to interfere. Then the chief broke into a broad smile again and said something to Thanh who turned to us. "Chief invite us."

"Okay, here we go," said Thomas with a grin. "This is the good part. I hope you got a strong stomach."

We walked into the nearest house—the chief apparently had the run of any house in the village—and sat around a crude wooden table. The chief clapped his hands and barked an order toward the back door. Soon an old barefoot woman appeared with a pitcher and four glasses on a tray. As she set the tray down I read a message from another world: "Seven-Up—You Like It, It Likes You." Apparently some of the villagers get into the big city, or American bases, more often than Thomas led me to believe with his they-don't-like-to-leave-the-hometown explanation.

The chief poured a round of clear liquid. "The local rice wine," Thomas explained. We raised our glasses in a toast. As we did, the sunlight from the doorway came through my glass and I noticed a variety of foreign objects suspended in the wine. It tasted oily in the mouth and started a fire in the stomach. The chief downed his glassful in two quick gulps, but I couldn't bring myself to follow his example. I kept looking at those floating particles and wondered what they would do to my insides. The chief poured himself another glass and urged Thomas and me to drink more.

After the chief had gulped several more glasses, the messenger stuck his head in the doorway and reported to the chief. He had brought the sick girl as directed but the mother had come along and was objecting more loudly than before. The chief, more than tipsy by now, went out to meet the distraught mother. What followed was a mad scene of tradition crashing into modern medical necessity and government authority, with plenty of emotional display. The mother made her arm-waving, wailing plea; the chief barked something in her face and tried to wave her away. The mother dropped to her knees on the bare earth and begged for a reversal of the corpsman's recommendation; the tottering chief raised his volume and his arm in a threatening gesture. The confrontation dragged on in the hot sun until the chief said something to Thanh in a drunken slur. "Chief say we can take girl, don't worry about mother."

"Okay, let's take the girl out of here before mother gets any worse or the chief gets any drunker," said Thomas. Back on the main road, Thomas turned around in his jeep seat. "How do you like that rice wine?"

"I didn't drink much but my head's really spinning."

"It can be strong, especially the first time."

"What was all that garbage floating in it?" I asked.

"I don't know but you can see why we call it rotgut. The first time I tried it I had a whole glass and barfed it up ten minutes later," said Thomas.

A week later the girl had recovered and Thomas took her back to Hoa Lam. The doctors who treated the girl attributed her recovery to the wonders of modern medical science. The girl's mother, this time crying tears of joy at seeing her daughter, attributed recovery to her own daily recitation of Buddhist chants before the family altar. Thomas didn't dare declare one side right and the other wrong. He simply chalked it up as another S-5 success and put it in his monthly report.

My first visit to a Vietnamese village was very educational and much appreciated. I looked forward to more, and if such jaunts never led to any closer relationship with Thanh, that was all right with me. At least they got me away from the compound and its dull routine for a couple of hours. But I still wondered why Thomas had never made any move for her. Abstention must have been more difficult for him; he saw her at close range every day. One day I got tired of wondering and asked outside his hooch. "Impossible," he said without hesitation.

"Why?" I asked.

"First of all, like I told you, she's not that kind of girl."

"Yeah, but you never know—you just might fit her definition of the right guy," I said.

"And secondly, she's not a Miss," he said, very matter-of-factly.

"What?" I was dumbfounded. "But she . . . I mean everybody calls her Miss Nguyen."

"That's just her name here in the compound, on the job," he explained. Thomas proceeded to tell me what he knew about Thanh. She was very married—six kids' worth! Her husband was in the South Vietnamese Army and she hadn't seen him in over three years. She lived with her mother and a sister who had three children of her own. The sister's husband was more responsible than Thanh's: he contributed some of his army pay to his family. The sister was not an interpreter, though she could speak some English. Her main job was running the laundry and souvenir shop inside our compound. So the two sisters were supporting a total of twelve people. I stood there in the late afternoon heat, sweating and wondering how two young mothers could support twelve people in the midst of war without resorting to the world's oldest profession. "You surprised? Disappointed?" asked Thomas.

"Surprised, yes. Disappointed, no. Actually it's pretty impressive when you think about it—she and her sister raising all those kids and not taking in any, ah, outside work with us horny GIs."

"Yeah, it is. She's lucky she learned English so well," said Thomas. "That's the key, since we're here."

The question of intimacies settled once and for all, I formulated a different image of Thanh the interpreter. She became for me an interpreter not only of languages but of her entire Vietnamese culture. There were more MEDCAPs, more fifteen- and twenty-minute sessions in her office after lunch. I asked why the Vietnamese, despite centuries of Chinese influence, do not write with Chinese ideographs and learned that French missionaries introduced the Roman alphabet in the nineteenth century. I asked why the Vietnamese keep their own houses so immaculate but throw garbage anywhere outside, and learned they feel no obligation to show any concern for areas that were not handed down from their ancestors. The Vietnamese also make the same type of distinction in their interpersonal relations: people from other villages are viewed as the enemy.

She also taught me to see differences between types of Vietnamese. The difference between country and city people was obvious to anyone since it was virtually the same as the difference between barely surviving and being almost comfortable, but other differences were not so obvious. Northern and southern Vietnamese were much different through the eyes of each other, northerners being more ambitious, pragmatic, and direct in communication; southerners being more easygoing and emotional. There were also many differences—physical, conceptual, and linguistic—between Vietnamese of different provinces, and sometimes between people living in villages only twenty miles apart. All of such differences carried significance to the Vietnamese, and a knowledge of them would have enabled Americans to deal much more effectively with the Vietnamese. Most Americans, however, were completely blind and deaf to them.

After I had been asking questions for a few days, Thanh started asking her own. Most of hers concerned the American standard of living. What little she knew about American life had come from magazines, movies, and comments from Thomas and others in the battalion. She heard that each American family has "many" houses and cars and wanted confirmation. After I straightened her out about that, she wanted to know if Americans, like Vietnamese, had to carry government ID cards, if it was true Americans could change jobs and residences anytime they wanted, the ages of my parents, and the name of the church we attended.

But not all of Thanh's questions were so naive or gentle. She asked some pointed ones, too, and they helped fill in the story of what I was seeing in the villages. Her sharpest comments were about the mismanaged American aid program. "Don't you know President Thieu he take all best thing and many dollar for ownself and family, then province chief he take all best thing and many dollar after that, then village chief he take all best thing and many dollar, then nothing left for people and Vietnam stay poor? Don't American know how that custom work? Why don't American president stop that custom? He should make President Thieu and province chief and village chief to quit that custom. He should make only American to give money and rice and new house to people. Now Vietnamese people we think President Thieu he make fool of American."

After hearing that, I had to ask if there was anything we Americans were doing right. "Oh yes, you do many good thing for my country. You teach us many thing in school, on base, in hospital, how to do in office like this. Many thing we don't know before you come Vietnam. Vietnamese people we like American man like you very much. You are kind, have big heart, big smile, give us so many thing. We like American very much.

"But we know you don't understand Vietnam history and custom. You try give us democracy but we never know democracy. We never had before but you have long time in America. We always have emperor in Hue City, he control all thing in Vietnam. And every province and every village have small emperor who control all thing. Common people in village never say no to village chief, never vote anything. Village chief he is like small emperor, even like god in village. People never ask question, never say no. I think you American never understand that way. Maybe Vietnamese never understand democracy. But we like American very much, we like big heart American."

So that was it—the old too-much-enthusiasm-and-too-little-expertise story. We were twentieth-century crusaders, and mostly blind crusaders at that. Painful as they were, such sessions with Thanh showed me why the numbers coming out of the computers in the command centers in Saigon and the Pentagon were not adding up to an American victory or, at least, an end to the fighting.

Thanh also introduced me to the most shameful facet of the American involvement in Vietnam, the side of the war that never made it on the evening news. The unmentioned result of sending over two and a half million Americans to Vietnam without wives was several hundred thousand illegitimate children. Very few fathers of such children acknowledged and helped support them. Most fathers simply deserted by following their transfer orders back to the States. Mothers left with mixed-blood illegitimate children were usually ill-equipped to support young children—the only job "skills" most had were those required by bar hostesses and prostitutes. More devastating was the humiliation and discrimination to which unmarried mothers and their illegitimate offspring were subjected. Children born of white or black Western men and Vietnamese women stand out in a Vietnamese crowd. They are immediately noticed, pointed at, and gossiped about for their "strange" looks, and rejected for their racial "impurity." Their mothers are shunned for prostituting themselves to foreign soldiers. Under such severe social pressure many mothers abandoned their children, and every Vietnamese city had its colony of mixed-blood orphans living in the streets.

Our jeep wound its way down a narrow street, trying to avoid the deepest potholes. Motorcycles putt-putted past, raising dust from the unpaved street glaring in the Sunday afternoon sun, dust that never seemed to settle back down. The jeep driver and I were the only Americans on the street. Thanh sat in the back seat shielding her face against the dust with the front flap of her *ao-dai.* Thomas wasn't with us today. This part of town was off limits to Americans and he knew the colonel would never believe he had lost his way if army MPs stopped him and sent a report back to 3d MPs. But I was still new enough to use that excuse if I had to, so he had encouraged Thanh to show me around.

The tallest building on the street was a Catholic church, a large concrete structure painted yellow. The bell tower held a white cross sixty feet above the roofs of the neighborhood. We stopped in front of the church, looked at it awhile, then turned into an iron gate on the opposite side of the street. The gate was topped by a sign in Vietnamese. We drove into a courtyard and parked beside a statue of the Virgin Mary. "Many children living here," said Thanh. "Have no mother and father."

A nun came out of an office next to the gate and greeted Thanh. She was a large white woman wearing rimless glasses and a perpetual smile. She spoke Vietnamese well enough for Thanh to understand. I was thinking how uncomfortable she must be in this heat under her full-length black nun's habit when she turned to me and switched to English. "Welcome, Lieutenant. The children will be glad to see a new friend."

"Thank you. I didn't know about your, ah, facility here until today."

"Yes, we haven't seen you before. We have been here a long time."

"Oh, I see."

"Look at anything you like while you're here. And come to my office before you leave."

"Thank you. I hope we're not interrupting anything."

"No, no. Today is Sunday, our day of rest," said the nun.

I followed Thanh through a doorway in the concrete enclosing the courtyard. The long narrow room was full of metal GI-style bunk beds, and each bed was full of children. No bed had less than four children. They were all sizes and colors and seemed to range in age from about two to seventeen. Most had been fathered by white Americans but there was no lack of black skin, and the features of some suggested Mexican fathers. A few were sleeping and a couple were crying but most were just lying on the dirty mattresses, staring blankly through the heat and occasionally raising a hand to chase a fly away from the face. Few of the children noticed when we walked in and only one did anything about our presence. A boy about seven years old walked over to me warily, reached out and pulled the hair on my arm, then ran squealing back to his bunkmates to report on the hirsute character of Westerners. "How do you think?" asked Thanh.

"Well, ah, I don't know. I never knew about this before. How many children are living here?" I asked.

"More than three hundred," said Thanh.

So here it is, another kind of body count. More than three hundred. Most Americans in Vietnam were interested in the body count of dead enemy troops. But here was another kind of body count produced by Americans, a body count of the living, not the dead. The living and the rejected—rejected by all the world except a handful of French Catholic priests and nuns.

We walked through more dormitory rooms full of dirty beds overflowing with orphans. All looked the same: dirty floors, paint peeling off concrete walls, small green lizards running across the ceilings, broken fan collecting spider webs in a corner. I started counting rooms and beds but soon lost count. The last bedroom we went through was full of cribs. Here the youngest orphans were cared for after being picked up wherever they were abandoned in the city. Sometimes the nuns didn't have to go through the city to find new orphans. Many had been abandoned outside the gate at night and discovered the next morning.

A small room with an open fire in one corner and a washbasin in another was identified as the kitchen. Over the fire was a cauldron full of a thin oily soup. On another side of the courtyard were three rooms full of wooden benches and chairs. These were the classrooms where orphans were taught how to read, write, and count. They also learned about Christianity and how the French Catholics had come to Vietnam. At the front of each classroom, above the teacher's podium, was a crucifix.

The big smiling nun came out of her office again as we walked toward the jeep. This time she focused all her attention on me. With a pleading expression on her face she asked me to please come back often and please bring whatever food, blankets, wood, and cement I could spare or scrounge. "You Americans have so much . . . you have a car to carry things. Perhaps you could bring some of the things we need . . . for the children . . . for the children. . . ."

I returned to the orphanage several times but was never able to bring any of the supplies the nuns asked for. Orphanages sponsored by private or religious groups were ineligible for U.S. government appropriations, and assistance from uniformed personnel was not encouraged. All I could do was contribute a few dollars of my own money and try to make a few orphans smile through their misery. It would be nice to believe the orphans remember me and my concern, but they probably have had more than enough problems to block out any memories of visiting Americans, in the years since I met them. By their appearance alone, they are reminders of years of war and suffering, most unwelcome reminders. And as for the postwar Vietnamese regime, I suspect that discrimination in the streets is stronger than Marxist preachings about equality among the workers.

After the village and the orphange, Thanh introduced me to her own family history. The lesson began in what I thought an unlikely way. At the end of one of our noon-hour sessions in the S-5 office she abruptly changed the subject with an invitation. "Would you like come to my house Sunday?"

"Would I what? Well, ah, sure, if I'm not busy. I'll check and let you know."

The next time I saw Thomas, I asked him what it meant. I was tempted to conclude her invitation carried the same connotation as if it had come from an attractive single girl back in the States, but felt I should confirm the matter. "You did say Thanh wasn't that kind of girl, didn't you?"

"Sure did," said Thomas. "But don't worry about it. Just go and consider it a ticket out of Colonel Palooka's concentration camp for a day."

Once again I was heading for an off limits area, and a credible cover story had to be arranged. We decided to say we were going to the Da Nang MARS station to call our families back in the World.

After a long hot ride down streets paved in potholes, our jeep stopped in front of an alley. At the corner of the alley and the street was a wooden booth with sandbags piled around the bottom. The booth could have been a lemonade stand back in the States except that the two teenage boys inside were wearing flak jackets and helmets and holding rifles. Above the booth a banner waved in the breeze. "What does it say?" I asked.

"It mean we hate VC—VC not come in this place," said Thanh.

Unknown to me, the driver had made other plans for the day. When he did not get out with Thanh and me, I asked why. He smiled and said he was meeting someone downtown. "I'll pick you up here at five, Lieutenant," he said as he drove away.

As we walked down the alley I collected an entourage of neighborhood kids, all squealing about the oversize green foreigner who had just arrived. Most sneaked up from behind and pulled the hair on my arms. I made the mistake of picking one kid up over my head. Every other one in the neighborhood immediately and loudly demanded the same treatment, and I had to pick up over twenty young squealers. Every house in this neighborhood had a concrete wall around it about five feet high, so it was difficult to see any more than red tile roofs. Broken glass and rusty barbed wire were set into the top of each wall, giving a forbidding appearance to the whole area, at least to my mind, which associated walls with medieval castles. We had to squeeze through Thanh's gate to make sure none of the uninvited, demanding another lift into the atmosphere over my head, came in.

The last person I expected to see came out to meet us. "Have trouble finding the place?" said Thomas, a pronounced slur in his voice.

"What are you doing here?" I asked. "Thought you were too busy today."

"I am. But I found another driver anxious for an excuse to get out of the compound, and besides, I didn't think you two would mind a chaperon."

"How gallant of you," I said. "Where's your driver?"

"Probably the same place as yours—getting the pipes and pores cleaned out in some steam bath downtown."

"But we're too proper for such base activities, aren't we?" I said.

"You know what they say—enlisted men have all the fun! But Thanh's got some good stuff here," said Thomas, raising his glass. "Come on in and try it."

We walked across a small concrete courtyard, under a shade roof, and into a house that looked more Spanish than Vietnamese. The walls were concrete or stucco painted white, and strings of beads served as doors. I would not have been surprised to hear guitar music coming from inside. We sat in low chairs around a low table. Thanh reached into a cabinet for another glass. Thomas reached into an ice bucket, clinked another cube into his glass, pulled a bottle of Johnnie Walker Black off the floor and splashed in another shot. "Help yourself," he said, pushing the ice and bottle toward me. Piled on the table beside the ice were several copies of *House Beautiful* dated three years before and more recent issues of *Life* and *Playboy*. Thomas and I had obviously been preceded by other Americans.

This was the first time I had had a mixed drink in mixed company since I had left the States four months before and it was obvious to Thomas. "Sit back and relax," he urged. "You can forget all about 3d MPs here."

"I think I forgot how to relax," I said. "But I'll sure try."

A group of curious children gathered around the doorway and Thomas asked for introductions. They turned out to be the five youngest of Thanh and her sister. The older brothers and sisters were out playing in the neighborhood with friends or studying. A time-out was called and we stepped outside to take pictures of the clowning kids.

The company, whiskey, and sense of freedom soon combined to create an unmilitary atmosphere, though two of us were in uniform. With no regulation or person to discourage me I began asking Thanh about who she really was and how she had come to be an interpreter in 3d MPs. The more she talked, the more I learned what the word "war" meant to her. For most of the time we Americans had been aware of it, the war was a faraway event we had read about in the papers back in the World. Even now in Vietnam the war was not always close to us. We were in the rear, insulated from its most brutal effects, and unless we were wounded or killed, there was no chance our families would be touched by it. But to Thanh, the word "war" meant something completely different. She was not, as I suspected the first time I saw her, above the war. She was very much subject to its influence and her family had already been touched by it very heavily.

To us Americans listening to Thanh's story the war had begun a few months ago when we were flown into it, and it would end a few months later when we would be flown out of it. But to Thanh's family the war had begun back in the 1920s and the end was not yet in sight. Thanh's father had been one of several hundred Vietnamese the French had exposed to a smattering of education and then denied the chance to use it. He had attended Catholic mission schools for seven or eight years, enough time to learn about the French Revolution and its ideology of liberty, equality, and fraternity. As soon as his formal schooling ended, he learned that such ideas were for Frenchmen only. He and many fellow Vietnamese were qualified for a wide range of jobs in the French colonial administration, and they could have formed the nucleus of a Vietnamese administration capable of making a smooth transition from a colonial to a post-colonial government without the disastrous two and a half decades of war that resulted. But the French couldn't bring themselves to think of Vietnamese as any more than servants. They persisted in reserving responsible jobs for adventurers and ne'er-do-wells from the lower rungs of French society. Thanh's father and his colleagues then took the only route open for men of education and patriotism. They joined the Vietnamese nationalist movement. Throughout the 1920s and 1930s the French were beset by strikes and acts of sabotage, several of which Thanh's father had helped organize and lead. He was jailed on several occasions and blacklisted by French factory and plantation owners. His career and health ruined by years of harassment and maltreatment by first the French and then the Japanese, he died shortly after the end of World War II.

Thanh was born in 1938 or 1939, she wasn't sure which, and maybe it was neither of those years, for on at least one document 1943 is the year given for her birth. But of the place she was certain—a village in the Red River Valley between the port of Haiphong and the city of Hanoi, one of the most heavily Catholic areas in Asia. She attended mission schools and learned French. From her father she learned to hate the French, but Vietnamese society prescribed very different roles for women and men. While still a high school student, Thanh was engaged to a man she had never seen. Her reaction to this development was surprisingly docile by Western standards. "If I were a man I would have fought against French like my father. But I am only a woman so I had to marry."

Shortly after her engagement the Indochina War came to a climax that interrupted both her education and marriage plans. Ho Chi Minh defeated the French at Dien Bien Phu in 1954, Vietnam was partitioned into a communist northern and noncommunist southern zone, and the people were allowed to choose which zone they wanted to live in. Thanh's family knew the communist regime in Hanoi would show little tolerance for their Western religion and attitudes about personal freedom, so they left their home village and boarded a refugee ship at Haiphong one night. The next morning they stepped off the ship in Saigon and into an uncertain future. Thanh finished high school in Saigon, then staged her last stand for freedom. She ran away to avoid her arranged marriage. She didn't run far enough, however, and was brought back after a couple of weeks.

At the age of seventeen Nguyen Thi Thanh was married to the

stranger her parents had chosen. As soon as it was physically possible and socially acceptable she became pregnant. Shortly thereafter her husband was drafted into the South Vietnamese Army and sent to an endless series of bases away from his young wife. He came home long enough to either witness the birth of one of his children or make his wife pregnant with the next. Desperate for support, the young mother began taking jobs on American bases, and learned English. By the time I arrived in Vietnam, Thanh had worked a total of twelve years for half a dozen American bases.

I listened in silent amazement as this slight woman across from me told the story of her family. She looked thin and weak but she had proven herself very strong through years of hardship. If I had experienced the dislocation and abuse she had, I expect I would be extremely bitter about the unfairness of life. But Thanh didn't seem bitter at all. What amazed me about her was that she could preserve an air of dignified optimism when all around her was chaos and suffering. Somehow, she could still smile and laugh, and anyone nearby found her attitude contagious. I guess the secret was that she had simply accepted war as part of life, like bad weather and illness, and had adjusted to it.

The first time I saw Thanh gliding through the heat waves on a dusty road, and for years after, I was struck by the great contrast between the clean image and optimistic attitude she maintained and the dirty and painful revolution her country was undergoing. The most accurate analogy to that contrast I can think of would be the sight of a rose blooming in a garbage dump.

There were more sessions with Thanh in my remaining weeks in 3d MPs, not always in a relaxed off-base atmosphere seasoned with whiskey, but always informative of some facet of Vietnam. She had turned out to be a great teacher of her country. She had introduced me to things I would never have learned had I never met her, things every American in Vietnam would have benefited greatly from seeing and knowing. The most memorable lessons, of course, were the village, the orphanage, and her family history. Without Thanh I would never have seen the war through Vietnamese eyes.

8 Just for Laughs

Units like 3d MPs were the models for all the military comedies that have appeared in movies and on television since World War II. In six months we produced enough humor to keep a TV series going for years. Some of that humor had its origin in the numerous forms of competition conducted in the battalion for the purpose of raising morale. But even more humor came from contests designed to satirize those official attempts to raise what many of us felt could not be raised by staying in the rear.

A typical example was the Sweat Stain Contest. All one needed to join was a clean shirt and a mostly normal body. The contest began at seven in the morning, when everyone reported to his office or place of work, and ended when the evening meal began at five-thirty. During those ten and one-half hours contestants used the heat of Vietnam and as much liquid as they could consume to push their sweat glands to the limits of production. The man who at five-thirty had the longest sweat stain stretching downward from the armpit of his shirt was declared winner and Sweater of the Week. First prize was the choice of a free six-pack at the club or first look at the next skin magazine received in the mail room.

Another kind of humor came from the offices in which many of us spent most of our working hours. Almost every day each company and staff section office received a dozen or more memos and directives from any one of several echelons of command between the Pentagon and Da Nang. We always marveled at the way those directives could make the most humdrum aspects of life seem so life-and-death important. What form of life acting on what value system could make one wonder if things like intercommand volleyball tournaments and the disposal of broken broom handles really determined the course of the planets?

A repeating source of humor was that which resulted from the occasional meetings between one of our excess staff sergeants and his company first sergeant. S. Sgt. Mervin Azdale was the only career member of the battalion who retained the athlete's build he had brought to and taken from boot camp more than a decade before. He stood six-three and his two hundred pounds were still distributed in such a way that the lines from his waist to his shoulders described a distinct "V."

Staff Sergeant Azdale had seen two things in his life that impressed him deeply. He saw the first when he was thirteen years old. It was during summer vacation in Philadelphia. He was wandering around his neighborhood looking for ways to kill time when he heard shouts and cheers coming from a building across the street. Just as he walked in, he saw it—a victorious boxer raising his arms overhead to acknowledge the cheers of a small crowd. He had never seen anything like it—dozens of pairs of eyes looking up at the gleaming muscular figure on the shoulders of his handlers in the ring, the whole scene wrapped in continuing shouting and cheering and clapping in approval of the just-finished display of disciplined speed and power. This is glory itself, thought young Mervin Azdale, the cheers of the crowd ringing in his ears, the vision of victory blocking out everything else he had ever seen, and anybody would be a fool not to dedicate himself to finding it. He did not see the defeated boxer lying unconscious and bleeding under the cheering.

That summer the inner-city teenager began preparing himself for the day when he too would receive glory. He trained hard, and for the first few years things went well. He won almost all his fights and he got a big break—an invitation to be a sparring partner for the great light-heavyweight, Hurricane Jackson. Things were falling in place for Mervin Azdale, and he began to think it was possible for him to surpass Hurricane Jackson someday and maybe even become another—there's no law against dreaming, is there?—Sugar Ray Robinson. But then things stopped going his way. His boxing career leveled off into that plateau populated by the ninety-nine boxers out of a hundred who try to make it big but don't. Nights when he heard the crowd cheering his victorious opponent became more frequent.

Mervin Azdale saw the second impressive sight of his life on a dark December afternoon in the twenty-fourth year of his life. He had lost another fight the night before, a loss he had decided would be his last, and was wandering around the neighborhood trying to make something of the few remaining career choices open to him. As he passed the post office, a Marine Corps recruiting poster caught his eye. The dress blue uniform on the stern-faced character in the picture was the most beautiful thing he had ever seen outside the ring—the white hat with the gold insignia, the dark blue coat with the row of medals, the light blue trousers with the red stripe down the outside. But it was the medals, the medals especially—those colorful little ribbons and pieces of bronze and silver which proved one's courage and worth—that he noticed. This guy looks like real class, like a real champ, thought high school dropout Azdale as he stared at the poster. "If I can't be a champ in the ring then I'll at least look like a champ outside the ring, and maybe someday I'll even be a real hero, too," he said to himself. He was ready to sign even before he talked to the recruiting sergeant.

The other half of the humorous situation created by Staff Sergeant Azdale was his company first sergeant. To understand why his first sergeant reacted to Staff Sergeant Azdale the way he did, and why the rest of us thought that reaction was funny, you have to understand a few things about the highest-ranking enlisted man in a company. First sergeants are different from other ranks in the military. For one thing, they are more stern and less given to displays of laughter and friendship than others, at least during working hours. For another, they have a more obvious sense of pride than most others. What they are most proud of is their company office, a collection of five or six clerks, five typewriters, and two file cabinets. In the file cabinets are kept the service record books of all men in the company, and all manuals and directives pertaining to the maintenance of those record books. First sergeants are extremely sensitive about the accuracy of records in their care.

There are three ways to quickly move a first sergeant into the range of anger and to the edge of violence. First, if you are one of his clerks, you can make a mistake on a service record book entry, like putting something about a promotion on the page for disciplinary actions and courts-martial. Second, again if you are one of his clerks, you can come to work hung over, thereby causing your typewriter to make too many spelling mistakes. Third, if you are anyone else, you can come into the company office and question in any way the competence of the first sergeant or the accuracy of work done by his staff.

It was the third of those mistakes that Staff Sergeant Azdale committed repeatedly, though he never did it intentionally. Staff Sergeant Azdale was always on the lookout for another medal to pin on his broad chest. Upon hearing even the vaguest rumor of another award being authorized by Headquarters Marine Corps or any other authority, he would rush to his company office and order one of the clerks to enter it in his record book.

Staff Sergeant Azdale's first sergeant was one Clifton Michaels, a short, thin, and mostly bald man who would not look out of place behind the lectern of a university classroom. A long, thin nose supported a pair of very thick eyeglasses which were replaced no less than once a year; very few mistakes got by his magnified vision.

First Sergeant Michaels was never very receptive to the unsolicited visits of Staff Sergeant Azdale. He saw them as intrusions which threatened to puncture the delicate atmosphere of quiet concentration his clerks needed to do their jobs accurately and efficiently. In the first place, he was completely unwilling to make an entry in a service record book without specific authorization in the form of a Navy or Marine Corps letter from Washington. A rumor from the club or a paragraph from a military magazine or newspaper was not enough. Secondly, the first sergeant saw more than searches for ribbons and medals in Staff Sergeant Azdale's actions. He saw in such actions the implication that he and his clerks were not keeping up to date on the latest directives, and that touched in a painful way the first sergeant's professional pride. Such an implication was unacceptable from any source, but the more so from someone a full two ranks down the hierarchy. Thus, whenever Staff Sergeant Azdale entered the company office and began talking about a new medal, First Sergeant Michaels would react with a demonstration of controlled professional rage and barracks profanity which, to those of us who had been in the Corps less than a year, was nothing less than wondrous. And since anything wondrous was a nice break from the dull routine of life in 3d MPs, someone in the battalion would drop a hint about a new medal in Staff Sergeant Azdale's direction no less than once a month.

The big ex-boxer was never less than bewildered at his first sergeant's angry reaction. He thought he was only claiming something he was already entitled to. "But, First Sergeant, Lieutenant Andrews told me just this morning and I figured he'd know. . . ."

First Sergeant Michaels had a different view of a new lieutenant's knowledge of administrative procedures. "Lieutenant Andrews don't know his ass from a . . . I mean the lieutenant didn't show you a letter from Headquarters when he told you, did he?"

"No, but he said it was in *Stars and Stripes* and . . ."

"Staff Sergeant Azdale, I told you just last week—something in a magazine or paper isn't good enough, the lieutenant don't know anything; I mean, nobody knows anything about a new medal until I get a letter from Headquarters, okay?"

"Yes, First Sergeant Michaels, I got it, I got it."

"Okay then, go on back to your duties."

With a confused look on his face, the big sergeant moved toward and through the door. As he ambled off into the heat waves he realized he was no closer now than twelve years before to answering a question that first occurred to him in boot camp: how does that huge, faceless building full of typewriters and clerks and files back in Washington, that organization calling itself Headquarters, ever get anything done right?

Not only humorous but easier to remember than most incidents occurring in 3d MPs was the only time we escaped from an inspection without being court-martialed. The occasion was the FLC Commanding General's semiannual inspection of all his subordinate units. The general himself didn't do the inspecting; he sent a small army of majors, captains, and staff NCOs around Da Nang to do the snooping. But the general received detailed reports on the condition of all units, so preparations for the inspection were as careful as if he were making the rounds himself.

For more than two weeks over two hundred troops and about fifty senior sergeants and officers washed, cleaned and oiled, spit-shined and polished, and brought up to date or corrected, everything the inspectors would be looking at, from belt buckles to plans in case of enemy attack, from rifles to service record books. Only those men whose duties could not be set aside without compromising the security of the battalion or allowing prisoners to escape were exempted from the inspection.

We didn't know it, but while we were getting ready for the general's inspection, preparations of a completely different order were going on a few miles away, preparations occasioned by an accident in our compound. A month before the scheduled date of the inspection, a PFC had begun to climb one of the guard towers around the brig to relieve another PFC and begin his four-hour period of staring down into the sun-bleached brig compound. As he put his weight on the third rung of the ladder, it gave way, and he fell back through the second and first rungs before hitting the ground and twisting an ankle.

The same day, the PFC's company commander told the battalion S-4 about the accident. The S-4 then inspected the tower himself, found most of the rest of it in the same condition as the rotten third rung, and put in an order for a new guard tower with the FLC logistics officer the same day. During the following week FLC had passed the order on to the Navy Seabees. Thus, while most of us in 3d MPs were washing, shining, or polishing, the Navy Seabees on the other side of Hill 327 were building a new thirty-foot-high telephone pole and two-by-four guard tower.

There is only one way to move a thirty-foot guard tower weighing over two tons in a country whose narrow roads are constantly jammed. It has to be airlifted from the construction site to the using unit. And, there is only one aircraft that can move a structure of such odd size—the largest helicopter in the Pentagon's inventory, the giant CH-53.

When the tower was completed the Seabees notified FLC, and FLC then put in a request with Marine Air for their largest helicopter. Unknown to the Marine Air Wing operations section was the date FLC had chosen for its inspection of 3d MPs, and unknown to the FLC inspectors was the date Marine Air had chosen to assign a helicopter. So, on the same morning that our troops were putting the finishing touches on rifles, uniforms, and boots, two marine pilots were lifting their chopper off the Da Nang airstrip and pointing it in the direction of the Seabees compound.

Within fifteen minutes the helicopter was hovering about forty feet over the new guard tower laying on its side. A cable with a heavy-duty hook was let out through a hatch in the helicopter floor, and a man on the ground snapped the hook on a cable wrapped around the top of the tower. Then the pilot changed the pitch of his rotor blades and slowly lifted away from the ground. He took up the slack in the cable and then carefully raised the tower to an upright position. Then he changed the rotor blade pitch again, applied more power, and lifted the tower off the sandy ground and above radio antennas and telephone wires.

The result of this joint service project was one of the strangest looking airborne cargoes ever put together—a thirty-foot-high timber and telephone pole apparatus dangling by a thirty-foot cable from a green box topped by a spinning propeller, and the whole contraption emitting an extended groaning sound. It all looked more like some excessively tall and awkward insect that had somehow survived the Ice Age than a modern military operation.

On the other side of Hill 327, over one hundred troops were filing out of their hooches onto the main road of the battalion compound. They walked slowly, trying not to bend their knees, in an effort to preserve the starched crease in their trousers.

Platoon sergeants and squad leaders then began lining up the rows of shining, scrubbed, and starched troops. They gave orders in quiet tones and reminded troops to move slower than they did back in the States so as not to raise any dust that would settle back down on polished boots. The sergeants did not stop their minute adjustments of columns and files until the toe of every boot, the buckle of every belt, and the nose of every face were placed on the same line. Then the company commander came out of a nearby hooch, moved to the front of the formation with the same stiff-legged walk his troops had used, and waited. Thirty seconds later the inspecting party, led by a major, came out of the battalion commander's office and the company commander called his troops to attention.

When the major began inspecting the first man, the chopper bringing our new sentry tower came into view far above Hill 327. We could also hear it very clearly, but no one took any notice since the sound of helicopters was always present around bases in the rear. By the time the major reached the fifth man in the front file the helicopter had dropped down on our side of Hill 327 to an altitude of about one thousand feet, and the sound of its rotor was louder than we were accustomed to hearing from our position three miles west of the airstrip. The eyes of a few otherwise rigid troops began to roll in the direction of the roar from the sky. By the time the major reached the eighth man it was obvious the chopper was heading for our compound. The S-4 officer and a clerk ran from their office to the brig to direct the installation from the air of their new tower.

The CH-53 helicopter had the greatest lifting power of any in the American inventory during the Vietnam War. That lifting power came from a powerful engine connected to four long and broad rotor blades, which created a down draft much stronger than that made by any other chopper. Depending on how close you were to it, the down draft could be merely surprising, irritating, or downright dangerous. If you tried to stand within fifty feet of a point directly beneath a CH-53 hanging less than one hundred feet above the ground, you didn't remain in the upright position for long. If you moved a couple of hundred feet away you were still trying to stand in a tornado, and your eyes, ears, nose, and mouth were fast filling up with all kinds of garbage. For those of us involved in an inspection two hundred meters away from it, that down draft resulted in a measure of humor.

When the tower was about three hundred feet above the brig, the entire battalion compound was swept by a nice gentle breeze which allowed us to forget for a few seconds the wilting heat of Vietnam. But as the chopper dropped to within two hundred feet of the ground, and then one hundred fifty feet, the gentle breeze became a stiff gust which was picking up and throwing a dark cloud of dust and small stones at our inspection. When the building dust storm blew the inspecting officer's hat off, that was the signal to suspend the inspection and head for the nearest hooch. The noise from the chopper drowned out the laughter that the troops let out at the sight of the major chasing his hat down the road. I don't know what kind of report the major wrote for the general about our disrupted inspection, but those of us who laughed loudest and longest about the scheduling foul-up scored it like this: Us-1; The System-0.

Then there was the night the VC chose to bother us at a most awkward time. FLC headquarters had a system of notifying units in the Da Nang area of the local security situation. All units were linked to FLC by radio. Every evening between seven and eight o'clock Flick Intelligence sent out a coded message indicating what kind of a night we could expect. The message consisted of only two words: "Condition" and a color. "Green" translated as no enemy activity expected; "yellow," as possibility of enemy activity during next 24 hours; "red," as enemy attack imminent. If a unit received a Condition Red message, all members of that unit were to stop whatever they were doing, put on combat gear, and go to the position they were assigned in their unit defense plan.

The security situation during more than ninety percent of the nights I passed in 3d MPs was described as Condition Green. On a few nights Condition Green was changed to Condition Yellow. On two nights in my time in the rear Condition Yellow became Condition Red. One of those two times the definition of Condition Red came true—our two nude sappers attacked. The other time the VC never appeared, and the result was a higher brand of comedy than one usually witnessed in the combat zone.

The Condition Red call came through on an ordinary week-night three and a half hours after we had received a Condition Green message. With visions of an irresistible human wave attack filling his crew-cut head, the young duty officer ran from the communications bunker to the colonel's hooch. There he found his commanding officer dressed in no more than his standard issue Marine Corps green undershorts, stirring his seventh highball of the evening with a ball-point pen and trying to lead the XO in a complete singing of the "Marine Corps Hymn."

The colonel could not bring himself to share his young lieuten-ant's alarm at the flash message from Flick. "Stand easy there, Lieutenant, just stand easy . . . we get them things all the time . . . don't mean nothing . . . do you really think those little VC bastards would dare attack the finest fighting force the world has ever seen? Say, Lieutenant, not to change the subject or any-thing, but do you remember the second line of the hymn? I forgot the damn thing."

The young officer did not react very well to having his image of a combat zone battalion commander so quickly and so thor-oughly shattered.

"Oh . . . no sir . . . but this message just came in and the guy at Flick said it was urgent, and . . ."

"Yes, yes, I know, all them calls and all them little pieces of paper from the general are always urgent, right XO?"

"Oh yessir, absolutely," chimed in the second-in-command, as befitted his position.

"Why, do you know what that general is doing right now as we stand here, Lieutenant, do you know?"

"No, sir, I don't know, but this message . . ."

"I'll tell you what he's doing . . . he's probably in his air-conditioned, bombproof bunker with nobody else but the prov-ince chief's daughter is what he's probably doing. . . . He's a sly bastard, that general . . . a sly bastard. . . . I guess that's why he's a general, eh XO?"

"Oh, yessir, absolutely," chimed in you-know-who.

Convinced there was no progress to be made at the CO's

hooch, the young officer began a backward movement to the door. "Ah, Colonel, sir, I better go tell the rest of the men so they can get ready for the, ah . . . attack . . . I mean if that's alright with the Colonel."

"Oh sure, sure, Lieutenant, go right ahead . . . thanks for stopping by anyway . . . drop in again sometime if you get the chance."

"Yeah, drop in again sometime, Lieutenant," echoed the XO.

"Oh, yessir, I will, I will."

With visions of that human wave attack getting larger each second, the frantic duty officer ran to the club. There he found everyone except the two Vietnamese waitresses in the same condition or worse than the colonel. Desperate to find someone who would take his urgent message seriously, the young lieutenant then ran to the adjutant's hooch. There he found one of the few men in the battalion who did not use beer or whiskey to help him through the night. Lieutenant McLucas had finished writing his daily letter to his wife and was studying a paperback book about how to win more bridge games.

"Well, look who's here—it's Lieutenant Hard-Charger, the new guy! What brings you to the solitude of my quarters at this hour?"

"Evening, Lieutenant McLucas, sir. I just got this Red Alert message in from Flick and I went to the colonel's hooch but he . . ."

"Yes, yes, I know all about the colonel at this time of night. . . ."

"And then I went to the club but . . ."

"Yes, yes, the club too, the club too. Well it's a damn good thing you came to my place, a damn good thing. Okay, Lieutenant, you and I got about two minutes to get this battalion straightened out. . . . I'll get this side of the compound in their gear and where they're supposed to be, and you go tell the sergeant major about the Red Alert. . . . He'll take care of the other side."

For the next fifteen minutes the adjutant and the sergeant major pushed about twenty-five officers and staff NCOs to get themselves and their troops in combat gear and out at their assigned places on the battalion's perimeter trench and bunker line. For fifteen minutes, more than one hundred troops of almost all ranks fought through the enveloping fog of whatever they had been drinking for the past three or four or six hours to put on flak jackets and helmets and load rifles and pistols. Then those same troops created a scene more appropriate to the theater of the absurd than a well-trained modern military unit as they staggered out to the line, bumping into each other, tripping each other, stumbling over the smallest undulations in the ground, a few here and there dropping out of the drunken procession to vomit or pass out. Preparations, which we had rehearsed until they took less than two minutes, had taken more than half an hour. By some miracle, no American shot another American.

Finally in place behind rifles and machine guns in the trench and bunkers, there was nothing to do but wait until another message came from Flick downgrading the Condition Red to Condition Yellow. In the twenty minutes before the message came through, the loudest sound was not that of the VC crawling through the grass and under our wire or shrieking their way toward us in a suicidal charge, but the snoring of those who had passed out crouching in our trench line. We waited, index fingers nervously stroking triggers. Above and behind us men waited in the guard towers around the brig, ready to turn searchlights on the kill zone in front of us if any enemy forms should materialize from the darkness. We waited and waited but the only attack that night came from the mosquitoes.

During that frantic half hour or so, a massive conflict was going on in about 150 American minds, a desperate three-cornered struggle between the sense of duty, the desire to survive, and the alcohol-soaked effects of trying to escape for a few hours the new and mostly incomprehensible kind of war that Vietnam was. In the background of that struggle mechanical, static-laced voices from Flick came through plastic radio receivers, and a confused collection of glowing visions of happy hometown yesterdays and shiny views of triumphant tomorrows ballooned out of the quiet, warm night air. And as those minds moved to the dreaded conclusion-question of what this night might turn into, more than a few pairs of pants were filled with the feces of fear. If the VC had really hit us that night as we stumbled and laughed and cursed our way through preparations, they could have chalked up an impressive body count at our expense. In the days and weeks after our Red Alert many members of the battalion, including those not normally given to contemplation, had ample cause to reflect on how close to each other the springs of comedy and tragedy are located.

9 Cumshaw*

Anyone who has ever been in the military has had daily contact with a comprehensive system of regulations governing everything from knocking out an enemy machine gun to disposing of broken broom handles. There is a civilian way of doing things and a military way, and according to the military the civilian way is almost always wrong. But to the continual embarrassment of those in uniform, the military way of doing things is not always the most efficient. Realization of that fact was the beginning of the cumshaw system.

The cumshaw system grew out of the views held by career-oriented members of the battalion, the lifers, about the military bureaucracy to whose service they were giving their best years. In the view of any senior enlisted man, there are official ways of doing things and there are effective ways of doing things. Official systems are things on paper which do not work but which give high-ranking officers something to talk about. As a gunnery sergeant once told me, "No officer is happy unless he's got four million papers to shuffle around and none of them has anything important wrote on it." In contrast, effective systems are things never put on paper which allow people and units to get things done and which let high-ranking officers think the official system is getting things done.

* From the Chinese word meaning tip or bribe. Westerners use it to mean theft or corruption.

The official system was and is called the SOP—Standing Operating Procedure. The SOP is activated by the signatures of commanding officers. The effective system was and is called cumshaw, a term borrowed from Chinese and referring to extralegal means of avoiding red tape. The cumshaw system begins to work when a senior sergeant looks you straight in the eye and lets slip from a corner of his mouth one simple sentence in hushed tones: "I know some people."

The SOP and cumshaw systems differed greatly in terms of range of concern and methods of operation. While under the label SOP the headquarters of each branch of the military placed recommendations on virtually every facet of modern life from promoting people up the rank ladder to disposing of garbage, the cumshaw system was concerned primarily with only one of those activities—the supply of food and equipment. There were cumshaw methods of doing other things but they were not so frequently used because the military could accomplish other things much more efficiently than supply.

The SOP supply system was a rather ponderous thing to operate. First you had to fill out requisition forms in duplicate or triplicate and submit same at counters four through ten of building 2614 between the hours of ten hundred and sixteen-thirty. Then you had to wait a month for something which might be about a foot long but which had a Federal Stock Number two and a half feet long. Then after about five weeks a computer somewhere in Hawaii would send a card which read that part number 74XT43–12933–443016 is no longer in stock but we recommend using part number 74XT43–12933–443016A in its place, and if you concur with our recommendation, simply fill out Form 7718 in duplicate (Use black ink only—Press hard) and forward to the nearest Supply Command via normal channels. Then after doing that and receiving nothing for five more weeks you had to send a tracer card to find the presumably lost order, and then after receiving nothing for six more weeks, send another tracer card to find the first tracer card, and, possibly before your tour in Vietnam was half over, the needed piece of equipment would finally come through. According to some people sitting in offices back in Washington, that system was efficient.

According to many more people in working units both in and outside the continental United States, there was a better way to get needed equipment. The better way was, of course, the cumshaw system. It was the cumshaw system that allowed friends of approximately the same rank in different units to barter among themselves to get things that they were not authorized to have by the Table of Organization or, if authorized, that they would have to wait for longer than they were willing to wait. In short, the cumshaw system speeded things up.

Those who are given to quick judgments or are enamored of clean organization charts drawn in perfect geometric patterns might be tempted to label cumshaw at best a threat to the effectiveness of official, organized systems, or at worst, institutionalized thievery. However, those who observed it at close range, or those who were saved by it from being made a scapegoat for some minor disaster occasioned by a breakdown of the SOP system, saw cumshaw in a different light. They saw it as a necessary augmentation of an official system that was in fact not as efficient as its designers and managers claimed. They also rightly maintained that anyone who considered cumshaw nothing more than thievery was confusing it with another system that has always existed in the background of war, a system that really was thievery—the black market. To confuse cumshaw with the black market was to overlook several differences between the two systems. Unlike black marketeers, no one who used the cumshaw system ever became rich. In addition, whereas the black market handled any commodity, including items needed by troops in the field, cumshaw dealt in items on which comfort, not life, depended. No one ever starved, ran out of ammunition, or bled to death because of it.

The cumshaw system was quite impressive in action. It could miraculously transform a captured enemy rifle into an air conditioner, a few hundred square feet of plywood into a water pump, ten reams of typing paper into three electric fans, or a case of whiskey and five dozen frozen steaks into a real live round-eye strip show. After observing the cumshaw system in operation, one almost began to believe in alchemy.

The cumshaw system was one of pure barter. As such it depended on an unwritten exchange rate. Allowing for variations of region and time, among all rear-echelon units in South Vietnam certain terms of exchange were generally agreed upon. The basis of the exchange rate was the most highly prized war souvenir among the men in the rear—one of the enemy's Chinese-made AK-47 rifles. One AK-47 would usually get you any one of the following: one case of American or Canadian whiskey, five cases of beer of brand names not available in the club, at least ten cases of Vietnamese beer, one new or two used air conditioners, five fans, ten cases of frozen steaks, three hundred square feet of linoleum, or twenty-five gallons of paint.

Most transactions, of course, did not fit exactly the AK-47 rate of exchange, either because one did not need the quantity that one captured rifle would bring, or one could not get his hands on an AK-47. The most common transaction involved fractions of the base rate, such as one bottle of whiskey for a case of light bulbs, one truck generator for the fifteen feet of pipe and one napalm bomb canister which could become a shower, one mess hall stove for a set of jeep tires and a long-distance radio antenna, two blankets with mosquito netting and five new radio batteries for one hundred rolls of toilet paper and a set of spark plugs, and so on.

None of those items acquired was exactly worth what was given up. Thus after each transaction was completed, there remained an inexact amount of value to be repaid. The use of money to clear up debts acquired in a cumshaw deal was generally looked down upon. Resort to the use of hard currency was taken as an admission of one's lack of expertise in cumshaw dealings. The only situation in which money was an accepted part of the compensation was that in which one of the traders was due to rotate back to the States within a few weeks of the deal.

The imprecise but mutually recognized and obligatory debt leftovers comprised one of the two forces that kept the cumshaw system going. The man who had accepted something worth more than what he had traded away was anxious to clear up his debt. He was therefore easy prey the next time the other party needed something.

The other force that kept the cumshaw system going was the pride of each man who was successful at operating it. The cumshaw operators received two kinds of reward for their efforts. The first and most obvious was material—the piece of equipment they needed for the moment. The other reward was intangible but longer lasting—the ego-boosting satisfaction that results from getting something done outside cumbersome official channels and not getting caught at it. Thus, the cumshaw system rolled on, with no visible hierarchy of authority to set it in motion and no regulatory apparatus to keep it on track.

There was considerable status attached to the ability to successfully operate the cumshaw system. Those individuals who had demonstrated such a "talent" were considered to have gone further than the rest of us in overcoming the frustration that so often resulted from the attempt to get some desirable response from the SOP. They had overcome the many shortcomings of the least efficient and most maddening component of the military bureaucracy, the supply system. In recognition of that success, the rest of us accorded them a measure of respect which generously exceeded that implied in the particular rank each had reached. These few individuals comprised an elite within the battalion, a local high society, and with good reason. This handful of men were the experts at acquiring not only needed military equipment, but the items of comfort and recreation—the whiskey, steaks, air conditioners, and hooch accoutrements—which nearly everyone wanted desperately to help insulate himself from the war and Vietnam. The cumshaw operators, then, were granted the high status that naturally flows from such basically materialistic values.

Given such values, needs and pressures, there grew up an invisible, effective organization parallel to the visible, official organization. If a man needed something either for himself or his unit, he still typed out the long Federal Stock Number on the official requisition form and took it over to the supply hooch. But after those formalities were dispensed with, the same man, if he knew what was best for him and whatever project he was involved in, then went to his hooch, reached behind his wall locker, pulled out an unopened bottle of Seagram's Seven or maybe even Canadian Club. The man then went over to the hooch of one of the known managers of the cumshaw system, put the bottle in a place impossible not to notice, and described what it was he needed. That's the kind of action that put the cumshaw system into operation—no paper, no Federal Stock Number catalog, no long wait.

The most dramatic cumshaw transaction I saw during my time in 3d MPs occurred while preparations were being made for an official reception at FLC headquarters. The commanding general of FLC was giving a reception for a group of officials, both Vietnamese and American, and military and civilian, from the Da Nang area. Included were a group of South Vietnamese generals, Buddhist sect leaders, and province and village chiefs. On the American side were about fifteen commanders of service and support units around Da Nang, and a few U.S. Agency for International Development and Red Cross people. That came to a total of about fifty people.

The importance of this event might be easily overlooked by those who were never in the military or Vietnam. Such a gathering of warriors, politicians, religious leaders, administrators, and assorted bootlickers was not too common even in areas untouched by war. In a combat zone it was rare enough that the previous one could easily have been forgotten. Outside MACV headquarters in Saigon such events never occurred more than once a year. This general's reception was the social event of the year, the Eye Corps version of a Celebrities Ball.

Obviously, preparations for the FLC reception had to be of the highest order. All units around Da Nang would, of course, continue their normal combat-support operations, but in the weeks before the reception all local units were expected to devote their spare time and personnel to its preparation. No omission was excusable; the reception had to be a success.

Since the reception was taking place in a combat zone, where items appropriate for receptions and cocktail hours were not easily secured, there was an obvious need for a method of procurement that could reach the less common items in the supply inventory. There was only one institution with such a capability, and it was, of course, the cumshaw system.

Accordingly, when notification of the reception went out, all the subordinate commanders in the FLC service and support network called meetings in their offices to pass the word on to staff section officers and chiefs. The significant part of this notification process was not so much the calling of a meeting. The significant part was the wording chosen to convey the message. Only the date, time, and place of the reception were given in specific terms. Everything else was given in the vaguest of terms: "Okay, gentlemen, have a seat there . . . I got this message from Flick I wanna tell you about. There's gonna be a reception over at the general's mess hall from seventeen hundred to twenty hundred on the twenty-fourth. Now, the general don't give receptions every day . . . there's gonna be a lotta big people there and the general and I think it would be a good idea if it all comes off smooth with nothing going wrong to ruin it. Now, we all gotta do our part to make sure it all comes off okay because it's the kind of thing that could help everyone concerned . . . so let's see if we can't do our best. Do I have any questions? Okay, go on back to your units there and carry on."

While the words of such an address were vague, the meaning behind them was perfectly clear: Crank up the cumshaw system, and fast! That's the way cumshaw was activated for the big projects. No commander could openly and directly use the unofficial but effective cumshaw system; to do so would be to admit the ineffectiveness of his own command. While it was, of course, undeniable that some commanders were more effective than others, none was willing, or dumb enough, to make so obvious an admission of membership in the less effective category as open and direct use of the cumshaw system would imply.

To be sure, even the best commanders were plagued by delays and breakdowns of the official supply system. But no commander, whether he had a big-name, headline-making front-line field unit or an unheard-of, going-nowhere, rear-echelon outfit, could afford to just sit back and wait for the SOP system to work itself out of a screw-up. Schedules of combat operations and general's receptions could not be changed in response to bureaucratic snafus. To meet tight and unbending schedules, the cumshaw system had to be leaned on sometimes. But it had to be done indirectly, covertly, so that if some unforeseen difficulty should arise, it could all be denied.

The most successful cumshaw operator in 3d MPs was Gun. Sgt. George Howard. Managing the cumshaw system was not Gunny Howard's only talent. His other abilities could be adequately described by identifying him as a member of the 1956 U.S. Olympic Wrestling Team. I don't know if there was any connection between his wrestling ability and his cumshaw ability, but I do know that Gunny Howard was never troubled with extended discussions over terms of trade or schedules of repayment. Things usually happened according to his schedule.

Whoever thought up the term "command presence" must have had Gunny Howard in mind. The only thing average about him was his height, about five-foot ten. To describe every other feature, one had to use superlatives. He had the biggest barrel chest, the broadest back, the brawniest arms, the widest shoulders, and the thickest neck I ever saw up close. He literally filled a door frame. The sweatband of even the largest size cover had to be let out and resewn to reach around his head. On the frequent occasions when he laughed, Gunny Howard's thick, bushy mustache would stretch across his face, and his opening mouth would reveal a big space between the upper front teeth. The only flaw in his physique was a slight limp caused by the loss of part of his right heel. During his first Vietnam tour three years before, Gunny Howard had stepped on a mine while fighting his way up Hill 327, the very same Hill 327 that now sheltered him and the rest of 3d MPs from the worst effects of typhoons, and separated us from the Freedom Hill PX.

Obviously then, Gunny Howard was invited to Colonel Palooka's briefing about the Flick general's reception. Other senior sergeants and officers were invited too, but their presence was more for the purpose of keeping cognizant officers cognizant than insuring that preparations for the reception were properly initiated. Colonel Palooka had been around long enough to know that just as there are official SOP systems and effective systems, so too there are cognizant authorities and actual authorities; sometimes one person carries the title and another person carries the job. Thus it was no accident that Gunny Howard had a front-row seat at the briefing. Nor was it any accident that Colonel Palooka jerked his eyebrows up and down and rolled his big dark Italian eyes in Gunny Howard's direction more than in any other.

Even before the colonel's briefing was over, Gunny Howard's cumshaw mind was in gear. So confident of his cumshaw contacts all over the Da Nang area was the Gunny that he decided he would make the Flick general's reception the cumshaw masterpiece of his career. He would manipulate the back-door supply system so well that no matter how long this war went on—five more years, ten—men would still talk about it. He would come up with all the things that give real class to an official function. He would produce all the things nobody thought could be had from a supply system in a combat zone—cloth napkins, name-cards in fancy gold lettering, miniature silk flags of the countries and religions represented, a big centerpiece for the hors d'oeuvre table, a choice of whiskeys and wines, and, instead of paper cups or coffee mugs emblazoned with boisterous slogans, real wine glasses.

Most of those items were relatively easy to find, even though there was a war going on at the time. It was the last item—the wine glasses—that was the rare one on the list. To understand the difficulty of Gunny Howard's task, you have to understand how rare wine glasses were among marine, army, and navy units in the rear. It would probably be easier to locate and capture alive the Eye Corps Viet Cong commander than to find fifty wine glasses among those three organizations. There was only one branch of the American military in Vietnam that used large numbers of wine glasses—the Air Force, those richly supplied guys with the slack jobs. (At least all the rest of us in the rear thought an airman's job was slack.)

The Air Force had wine glasses because they operated on a different definition of the term "essential combat-zone equipment," a definition the rest of us found incredible. I once heard a Green Beret captain describe an Air Force club he had been in. His eyes became big, his speech became slow and hushed, and he underlined almost every word by tapping a forefinger on the table. He talked about carpeting two inches thick, about perfumed women, about soft violin music piped into the dining room. "And can you believe it, there I was sitting there and this guy in a white coat walks up and says, 'How would you like your steak, sir, and what kind of wine would you care for this evening, sir?' I couldn't believe it . . . I didn't know whether to shit or go blind!"

But Gunny Howard was certain he had that problem solved. In a deal a couple of months before, he had received two cases of wine glasses. He had accepted them knowing they were next to worthless among marine, army, and navy units but also knowing they might be useful in a deal with the Air Force someday. So Gunny Howard decided to begin preparing his reception contribution by gathering in one place those items he thought he already had or those he considered easiest to get. He went to the battalion supply hooch, walked past the corporal on duty absorbed in a skin magazine to the back corner where he remembered hiding his two cases of wine glasses. He wrapped his massive tatooed arms around a bin holding between one and two hundred pounds of underwear and flipped it out of his way, scattering half the contents into other bins or onto the floor. He did the same to bins of helmets and boots but found no wine glasses. Then he hollered at the corporal at the other end of the hooch, "Hey, stud, where's Staff Sergeant Davis?"

"I don't know, Gunny, he left about a half hour ago and . . ."

"You don't know, huh? Well I'm not surprised. What the hell does the younger generation know nowadays besides how to grow long hair and demonstrate, huh?"

Gunny Howard drew up beside the corporal and underlined his question with a big grin which stretched his mustache almost from ear to ear.

"Yes, Gunny Howard, sure thing . . . I'll tell Staff Sergeant Davis you were here."

By now Gunny Howard had noticed the corporal's choice of reading matter. Pointing to one of the nude round-eyed girls on the page, he asked, "Tell me, young man, do you think you'll ever touch anything like that, I mean really touch anything that good."

The corporal answered with a tone of assurance the gunnery sergeant found disturbing. "It's just a matter of time, Gunny, just a matter of time."

"Yeah, you shit green apples, too. You young guys all think you got it made. You just wait . . . you'll get back to the World and nothing that nice will even give you the time of day . . . you just wait."

"I'll get mine, Gunny, don't worry. And when I do I'll take a picture of it and send it to you."

"I'm not gonna hold my breath waiting for that to happen . . . dream on, young man, dream on."

On his way out the door Gunny Howard turned back in the corporal's direction. "Oh, and one more thing, Corporal. You better police up that back corner of your hooch . . . you got a helluva mess back there."

When the corporal was sure the older sergeant was out of hearing range he muttered his real reaction to the meeting just concluded. "Thanks for dropping in, you fucking lifer!"

Before resuming his search for wine glasses, Gunny Howard decided to answer the call of nature. He headed for the Marine Corps' version of an outhouse, called the "shitter." The plywood and sheet metal shitters were always screened, so one had to open the door to see if a hole in the plank seat was open. Gunny Howard jerked the door open and found the supply chief planted on a hole next to an unoccupied space. He entered, unbuttoned, and sat down.

"Well, Davis . . . exercising your brain again? You were in here yesterday, too, weren't you? You ought to be more careful . . . don't want to strain that gray matter, you know."

"Your concern is touching, Gunny, really touching."

"Seriously, Davis, I was over to your place a few minutes ago looking for them wine glasses I was keeping there . . . you know, there's that big reception over at Flick in a couple weeks and I was gonna . . ."

"Yeah, I know all about it, but we don't have them anymore. I had to use them as part of the deal to get our new hooch fans."

"You what? Shit, Davis, I need them things now . . . I told the sergeant major over at Flick I could get them. What are we going to do now?"

"There's only one outfit around here that's got wine glasses and you know who it is—the Air Force. I know a master sergeant over there. But you can bet he knows about the reception, too, so the price will be high."

"Shit, Davis, you got my ass in a wringer now . . . I might have to trade away your whole supply hooch to get them glasses, but that won't be no loss, considering the half-assed way supply works anyway."

"Supply don't screw up nearly as much as your boys running that brig over there . . . how many of those brig-rats have you reformed so far—ha!"

"Okay, Davis, okay . . . I'll let you know what the price is, I'll let you know."

This was the first time in a long time that things were not happening according to Gunny Howard's schedule, and he was momentarily taken aback by it all. As soon as he regained his balance, he grabbed one of the brig's jeeps and drivers and headed for the Air Force compound next to the airstrip.

Gunny Howard wasn't smiling after he talked to the master sergeant. The price was high—a complete North Vietnamese Army uniform, one of the rarest souvenirs in all of South Vietnam. He knew exactly where to get one, but like the price of the wine glasses, the price of the uniform would be high. He told his driver he would be going to the hospital the next morning.

The Naval Support Activity operated the largest American hospital in the Da Nang area, large enough to have real American female nurses on its staff. One ward of the hospital was devoted to the care of wounded Viet Cong and North Vietnamese prisoners. When some of those prisoners died, the hospital staff went into the souvenir business.

Fortunately, the chief corpsman of the POW ward was not busy when Gunny Howard arrived.

"Yeah, Gunny, I got a uniform now . . . got three of them, as a matter of fact. How many you need?"

"Oh just one, Doc, just one."

"I see. Well, let's step back here to my office and talk it over."

Gunny Howard wasn't smiling after this meeting, either. The price was high—a case of Canadian Club, one hundred square feet of linoleum, one hundred square feet of plywood, two gallons of varnish, an air conditioner ("It's okay if it's used"), and a new desk, mattress, and wall locker. That amounted to a complete remodeling of the chief corpsman's office and sleeping quarters.

With the price that high, and only ten days remaining until the reception, there was only one thing to do. Gunny Howard would have to visit every friend in every unit in the Da Nang area and pick up anything that would put him closer to the NVA uniform. And that is what the gunny and his driver did. Others had to take the gunny's duty at the brig, and other drivers had to help out the one remaining brig driver.

Gunny Howard was not alone during those ten days. Every cumshaw operator in 3d MPs did all he could to help, and the rest of us gave him our hopes and held our collective breath while he scrambled around Da Nang informing all his debtors from previous cumshaw deals in no uncertain terms that the time to pay off had come. In the course of three frantic trips the generally accepted concept of a normal trade was completely redefined. A used air conditioner became two truck generators. A case of new spark plugs became a set of weight-lifter barbells. A wall locker and a used typewriter became a cook-stove. A pallet of beer became a pallet of cement. Five reams of carbon paper and blank service record book pages became three cases of mosquito repellent. Four boxes of photographic paper and two gallons of developing chemicals became two dozen searchlight batteries and ten pounds of rat poison.

At one point Gunny Howard even had to accept half a ton of sand and the trailer it was in. "How the hell am I gonna get rid of a pile of sand? This whole city's sitting on sand—nobody's short of it."

"Take it over to 1st Division. They can use it out on their hill perimeter," replied the supply sergeant he got it from.

The gunny was able to move the sand when he found someone who needed a trailer. "You can't have the trailer without the sand." One of the gunny's definitions of a fool was a guy who failed to make the most of a strong bargaining position.

At last Gunny Howard had the things he needed to get the NVA uniform from the chief corpsman at the NSA hospital. With only two days remaining until the reception, the gunny took the NVA uniform to the Air Force master sergeant. After eight days of running and sweating and blustering his way through more than a dozen deals all over and around Da Nang, Gunny Howard put his hands on the wine glasses he knew would add that extra touch of class to the general's reception. He carefully wrapped the two cases of glasses in a poncho liner and instructed his driver to hit the minimum number of ruts and go no faster than the slowest vehicle on the road back to 3d MPs. Back in the compound just as the sun dropped behind Hill 327, the gunny carried his fragile package into the supply hooch past the duty corporal absorbed in a skin magazine, and hid them in the back corner behind the underwear.

His task finally completed, Gunny Howard walked to his hooch wearing a mustache-stretching smile. He reached behind his wall locker, pulled out a bottle of Canadian Club and poured himself an extra strong before-dinner drink. He lay back on his bed and closed his eyes in complete satisfaction. He had just pulled off the cumshaw coup everyone else in the rear thought was impossible. He had come up with the gear no one thought could be had in a combat zone in the short space of only eight days. If anyone ever wrote a history of cumshaw transactions in the Vietnam War, the name of Gun. Sgt. George Howard would surely appear more frequently than any other.

At this point in Gunny Howard's latest campaign against SOP systems, a large number of people he had never met intruded and deprived him of his greatest victory—the Viet Cong. On the night before the reception was to be held, the local VC command decided to send their troops across the river south of Da Nang and see how much of the airstrip they could destroy. The result was the Battle of the Bridge, the event that jerked our attention away from a general's reception and the cumshaw system faster than anything else could.

The morning after the battle, FLC sent to all Da Nang area

commanders a message that surprised no one: the general's reception was canceled due to "the uncertain situation in Eye Corps Tactical Zone." To the PFC who gave him the message Gunny Howard replied in a flat voice, "I know, young man, I know." To the PFC's question about how he knew before the message came through, the massive gunnery sergeant did not reply.

Later that afternoon Gunny Howard went to the supply hooch, walked past the duty corporal absorbed in a skin magazine to the back corner where he had hid his wine glasses the day before. He muscled a bin of helmets off to the side, exposing the two cases of wine glasses. Then he took one of the helmets from the bin, swung it high over his head and slammed it into the delicate glass in front of him. The resulting sound was loud enough to break the duty corporal's concentration on pictures of nude female skin. Afraid the gunny had fallen and broken the leg brace which allowed him to walk with less than a complete foot, the corporal ran to the back of the hooch. He found the older man still bashing a helmet into the pile of broken glass and wrapping paper which only a few seconds before had been two cases of wine glasses. "Gunny Howard, what are you . . . are you okay?"

Gunny Howard was too engrossed in feelings of guilt to answer. He now felt that what he had done during the last eight days constituted a serious breakdown of the commitment to professionalism he had made years before, a grave lapse in the responsibility he as a senior sergeant and combat veteran felt for all young marines, even though the troops who were wounded and killed at the bridge were not in his company. "There I was running my ass off all over this fucking town, trying to get things ready for a fucking reception for a bunch of candy-asses who never got shot at or even got their hands dirty, while the fucking VC were getting things ready to shoot up our troops, and two of them got killed and another one will never see again, and another one will never walk on his own legs again . . . and I never figured what them filthy little VC commie bastards was doing all that time . . . I never figured . . . shit, what's this place doing to me?"

Gunny Howard finally stopped after many of the glass fragments had been hammered deep into the floorboards and nothing larger than a dime remained. He stood, dropped the helmet, and walked toward the door. As he turned sideways to fit his body through the door frame, he stopped and turned back to the baffled man on duty. "Corporal, you got a helluva mess back there but don't you clean it up. I'm gonna find an Air Force guy and a VC, and I'm gonna stick it up their ass!"

10 The Thing Most Missed

To the continuing frustration of American men in Vietnam, not all social needs could be answered in the rear. The lack of women was a constant problem, gnawing away at the composure of nearly every man. Since the average age of battalion members was under thirty, almost every man would be sexually active if he were back in the World around girls and wives. In Vietnam, of course, that pattern of activity was disrupted completely. The desire was there but opportunities for expression were virtually nonexistent. Strip shows were hardly satisfying since they were all look and no touch. In this respect alone assignment to the rear was worse than duty in the field. The grunts had their desire for women either eliminated or reduced to a minimum by the danger and the exhausting work involved in surviving in the bush. But the men in the rear had plenty of time, and they were rarely too tired to think about the girl or wife they wanted to be with.

There were several ways of dealing with the sex drive in the rear, none of which was any more than temporarily adequate. For one, a guy could reread the battalion's circulating library of pornographic novels and "skin mags"—magazines containing little more than pictures of female skin. Or, if all issues were checked out, a guy could rearrange and stare at his personal collection of pictures which he had thumbtacked to the wall beside his rack at bed-top level. The pictures were of completely or half-nude girl friends or wives.

If a man couldn't find a girl in the States willing to pose nude in front of a camera, he would have no choice but to resort to the simplest and most widely practiced method of dealing with the desire for women. He could stare at an underfed, prematurely aged, Vietnamese woman and fantasize her into Raquel Welch.

If a guy wanted a real girl, not a fantasy, he had to break the rules. Every base in the rear had a rule against anyone being outside the compound after dark. To enforce the rule every base had a high fence around it and an armed guard force on duty twenty-four hours a day at all entrances. But the guards were human, too, and they felt the same needs as everyone else in the compound. They could usually be counted on to look the other way at night while a hole developed in the fence between gates and a few men snuck out for some boom-boom time down the road in Dogpatch. The military's response was to put Dogpatch off limits. Any GI caught in or only walking past such an area at any time, not only at night, was subject to arrest and court-martial.

Those who headed for Dogpatch at night had to think about another, though unofficial, kind of penalty. A collection of some of the wildest rumors ever dreamed up were in constant circulation among troops in the rear. While it is most probable the rumors did not originate in the military, it is just as probable their circulation was never discouraged, for they promised such horrible experiences for any American venturing into Dogpatch that their effect was to help enforce the off-limits directive. According to one, the residents of Dogpatch were very anxious to slit American throats. Another warned that the Vietnamese offered GIs whiskey mixed with ground glass. Another had it that local prostitutes had broken glass in their vaginas. According to still another, prostitutes not fitted with broken glass would give GIs incurable varieties of VD, and the victims would be quarantined for life on a small island in the South China Sea, never to see the States again. But official policy and unofficial propaganda had little effect, and periodic MP sweeps through Dogpatch areas netted the unbelievers and deserters.

A more satisfying way of dealing with the sex drive, and one that did not involve the risk of arrest and court-martial, was related to making that run over to the Freedom Hill PX. On the way back to 3d MPs, the driver would often decide that since Vietnam was such a dirty, dusty country, and since the colonel hated to see his vehicles get dirty, he had to stop at a water point for a quick wash and service. A water point was a place near a well or a small stream where the Vietnamese washed jeeps and trucks for the Americans. The groups of Vietnamese working at the wash point always included two or three women somewhere between the ages of fifteen and forty-five, and four or five boys about seven to twelve years old. There was no official connection between the wash points and the Americans; the former were strictly free-lance operations.

The wash points were not really wash points. True, the boys splashed water on the jeeps and trucks but they didn't pay much attention to how much dirt they left on the vehicles. The wash points were only the newest variations on the old prostitution theme. While the young boys splashed water on the jeep, the driver went back into a shanty made of Coca-Cola cases with one of the women. That's what he meant by "service" when he said he had to stop for "a quick wash and service." If you could have seen what the wash point girls looked like, you would understand how desperate Vietnam could make a guy.

None of those methods of dealing with the lack of women was particularly involved. None of them was very risky, and none was new. They had been practiced by troops far from home in nearly every time and place. But there was one man in 3d MPs who used considerable imagination in solving his problem. The most elaborate scheme for dealing with the need for women that I ever heard of was dreamed up by one of our excess career sergeants. His plan was also one of the most damaging to the American effort in Vietnam, and to postwar Vietnamese-American relations.

We all knew him as Sergeant Ski because none of us could pronounce or remember any more than the last three letters of his very long Polish name. And as far as we knew, no one except his parents and the administrative clerks, who kept all the service record books up to date, ever even knew his complete name.

Sergeant Ski had begun his first tour as a skinny and scared PFC more than three years before; he had finished as a skinny, but not so scared, corporal. He had begun his second tour as a lean and mean senior corporal. That tour was cut off after five months when Sergeant Ski stopped several hundred steel fragments from a North Vietnamese mortar round—with his buttocks. Back in the World Sergeant Ski had liked the Purple Heart medal, the American food and the promotion to sergeant he was awarded, but he hated the desk he had to drive and the papers he had to shuffle in his postconvalescent leave assignment. The personnel officers at Marine Corps Headquarters probably drooled when they saw Sergeant Ski's request to go back to Vietnam—not very many men wanted another year of the Nam after their first. Even fewer wanted another tour after their second, especially after the *Tet* offensive of 1968. Sergeant Ski began his third tour in the Nam no longer lean and no longer mean. He came prepared to collect the benefits he felt the U.S. government and Vietnam owed him from his first two tours. He had served his time in hell—he had already walked through miles of rice paddy and over dozens of hills, and he had caught an assful of hot metal. Now he was going to cash in.

Shortly after Sergeant Ski joined the 3d MPs the bennies started rolling in. There was all the steak and ice cream and beer he wanted plus the club, movies, USO shows, and the Freedom Hill PX. And after he was back only one month Sergeant Ski was notified that very soon he could announce himself as *Staff* Sergeant Ski. With combat pay—an extra seventy-five dollars a month—and a promotion in his pocket, Sergeant Ski was beginning to feel like somebody. "Who was it said 'war is good business?' . . . yessir, I sure would like to meet that guy someday," he could be heard to say in the club some nights.

Unknowingly, General Westmoreland, General Walt, and Lieutenant Colonel Palooka helped Sergeant Ski make up for the lack of female companionship in his life. Those commanders had for years been letting Vietnamese enter American bases during the day to earn a subsistence income by performing a variety of services for American troops—translate English to Vietnamese and vice versa, serve food and drinks, cut grass and hair, wash and iron uniforms, polish boots, make beds, and sweep out hooches. About ninety percent of the Vietnamese who came onto the bases were women and most of those were hooch-maids engaged in the last four of those jobs. Every day about fifty Vietnamese came into the 3d MP compound.

Sergeant Ski was in the battalion less than one day before he discovered that two Vietnamese women were the maids for his hooch. One was about forty-five, the other about twenty. Neither was attractive by either Vietnamese or American standards, but after two weeks Sergeant Ski's impression of the younger woman changed from "ugly and filthy" to "acceptable" ("She'll do in a pinch—Ha!") to "pretty damn sexy when you really take a look at her."

Sergeant Ski's job was to counsel prisoners in the brig every day and to serve as duty warden for one eight-hour shift every other day. The counseling never took more than three hours, and Sergeant Ski preferred to serve as warden at night, so he usually had every afternoon to himself. That was plenty of time for him to think of a way to get at the girl in his hooch. His first move was to visit, at night, the hooch of the navy medical corpsmen attached to the battalion. For a bribe of a bottle of whiskey, a luxury not allowed junior enlisted men in the combat zone, one of the corpsmen gave Sergeant Ski a broken stethoscope, an operating room mask, and the Vietnamese word for doctor, *bac-si.*

The next morning after finishing with his prisoner, Sergeant Ski tried out his technique. He went to his hooch at about eleven. The hooch was empty except for the two women. Sergeant Ski took an extra pair of boots from under his bed and gestured the older woman outside to polish them. Now only the younger girl was inside. Sergeant Ski went back inside, put the mask over his mouth and nose, and hung the stethoscope around his neck. Then he walked over to the younger girl and announced his new profession: *"Bac-si, bac-si!"* The girl turned to him with what would be judged an expression of complete bewilderment in any culture. She understood his words but not his costume, not his timing, and not the place. She might have understood his purpose if she could have seen the lascivious leer behind his mask. Sergeant Ski repeated himself. *"Bac-si, bac-si!"*

When the girl failed to move, Sergeant Ski moved her. He led her over beside the bed, sat down, and stood the girl in front of himself. Then he began a longer speech, mostly in English. "Now just relax, sweetheart . . . I'm a *bac-si,* see? And I gotta make sure you got none of them weird diseases people get over here, see? Now just hold still."

Sergeant Ski began somewhat professionally. He took the girl's hands and pretended to examine the backs, the palms, the fingers. Then he went to her head and looked into eyes, ears, and nose, and down the throat. While he "examined," Sergeant Ski kept talking. "What's your name, sweetie?" The terrified girl could neither understand nor formulate an answer the American "doctor" would understand.

"You don't have no name, huh? Okay, I'll give you one." Sergeant Ski then pronounced several times a slang word for the female genitalia. "That's your new name." He repeated the word until the girl said it a few times, then he proceeded with his assault.

Now Sergeant Ski was ready for other areas, the areas whose existence had caused him to devise this whole charade. He raised the girl's blouse above breasts that had probably never been covered by a bra. "Here, hold up your shirt so I can check your heartbeat . . . oo, not bad, not bad at all." He touched the end of the stethoscope at a few places on and around the soft brown mounds before him. Then he dropped all pretense of medical concern and covered the bare skin before him with both hands for a long time.

By now Sergeant Ski was breathing heavily and sweating freely. He no longer saw any need to hold up a facade of professionalism; he ripped off the face mask and stethoscope. And the girl now knew that the foreigner who could not control himself was not a doctor. But, comparing his size with hers, and fully aware that there were very few men inside the 3d MP compound willing to help her, she let the attack continue.

"Everything's all right up front, now let's check down here."

Sergeant Ski let the girl's blouse drop and jerked her black silk peasant's pants down around her knees. Here he found the only undergarment the girl wore, a pair of plain white cotton panties. The plainness of the panties took his mind off what he was doing for a fraction of a second. There was nothing embroidered on the white cotton—no little pink hearts or cutesy messages ("Never on Sunday") as he had found at other times and places. The panties soon joined the pants around her knees.

The fat, panting sergeant couldn't believe what was happening—this girl, this real live female, was standing before him naked as a jaybird and not saying or doing anything to stop him! He had put on the doctor act half expecting it would do no more than get the girl's attention. He had come prepared to struggle for every feel. But here he was experiencing something as good as the wildest fantasy he had dreamed up in a long time!

As fast as he could cover the short distance to the target area, Sergeant Ski's hand was between her thighs squeezing, probing. At this new extension of the assault the girl's leg muscles tightened and she turned to one side, falling away from, more than protesting, the continuation of her humiliation. Sergeant Ski quickly killed what he thought was the beginning of a delayed protest with a twist of his probing hand and a viselike grip on the thigh which was moving away. The girl's hips jerked back to the proper position and the sergeant continued.

Through all of this the girl was thinking, but of things much different than those racing through the frenzied mind of her tormentor. In her naive farmer's daughter's mind, a mind that had never been exposed to formal education, she was wondering why it had taken so long for something like this to happen. She had heard from her friends that this kind of thing happened all the time. But her first time had not happened until today, over two months after she began coming to this camp. "I am luckier than most girls," she concluded.

She was also wondering if there was some way to stop this kind of activity. Ever since she had been working here she had thought American men were much nicer than Vietnamese men, but now she wasn't sure, she wasn't sure. She had heard that girls who tried to stop men like this lost their jobs and could not work in any other American camp, but if she lost her job her six younger brothers and sisters wouldn't have enough to eat. She had to keep her job, she had to. But there must be a way to stop this unkind behavior, there must be a way. If only she had been able to go to school, then maybe she could think of a way, but that was not to be. As the oldest daughter she had had to begin working almost as soon as she could walk. Such was the fate of the poor in a country that knew little else but war and bad harvests. But there must be a way to stop this unkind behavior, there must . . . there must.

After many more long seconds, a combination of associations and impulses came together in the gray fog of Sergeant Ski's brain and reminded him that it was time to refill his huge stomach. The sergeant took his hands away from his victim. "Everything seems to be okay, sweetie, but I'll have to check every once in a while just to make sure," he announced, his entire body running in sweat. Then he ambled out the door toward the mess hall, his wet face framing the broad smile that all men without women recognize as "conquest completed."

The girl slumped to the floor, crying softly into a sleeve of her blouse. With the other hand she gradually pulled her clothes back in place. She slowly stood up, took a deep breath to suppress her sobs and began remaking the bed her attacker had wrinkled with his excessive weight.

In the next few days there were more "examinations" by the self-appointed "doctor." They were finally interrupted one morning when Sergeant Ski was met on the way to his hooch by Bill Thomas, the battalion S-5 officer. Sergeant Ski straightened out of his slouching walk and saluted. "Morning, Lieutenant."

"Morning, Sergeant Ski . . . I want to talk to you for a few minutes."

"Sure, Lieutenant . . . come on over to my hooch. I was just gonna wash up for chow."

"Right here is fine," Thomas snapped. "You better keep your hands off the hooch-maids; they got plenty to do without you manhandling them."

Sergeant Ski reacted to Thomas's reprimand as he reacted to all criticism—he turned his eyes off Thomas to the dark hills in the hot distance behind the brig. He found he didn't hear very well if he wasn't looking at the source of a sound. Thomas continued through a lecture he had delivered many times before and expected to deliver many times more.

"And every time one of you guys grabs a hooch-maid or a waitress they go home and tell their family and pretty soon they hate us as much as they say they hate the VC, and when the VC come along and ask if they want to help fight the Americans they're more than willing, more than willing, so this fucking war goes on and on. . . ."

Sergeant Ski responded as he had been conditioned. He saluted, barked a "Yessir!" and stomped off to his hooch.

The sergeant was already in a rage when he reached the entrance to his hooch. He marched in muttering, "Where is that little bitch!" When he found her, he grabbed the collar of the maid's blouse and jerked her away from the row of boots she was polishing. Her blouse tore and she uttered a small scream. "You better learn to keep your mouth shut!" He underlined his words with a hard slap across the girl's face and a kick on her shins. The beating probably would have continued had another sergeant not entered the hooch and reminded Sergeant Ski of the time. "Hey Ski, let's go to chow."

After a few days, when no punishment of any kind came from the colonel or anyone else, Sergeant Ski knew he was free to grab his hooch-maid anytime he wanted. And there was no longer any need for the elaborate doctor act. The only change Sergeant Ski made in his actions after Lieutenant Thomas told him to leave the girl alone was to drop the crude name he had given her and call her Baby-san. There wasn't much the 85-pound girl could do against the unwanted advances of the 230-pound sergeant, and so they continued.

Most members of the battalion thought Sergeant Ski's assaults on his maid were funny, a light break in a boring routine. And many others in 3d MPs were doing the same thing. The few who worked for or supported S-5 and the Civic Action Program thought otherwise, and Bill Thomas put their thoughts into words.

"That fucking perverted sex maniac Sergeant Ski did it again this morning. I'd have to run five MEDCAPs to make up for every one time he grabs his hooch-maid, and to do that I'd have to stay in this fucking war twenty-five years!"

The attitude of those who were doing the same thing Sergeant Ski was doing was "we Americans left the highest standard of living in the world, we came ten thousand miles to one of the most fucked-up countries there ever was to save these people from communist brutality and to show them how to raise themselves to our level of civilization. We Americans are doing these Vietnamese a favor by just coming over here and the least they could do to show their appreciation is put out with a little nooky now and then and keep their mouths shut."

So, because of people like Sergeant Ski, the Vietnamese hated most of us a little more each day, S-5 fell further and further behind in its efforts to win friends, and the war went on.

None of us who sympathized with her knew how Baby-san continued to take all of Sergeant Ski's abuse, but she did. She never said anything and she never looked at him. Her self-control, her hiding of her real reaction to what was happening to her, was both amazing and pathetic. She just kept ironing or sweeping as Sergeant Ski's hands roamed over her, probing, pinching, massaging. She probably told herself Sergeant Ski's abuse was preferable to starvation. Our Western minds couldn't think of any other rationalization.

Those of us who tried to protect her from such abuse gave Baby-san our respect as a consolation for her humiliation and our failure. She would always be reserved a special corner in our overall memories of Vietnam.

When word about Sergeant Ski's doctor charade got around, most members of the battalion expressed sympathy with his need for women and admiration for the novel way he had used to satisfy that need. One of the senior sergeants, however, laughed when he heard about it and considered it a waste of time and effort. Sgt.-Maj. Garrett Snell knew there was a better way to get around the colonel's regulations and get some female companionship inside the compound, a way that did not involve the risk of getting caught. It was Sergeant-Major Snell's belief that a staff

NCO, if he really was worthy of being a staff NCO, that is, should be able to satisfy his need for women without attracting the attention of young lieutenants and other incompetent do-gooders. Sergeant-Major Snell immediately set about acting on his belief, and because of his position in the battalion he could be sure of cooperation from many quarters. Sergeant-Major Snell was not only the senior enlisted man in 3d MPs—there is only one sergeant-major in a battalion—but also the marine with the most seniority in the entire battalion. He had enlisted in the Marines in mid-1940, more than a year before the attack on Pearl Harbor, according to the way most of us referred to that era. Sergeant-Major Snell, however, dated his entry as "back about the time Christ made corporal." Now serving in his third war, the sergeant-major had over twenty-eight years in service, a full decade more than the colonel. Understandably, when Sergeant-Major Snell talked about what it was like in "the Old Corps," everyone listened.

The first thing Sergeant-Major Snell did to remedy the lack of women in 3d MPs was contact a couple of other sergeant-majors in the area, longtime buddies with whom he had served on several occasions before. From them he got the materials to build a small storage shed. Then he went to the colonel and commented on the growing volume of business in the club and how much they needed another Vietnamese girl to help wait on tables and how nice it would be to have another cute young female face around to take everyone's mind off the war. As Sergeant-Major Snell knew would happen, the colonel agreed and directed the XO to order another Vietnamese waitress from the FLC Indigenous Personnel Office. To make sure the system coughed up the right body, that is, a shapely, willing body, Sergeant-Major Snell went and talked to still another senior sergeant he knew in a strategic place, one in the office dealing with civilian labor relations, and told him to send along to 3d MPs the first likely candidate who walked in the door. The result appeared in the club one week later. Lulu could have made a priest forget his vows of celibacy. She was too shapely for a Vietnamese, mainly because she was half-Chinese. With her blouse-busting figure and rolling hips, all eyes were upon her as she walked to and from tables.

By the time Lulu came on the job, the new storage shed was ready for use, and it had been placed directly behind the club. That location, pointed out by the sergeant-major, was the most convenient, since the official purpose of the facility was to hold the extra cases of beer, whiskey, and soft drinks supposedly ordered to answer the alleged increase in demand in the club. In spite of that official purpose, the sergeant-major had a bed installed in the shed. At a secret briefing in the shed one afternoon Lulu was taught how to explain her trips from club to storage shed—"If anyone asks, just say you gotta get some more Seven-Up." The going rate for a quick roll in the rack with Lulu was passed around by word of mouth and business was off to a roaring start. On a typical night Lulu made between five and ten trips to the shed. She was allowed to keep half of her ten-dollar fee, and the rest went into a club "Improvement Fund," to which, no doubt, there was connected a pipe leading directly to Sergeant-Major Snell's pocket.

As everyone feared, word about Lulu and the storage shed spread throughout the battalion, and the lower-ranking enlisted men made known their desire that a similar arrangement be made at their club. Sergeant-Major Snell immediately rejected the idea and explained the exclusivity of the deal with one of the oldest truisms in the military: "Rank has its privileges."

11 Black and White

When viewed by outsiders, a military unit looks the epitome of conformity. All members work toward the same goal and under the same regulations, all activities are carefully coordinated, all members move together much of the time, and everyone even dresses and talks alike. To the outsider it appears that nothing divides the closed society of the military unit. Insiders, however, get a different view. They can see very clearly the differences between individual members: differences of age, regional or national origin, economic status, educational achievement, race, religion, and, of course, personality. During the Vietnam War the differences to be seen were especially sharp, not because of anything happening in Vietnam but because of developments back in American society.

The Vietnam War era was a time of rapid social change in the United States. Racial and ethnic minorities—American Indians, Mexican-Americans, Puerto Ricans, and especially blacks—were claiming the right to participate in every sphere of American life on the basis of equality with the white majority. Behind the rapid social changes of the 1960s were decades of gradually changing attitudes. In the years between the end of World War II and the beginning of the Vietnam War the view of minority members held by the white American majority changed. The picture of minority Americans, particularly blacks, as simple people of limited ambition who would eventually enter the mainstream of

American society and support white values was questioned. Excessive sympathy and condescension were dropped from white thinking. Persons of Afro-American, Latin American, and American Indian ancestry gradually came to be viewed as possessing the same talents as those in the majority.

At the same time, of course, the views that minority Americans held of themselves were also changing. Pride in the accident of being born into an ethnic minority group replaced shame. Assertive display of ethnic modes of behavior and styles of dress replaced resigned acceptance of imposed norms. A "get-it-now" urge to claim and exercise rights replaced a docile patience with their subversion.

During the same period, and especially in the years between the end of the Korean War and the beginning of the Vietnam War, the views of minority persons held by American military leaders changed less dramatically. Although the military led the way in ending racial segregation when the president ordered integration in 1948, the effects of the policy were diluted by an unwritten quota system which governed the assignment and promotion of minority members. Whatever complaints blacks and other minority members could have made against the discrimination they endured were effectively muted, and the overwhelmingly white upper reaches of the command structure continued in their belief that equality of opportunity really existed and all was well in the ranks down below.

Throughout the period between the Korean and Vietnam wars the proportion of minority members in the military remained far below the minority proportion for the general population. Those minority members who did enter the military in this period generally accepted the values of the white majority and viewed military service as a method of gaining acceptance by the social majority. For the most part, they reinforced the stereotypes of minority personnel held by the military establishment. Those minority members whose self-view was changing in this period avoided military service because they believed it represented the surrender of one's individuality—one's "soul"—to the adversary social majority.

The change of values that occurred in civilian society in the decades before the Vietnam War and the most conservative views prevailing in the military set the stage for a confrontation between younger generation minority personnel and the military. What brought about racial confrontation in the military was the expanded draft call of the Vietnam War. Draft policy during the war exempted from military service those men who either were students or held certain jobs, such as teaching, that required a university degree. Since the proportion of minority members in universities during the 1960s was far below the minority proportion for the general population, the draft policy amounted to a form of discrimination. In terms proportionate to the white-to-minority distribution in civilian society, more minority members than whites were drafted. Large numbers of minority Americans who would never have entered the military if there had not been a war, those whose self-view had changed so drastically in the decades preceding the war, were brought out of the inner cities and into direct and daily contact with an authority structure not equipped to understand or deal with them. Minority personnel, especially blacks, who answered the draft in the 1960s were much different from those who answered the call in the 1940s and 1950s. The former were highly sensitive to discriminatory treatment and not at all reluctant to complain whenever it occurred. The result was a double clash between, on one level, young black draftees and the nearly all-white military command structure and, on the other, the same young blacks who had no interest in a military career and older blacks who were making a career of the armed forces.

While young minority draftees were expressing their ethnic differences, the military establishment gave its traditional response to individualism: "All military personnel are the same and will be treated the same. No exceptions." On the individual level, servicemen learned of the official policy when an NCO hollered at them, "There are no white marines or black marines in this unit! I see only green marines!" As is so often the case, however, there was a considerable gap between official policy and actual conditions. All of us in Vietnam wore the same green uniform but we were aware of other colors as well, chiefly black and white.

Although most members of all minorities exhibited some degree of ethnic identity, it was the behavior of young blacks that was most noticeable and that consequently contributed most to misunderstanding and confrontation. Five forms of behavior in particular brought about confrontations between young recruits or draftees from minorities and military authority figures. The first concerned styles of grooming. One of the first visible manifestations of the new pride among blacks was the "Afro" hairstyle. Preference for that hairstyle carried over from civilian to military life. But whereas in civilian life there is no printed and enforced regulation concerning the length and style of hair, in military life there definitely is. That regulation was one of the first challenged by young blacks on American bases the world over, and small unit leaders found themselves spending more and more time explaining and enforcing it.

Along with the new hairstyle came a new style of comb. The Afro comb was shaped differently than its merely functional predecessor. Having few teeth and a long handle, it looked more like a stiff paintbrush than what most people recognize as a comb. The shape of the Afro comb made it difficult to fit in a uniform pocket, and that was why the new comb became a cause of confrontation. Uniform regulations of the Vietnam War period forbade putting anything in pockets that either made an outline of the object visible from the outside or protruded from the top of the pocket. The Afro comb was too long for uniform hip pockets; the black handle stuck out above the pocket flap.

Three additional practices did not violate any regulations but were so radically different from what racist authority figures considered proper conduct for minority members and what unprejudiced authority figures considered proper conduct for anyone in uniform that they made the entire command structure overly sensitive to actual violations. First was a style of walking called the ditty-bop. A direct expression of the new "I-am-somebody" pride among minority personnel, the ditty-bop was accomplished by exaggerating the normal roll and swing of hips, shoulders, and arms, and locking one knee.

A second unconventional but not illegal practice resulted when two blacks were ditty-bopping toward each other. Instead of greeting each other with a salute or a wave and continuing on their way, the two would usually stop and go through the elaborate ritual of "looking after my brother," as it was usually explained. The soul greeting began with the raised-fist Black Power salute, which then evolved into a rhythmical pattern of tapping each other's fists, palms, backs of hands, and chests, the entire sequence accompanied by equally pro forma phrases and questions: "What's happening, baby? . . . how's the (white) man treating you, brother? . . . keep them off your back, man, . . ." The complete soul greeting between two men might take as much as two minutes, and if one man or group met another group, as much as ten minutes might be taken up in a process of recognition that whites usually accomplish with a one-second wave or nod of the head.

The third unconventional form of behavior was even more misunderstood than others. On off-duty time young blacks and other minority members would frequently gather by themselves in a hooch or, more commonly, outside around a bunker on their unit's defensive perimeter or in a bomb shelter, and talk about anything but the war or their unit's mission. The facts that no whites were invited to these meetings and that they usually took place at night added to the wondering and suspicion with which they were viewed by white authority figures. It looked as if young blacks were voluntarily segregating themselves, rejecting association with the white society their parents and grandparents had openly aspired to join. Whereas blacks had once fought against racial segregation, it looked as if they were now promoting it. To whites and older blacks who had for decades considered valid the goal of racial integration, the after-dark closed meetings were an upsetting development to witness.

Most white observers assumed, on the basis of little evidence and no verification, that such meetings and other new forms of ethnic behavior represented rejection of the goal of integration. The same observers then piled another unverified assumption on top of the first: since blacks were rejecting integration, they were therefore plotting its violent opposite—all-out war on white society and its military organization. Old fears about campaigns of vengeance against the white majority were aroused in the minds of many. Carrying such questions and suspicions, many small unit staff members and commanders were unable to see the new patterns of behavior exhibited by minority personnel as expressions of pride. Instead, they were viewed variously as evidence of disloyalty, unnecessarily provocative actions deserving a swift and harsh response, or outright violations of regulations.

Compounding the anger of whites who witnessed ethnic pride was the selectivity employed by blacks as to the place of its expression. During combat operations in the field the behavior of black and white troops was indistinguishable. Everyone cooperated and many blacks and whites formed what the latter mistakenly considered close friendships. Once back in rear echelon areas, however, a change came over many blacks. They segregated themselves from whites during free time and occasionally became insubordinate. Many whites were bewildered to find blacks who had been friendly in the field suddenly turn hostile in the rear. The presence of the enemy in the field apparently caused blacks to postpone expression of their ethnic pride.

When the military made its legal response to those prideful expressions which were violations of regulations and orders—court-martial—the result was that a disproportionately large number of men arrested and confined to military prisons were blacks or members of other minorities. The proportion of prisoners from minorities in the 3d MP brig was consistently between forty and fifty percent, and the minority proportion in the Army Stockade at Long Binh occasionally went over fifty percent, although the proportion of blacks in the Marine Corps and the Army remained at or near fifteen percent.

Minority members who expressed their ethnic pride in various ways were not, in the early years of the Vietnam increased-draft period, consciously confronting the military authority structure. To their own minds they were only expressing pride, exchanging common experiences, or building up each other's shaky confidence. But later, when they saw how infuriating that behavior was to most white sergeants and officers, and how rigid the military's response to their prideful behavior was, increasing numbers of blacks and other minority members stopped thinking about contributing to the accomplishment of their unit mission or serving their country, and began playing a game with the adversary, mostly white military authority structure. The object of the game was to see how many authority figures one could anger and how close one could come to open violation of regulations without getting court-martialed. The reward was considerable prestige among one's peers. As more players entered, the game became more elaborate. What evolved was a kind of continuing tournament for underachievers. All definitions of achievement put forward by the military establishment were rejected. All rewards were shunned: liberty passes, duty assignments to which extra pay was attached, even promotions. To accept such rewards was taken as proof that one had renounced his ethnic identity and "sold out" to the adversary.

In time, reluctance to cross the line separating legal from illegal activities was dropped. Among the most bitter, minority ingroup standards even developed to the point that one had to willfully violate regulations and be arrested in order to prove one's ethnic purity. According to this standard, one who had served a sentence in a stockade or brig was ethnically purer than one who had only been fined or verbally reprimanded.

During the Vietnam War then, the American military faced an unprecedented set of circumstances. At the same time that it was dealing with a numerically superior enemy force and a baffling cultural environment in Vietnam, as well as an indifferent or hostile civilian population in America, it was faced with a challenge from within—the possibility that military members from social minorities would withhold their loyalty from national policy goals and the military force pledged to carry out those goals. The irony, even the tragedy, of this development is difficult to overemphasize. The single social institution that had offered minority group members more opportunity than any other in American society since the very earliest days of the Republic was suddenly accused of being as discriminatory as the most unreconstructed corners of the nation, and was beset with an unprecedented level of insubordination by minority members.

While race relations in the military in general were a faithful reflection of those in civilian society, there were certain differences in the racial situation between the various branches of service comprising the military establishment. Racial friction in the Marine Corps occasionally became sharp because of two features of that branch, one structural, the other regional. Because of its comparatively limited mission—to conduct and support amphibious operations—the Marine Corps offers training in fewer occupational specialties than the Army, Navy, Air Force, or Coast Guard. The needs of the Marine Corps are primarily in the ground combat and support specialties: motor transport, supply, armor, artillery, and infantry. Until the 1970s minority personnel in general had fewer educational and occupational advantages in civilian American society. Such persons had long recognized a side benefit of military service: the chance to learn useful job skills while at the same time being paid. But those who entered the Marine Corps in hopes of learning a marketable skill were highly disappointed to learn that no meaningful job training would be made available to them until after they had served a year or two, or (often) the entire initial enlistment period, in a field unit. There is, of course, no need in a civilian economy for infantrymen or artillerymen. Feeling deceived and used, many minority members were quick to see such policies as evidence of racism rather than the result of the "needs of the service" taking priority over personal desires.

American regionalism also contributed to racial tension during the Vietnam War. In the American South military service has long been considered not only a duty but an honor. While there has been no lack of persons from the North and West who consider military service an honorable activity, most conscientious objectors, draft-dodgers, and war protesters have tended to come from those regions. This regional difference in attitude became especially obvious during the Vietnam War, when every sizable antiwar demonstration took place in the North or far West. These regional attitudes affected personnel composition of the military: during the Vietnam War there was a higher proportion of southerners in uniform than the regional distribution of the American population would lead one to expect. Disproportionate representation in the military led in some quarters to a faithful reflection of the conservative racial views long characteristic of the American South.

The result of the southern character of the military was to

heighten the suspicion and tension between young blacks in the lower ranks and white authority figures. Young blacks from large northern cities were brought into close contact with a kind of white man they had only heard about secondhand from parents or grandparents who had migrated from the rural South. White sergeants and officers from the South were brought into close contact with a new kind of black American—a young man completely unlike the docile figure they had seen in the formative period of their lives. Upon hearing a southern accent, many young blacks unjustifiably concluded that a cooperative stance toward the mostly white authority structure was futile; many felt justified in adopting a belligerent stance. Some senior sergeants and officers, unfortunately, fit quite well the stereotype of the racist red-neck of the rural South. The fact that many others did not fit that stereotype was overlooked by many suspicious and frustrated young blacks. Too often, southern accents and strict enforcement of regulations were taken as proof of racist intentions. What occurred with increasing frequency during the Vietnam War were sharp confrontations between the marine command and belligerent blacks over a wide variety of issues, including violations of uniform regulations, use of marijuana or drugs, and refusal to participate in combat operations.

In the 3d MP brig we had the worst offenders of all regulations, and judging from their actions in the brig, racial hatred was a contributing cause of their offenses. The guard force and anyone in a position of authority were subjected to a daily stream of abuse, much of it expressed in racist epithets. Every guard had heard at least one prisoner accuse him of being a "tool of the imperialist, racist, American establishment" or simply a "honky" or "white beast." Death threats by the least cooperative prisoners against guards were common and kept all alert for the possibility of a riot. The atmosphere in and around the brig was charged with a dangerous amount of tension, and the situation was not much different at brigs in other units and in other services. Clearly, something had to be done.

The response came from the Pentagon and applied not only to 3d MPs but to the entire American military. Instead of reinforcing the traditional response of arrest and court-martial, the military tried a new approach, by ordering each unit down to battalion level to form a Human Relations Committee. Between five and ten individuals representing all ethnic groups, and most ranks, were chosen to meet at least once a month. Given various labels (Race Relations Board, Equal Opportunity Conference), these committees all shared the same purpose—to improve race relations in each unit by encouraging members of all ethnic groups to openly discuss their views of each other.

The Human Relations Committees contributed much to the easing of racial tensions both in Vietnam and the United States. The unit committees offered the only informal setting in which military personnel of all ages, ranks, and ethnic groups could discuss behavior patterns they had seen each other exhibit without provoking derision or violence. By being given the chance to ask simple questions like "Why do you call each other brothers?" and "What did your parents teach you about black people?" both blacks and whites and other ethnic group members learned much about the perspectives of the others. As reports of Human Relations Committee meetings were sent up the chain of command and finally to the Pentagon, a number of Defense Department policies were changed. Soul and Latin music were added to jukebox selection lists to supplement the traditional country and western and rock and roll in all clubs on American bases the world over. Clothing, beauty products, records, and magazines appealing to minority tastes were added to the inventory of Post Exchanges. Clothing and grooming regulations for off-duty time were relaxed to permit use of ethnic fashions. But the Human Relations committees could not eliminate all racial friction. Despite the progress made, racially motivated incidents of violence remained depressingly common in the military.

While the idea of such committees was approved by nearly everyone concerned about race relations at the outset, some of the decisions with which they were initiated served to compromise their effectiveness. In most units, higher-ranking minority members were chosen to chair the committees. The reasons such personnel were chosen did not always reflect the spirit in which the Human Relations Committee program was initiated. Many commanders feared that minority personnel in their units were on the verge of open rebellion and they would, if faced with a situation in which they had to choose, give greater loyalty to their own ethnic identity than to their unit's mission or their nation's policy. They felt that by putting a black or Puerto Rican or Mexican-American in front of a group of younger generation minority members, the latter would somehow be less inclined to break regulations; the feared revolt, in effect, would be defused. By making such a decision, these commanders revealed their feeling that it was more important to forestall a revolt than to lay bare and examine the ignorance and suspicion which caused them (and many others) to fear a mass disaffection.

Other commanders threw the problem of race relations into the laps of higher-ranking blacks for a different reason. Some seriously believed that only blacks could really understand blacks and, by extension, older blacks had some special inherent ability to control younger blacks. One of the greatest successes of the Human Relations committees was the revelation to members of many ethnic groups the racial myths that each preserves in an era generally considered "modern."

The effects of the practice of naming older minority members to chair committees and meetings of younger minority members were to only partially alleviate the reluctance of the latter to freely express themselves with a white chairman, to overlay the racial problem with the phenomenon of the generation gap, and to present the minority chairmen selected to solve this deep-seated, centuries-old social problem with a painful identity crisis.

Since higher-ranking blacks had decided years before the Vietnam War to make a career of military service (or they would not, of course, have reached a higher rank by the time of that war), young blacks usually viewed them as moral weaklings who had sold out to what was labeled the "white racist establishment." They were considered "bought men," shuffling Uncle Toms who answered "yassah" to everything the white CO ordered. Higher-ranking blacks were also, of course, older than first-term enlistees or draftees. They were thus subject to one of the truisms that so many young people of the 1960s accepted without question—"you can't trust anyone over thirty." Thus, for both their choice of career and their age, higher-ranking minority members were denied the confidence that could have enabled them to be more effective.

In addition, higher-ranking minority members chosen to chair the new committees were compromised by attitudes which they themselves brought to their new duty, as well as by tensions arising from their being placed between two groups to both of which they had long been paying loyalty. Most chairmen genuinely wanted to make a contribution to the solution of racial problems in both the military and American society at large. But at the same time, most felt they were being placed in an impossible position—between a conservative authority structure trying to preserve itself and a radical force trying to alter significantly that authority structure. To support one side was to tear down the other. To favor the white authority structure was to deny the ethnic group that had given one life; to favor one's ethnic brothers was to reject the organization that had allowed one the best career opportunity open at the time of choosing. Torn between loyalty to country and career on the one hand and ethnic identity on the other, many committee chairmen were less than enthusiastic about their new assignment. Some decided to do no more than make a show of concern for their commanders to see and leave the real issues to someone else. Others felt they had been wrongly singled out to solve a national problem not of their making. Still others viewed young minority members as no more than loudmouthed troublemakers who had only exaggerated their own problems and were undeserving of all the official attention. Varying arrangements of such personal feelings and fears as well as other, extrapersonal forces, not the least of which was the fact that much of the effort to improve race relations was undertaken at the same time and place in which the military was trying to defeat an enemy and befriend a very foreign civilian population, combined to limit the effectiveness of the Human Relations program in its first years of operation.

12 EPD

Any human community, whether large or small, carefully or loosely organized, sooner or later has to deal with nonconformity to accepted standards of behavior. Sociologists and criminologists have shown themselves adept at analyzing and labeling what they call "deviant behavior" and "recidivism," and eager to investigate the causes of and to reform such phenomena by a lengthy process of psychological testing and counseling. The military describes and deals with the same phenomena in terms much less scholarly and methods much more direct. Every unit, it seems, has its "ten percent who don't go along with the program." Such individuals, usually referred to by their sergeants as "shit-birds," are promptly charged with a violation of some article of the Uniform Code of Military Justice, and marched before their company commander who, without the aid of lawyers and a jury, listens to the offender's side of the story, decides guilt or innocence, and passes sentence. Probably three-fourths of all violations of military regulations are dealt with by this accelerated type of trial, known in the Marine Corps as "office hours." Serious offenses, such as armed robbery and assault, are tried by formal court-martial, complete with trained lawyers and a panel of officers acting as jury.

In a military unit, governed as it is by a lengthy list of regulations, it doesn't take long for someone to violate, intentionally or not, prescribed procedures. When such violations occur in a combat zone they are usually handled differently than if they had occurred in a secure area. In general, fewer brig sentences are handed down in the combat zone. Since there is never a shortage of work to do in a combat zone, most offenders are given several days or weeks of extra police duty, or EPD. In a field unit, EPD jobs are given out with a view toward improving combat effectiveness: cleaning weapons, carrying ammunition, improving defensive positions. In a rear-echelon unit, however, the priorities are different and EPD jobs have more in common with public utilities in civilian communities. Rather than being necessary in a strictly military sense, EPD jobs in the rear are merely the least desirable, things like painting hooches, laying water pipes, digging grease pits for the mess hall, carrying cans of garbage to dumping points.

The most distasteful noncombat job in Vietnam was necessitated by the lack of plumbing in the rear bases. Several hundred or several thousand men in each base camp produced every day several hundred or several thousand pounds of feces which had to be disposed of as fast and as cheaply as possible before it became a health hazard. The most common method of disposal was to pour kerosene or used oil from the motor pool over the matter and burn it. Once a week two men who had somehow failed to satisfy their company first sergeant drove a jeep and trailer around to all the outhouses, or "shitters" as they were called, pulled the 55-gallon drum halves in which the fecal matter was deposited out from under the two- or three-hole seats, put them into the trailer, and took them to a designated burning point. Base commanders always dictated that waste matter be burned at a place that would not interfere with the defense of the base compound should it come under attack by an enemy seeking to take advantage of the disarming smell caused by the operation. The problem with this requirement was that a strategically acceptable burning point was not always downwind from the compound. On many days billowing clouds of putrid black smoke would pass through the offices and supply sheds and barracks and mess halls of the rear, forcing everyone to share a punishment intended for a few. The only thing a trooper could do if he had been assigned to the "shitter-burning detail" was put on his oldest field uniform, hold his nose, and bear it, so to speak. The best thing a guy could hope for out of the deal was that the other guy would be reasonably easy to get along with and the two could take their minds off the repulsive duty with some fairly informative, or at least entertaining, conversation.

"You the guy burnin' shitters today?"

"You guessed it. Jump in."

"You got a license to drive this thing?"

"No. But I drive anyway. Sometimes I take the CO and first sergeant over to the PX."

"No shit?"

"No shit. Ain't nothin' special, though. Anybody can learn to drive, if the first sergeant likes you, that is. If he don't, you just keep on walkin'. What's your name anyway?"

"Duggan."

"Mine's Altizer. This your first time burnin' shitters?"

"Yeah."

"Don't worry none . . . I'll show you all you need to know. There's nothin' hard about it. Just smells so fuckin' bad is all."

"Yeah. This your first time?"

"No. I done it before . . . a few times. How did you get put on this duty, anyway?"

"I forgot to sweep out my squad's hooch when Staff Sergeant Loftus told me to, and I didn't salute an officer."

"Which one?"

"The third hooch beyond the mess hall."

"No, dumbass. I mean which officer didn't you salute?"

"Oh. I thought you meant . . ."

"I know what you thought I meant, Duggan. Which officer didn't you salute?"

"Springer."

"Yeah, I know what you mean. He's such a little shit, a guy can't find him half the time."

"Yeah, and he was way across the road half behind a jeep, but all the first sergeant said was I should look harder."

"Whadja expect? Of course a first sergeant would say somethin' like that. Them lifers always say somethin' like that.

Okay, here we are. Get out and I'll show you what to do. You know whose shitter this is, Duggan?"

"No."

"This is the colonel's very own private shitter. Only for him and the XO."

"No shit?"

"No shit, Duggan. You know, every time I had this duty I never could figure out why there's separate shitters for the colonel and the staff NCOs and other officers and then other ones for peons like us. I mean the colonel's shit and the first sergeant's shit and our shit is all the same, ain't it?"

"I guess so."

"Of course it's the same! It all looks like shit, it all smells like shit, and it all tastes like shit, right?"

"I guess so."

"You guess so? You know anybody who ever tasted shit?"

"No."

"You ever tasted shit yourself?"

"No."

"Okay, Duggan, it's just a joke, see?"

"Yeah, I see now."

"That's okay, Duggan, forget it . . . it's just a joke, see?"

"Yeah, I see."

"Okay, now the first thing is to open this door at the back, and you see them two tubs in there? Okay, put your gloves on there . . . and then just reach in, grab one and pull it out. But don't pull too fast . . . pull easy like this, see?"

"Yeah, I see."

"So the crap don't splash none. Okay, pull yours out there . . . easy now."

"Goddam, that shit stinks!"

"Well, whadja expect? It's pure shit, Duggan. One hundred percent pure, U.S. Government-inspected shit. But I found a way to cut the smell a little. I always pour some of this diesel over the top. It ain't so bad then."

"Goddam, that's the worst thing I ever smelled in my life, Altizer!"

"Welcome to the shitter-burnin' detail, Duggan. Okay, now

comes the tricky part. We gotta lift these tubs up into the trailer, okay?"

"Okay. How?"

"We gotta work together careful, Duggan. You get on one side and I'm on the other. Then we lift careful at the same time and slide it in the trailer. Okay?"

"Okay."

"Okay, start to lift . . . careful . . . and don't tip it, whatever you do. If any of that shit spills on you, you'll stink for a month! Okay, set the edge on the trailer there . . . now just slide her in real easy."

"Goddam, Altizer! A guy needs a gas mask for this job!"

"No shit, Duggan. But don't worry. You'll live through it. Okay, let's get the other one . . . okay, up and in . . . that's good. Okay, get in."

"Do we go burn it now?"

"Not yet, Duggan. We got a lot more to collect first. Next is the staff NCOs' shitter."

"How long does this job take, anyway?"

"Oh, we should be done by two or three in the afternoon, why? You in a hurry, or somethin'? You got a date this afternoon?"

"Fuck no, I ain't got a date. I just don't wanna spend anymore time around this shit than I have to, is all."

"Well, you may as well relax, Duggan. This job's gonna take about six or seven hours any way you cut it. Course if all the shit was in only one or two shitters like it should be instead of this shit about a separate shitter for the colonel and another one for the staff NCOs and all, this job wouldn't take half as long. But that's the Marine Corps for you . . . they gotta see how much time and everything else they can waste, you know?"

"Yeah, I guess so. Hey, Altizer."

"Yeah, what?"

"Okay I ask you a question?"

"Sure it's okay."

"What about you?"

"What about my what?"

"The same question you asked me—how did you get put on this duty?"

"Oh, that. I got caught sneakin' back in the compound after hours last week. I was comin' through that hole in the wire down by Delta Company. You seen it yet?"

"Yeah, I see Delta Company a lotta times."

"No dumbass. I mean you ever seen the hole in the wire?"

"Don't go callin' me dumb, Altizer. That's the second time you done it and I don't like it."

"Okay, Duggan, okay, for crissakes. I'll show it to you sometime. Comes in very handy. It's been there about two months and they ain't fixed it yet. I'll show it to you sometime."

"Thanks."

"Yeah, I went down to Dogpatch for some pussy one night and they got me when I was comin' back in. You been to Dogpatch yet?"

"No, not yet, but I heard about it."

"You oughta go down there sometime. It's that bunch of cardboard and plywood shacks about a mile and a half down the road. There's a couple broads down there will do anything for a couple bucks. Not too old, either."

"Yeah, I heard about it."

"Well, here we are . . . you know this place, don'cha?"

"Yeah, I know. Staff NCO shitters."

"Right. There's more tubs to lift here, but we'll get her. Okay, grab your gloves and the diesel."

After lifting tubs of feces into the jeep trailer for half an hour, during which time the dominant smell was too obvious and the dominant sound was that of Altizer giving his partner Duggan what was fast becoming superfluous supervision, the two were back in the jeep and on their way to the last group of outhouses on their morning round. Once again Altizer was in charge of both the vehicle and the conversation. "Yeah, like I was sayin', first sergeant says next time I fuck up, he's gonna send me back to the bush, but I doubt it. Look at this."

"What?"

"My finger, see?"

"I see five, just like everybody else got."

"Look at this one. It don't move, see?"

"Why not?"

"I was out in the bush with 9th Marines a few months back and the gooks hit us one night with mortars. I got a piece of steel in this hand and it fucked up the nerves to this finger so I can't move it none."

"No shit?"

"No shit. Even if Racquel Welch dropped her pants and told me she wanted this finger up her cunt, I couldn't do it."

"Yeah, but you could go back to the World with that injury, couldn't you?"

"Yeah, I guess so, but they gave me a choice of goin' back to the States or comin' here to the rear and I chose here."

"You mean you'd rather be in the Nam than the World? You like bein' in the Nam?"

"Yeah, I like it a little. I mean bein' in the rear, not out in the bush."

"Why?"

"It's a lot safer than the bush and I still get my extra combat pay."

"Course you get the pay but you're still in the fuckin' Nam!"

"I don't mind it so bad. It ain't so bad if you don't let it get to you like some guys do. Okay, here we are. Now we get to pick up our own shit."

"I can't wait, Altizer."

"I just knew you'd like the idea, I just knew it . . . say, Duggan . . ."

"Yeah?"

"Lemme ask you . . ."

"Ask me what?"

"You been doin' this job for a couple of hours now. Whadya think of it?"

"I think it stinks and I don't wanna think nothin' about it, is what I think of it."

"That ain't exactly what I mean."

"Well, whadya mean then?"

"Like yesterday I got this idea while I was out here . . ."

"Yeah?"

"And I got to really lookin' at this shit for some reason . . ."

"Yeah?"

"And it just hit me."

"What hitcha, Altizer?"

"It just hit me. We eat that crap they dish out at the mess hall and then we shit this crap you see right in front of you there. . . ."

"But that's natural, ain't it? Everybody eats and everybody shits, right?"

"Right, but that ain't the point, Duggan."

"Well, just what is the fuckin' point?"

"The point is this. We eat that crap in the mess hall and it supposedly turns into that shit right there in front of you, but they don't look any different, do they?"

"So?"

"So they look just about the same, which means that crap they serve in the mess hall is almost pure . . ."

"Okay, Altizer, I heard enough of your crazy fuckin' ideas. . . ."

"But look right there, Duggan, there's some hamburgers and potatoes and gravy . . ."

"Shut up, Altizer. . . ."

"And there's some peas and carrots and there's some of that apple pie we had last Sunday. . . . Shit, I never wanna eat that mess hall crap again!"

"Shut up, Altizer! Will you just shut the fuck up? You're makin' me sick!"

"Yeah, well it makes me sick too, Duggan, but don't you ever think about what you're doin'?"

"All I know, Altizer, is if I think about this job, I can't do it. And if I don't think about doin' it, then I can do it. It's as simple as that."

"You mean you just go through the motions like a machine or somethin'?"

"Yeah, that's what I do. I don't think about it none. Now get over there and help me lift these fuckin' things into the trailer."

"Okay, Duggan, okay, for crissakes."

After another half hour of pulling tubs out from under outhouses and lifting them into their trailer, Altizer and Duggan arrive at the battalion burn-point.

"Okay, Duggan, here we are. This is where we burn 'em. Now the way we do it is we set these tubs out there in two rows, pour more diesel in 'em, light 'em up and stand back. Okay?"

"Okay. Let's stop talkin' about it and hurry up and get this fuckin' job over with."

"There ain't no use hurryin', Duggan. We're gonna be out here until two or three this afternoon anyway . . . ain't no use hurryin' any."

"Yeah, but we don't have to be so close to these fuckin' tubs of shit til two or three, do we? Let's get 'em over there."

"Okay, Duggan, okay, for crissakes. Just let me get my gloves on a minute. . . . Say, Duggan."

"Yeah?"

"You ain't been talkin' much this mornin'."

"Well, I'll tell you what, Altizer. After hearin' some of your crazy fuckin' ideas, I'm not sure I wanna talk to you."

"Now just take it easy, Duggan, just take it easy a minute. I was just wonderin' where you're from, is all."

"Where am I from? What's that got to do with burnin' shitters?"

"Just answer the question, Duggan. Where you from?"

"West Virginia—God's Country—if you wanna know."

"God's Country?"

"That's what I said. God's Country, by God."

"Shit, Duggan! And you was tellin' me a little while back I got some crazy ideas! Shit, if you keep talkin' like that you're gonna make me drop this tub of shit!"

"If you drop this thing, Altizer, you can find somebody else to help you."

"Okay, Duggan, okay for crissakes. But that does seem to explain it."

"Explain what?"

"What you said before about not thinkin' about what you're doin', and just now you said you're from God's Country."

"So?"

"So that explains why you don't think nothin' about what you're doin'. I mean you people up there in West Hillbilly country don't have no plumbin' or . . ."

"Whadya mean 'no plumbin'? We got all the plumbin' we need!"

". . . or other modern conveniences like civilized people, so when you wanna take a shit you just step off the back porch of your shack . . ."

"Whadya mean 'shack'? We got . . ."

". . . drop your pants and shit bareass naked in the woods! And then when you're done you just tear a page out of the Sears and Roebuck catalog and wipe your ass and it's all done and you don't think nothin' of it!"

"You're full of shit, Altizer! Completely full!"

"And that's why you don't think nothin' about what you're doin' here. You see shit all the time at home and so it ain't nothin' new here in the Nam. You're right at home, eh Duggan? Ha!"

"Altizer, you gotta be the biggest bullshitter in the whole battalion, you just gotta be."

"Not half as big as you, Duggan, with your West Virginia God's Country shit."

"Sounds to me like you're goin' off your nut, Altizer. Sounds like the Nam is gettin' to you. I figure in a couple, three more weeks we'll be carryin' you over to the Navy hospital and one of them psychiatric guys will be talkin' to you . . . that's what it sounds like to me."

"You don't have to worry none about me. . . . Okay, stand back there, Duggan. I'm gonna light 'em up. From now on the trick is to watch which way the smoke goes and stay on the other side of the tubs. Sometimes the wind changes."

"Goddam! They really blow up, don't they?"

"They start out hot, but they burn down fast. Gotta keep pourin' juice on 'em. Goddam, look at that!"

"What?"

"That can of diesel is kind of close to that burnin' tub on the end. Run down there and pull it away over by the jeep, will you?"

"Okay. . . . Goddam, that smoke stinks, don't it?"

"Fuckin' A, it stinks. That's why you wanna stay away from it."

"Yeah . . . by the way, Altizer, not to change the subject or anything, but where you from?"

"Me? I'm from the capital of the West in the Golden State. Los

Angeles, California. And we don't have to say it's God's Country 'cause everybody knows. Everybody except you West Virginny stump-jumpers, that is."

"All right, Altizer. Just tell me one thing Los Angeles got that West Virginia don't. Just one thing."

"Be glad to. Take, for example, Hollywood. The movie capital of the world. You've seen movies in West Virginny, ain't you, Duggan? I mean you got electricity don'tcha?"

"Yeah, Mr. Smart-Ass. We got electricity and I seen plenty of movies."

"Courtesy of Los Angeles and Hollywood."

"Name somethin' else."

"Disneyland. The world's largest amusement park. People come from all over the world to see it."

"That's it, Altizer, that's what I mean. Disneyland."

"So what's wrong with Disneyland? It's the world's largest . . ."

"That's what I mean, Altizer. Sure it's the world's largest amusement park because you people out there are all the time screwin' and havin' babies and . . ."

"So what? Everybody has babies, even you hillbillies."

"Yeah, but you got so many that pretty soon you need some place to take 'em, and so you cut down all your trees and build somethin' like Disneyland so you'll have a place to put all the fuckin' kids!"

"So what the fuck does that mean, Duggan?"

"What it means, Mr. Smart-Ass, is that you got no more trees or clean air in Los Angeles. In West Virginia we got trees, mountains covered with trees—big tall green trees that reach up in the air, the clean air. . . ."

"Duggan, I can't even begin to believe you. . . ."

"We got clean air in West Virginia, Altizer. I heard the air in Los Angeles smells as bad as that shit burnin' in front of you there."

"You don't even know what you're sayin' anymore, Duggan."

"That's okay, Mr. Smart-Ass, keep right on talkin' if you want. But don't forget to tell us about the clean air and the tall trees in Los Angeles—ha!"

"I swear to God, Duggan, you must be the dumbest fucker in this whole fuckin' battalion."

"Altizer, I told you—don't go callin' me dumb. That's about the tenth time you said it this mornin'."

"Okay, Duggan, okay for crissakes. But the things you been sayin', I mean about havin' babies and cuttin' down trees and Disneyland—I never heard anything like that!"

"Yeah, well think about it sometime, only don't go callin' me dumb, is all."

"Okay, Duggan, okay, for crissakes. Here, pour some more juice in them tubs over there . . . they're dyin' out. . . . Let's just change the subject, okay Duggan? I can't make no sense outa what you say anyway."

"That's the best idea you come up with all mornin', Altizer, 'cause I can't make no sense outa what you been sayin' either."

"I'm not surprised, Duggan. I'm not surprised."

"What? Whadya mean by that?"

"Nothin', Duggan, nothin'. You know what I'm gonna do as soon as I get off this fuckin' duty?"

"No. What?"

"I'm gonna ask the first sergeant if I can work with the battalion carpenter."

"Why you wanna do that?"

"So I can learn somethin' useful from this fuckin' Green Machine, somethin' . . ."

"You already got somethin' useful, don'tcha? You can drive a truck and jeep and talk on the radio, and all the weapons . . . What else you need to be in the Nam?"

"That's what the lifers say is useful, not what I say is useful. Besides, I ain't gonna be in the Nam forever. I mean somethin' useful for when I'm back in the World."

"Oh, you mean that way useful."

"Yeah, for when I'm back in the World. I figure if I learn me a trade, I'll make out all right back in the World . . . people are always buildin' houses and shit and they'll always need guys who know a trade, right?"

"I guess so."

"Whadya mean you guess so? Don'tcha ever think about things like that?"

"Not much."

"Not much? Why not?"

"Don't see no reason to, at least not yet."

"Not yet? Well just how long you figure we're gonna be here? How long you think this fucked-up war's gonna last, anyway, Duggan?"

"Don't know. Nobody don't know that, do they? You know how long it's gonna last, Altizer?"

"Course I don't know, but I know I'm goin' back to the World in eighty-eight more days. No, wait—eighty-seven days and thirteen hours and twenty-two minutes. And after that the fuckin' war can go on as long as it wants. I won't give a shit then. Here, stand back a ways, I gotta light this one again."

"Okay."

"Okay? Whadya mean 'okay'? Say, just how long you figure on stayin' in this fucked-up place, anyway, Duggan?"

"I figured it up last night. Two hundred and eighty-one days."

"You got two hundred and eighty-one days to go?"

"That's what I said. Two hundred eighty-one."

"Shit, what am I doin' wastin' my time talkin' to you about what to do back in the World? I thought you was short."

"Well I'm not yet, but I will be soon."

"Soon! Shit, Duggan, you'll never be short if you got two hundred eighty-one days to go! Never!"

"Whadya mean 'never'? You had two hundred eighty-one days to go at one time, didn't you?"

"Fuckin' A, I did, but that was a long time ago, a long time ago."

"Right. And someday today will be a long time ago, right?"

"What? Say that again, Duggan."

"For your benefit I'll say it again. I said, someday today will be a long time ago."

"Maybe you understand that, but I sure as hell don't. Must be your fucked-up way of thinkin'."

"Whadya mean 'fucked-up' way of thinkin'? If you just think about it, you can understand it . . . if you can think, that is."

"Don'tchew worry none about me, Duggan. I can think all I need to, all I need to."

"I hope so, Altizer. I hope so. For your sake I hope you can think enough so you don't get yourself back on this shitter-burnin' detail."

"You don't have to worry none about me, Duggan. You won't see me back here again."

"Well I hope not. For your sake I hope not."

"You don't have to hope none, either."

"Okay, since you got it all figured out."

"Yeah, I got it all figured out. . . . Actually though, Duggan, that is too bad, a young guy like you with his future all ahead of him still got two hundred eighty-one days to go. I really feel sorry for you."

"Thanks a lot, Altizer. Thanks a fuck of a lot."

"Anytime, numbnuts, anytime. But seriously, Duggan, I'm really tryin' to help you."

"How you tryin' to help me?"

"I'm tryin' to tell you somethin'."

"What?"

"Shut up a minute so I can finish. What I'm tryin' to tell you is if I was you, I'd clean up my act fast."

"Why?"

"Why? Goddam, you're dumber than I thought!"

"I already told you, Altizer. Don't go callin' me dumb!"

"Okay, Duggan, okay, for crissakes."

"Besides, if you're so smart, how come you're burnin' shitters, too?"

"Okay, Duggan, okay for crissakes. But look, you been here only about, what? . . . three or four months?"

"Three months and nineteen days."

"Okay, but that ain't the point."

"It ain't? Then whyja ask me?"

"Just listen a minute. You know when the first sergeant's goin' back to the World?"

"I heard about five weeks."

"You heard right. You think your troubles are over soon as he leaves?"

"Why not?"

"Why not? Goddam, you are . . ."

"Don't go callin' me dumb, Altizer."

"Okay, Duggan, okay, for crissakes. I'm just tryin' to help you. The point is there's plenty more first sergeants where ours came from and they do talk to each other just like we're talkin' today."

"So?"

"So if our first sergeant tells the next first sergeant you're a shit-bird, you'll be burnin' shitters just like today for the next two hundred eighty-one days."

"Oh yeah?"

"Yeah. You ever think about that?"

"Well, no, but . . ."

"See, I'm just tryin' to help you. What that means, Duggan, is you got five weeks to get your shit together so the first sergeant don't tell the next first sergeant you're a shit-bird, okay?"

"Okay, I'll try."

"Okay. So the next time Staff Sergeant Loftus tells you to sweep out the hooch, you'll do it, right?"

"Right."

"And the next time an officer—any officer—walks by, you'll salute, right?"

"But that Lieutenant Springer's such a little shit, I swear I didn't see him. . . ."

"I know he's hard to see, but you don't wanna be burnin' shitters again, do you?"

"Fuck no!"

"Okay, then look extra hard for him next time, and if I'm around I'll tip you off when he's in the area, okay?"

"Okay, I'll try. But I got a question for you, Altizer."

"What?"

"If the first sergeant can tell the next first sergeant I'm a shit-bird, then he can tell him you're a shit-bird, too, right? I mean here you are just like me. . . ."

"I know what you mean, but it ain't gonna happen."

"Why?"

"Because by the time the next first sergeant gets here I'll be over helpin' that battalion carpenter and learnin' my trade, like I told you."

"Well, I hope so. For your sake I hope so."

"You don't have to hope none for me, Duggan. I got it all figured out."

"Well, I hope so, but I got another question for you."

"Go ahead, ask your question."

"Shut up a minute and I will! What if you get zapped before you ever get back to the World? You ever think about that, Altizer? Then where would your learnin' a trade be?"

"I knew you'd ask somethin' like that, Duggan. I knew sooner or later a guy like you would . . ."

"Don't go callin' me dumb, Altizer."

"Relax, Duggan, for crissakes. I didn't call you dumb."

"Well?"

"Well what, Duggan?"

"Well, what about my question? What if you get zapped before you ever get back to the World?"

"That ain't gonna happen."

"How do you know? It already happened to a lotta guys, didn't it?"

"Yeah, but it ain't gonna happen to me."

"How do you know that?"

"I just know. It ain't somethin' you can put into words. I just know."

"Well, I hope so, Altizer, for your sake I hope . . ."

"Hey look! Here comes the first sergeant! Get busy doin' somethin'!"

"Doin' what?"

"Any goddam thing, Duggan. Just *do* somethin'! Here, grab this one, it's done. Help me pull it over here. . . ."

"Okay, you two, as soon as those tubs burn out you can knock off for chow," said the first sergeant. "Hey, whadya got over there? I told you to keep them diesel cans at least twenty-five meters away from burning tubs, didn't I?"

"Yes, first sergeant," answered Altizer and Duggan in unison.

"You wanna blow yourselves and that shit up both?"

"No, first sergeant."

"Well, put 'em away there."

"Yes, first sergeant."

"And don't forget—over at the mess hall you two go through the line and fill up your mess kits like everybody else but then you take it outside and eat behind the kitchen . . . can't have you two stinkin' up the whole damn dinin' room. You two got that?"

"Yes, first sergeant."

13 R & R

Vietnam was an unpopular war, and to help make it more palatable to those fighting it the Defense Department added a few "sweeteners" to its personnel policies. The main one was the rotation system, according to which no serviceman or woman had to stay in Vietnam more than one year, thirteen months in the case of Marines, unless he or she wanted to extend. The Rotation Tour Date, or RTD, the date one could leave Vietnam, was on the mind of everyone in the war from the day he stepped off the plane at Saigon, Cam Ranh Bay or Da Nang. In between the date of arrival and the RTD was another sweetener: Rest and Recreation leave, or R & R, a five-day vacation from the war spent in a different country.

The R & R policy made Asian politicians and businessmen just as happy as American GIs. One can imagine platoons of government functionaries and foreign ministers from about half the countries in the Pacific basin begging and trying to bribe American officials to get their larger cities approved as R & R sites by the Defense Department. And with the potential financial benefits so attractive, it is understandable why no effort was spared to win R & R designation. American servicemen were taken to the R & R city of their choice by government-contract commercial liners, usually Boeing 707s. Most men took between four hundred and twelve hundred dollars for their five-day vacations from the war. With between 165 and 185 men aboard, each plane brought in anything from $66 thousand to $222 thousand. Depending on the popularity of the city, from one to five planeloads of GIs arrived every week, and that represented, potentially, over one million dollars in free, no-strings-attached foreign aid. During the peak years of American involvement in the war, the better-developed pleasure haunts like Bangkok and Hong Kong made $100 million a year from visits by Vietnam-based GIs.

When the dealing was done, there was a total of ten cities on the R & R list: Tokyo, Manila, Singapore, Kuala Lumpur, Hong Kong, Bangkok, Taipei, Naha, Sydney, and Honolulu. Married men were given first chance at Honolulu, the idea being that it was the most convenient location for wives coming from the continental United States. But if a seat was open on a Honolulu flight, a single man could take it.

As soon as a city won R & R designation, a flurry of commercial activity was touched off. Government ministers and their rich patrons bought up desirable land and established construction companies. Hundreds of Western-style hotels went up overnight all over Asia, cheap five- and six-story buildings named to attract homesick GIs—"Hotel Tennessee"—structures that couldn't pass a building inspection without a bribe. Many cracked and collapsed in earthquake-prone areas like Manila, but they were great for the economy, both local and faraway. Thousands of unskilled people became maids, cooks, bartenders, waitresses and waiters, and cashiers. And in every hotel room was a Japanese or American television set and an air conditioner. Souvenir industries boomed and thousands of people working in villages or back room city sweatshops turned out tons of genuine junk which included such best-sellers as wood carvings of fierce water buffalo, rattan furniture, "real" jade and ivory jewelry, and tapestries of the Last Supper that glowed in the dark.

Tours were organized to local places of interest, which meant roads were paved, Japanese buses imported, and drivers and guides trained and uniformed. At every stop, souvenir and cold drink and film stands sprang up. And few GIs went on a tour before buying a Japanese camera. Even elephant handlers and snake charmers got into the act. GIs who went to Bangkok could see a demonstration of a logging operation using elephants to pick up teakwood. In Singapore turbaned Indian immigrants eagerly tootled flutes and pulled drowsy snakes out of baskets for curious GIs on the street. But whether the Americans spent their five days in hotels or outside touring, they consumed thousands of tons of Australian and American steak plus millions of bottles of American, Canadian, and Scotch whiskey and American beer.

The number of taxis in R & R cities increased dramatically, which pleased Japanese and Taiwanese car manufacturers no end. Hundreds of American-style bars and restaurants were built outside the R & R hotels, providing thousands of jobs. To satisfy American tastes in music, several thousand Asian teenagers started banging drums, strumming guitars, and yelling into microphones, thinking they were the successors to the Beatles. Several hundred Chinese, Filipinos, and Thais put on sequined shirts and cowboy hats and declared themselves country and western singers. And although legitimate foreign exchange services were offered in approved hotels, a black market money-changing operation flourished. If my experience was representative, almost every street in an R & R city had its underling waiting in the shadows, ready to "changee dollah."

But the biggest R & R business of all, by far, was prostitution. Never a negligible social phenomenon in Asia, prostitution was greatly expanded to accommodate the 2.6 million Americans in Vietnam, most of whom went on R & R once and many of whom wangled a second five-day vacation. Finding the girls to answer the desires of the GIs was no problem, since the values that made the whole trade possible had already existed for centuries: daughters are far less valuable than sons. The local underworld, usually Chinese-dominated, simply sent a few flunkies into the countryside to make the offer to ignorant and nearly starving rural families. Hungry parents "sold" excess daughters for a few dollars into a kind of indentured labor system that came pretty close to fitting the United Nations definition of slavery. Only if the girl were unusually unattractive, or smart, could she be hired for a different job: maid, laundry girl, seamstress in a dressmaker's, or assembly line cipher in a candy or toy factory. That system pulled hundreds of thousands of girls from villages into the big cities, with their R & R hotels, steam bath houses, and red-light districts. Once settled, the girls learned the ancient fact of life for their "occupation": most of their earnings went into the procurers' pockets. The essential link between GIs and girls—the pimps—were even easier to come by, for the organization didn't even have to leave its urban base. Just round up homeless street urchins and teach them a couple of sentences: "Hey GI, you want gell? Numbah one gell ten dollah this way you come." And the boom in prostitution sparked a boom among manufacturers of prophylactics and birth control devices.

I asked for Manila so they gave me Singapore. When the shiny 707 lifted off the Da Nang airstrip I felt about a thousand pounds lighter. Everyone else apparently felt the same, for there was an immediate lightening of the atmosphere, and the laughter-studded chatter of tourists filled the cabin. For five days we were free. We had money and young ideas and nothing and nobody better stand in our way! We might be dead in two weeks so we're going to get it all this week! Keep the booze flowing and bring on the broads!

The captain quickly reined us in with a warning: no alcoholic beverages would be served during the flight and if anyone was found sipping something he had sneaked aboard, the plane would go straight back to Vietnam! We indicated our willingness to comply, with immediate silence.

Four hours later a winding, green coastline came into view and the seatbelt light came on. As the plane dipped we looked down on palm trees and thatched villages along clear coastal waters. Deep green jungle stretched for miles inland. We landed but the plane did not taxi to a place beside the commercial liners. We had just come from the war so we were quarantined, segregated at the far end of the airstrip. A bus delivered us to the main airport building. In exchange for our being segregated from normal people we were granted one privilege: we didn't have to go through a customs check.

While waiting for buses to our hotel we looked into the waiting area and saw a form of life we had not seen for months: civilians. They were of all sizes and colors and they wore everything from pith helmets to fezes, saris, sarongs, and business suits. They were standing or sitting in no approved formation: talking, smoking, drinking, staring. There was no rush-rush, no regulations; and I wasn't sure I knew how to act in so free an atmosphere.

We got out of our buses and looked up at a six-story building. A sign hung over the entrance between two palm trees: Seaview Hotel. A handsome young man in civilian clothes and carrying a clipboard hollered "This way!" We walked in and down a flight of stairs to a dance floor covered with folding chairs. When we were seated, the man with the clipboard stepped up onto the bandstand and introduced himself as Navy Lieutenant Allen, the R & R officer here in Singapore. Smiles of envy and audible murmurs came from the audience: "Talk about the perfect assignment! . . . Wonder how he swung it?"

Lieutenant Allen welcomed us to Singapore and said he hoped we would have a good time. Then he took the smile off his face and got to the meat of his message: anybody who screws up in the hotel or on R & R-sponsored tours will be sent back to the Nam immediately. Anybody who screws up outside the hotel is subject to arrest, trial, and imprisonment in a local jail, and the Singaporean police haven't yet heard of the idea that prisoners have rights. And Singapore has some of the toughest drug laws in the world. Anybody caught using or dealing in marijuana or drugs would likely be locked up and forgotten about, and there is nothing the Defense Department can do about it. Lieutenant Allen's attention-getter was very effective. No one fell asleep during the rest of the briefing.

Lieutenant Allen sat down and a Chinese girl in miniskirt took his place. Smiles and murmurs once again rippled over us: "O-o-o-o, look at that chickee . . . I'd never kick her out of bed!" Miss Lee welcomed us to Singapore and said she would now explain the various facilities available to us. A curtain parted behind her revealing a screen, the lights went out, and a slide projector came on. "Come here, Miss Lee," said a voice from the dark. "At ease!" barked Lieutenant Allen.

Miss Lee explained that we could stay at any one of five R & R hotels. She showed us slides of single and double rooms, lounges, and dining rooms and quoted prices. She also said we could stay in other hotels if we wanted but the R & R staff could not guarantee our safety or the security of our possessions. The lights came on and Lieutenant Allen again took the bandstand. "You can also spend your week in a different kind of setting than a hotel here in the city." He then introduced a character who looked like he had just stepped out of *Robinson Crusoe.* He was dressed like the stereotyped beach bum: tennis shoes, dirty white sailing trousers, open-neck shirt, pipe, and a ship captain's cap at a jaunty angle. He told us a story straight out of a volume of adventures written for early teens. A thick Australian accent added a note of credibility to the account.

He first came to Singapore as a merchant seaman on a freighter out of Sydney. He wrote his wife that he would be back in about six months. That was fifteen years ago. He had still not been back home and had no intention of going. As he put it, "I ran into a bit of luck, I did." He bought some land a few miles outside the city on the coast, complete with sand beach and palm trees. He put up a house and sat back to enjoy his own private paradise. When GIs started coming to Singapore from the new war in Vietnam, he decided to share his paradise. "I've got everything you want. Come along with me and you can be on the beach with a cold beer in one hand and a warm girl in the other in only thirty minutes!" he said with a leer and a wink.

After the beachcomber made his pitch for war profits, Lieutenant Allen came back with final instructions. "Now here's the most important part of all," he intoned. The lights went off again and a new slide was projected. There was no picture, only words and numbers: "Tuesday, June 3, 0900."

"This is your departure time. Write it down. Memorize it. You will be packed and ready to go at this time at the front desk of whatever hotel you stay in. If you miss it, we notify the Singapore police to look for you and we send an AWOL notice to your unit! That's all. Have a nice time."

The lights came on and we went upstairs. About one-third of our number got on other buses to go to other hotels or to the beachcomber's paradise. The rest of us, about one hundred bodies, lined up single file at the front desk to register. The line stretched out the door, across the parking lot, past our buses, and almost to the street—long enough to provoke plenty of bitching: "I thought I was getting away from this kind of shit for a few days!"

By the time I got up to the front desk the first men to sign in had changed clothes and were on their way out, carrying cameras and trailing the scent of beer. When my turn came I got another reminder of the military I wanted to forget for a few days. Propped up on the counter beside the smiling girl asking my name was an official Navy photograph. It showed an officer in the standard pose: wearing dress uniform, seated, holding left hand over right on the chair arm. In the background were an American flag and a globe. Beside the picture was a letter on Navy stationery, under plastic: "To Our R & R Personnel: I recommend, without reservation, the Seaview Hotel. Signed B. L. Smith, Commander, Chaplain's Corps, United States Navy." I wondered if Chaplain Smith knew the troops did not attend prayer meetings while on R & R.

I signed my name, took my key, and headed for the elevator at a brisk pace. As I went up, my vacation timer started counting down . . . 120 hours . . . 119 hours 59 minutes . . . 119 hours 58 minutes . . .

The howls of the newly drunk filled the hall on my floor. I walked into my room looking forward to a long nap in a double bed. Then I would begin a careful search for my R & R dream girl. It was important not to make such an important decision under fatigue. But the bellboy had other ideas. Without knocking, he stepped into my room. "Sir, please come. I show you."

"What? Show me what?" I asked, in true ignorance of what he was getting at.

"I show you gell," he said, amused that I didn't catch on the first time.

"No, thanks. I'll look later," I said.

But he insisted. "Sir, please come now. Best gell be gone quick."

So I went and it was an eye-opener. A banquet room was being used as a . . . what else could it be called but a girl market? This was the one facility of the Seaview that Miss Lee had left out of her briefing, the place where the lonely and horny GIs far from home could meet their five-day girl friends. Young Americans in civilian clothes were nudging and excusing their way out with laughing girls, eager to get back to their rooms and try out their choices. The bustle of activity in the room reminded me of a fish market. Sitting on chairs along the walls and at small tables in the center of the room were about fifty girls. They represented just about every physical and racial type in Singapore, one of the most cosmopolitan cities in the world: short, tall, slim, plump, brown Malay, yellow Chinese, and every possible combination thereof.

Most of the girls were dressed in the sexiest clothes imaginable, working hard to show off their charms. A few were dressed for church, but all had too much makeup on. Some smoked, some chewed gum, some gossiped, some stared blankly. All could put on the happy face for potential buyers but I had a hard time believing the girls were not feeling extreme humiliation as they waited to be rented for the week. Each girl had a number pinned to her dress. GIs milled around, trying to evaluate what they saw and make a choice as fast as possible. "O-o-o-o, look at the tits on sixty-three!" "Yeah, but check the ass on forty-nine! I'm gonna grab her quick! Ah shit, some dude just got her!"

When a GI made his choice, he took the girl to the far end of the room. Seated at a table was the boss of the girl market, a well-fed Chinese woman with a pen in one hand and a thick wad of American dollars in the other. A cigarette dangled from one side of her mouth. Behind her stood the bodyguard, a crew-cut Chinese man, broad shouldered and heavily muscled around the neck. No doubt a kung-fu master, I thought. The boss-lady took the girl's number and the GI's name, ID card number, room number, and money: twenty-five dollars a day, please. I took number seventy-eight for two days. The Chinese madam urged me to take her for all five days but I wanted to preserve an out, just in case we didn't get along.

On the way back upstairs my choice smiled blankly and gave me her alias. "I Linda." In the room she pulled a card out of her purse and thrust it in my face. It was a plastic envelope. A strange writing system was printed on it. The only part I could read was a list of dates. My mind fumbled to figure it out. Was it a driver's license? Lottery ticket? Library card?

Linda laughed at the puzzled look on my face. Then she moved a hand below her waist and said, "No sick. Ha-ha-ha!" So that's it! The VD exam card, required of all girls working in Linda's profession. She had last been examined two days before. How honest of her to show me! And how considerate of the R & R authorities to insure the cleanliness of the women they were allowing to contact us all-American boys!

I ordered a couple of beers from the bellboy. While gulping the cold freshness and savoring the miracle of air conditioning I looked at Linda sitting on the bed. Above her blank smile she had a tiny nose, wide-set eyes framed in false eyelashes, gobs of thick black hair, plus gobs of makeup. This is one of them, I thought. One of the mysterious women who perform the fantastic services we used to talk about in the locker room, the frat house, and the barracks, back in the World. As the beer took effect, a network of thin steel threads tightened around my stomach and sent quivering impulses shooting down through my crotch to the back of my kneecaps.

I moved for Linda. But she didn't begin any fantastic performance. She was completely passive about the whole thing. She kind of "serviced" me, as one services broken toasters or washing machines. But I was rid of months of accumulated tension and so I slept deeply. I got up seventeen hours later and Linda was not there. I immediately checked my clothes but nothing was missing. I took a shower and went downstairs for some breakfast. Linda was sitting beside the swimming pool, gossiping with a girl friend.

After giving her initial service, Linda turned out to be a dud. Everything except eating tired or bored her. She didn't want to show me around the city. She didn't want to take me shopping. Every time I told her I wanted to go somewhere she gave a blank smile and said she would wait in the hotel. This wasn't the way R & R was supposed to go. According to everybody I had talked to about it, the girl was supposed to do everything. If she didn't want to help me enjoy Singapore, both in bed and out, why was she working as an R & R girl? On my second day I gave Linda her unconditional release. Her reaction was the same she had made to everything else I had said: the blank smile.

After the disaster of Linda something had to be done. I wasn't going to sit in my room, reading the novels of Charles Dickens for the rest of my R & R. Hell, I might be dead next week, and if my number was coming up, I was going to get my money's worth of a good time this week. But where to start? The bellboy and the woman who rented me Linda were out of the question—they couldn't be expected to introduce me to a competitor. While I was out touring the next afternoon, my taxi driver solved the problem for me. He was used to seeing R & R GIs with a girl showing them around, not alone as I was that day. He looked at me too many times in the rearview mirror and finally asked, "You no hab gell?"

"Not now I don't."

"You want?" he asked without a pause.

I wanted to say "No more Lindas please," but I doubted he would understand. "Sure, if she's nice."

"Oh yessir, vay nice numbah one gell I know. You see now?"

"Now?" Somehow it didn't seem proper to meet the kind of girl he was talking about at one-thirty in the afternoon. "No, not now. How about tonight?"

"Yessir! Anytime you say okay," he said with a strong note of enthusiasm.

For the rest of the afternoon the driver guided and I fired away with my Instamatic at temples, stately colonial mansions, slums, and sweating Indians in dockside labor gangs. On the way back to the hotel we set a time and place to meet that night. After a nap and a shower the sun was down, so I came out. The driver was all smiles when I got into his taxi, and as we lurched off into the night he assured me I had made a wise decision in taking advantage of his offer. "Yessir, vay nice numbah one gell I know. You like!"

We drove for what seemed a long time, across the city and down progressively narrower and darker streets. The driver parked the car at a place that made me think about muggers. We walked for about five minutes through dark streets full of hushed activity. Soon we were passing open doors. From some of the doors television noise came out, from others the glow of red light.

I looked in one and saw half a dozen bored women in miniskirts, slouched on a sofa before a television. This neighborhood was making no effort to disguise its true purpose.

After we passed a few more doorways, the driver raised a guiding hand and we entered one. The room was dark and barely furnished. Lounging on the lone sofa was a tall Chinese girl wearing an embroidered blouse, tight black pants, and high heels. She was very beautiful and must have been the highest-priced girl on the street.

From the dark far side of the room a short fat middle-aged Chinese man approached. He was the most perfect personification of greasy guile I had ever seen. The single red light bulb in the ceiling glared off the top of his bald moist head. Oversize sunglasses gave him a buglike appearance, and as he rubbed his hands together, a huge welcome-to-my-trap smile stretched across his face. "Good evening, sir. This way please." Introductions and the use of names are definitely out in a red-light district.

A thin, almost handsome man appeared from somewhere and escorted me to another room. The taxi driver remained in the outer room with the fat boss. The handsome man's English came out in melodious tones. "Would you care for a drink, sir?"

"A drink?" I was not prepared for that. "Oh, well, sure . . . ah, can you make a Seven-Seven?"

"Of course, sir. One moment, please." This guy was treating me like a real VIP instead of just another R & R GI. He walked briskly to a dark doorway and gave my order to someone out of sight. While I waited he made small talk about the terrible heat of the Singapore summer. A plump girl with a blank face brought my drink out on a tray and set it on a small table without looking at me. I took a sip and started to say it tasted fine when several women started walking into the room. "Please look, sir," my guide said.

The women walked in single file and lined up along the wall opposite me. When no more entered, there was a total of five facing me. There they are, I thought, the women who know all the secret pleasures of the flesh. And here I sit only ten feet away. Christ almighty—if the Congregational minister could see me now!

My guide provided a running commentary on the female line-up. "This one only nineteen . . . next one half-Malay, half-Chinese . . . that one just in from Kuala Lumpur . . ." I stopped listening when he mentioned Kuala Lumpur. I didn't know if coming from Kuala Lumpur meant the girl was any better than the others, but if her skill at dyeing hair was any indication, I would doubt it; hers had turned out orange. The half-Malay, half-Chinese girl was snapping her gum loudly. I looked and looked. All I could think of was a livestock auction at the county fair.

"Which one you like, sir? Choose anyone, please." I was apparently taking more time than previous customers, for my guide began pushing gently. "You like see more gell? What kine gell you like, sir?" I chose the least dangerous-looking girl in the line-up, the only one who had not dyed her hair, the only girl not wearing a tight miniskirt or making noise. I couldn't imagine waking up next to a pile of orange hair or snapping gum. I paid the man, gathered my taxi driver and said goodbye to the unctuous boss as he counted my money.

On the way back to the hotel I couldn't bring myself to turn and look at the girl I had chosen. I was wrestling with weighty feelings of guilt. Here you are, I lectured myself, contributing to vice and the exploitation of women. Hopefully the Great Scorekeeper in the Sky would write it off under the heading "Sins of the Well-Meaning; Pass Lighter Sentence."

Back in my hotel room, guilt was replaced by a sudden attack of chivalry. "Are you sure this is all right with you?" I asked. She gave a knowing smile and showed me her VD exam card.

Her name was Suzy and she quickly made me forget all feelings of guilt. She handled me gently and when I was conscious again it was almost noon the next day.

I didn't really look at her until the next afternoon. Then I could see why red-light districts always use red lights: it makes the girls look younger. But Suzy wasn't ancient, not at all old enough to embarrass me in the dining room. She just looked experienced, devoid of any illusion of what life is all about.

Suzy was a quiet, unpretentious personality undistorted by extravagant ambitions. Somehow, "prostitute" seemed an inappropriate term to use to describe her. She just didn't fit the stereotype. When she asked a few questions—Where are you from, How many brothers and sisters do you have, What is your job in Vietnam? . . .—she really listened to the answers, as if they were in fact coming from *me,* a real person, instead of a machine. She wasn't constantly trying to wheedle a few more bucks out of a guy like most girls in her position, and she didn't look through a guy's pants while he was in the shower. There was a resignation about her but it did not make her look weak. She took what life carried her way and asked little more than to be allowed to survive.

Suzy was refreshingly receptive to everything I suggested. She took me everywhere and showed me everything: a jade museum, a Hindu temple, a Moslem mosque, a Malay village built over water, even a crocodile farm. We walked along the bay and watched plodding lighters unload freighters from all over the world. We sat under shade trees on the deep grass of the polo field laid out by the subjects of Victoria. For dinner she took me to Chinese restaurants where Westerners are never seen, small, cluttered places where the food is cooked out in the street over open fires and brought in by shouting men running up flights of stairs on legs that look like rippled, polished bronze. She laughed when I ordered ice cream for dessert and said that on this side of the world it is for children only. Most memorable of all, she made me feel I was more than a machine to be serviced, a rare impression to be gained from a woman in her line of work.

Suzy grew on me. I didn't want to leave her, and I guess that's part of the R & R experience, too. I wanted to spend more time with her in this environment, and I wanted to know her away from the wake of war and an R & R hotel. But none of that could be. June third came too quickly. On the last morning I took a shower long before my departure time. Maybe there would be time for one more session with Suzy on the sheets. Coming out of the bathroom, I quickly put that idea aside. Suzy was sitting in front of the mirror making up. On her face, showing clearly through the cream and shadow, was a distant professional expression. She knew what I had not yet accepted: my contract time had expired. She was mentally preparing herself for the next guy.

She was still in my room but I was already part of her ancient history.

The only farewell Suzy would accept was a smile and one word: "Good-bye." That seemed laughably inadequate to me but that was the way she wanted it. After the way she had allowed me to feel human again, I felt she deserved official recognition of some kind. If I had my way I would order a full battalion formation with the band playing and everyone standing tall in dress uniform on the parade deck, and I'd have some colonel give her a medal at least, and a citation with heroic phrases describing her performance of duty . . . "for service above and beyond the call of duty in support of operations in the Western Pacific, the President of the United States takes pleasure in awarding the Silver Star Medal to Suzy Singapore." And after she had served twenty years in her profession I'd give her a pension for life, just like the guys in uniform were eligible for. Suzy and her thousands of sisters who took care of America's, and every other nation's, sons in uniform deserved such benefits just as much as the men who marched around and pulled the triggers. But for Suzy and her sisters there would be none of that. No pictures in hometown papers, no award ceremonies, no pensions. No one would ever recognize her sacrifice. For Suzy there would be only fading looks, less money, more abuse, more cheap whiskey, maybe a needleful of heroin, and an early death in a crowded, stinking tenement or a VD clinic. Some reward.

Downstairs in the lobby the line was forming. Lieutenant Allen stood at the end of the line and as more men joined it he checked off names. Few men talked and those who did conversed in tired tones and yawn-punctuated mumblings. Most wore rumpled, stained clothes and all were struggling with pronounced hangovers. We leaned against door frames or slouched in lobby chairs and sofas, staring bleary-eyed at the big fact hanging in the air: we were really going back to Vietnam. At nine Lieutenant Allen looked at his watch and his clipboard, then hollered that there were two men missing, and had anyone spent any time with two army men named Buxton and Wazlewski? No one had (or wanted to admit it), so we boarded the buses and headed for the airport. Our bus, and the other three no doubt, quickly filled up with the stench of sweaty clothes and hung over breath, and several windows were opened.

After making personnel pickups at the other hotels our caravan moved onto a four-lane expressway and picked up speed. Our dozing and gazing at palm trees were ended by frantic honking from behind. We looked out the back window and saw a taxi speeding in and out of traffic to catch up to us, horn blaring and lights blinking. Jammed in the front seat beside the driver was a laughing and waving American and a heavily made-up Chinese girl. The taxi passed us, horn still honking, and moved between two of our buses. In the back seat was another American, and Chinese girl, also laughing and waving. Buxton and Wazlewski had arrived.

In the airport waiting room our group became more talkative. One guy had four cameras and an accessories bag draped around his neck and was bragging about the bargains he had gotten on everything. Others were showing off their Hong Kong suits slapped together by Chinese tailors in twenty-four hours. Here and there small groups were forming and exchanging experiences of the last five days. Naturally, Buxton and Wazlewski attracted the largest throng. They hadn't slept the previous night and still smelled like a distillery. For the most hung over, there had been no tours, no camera clicking, no night, no day. They were drunk fifteen minutes after we checked in and they only sobered up long enough to eat. They had made a heroic effort to take every willing woman in town and, according to their loud-mouthed accounts, very nearly succeeded. For them the five days was not R & R. It was I & I: Intoxication and Intercourse.

No matter what the character of R & R, whether it really was Rest and Recreation or nothing more than Intoxication and Intercourse, those who went through it were left with a vague dehumanized feeling. Five days before, we had been put on an assembly line and now we were coming off the other end. Along the way we had been processed by different hands doing different things. First, inject plenty of booze, then attach a willing woman, guide the subject through the tourist routes, and add accessories as appropriate: cameras, stereo equipment, and genuine junk souvenirs. Certainly there were momentary pleasantries and pleasures. We had seen places we never would have seen on our own; we had been allowed to forget military regulations for a few days; and the girls were warm. But no matter how many of the R & R benefits were indulged, the impression remained: somebody else was getting more out of it than we were. The most likely beneficiaries were also the most traditional: the wide range of businesses without which war could not be waged. The R & R policy gave very clear illustration to a very old fact: war is good business.

At eleven-thirty a crew-cut Chinese ground attendant opened a gate and we filed out into the flight line and up the stairs into our 707 with the smiling stewardesses. Later in the day another planeload of GIs would land and the whacky R & R sideshow to the main event in Vietnam would start all over again.

14 The Worst of News

In the fifth month of my tour the occasional trips to the Freedom Hill PX ceased to be welcome breaks from the boring routine of life in 3d MPs. I ran into a friend from training days and thought I saw the chance to kill a couple of hours, talking about friends and where they were serving. But he wasn't smiling. "Did you hear?"

"Hear what?" I asked.

"About Bell and DJ."

"What about them?"

"They're dead," he said in a flat voice. Without my invitation, he launched into a description of how each of the two had died, but I didn't hear any of it. I looked through him and said nothing. Dead, I thought. Dead. No, there must be some mistake. Death is not for me and my friends. We had sweated and drunk and laughed together. Death is not for us. Death is for others whose names and faces we do not know. There must be some mistake. You must have the wrong number. Please dial again.

After my insane silent soliloquy I was still not ready to join reality. We were standing in front of the PX, next to a snack bar. Americans in dusty green uniforms milled around us, a slow motion tableau of sweaty squinting faces. I caught fragments of their conversations about stereo equipment and new cars, and their orders to the Vietnamese girl behind the counter. "Five hamburgers with everything on 'em . . . three ice cream cones . . ." When the thought of saying something finally formed, I mumbled something about picking up some razor blades and left.

For the next several days my main project was trying to fit the deaths of two friends into my mental suitcase. I went through the motions of my official duties but my mind was on the enormous fact of death touching close. Second Lieutenant Larry Bell—dead. Second Lieutenant D. J. Barton—dead. I had seen them only one month before. Only six months before, we had been sweating and laughing our way through war games and obstacle courses in the Virginia countryside. I felt the same trite and futile things just about everyone else has felt on hearing of the loss of close friends still in their youth. We've been cheated, all of us—our generation, the Marine Corps, the country, the world. And as if to underline the loss, the world will stumble on in all its mystery and blind chance and no one will remember these two small lives that embodied so many of the talents and foibles of their generation. Well, go ahead, world, go ahead and forget if you want. But as long as I live, their memory will never fade away.

Bell and DJ had come to the Marines by vastly different routes. Bell was an untamed young man, as wild as the rural Oklahoma that reared him. When he first told me he had spent a few nights in jail, I made a mental note to avoid him. But the more he explained, the more I understood. Bell couldn't find an outlet for all his restless energy. The work on his father's farm, more than sufficient exercise to most, wasn't enough. The girls and athletic teams of high school and college weren't enough. Approved activities exhausted, Bell turned to things frowned on: drinking, brawling, and racing cars through the center of his small hometown.

Although Bell could have been accused of much indiscretion, he was never guilty of any vile premeditation. His occasional brushes with the law were the result of schoolboy pranks getting out of hand. He once explained to me with wide-eyed adolescent innocence how one of his ideas had gone wrong. "I swear to God I didn't know the hill was that steep! We was just going to roll his car down the road a little ways while he was in picking up his date, then hide out in the bushes and laugh when he came out and couldn't find it. I swear to God I didn't know the car would roll all the way down the hill and into the river!"

After several years of this kind of thing, the local police chief paid a visit to Bell's father. "Mr. Bell, it's probably none of my business, but have you ever suggested the Army or the Marines to your son? I'm sure they'd be more than happy to have a young man as strong as Larry. Because to tell you the truth, Mr. Bell, me and the boys are getting pretty tired of his 'tricks,' as he calls them. Now you know, when he tears one on, it takes half the force to bring him in!" After completing three years of college at four schools, Bell took the police chief's suggestion.

DJ came to the military by a route much more direct. His father was a career Marine officer, so the idea of entering the corps was not a last resort to be considered if other things went wrong. His service was not dictated by parents, but after growing up around other military families and moving from base to base, he thought it a natural part of one's career pattern. DJ made it clear to all within hearing range, however, that a military career was out of the question. For him the Corps was an interlude of adventure between college and more serious career preparation, probably law school.

Bell and DJ displayed no outward similarities beyond the green of their uniforms. Their physical differences were those between a lithe gymnast and a ponderous weight lifter. In fact, lifting weights is exactly what Bell did to fill up any free time not taken in drinking beer or chasing women. When he first learned of Bell's iron-pumping, DJ was incredulous: "Say, what are you, some kind of masochist?"

DJ moved with a grace and assurance most of us found baffling. Bell lumbered and lurched. Both feet pointed outboard and one shoulder dipped too much. All who saw him walk came to the same conclusion: it was a miracle he achieved any forward motion at all. As for marching in formation, Bell was a disaster. We buried him in the middle of our ranks and prayed no one would notice him. DJ was the only one in our company who could call cadence like an experienced sergeant. When the strident tones of his natural commander's voice lofted over us and echoed through the pine trees, we wanted to march, not walk, everywhere we went. Bell marched us around in a high-pitched nasal twang more appropriate for square dances or calling hogs.

Their different upbringing stamped them with different imagery and prepared them to consider different situations comfortable or forbidding. Bell was the rural he-man; he could have easily been a model for "Marlboro Country" commercials. DJ was the urban sophisticate, inhibited by neither rank nor the pretense of it. Bell was completely out of place in a dress uniform at the stifling formal functions we occasionally had to attend. Like many of us, he hung around the edges of the gathering, wolfing hors d'oeuvres and gulping punch. Not until someone got drunk did he feel he could join in. DJ would have been right at home in the middle of a debutante ball. I once saw him charm a three-star general into telling a string of war stories about the Pacific campaigns against the Japanese.

DJ and Bell also had vastly different tastes in entertainment. On weekends they headed for the same metropolitan area—Washington, D.C.—but they ended up in widely separated neighborhoods. DJ went to the singles bars in Georgetown where he wooed the coeds and secretaries. Bell went drinking and whoring on Fourteenth Street. After a couple of months Bell's weekend routine was disrupted when he was involved in a traffic accident that claimed his Corvette. For the rest of our stay at TBS he was reduced to begging rides from classmates. I was targeted for much of his attention. Afraid that I would end up in a civilian jail and a Marine court-martial following one of his pranks, I tried to beg off. As it turned out, however, there was nothing much to worry about. His accident had apparently tamed him considerably, for he was satisfied to go to a movie in D.C. and then laugh at the hippies around Dupont Circle.

To distant observers, those differences in Bell and DJ looked great. But they were really only superficial. Their attitudes were not so different, and that is not at all surprising, for in a corps of volunteers there are basic similarities. Both were attracted by the personal challenges inherent in joining a corps they knew would test them in the extreme. The prospect of death interrupting that challenge concerned neither. Both found it easy to be selfless. Those of us who worked with them knew both would willingly put themselves in danger to help others out of it. In a time when it was fashionable to run away from responsibility and loudly criticize one's country, both sought heavy responsibility and the chance to serve the country that had given them life. And though neither had a well-developed political philosophy, both found it easy to consider communism the twentieth-century enemy of their country.

Both Bell and DJ were activists, as would be expected of young men in the military, but neither fit very closely the stereotype of the military man, thereby exposing the falsity of the stereotype. If some project were under consideration, whether an assault on an imaginary enemy position during a tactics problem, or the choice of a movie on weekend liberty, we heard different proposals from the two. Bell would blurt out "What the hell we waiting for? Let's go!" From DJ the same predicament brought forth "Wait a minute, we gotta figure this out." Neither Bell nor DJ were stupid, but neither would ever be accused of being especially intellectual. After every week of lectures we had a test on Saturday morning. The tests were always of the objective type—multiple choice and true/false. Since I had come to the marines from a public school teaching position, I was aware of the difference between a valid and an invalid test. I knew the objective tests were much less valid than, for example, essay tests, but they did fit the needs of the instruction staff—objective tests could be graded quickly and by anyone with an IQ over 80.

Such fine distinctions, however, were barely noticed by Bell and DJ. They knew that what the military called "academic work" wasn't really academic—it was just something that made the training schedule look good to the generals at Headquarters and unusually snoopy congressmen. "Do you know how they make these tests?" Bell asked me early in our time at TBS. "Hell, they just make up a bunch of questions and throw darts at them. And that's the only way to take them. Just close your eyes and stab the answer sheet!"

Alarmed at their lack of concern, I studied for the tests. Bell and DJ never did. Every night of the week they could be found in the bar. On Saturday morning they wrote their tests without worry, turned them in, and went on liberty. I sweated over every answer and compared them with classmates afterward. The results of our much different approaches never varied. We always scored within fifteen points of each other. "See Chuck, I told you it wasn't worth sweating. Just close your eyes and stab!"

For the sake of accuracy, however, it must be noted that Bell's system was not completely successful. Officers who scored below seventy percent were required to study in the lecture hall for two hours each night. Instructors were on hand to answer questions. Anyone scoring above seventy on the next test was excused from the "Dummy Detail," as the mandatory study hall was dubbed. Bell earned a seat quickly and rarely worked himself out. DJ and I took longer but we did make a few appearances.

Despite a poor academic record, Bell never gave up his hope of entering a reconnaissance unit. In an infantry division the recon battalion was used to "snoop and poop" behind enemy lines in an effort to determine the enemy's capabilities before a major operation was staged. Recon patrols were "inserted" into hostile territory by helicopter. After spying on and occasionally harassing the enemy for a few days they were "extracted" from a prearranged point, also by helicopter. Many patrols never made it to their extract point before being discovered and wiped out by the enemy. For the extra danger they faced, recon unit members were accorded extra respect. Recon was considered the elite of the elite, something like the Marine Corps' answer to the Army's Green Berets.

Recon had the pick of the entire corps and they set high standards for entrants, much higher than the recruiters. According to official policy only the top ten percent of a TBS class was even eligible for consideration, and Bell wasn't even close to that percentile, due, of course, to his low academic standing. But when our company reached the patrolling section of the curriculum he met an instructor who saw something in him that official standards could not measure. The instructor was a major, three full ranks above us, but that huge gap didn't blind him to any leadership potential in the unpolished Bell. Maybe the key was the fact that the major was also a former All-American football player and he thus quickly recognized the reckless enthusiasm of another former jock. Whatever. Bell went to Recon school after TBS, no doubt because the major had made it plain to headquarters that the official criteria must be set aside in Bell's case. DJ was also picked for some post-TBS training before getting to Vietnam, but without any rules being bent. A test had revealed some language aptitude, so he was enrolled in an intensive course in Vietnamese. Beyond the fact that I had two strong legs, no noteworthy potential was seen in me and I was shipped out to the infantry right after TBS.

Bell and DJ also shared a sense of humor and they expended much energy in expressing it, with the result that the rest of us could enjoy an occasional respite from dry classroom lectures and make-believe field problems. Bell leaned toward practical jokes that pushed the victim to the brink of violent retaliation, and he always scheduled his pranks for the most inappropriate times. Whenever he found someone racing toward a door he would quickly offer to assist the other's entrance or exit, only to hold the door half open and laugh like hell when the victim crashed into the edge of it. Or if someone were involved in frantic last-minute preparations for an inspection, Bell thought it was hilarious to hide an essential like rank insignia or a tie. Then, while the victim tore through an equipment display he had only minutes before carefully assembled, the ever-helpful Lieutenant Bell would give a countdown to certain failure. "You better hurry up, here comes your captain . . . he's almost at the door now . . . you better find it quick!"

DJ had the steel-trap mind that could easily identify the absurd in any situation, and the sharp tongue to voice it. Early in the training cycle he turned his "talents" on me. Our company was divided alphabetically into four platoons of about sixty each. At our first formation everyone in first platoon noticed we had two Andersons. Since we were the same size the problem of identity could not be solved by labels like "Big Anderson" and "Little Anderson." DJ seized on the issue with characteristic vigor. "What are your initials?" he asked each of us. He mulled over our initials for a few seconds. "W. D. and C. R. . . . hm . . . Okay, listen up! W. D., since you're always standin' around watchin' things, you're gonna be the 'Watch Dog' from now on—you got it? And C. R.," he turned to me, "with initials like that, you can only be 'Crotch Rot!' " The platoon conferred its approval with a chorus of guffaws.

Within our ranks the names DJ gave us were appreciated for the mix of irreverence and the ridiculous they conveyed. But such was not always the case among outsiders. One day our platoon commander, a captain, two ranks above us, told DJ to summon Anderson. Without thinking carefully enough, DJ sought to clarify which Anderson the captain wanted by use of our unofficial names. "Which Anderson, sir, Crotch Rot or Watch Dog? Ah, I mean C. R. or . . ."

The captain was in no mood for humor that day. "What? What did you say, Lieutenant? Say that again!"

"C. R. or W. D., sir?"

"No no. What you said before! Say it again!"

DJ reluctantly repeated our unofficial names and all of us within earshot braced for the lecture that would surely follow. The captain concluded with an admonition we would hear several more times during our stay at TBS, "and in the future, Lieutenant Barton, you will restrict your humor to situations in which it is more appropriate. We've got a training schedule to complete!" DJ barked "Yes, sir" and rejoined us. But he had the last word. That night in the mess hall he brushed off the platoon commander's lecture. "Ah, these terminal captains—you can't take them too serious."

DJ reserved his best efforts for new arrivals at TBS. Having been brought up on military bases, he was much less awed by military traditions, hardware, and campaign ribbons than the rest of us. His favorite prank was an unexpected upset of custom regarding the salute. According to timeless tradition, a salute is initiated by one of lower rank toward one of higher rank. Officers of equal rank never salute each other. Once a month a company of officer-students graduated and a new company began the training cycle. DJ liked to find a new arrival burdened with luggage, textbooks, and a pile of orders, and a girl friend at his side. Both hands full and not sure where he was supposed to go, the new student was completely unprepared.

DJ approached at a brisk pace, saluted sharply, and bellowed "Morning, Lieutenant!" The unsuspecting victim fumbled frantically to return the salute of one he assumed was an officer of higher rank, and usually managed to drop something before noticing that the source of his irritation was, like himself, a mere lieutenant. DJ would then turn and add insult to injury with some superfluous advice: "Keep your eyes open, Lieutenant. Anything can happen around here!" Among DJ's more memorable victims were the officer who dropped all copies of his orders in the snow and the young man who dropped a suitcase on his girl friend's foot.

Bell and DJ often combined for some effective humor, the most notable example of which concerned part of our uniform. In Marine Corps terminology, a hat was a "cover." The green cover for the field uniform had less shape than a baseball cap. We were required to block our covers by stretching them over a plastic frame and painting them with starch. The dry cover was stiff as a board and presented the "squared-away" appearance we were constantly admonished to display. To Bell and DJ, however, no starched cover was complete unless it had been subjected to the "grrr" treatment. The two would approach their intended victim full of praise for his cover. "That's a real nice cover you got there, Lieutenant."

"Real squared-away, isn't it?" chimed in Bell.

"But there's only one thing missing," counseled DJ.

"What's that?" asked the unsuspecting one.

"Here, let me see it a minute. I'll show you," offered DJ. "It needs some grrr."

"Some what?"

"Some grrr. Like this." DJ proceeded to crush, twist, and mutilate the once squared-away cover, all the while making the growling sound the treatment was known for. Bell cheered his partner on with shouts of "More grrr, more grrr!" A crushed look came over the victim's face as he watched two hours of patient labor disappear in DJ's hands. Most targeted lieutenants were too stunned to respond as DJ handed them the ball of green cloth that had recently been a perfectly blocked cover, but not too many minutes later they were after blood.

As the training cycle wore on, some of our classmates began showing obvious concern about the raging war in Vietnam that lay in the very near future of all of us. Some were laughing less, others were found gazing out of windows for extended periods. Those in the advanced stages of their foreboding could be heard asking questions like "What percent of our platoon do you think will come back from it?" Neither Bell nor DJ could stand to see anyone brooding about anything, their view of such being that it was at best futile speculation and at worst mawkish self-pity. Whenever they found it in anyone, they attacked with a demonstration of fatalism and gallows humor that had a surprisingly uplifting effect. "What the hell—you can't live forever!" Bell would bellow at the depressed man.

"That's right," DJ would agree. "Besides, didn't you know Bell here's gonna get a CMH when he gets to Nam?"

All of us understood the letters CMH to mean Congressional Medal of Honor, the highest military decoration, so the man was naturally skeptical that such an award could be arranged in advance. "What makes you think he'll get the big medal?"

"No no, not that. For Bell, CMH means Coffin with Metal Handles!" DJ would explain with a laugh. "Come on, pal, let's go get a beer!"

I saw Bell and DJ once each in Vietnam and on each occasion they expressed once again their gallows humor. Like all other Americans in the combat zone, we wore helmets and flak jackets and carried a weapon, either the M-16 rifle or .45-caliber pistol. The uncomfortable combat uniform evoked derisive comment from DJ when I ran into him in Da Nang. "What do you think of my clown suit, C.R.? Real appropriate, eh?"

"Yeah, but for what?" I asked.

"For getting greased in! Hell, I couldn't run for cover in this thing if I had to!"

I last saw Bell when he came to the 3d MP brig to pick up one of his men who had completed a brief term. He told me about his new operation, scheduled to start the next day. As his jeep backed out of the parking lot he threw his head back and laughed at his fate. "Hell, I'll never see my twenty-sixth birthday!"

The more admiring among those who knew Bell and DJ would have no trouble at all speculating on the successes they might have achieved after the war. Many saw DJ as the future corporate lawyer and Bell as the big-time rancher with more oil derricks than cattle on his land. But most considered it pointless to speculate on what the country lost with their deaths, especially since the country seemed so anxious to put Vietnam out of its awareness. Anyone who knew them, though, would agree with confidence that the world definitely lost a lot of laughter with their passing.

15 Season of Change, Season of Hope

Toward the end of the year things began to change in our usually boring, sometimes tragic, sometimes comic, sanctuary in the rear. Our compound was overrun by the rumor of an impending change of command. That might not sound like much, but in an organization where one personality can so directly influence hundreds of other personalities, the effect was similar to that of an earthquake great enough to cause reporters to use the adjective "devastating." There is only one rumor of greater impact—that of an imminent enemy attack. Colonel Palooka was being reassigned to Headquarters in Washington. We all prayed he would be surrounded by many talented subordinates, for a Headquarters assignment can be dangerous for officers of modest talent like our colonel. Nice guys like Colonel Palooka are the kind selected to be scapegoats when the schemes of the more ambitious and less principled go awry.

The differences between the out-going and in-coming commanders were striking—so striking as to make us wonder at length about the validity of the recruiting and promotion policies that had attracted and retained such contrasting types. That two such different personalities could occupy the same rank station in an organization that valued above all else conformity to a fixed set of values was a source of continuing amazement to the entire battalion, and probably to the two colonels as well.

Whereas Colonel Palooka's nickname came from an approximation of his real name, the new colonel's nickname was derived from his appearance. The new CO was smooth, pointed, and rather dangerous-looking on top, so he was called Colonel Bullethead—out of his presence, that is. The new CO wore the scowl of the perpetually dissatisfied inspector. He looked very uncomfortable during the few times he was observed smiling. Our beer-assisted theorizing led us to conclude that he probably *felt* very uncomfortable smiling, too, and so he didn't do it very often. Whereas Colonel Palooka was an easy-going grandfatherly type who liked to counsel subordinates over a bottle of whiskey, Colonel Bullethead was the stern and tireless critic who saw in the need for counsel proof of weakness. Whereas Colonel Palooka was perfectly content to let subordinate commanders run their own units however they thought best, Colonel Bullethead had to stick his bullethead into every office and endorse every decision. And whereas Colonel Palooka always appreciated a good strip show or beer party, his successor viewed such diversions as forms of dissipation required by lesser talents.

Colonel Bullethead was a little too high-powered for the slow and unspectacular pace of life in a rear-echelon unit. Assignment to the Pentagon or a unit in the field would have better fit his temperament, sense of duty, and idea of what a battalion commander should be. He wanted to go places and do things. There were in the combat zone many units that were going places and doing things, but 3d MPs was not one of them.

Colonel Bullethead began his tour of duty with a two-week inspection of everything in the battalion compound. He looked in everything from file cabinets to prisoners' sleeping quarters, from mess hall kitchens to club cash registers. Everyone smiled and held his breath for the flood of new policies and orders we knew would follow. And a flood it was. Bullethead wanted all cigarette butts picked up immediately. And to make sure no new butts replaced the old ones on the ground, he ordered "butt kits" placed beside every door of every hooch. A butt kit is an empty tin can painted red into which the remains of smoked cigarettes are thrown. And after inspecting the roofs of all the hooches, Bullethead ordered changed the sandbags that held the roofs in place during typhoons. Reportedly, he didn't like the color of the old sandbags. Then he upgraded the additional duty of career counselor to a full-time position, appointed a career sergeant to the job, gave him a typewriter and a clerk, and had a new hooch built to house the new office. Along the sidewalk leading to the new hooch were placed large stones painted white.

But the worst of all the new orders Bullethead issued was the one that locked the compound gate at five-thirty in the afternoon. There would be no more nighttime visits to the painted ladies of Dogpatch, or to friends in other units' clubs, nor would there be any more after-dinner escapes from the compound for no better reason than to get a change of scenery. Presumably to vent the increased frustration which he knew would result from his locking of the compound gate, Bullethead ordered an expansion of the intrabattalion sports program. The locking of the compound gate was all the more surprising to us since we knew how much Bullethead's predecessor had liked to escape the confines of his command on the slightest pretext. The new CO drank very little and had no use for the club. Not even a round-eye strip show could get his attention.

Colonel Bullethead apparently viewed himself as a mixture of the Eye Corps sheriff and the FLC general's personal cop, and he certainly looked the part. On his right hip he wore a snub-nosed .38 with prominent white plastic (some said pearl) handles. And on the front of the jeep that Colonel Palooka passed on to him, Bullethead had a big red sign mounted which announced in gold letters three inches high his rank, name, and command. No other of the many battalion commanders in the Da Nang area, and possibly in all of South Vietnam, announced himself quite so loudly.

On a warm November night Bullethead caught me in a moment in which my sense of discipline was relaxed more than usual. The Enlisted Men's Club occasionally had a "Boss's Night," on which any enlisted man could invite his platoon or company commander to his club and forget for a few hours the normally formidable barriers of rank. And since the EM Club had more and cuter Vietnamese waitresses than the Staff NCO/Officer's Club—they had five to our two—I was never less than extremely eager to accept an invitation.

Boss's Night itself went just fine—I got more than enough to drink, the Australian strip show was better than usual, and I got to talk to my favorite waitress. The problem came after it ended. Instead of everyone quietly walking back to his hooch, the men in my company made up a formation that looked more like a herd, and invited me to march them back to their hooches so as to maintain company integrity and pride and whatever else it was they felt was at stake. So, with some troops echoing my beery call of cadence, others trying to sing some ribald ballad they had picked up in boot camp, and all stumbling into each other, we marched off into the darkness with no discipline but plenty of noise. Too much noise, according to my company commander and Colonel Bullethead who were tailing us. Just as I dismissed the herd in front of the enlisted hooches, my company commander ran up to me and growled, "Be in a clean uniform tomorrow morning—we're going to see the colonel!"

With visions of the most terrible punishments flying through my head, I did not sleep very well that night. I was sure there would be a long lecture on how I had disgraced the officer corps of the finest fighting force the world has ever seen, and at the same time made enough noise for the Flick general and every VC in Eye Corps to hear. I would probably be thrown in the brig and put on bread and water for two weeks. And after all of that, Bullethead would hit me with a huge fine to insure that I would return to the World penniless.

After the sun had been up about an hour, I got up, shaved, and put on a clean uniform as per instructions. I walked on weak legs to my company commander's hooch and waited for him to finish dressing. Without a word he nodded to me to fall in step behind him. While I tried to rehearse a speech of explanation through the fog of my hung over brain, we paced off the distance to the headquarters hooch. Long before I was ready to face the man who held much of my life in his palm, my captain was at the foot of the stairs leading up to the headquarters entrance. He slowed his pace in preparation to turn and climb the stairs, looked up at the entrance, and—what was happening!—turned away and continued walking toward the brig. He let me off! He could have helped the colonel hang my ass but he let me off! Why?

In his office in the brig he told me. The colonel didn't like my captain and my captain returned the feeling in amplified form. After seeing the new colonel in action for a few weeks, the captain had decided to do all he could, short of getting himself relieved, to take care of breaches of discipline in his company by himself. He would tolerate no more outside interference than necessary. It was from such intracommand tensions that I had reaped a little benefit. Instead of a long lecture, confinement to quarters, and possibly a big fine, I was sentenced to stay out of the club for two weeks. All in all, it turned out to be a nice chance to catch up on some weight lifting and letter writing. I never told my parents why there was a sudden increase in the volume of mail they received in the fifth month of my tour.

Shortly after Colonel Palooka left, Major Nails left. That they should leave the war at about the same time seemed both logical and natural to all the rest of us watching from below, since they had complimented each other so well in their idiosyncrasies. We would not have been surprised to learn that they had been assigned to the same unit back in the States.

Major Nails' replacement was an even more striking contrast to him than Colonel Palooka's had been. There was nothing dumpy, nothing superfluous about Maj. William James Duke. Nor was there any attempt at bluff or any suggestion of incompetence about him. In the terminology current at the time, he was "a real one"—a really competent leader who had proven himself more than once. He looked the part, too. His 210 pounds were distributed in such a way that he had the physique of an athlete twenty years his junior. The top of his crew cut was slightly more than six feet above the ground. He was quiet, his darting eyes noticing much more than his voice expressed. When he did speak there was no encouragement of doubt. Major Duke personified all the qualities of a genuine leader which Hollywood has still not been able to teach any of its actors.

The story was that Major Duke had saved several American

lives on his previous tour in Vietnam. That fact was nothing much by itself—many others had done the same. But the method by which he had saved those lives had not been used by many others. On some nameless hill Major Duke's unit had come under enemy fire. That was soon followed by an enemy assault. The infantryman's nightmare was brought to reality—hand-to-hand combat in the confusion and horror of point-blank rifle fire and bursting hand grenades. An enemy hand grenade was thrown in the midst of a group of American troops. Without hesitation, Major Duke dove on it and held it to his stomach. If the grenade had exploded, Major Duke would have been a dead Medal of Honor winner. But for some unknown reason it did not explode, and Major Duke was a living recipient of the second highest American military decoration, the Navy Cross.

Christmas season was full of more of that whacky incongruity that no other environment but the rear of a sometimes sleeping, sometimes snarling, war could produce. One week there was a day that MACV radio and television announced as Christmas and the next week there was a day that the calendar labeled New Year's. But even without the help of the MACV studios and the calendar we still would have had a good idea of the coming of what people back in the States called "the holiday season." Colonel Bullethead was determined to recreate in Vietnam as much of the American way of life as possible. And with the help of a public address system, he came reasonably close. Beginning a week before Christmas and continuing until the end of the year the colonel ordered that Christmas music be played over a loudspeaker placed on the roof of the headquarters hooch. So, to the normal background sounds of a nearby army artillery battery, the scream of jets, and the whump-whump of helicopters overhead were added the amplified strains of "Rudolph the Red-Nosed Reindeer," "I Saw Mommy Kissing Santa Claus," "The Twelve Days of Christmas," and "Silent Night." However, no one in Eye Corps or even all of MACV had enough rank or enough pull with God to cause snow to fall and make it a white wartime Christmas.

There was other evidence of the change in seasons, too. Several hundred elementary schools back in the World had principals or teachers who thought about the troops in Vietnam, just as they had thought about the troops in World War II and the Korean War. They also thought about the reasons behind the war in much the same terms they had thought about the issues behind those earlier conflicts. We were, they apparently thought, soldiers in the Army of Righteousness fighting against the Forces of Evil—the communists—and they wanted us to know they were thinking about us this holiday season. They also wanted us to taste some of the benefits of the country whose way of life we were supposedly defending, so they sent us several hundred tons of baked bread and cakes and canned peas and corn and tomatoes and asparagus and boxes of Christmas cookies and all kinds of candy.

Attached to the crates of stale bread and canned goods were letters, and in the letters were sentiments more appropriate to the war America had entered nearly two decades before, when there really was an international communist conspiracy determined to bury the Western democracies. Typical was the message sent by Mrs. Poindexter's fourth grade class from Sam Houston Elementary School in Denton, Texas: "To Our Men in Uniform: We want all of you to know we are thinking of you in this Christmas season. We are deeply grateful that you brave men have volunteered to go so far away to fight and keep Communism far from the shores of our great American nation. We hope these home-made and canned goods reach you in time for Christmas. All of us pray everyday for your victory and so that all of you can be back home for next Christmas." Under the typed message were the signatures of two adults in a slanted, barely readable hand and those of twenty-eight students in an awkward, barely readable hand.

Unknown to the patriots who sent it, the groceries never reached the men in the foxholes. Instead, it was pushed off to the side of the Da Nang airstrip to make way for higher priority cargoes. There it baked and rotted for several days under a sun almost as hot in December as in July until it was dumped in whatever space the rear-echelon units could spare. Most of those units did the same thing with it as we did in 3d MPs: we ate the best and gave the rest to local farmers who used it to fatten their pigs and chickens.

No one had the heart to write to Mrs. Poindexter and her class and tell them what happened to their Christmas present to us. Nor did anyone have the heart to write her about what became of some of the food after we passed it on to the Vietnamese. More than a few farmers donated pigs and chickens fattened on the expression of Mrs. Poindexter's patriotism to local members of the organization dedicated to the defeat of the American effort in Vietnam: the Viet Cong.

Christmas 1968 in Vietnam was full of hope—Bob Hope, that is. The veteran entertainer brought his Christmas Special for the troops to two locations in the war zone, Tan Son Nhut Air Base near Saigon and Da Nang. The event was scheduled a few days before Christmas Day, and two weeks before that the local commanders' planning meeting was held. Every commander of a unit battalion-size or larger was present to hear the III MAF Chief of Staff explain where the Christmas Special would be held, what responsibilities local units would have, and how many tickets were available. Third MPs got a big responsibility—security for the entire event—and very few tickets. The general felt that since we would be manning all entrances we would already have a free view of the performance, so we didn't need any tickets. Half of the tickets were being reserved for two categories: field units in Eye Corps and patients at the Navy hospital in Da Nang. The rest of the tickets were to be divided among the thousands of troops stationed in Da Nang. Since there were many more troops who wanted to see the Christmas Special than there were tickets available, there immediately grew up an active scalper's market. The day before the performance, tickets for the best seats were going for twenty-five dollars.

Although the performance was officially known as the Bob Hope Christmas Special, the majority of the troops who wanted to see it thought of it in different terms. Bob Hope had been entertaining American servicemen and women for several years before most of the Americans in Vietnam were even born, so there existed between him and his mostly young audience a sizable generation gap. Most of the younger troops considered Mr. Hope's brand of humor a little corny. What they really liked was the group of singers and dancers the veteran comedian brought with him, a group that always included some of the most attractive up-and-coming female talent in show business. In 1968 the group included a stunning beauty who could also sing, Ann Margret. To a man, the young troopers thought of the show as the Ann Margret Christmas Special which included a comedian named Hope.

A few days before the performance a stage was set up facing Hill 327 and different colored tapes were laid out on the lower slopes of the hill to mark seating areas. Temporary fencing was set up around the entire seating area to keep non–ticket-holders out. At 6:00 A.M. on the day of the performance we MPs took up stations at all entrances and on all roads leading to the site. Two amphibian tractors growled into place at the side of the stage and lowered their mouthlike loading ramps. If the VC interrupted the show, performers were to take cover in the big vehicles. An hour before the show was to start, ambulances began arriving with a special category of spectators: hospital patients in light blue pajamas. All first row seats were reserved for the patients. Groups of other Da Nang area units arrived, showed their tickets, and took their seats in orderly files.

Fifteen minutes before show time, a line of trucks pulled up at one of the side entrances. The trucks were just like all the others that had been arriving for several hours, but the passengers were different. There were no shined boots and starched uniforms among these spectators. And they didn't enter the seating area in orderly files. They jumped out of the trucks and examined the hillside, as if they were figuring out the best way to rob a bank. They walked up to the entrance, looked at the fence around the seating area and smiled. They looked at our clean uniforms and sneered. They hesitated as the unvoiced plan spread through their number. Then they charged.

Our temporary fence was quickly trampled to the ground and we MPs were pushed out of the way. The troops from the field units had arrived. Numbering three or four hundred, the mob surged into the seating area and made their own seats by pushing the waiting crowd toward the middle. The field troops had come to see some young American womanhood and they were not going to be put off by the formalities of tickets and seating arrangements. Before we MPs and the crowd had recovered from the onslaught, a small helicopter approached from the airstrip, raised a dust cloud over us, and touched down on a small pad near the stage. Bob Hope stepped out, waved an oversize golf club toward the crowd, and the show was on.

"There he is!" said scattered voices in the crowd.

"Yeah, but where's Ann Margret?" answered many more voices.

Mr. Hope made us listen to a string of one-liners before he brought out his main attraction. When she finally came out on stage, the recognition in the crowd was immediate. "O-o-o-o-o-o," said over ten thousand voices. "Look at them legs! . . . and that ass! . . . and them knockers! . . . she can sit on me anytime," said thousands through the crowd. Ann Margret sang her first number in tight black pants, which she later changed for a bright red low-cut gown, which she changed for hot-pants, which just about drove the all-male crowd up the side of Freedom Hill. She must have realized she was mentally raped at least ten thousand times during the show, but she never betrayed the realization.

Everyone knew the show had to end but the crowd didn't let it happen before demanding two curtain calls by all the girls in the Hope troupe. As the crowd was warming up to another roar of "Encore!" the veteran comedian reminded us that he had another crowd waiting in Saigon. He ended with the wish that we would all be back in the States by next Christmas, to which many voices on the hillside answered with a sardonic laugh.

When the day arrived, we put on a Christmas party for all Vietnamese who worked for us, and their children. The party was conceived as a gesture of goodwill. Christmas was considered to be one of the very few things that Vietnam and America had in common. Due to an aggressive missionary effort by nineteenth-century French colonizers, it was not too difficult to find Christians in twentieth-century Vietnam. What better chance to win Vietnamese friends, our S-5 and the colonel reasoned, than to hold a joint celebration for an occasion that each of us would celebrate separately anyway? The colonel ordered our staff of cooks, who specialized in burning hamburger and eggs, to turn out roast turkey and cake.

The Christmas party was received by the Vietnamese in a far different spirit than it was given by us. Most of those who came to the party attended for reasons that had nothing to do with religion. Our guests were usually willing to attend an official American-style function when they found out it would be held in the battalion dining hall and refreshments would be served. For a few hours a group of people who had to get through most of the days of their lives on less than half the number of calories widely considered the minimum daily requirement were allowed inside the treasure trove of wondrous and tasty things called the mess hall. And since in the chaplain's view it would hardly do to have armed guards watching over people at an event occasioned by the birth of Christ, the Vietnamese were allowed to do just about anything they wanted in the large room. So, here and there, between smiles and Christmas carols, men could be seen stuffing fistfuls of turkey or ham sandwiches and cups of ice cream into pockets and shirtfronts. And every once in awhile a woman would discreetly turn away from the battalion photographer and jam an orange or a piece of cake downward into panties or upward into a brassiere. What we Americans considered merely appropriate accessories to a party the Vietnamese considered essentials of life.

When it was time to go, most of the adult Vietnamese looked as if they had been permanently deformed by their participation in the foreign custom of the Christmas party. As they moved to the jeeps and trucks that would take them home, they exhibited a variety of unnatural postures and limps in trying to conceal recently acquired bulges made by solid goodies, or expanding dark spots caused by soft drinks and melting ice cream poorly placed in undergarments.

Some of us observing the grotesque parade found new reason to sympathize with the Vietnamese for all the poverty and malnutrition and the many other forms of deprivation they had to put up with in trying to eke out an existence around the war. Others of us found reason to simply laugh at the weird shapes this group of human bodies had assumed over the past couple of hours. In their desperation to escape with as many edible treasures as possible, the Vietnamese certainly could not understand the great contrast in expressions exhibited by the audience before which they labored—about half the faces twisted in pity, the rest stretched in laughter. I am not sure what the Vietnamese definition of the profane is, but I have an idea we Americans gave illustration to it quite well on that Christmas Day.

16 Across the River and into the Unknown

About three weeks into the new year I bumped into the adjutant in the combination toilet/shower hooch. He pulled up to the urinal beside me.

"Your orders came through, Chuck. You're going up north to 3d Division. Drop into my office sometime today."

"Well, that's great, that's great . . . yeah, I will, Luke."

"So now you're gonna leave us back here and go up there and be a big hero . . . well, you remember everything you walked away from back here . . ." Luke then launched into a listing of all the benefits of life in 3d MPs, a recitation I had heard countless times before, and concluded with his standard question for anyone leaving 3d MPs, a question spoken in the most sarcastic tone of voice he could produce. "Now, how can you leave all of that behind, Chuckie-boy—how?"

I responded in like tones. "Yeah, Luke, I know—you got a nice little battalion here, a nice place to visit but I wouldn't want to . . . and you know how to finish that one."

"Yeah, Chuckie, I know, I know . . . but I hear those little guys on the other side are using real bullets on our guys . . . what if they point one of those things called rifles at you and pull the trigger?"

"Well, I'll just jump up and holler, if they get me, *you'll* leave 3d MPs and replace me!"

"No chance, Chuckie, no chance . . . I got a family, remember?"

By now we had buttoned up and were on the way out the door. "Seriously, though, Chuck, drop us a line now and then so we know how you're getting along."

"I will, Luke, I will."

"Oh, and one more thing."

"Yeah, Luke?"

"Be careful, okay?"

"Yeah, Luke, I will."

There it was—the most official word from the most official person. Those pieces of paper by which the government moves people really existed, and they had really been signed by real people.

I never had an experience that jammed so closely together humor, tragedy, pathos, boredom, and the dozen other emotions in between for which we have no names, as did my six months in the rear of the Vietnam War. And the way it ended was perfectly in keeping with its whacky character. I slept no more than three hours my last night in the 3d MPs. At five in the morning I threw a bag in the back of a light truck and climbed in beside the driver. The corporal was a friend but we said little. He had been in the bush before joining 3d MPs, so he knew well the mix of anticipation, anxiety, and a hangover young men carry on the eve of their blooding. As the truck moved out the gate and down the road I tried to see as much as possible of a place and time that were fast receding into the past. My eyes settled on the delicate pink flame trailing out the back of an all-weather fighter-bomber lifting off the Da Nang airstrip, and I thought I had at last seen something man-made beautiful enough to rival the emerald beauty of Vietnam.

That vision was shattered as the truck slowed before an intersection. From a cluster of shelters made of Coca-Cola cases and ammunition boxes came a single rifle shot. If the bullet had hit one of us we would have felt something before hearing anything.

But we heard something before we felt anything so we went ahead with reactions learned in training. The driver jammed the gas pedal to the floor and I put a hand on my .45. In the next few seconds, as our truck lurched into a left turn and that lone bullet tore through the cool morning stillness above and away from us, a confusion of shock, hopes, fears, and unfinished prayers shot through my foggy brain. The only one I remembered ten minutes after the shot was fired was my extreme surprise at my unseen enemy's lack of consideration for my condition at that hour. The least he could have done was wait until I was awake before trying to kill me!

That's how great the distance was between the rear and the war.

The next day I began learning what poor preparation the past six months in 3d MPs had been for my next six months in the field. I began to see that if I were to get through a field assignment successfully, I would have to unlearn the nonchalant ways of thinking and moving I had picked up in the rear. In the next six months there would be no more showers every day, no more nights of peaceful sleep on clean sheets and stateside mattresses, no more steaks in the mess hall, no more of the relaxed buddy-buddy summer camp atmosphere. And the worst enemy in the rear—boredom—would be the least threatening of a variety of irritations and dangers in the field. I would have to develop very thick skin and become coldly functional.

The first lesson in that unlearning process came at Quang Tri City, seventy-five miles north of Da Nang, in the tent city that was the headquarters of 3d Marine Division. A convoy was forming up to take ammunition, C-rations, mail, warm beer, and replacement troops to the forward support base at Camp Vandegrift. In the staging area I ran into the first grunt—a real live field marine—I would associate with in the new world of combat I was entering. There is nothing noteworthy about that fact, for the convoy was certainly not forming up for me alone. It was the activity Mr. Real Grunt was engaged in that struck me. He was sitting on the ground leaning against a wall of sandbags and he was doing the last thing I expected a battle-hardened marine to be doing in a combat zone. He was brushing his teeth. He moved the brush deliberately and thoroughly, as if he had much experience filling in dead time. I wondered: Is this how the troops prepare for search and destroy operations against the enemy? But the closer I looked, the more I found to support my expectations about men in war.

Except for the toothbrush, everything about Mr. Real Grunt supported the image of combat troops Hollywood had given me. His boots, once black, were white from innumerable scuffings against hillsides, tree stumps, and rocks and innumerable dunkings in streams. His pants, originally dark green, were now almost white at the knees and seat. One bare knee stuck out through a long tear in the material. About a dozen red scratches crossed the white kneecap at different angles. Instead of the long-sleeved green shirt he was issued along with the trousers, he wore a green T-shirt. Over that was a flak jacket, dark green when new, now white in places from abrasion, reddish-brown in others from dirt. One rank device was pinned to the zipper flap: the two parallel inverted "V"s of a corporal. The bottom row of fiberglass protective plates, the ones that might prevent several dozen white-hot shrapnel slivers from perforating his intestines and kidneys, were cut out.

His arms were bare and sunburned, the elbows crossed by many scratches from elephant grass and wait-a-minute vines. Under the T-shirt his skin was pale white. Hanging from each shoulder and crossing in front and back were four bandoleers of ammunition. Around the neck was a bead chain, at the end of which was one of his two dog tags. The other was on one of the boots, under the laces—in case he met death in an unusually violent, dismembering manner. Also around the neck, but more loosely, was a towel dyed dark green. Faint white streaks of dried salt ran through it from all the sweat it had absorbed.

The back of the neck, tip of the nose, and the earlobes were sunburned; everything else was pale. A well-tended mustache spaced the nose and upper lip. The hair was cut short, but only because he had just spent some time in a rear area; first sergeants tolerated unpolished boots, but not long hair, around their clubs and company offices.

The helmet shaded one side of the head more than the other.

The strap did not pass under the chin, as its manufacturer and the grunt's commander intended, but was fastened at the back along the helmet lip. Around the helmet was a section of inner tube. Under it were held a field bandage and a plastic vial of mosquito repellent. Several messages had been written on the helmet cover. Still legible were: "Columbus, Indiana—God's Country," "Marlene," and a list of thirteen months arranged in two columns. Eight of the months were crossed out.

On the ground on one side of him were his pack and his cartridge belt. Tied to each with extra pack straps and boot laces were several canteens and hand grenades. On the other side of him there was a large red canvas bag full of letters and packages for the rest of his company. Propped between the ground and his left shoulder, inside the arm, was an M-16 rifle.

Just about everything I was wearing that day contrasted with what Mr. Real Grunt was wearing. My boots were still black. My trousers were still dark green all over, and where he had a long tear, I still had a sharp pressed crease. My skin displayed no scratches, no sunburn. I had not yet learned that a grunt could not wear a long-sleeved shirt in a country where the temperature frequently goes over 110 degrees. My flak jacket was still clean and still had all its plates. I had not yet seen any reason to wear a green towel, write anything on my helmet cover, grow a mustache, or carry extra canteens and hand grenades. And, I had not yet learned to fill dead time or to relax in a foxhole or against a wall of sandbags. I stood like a traveler in an airport, not very smoothly shifting from one leg to the other, trying, and failing, to cover my anxiety and nervousness with an air of nonchalance.

I never learned Mr. Real Grunt's name. During most of the time I was inspecting him he was staring off into the hot distance, steadily working the toothbrush around inside his closed mouth. We exchanged no words, but more than a little communication passed between us. He looked at me once. It was a fast glance that began at the rank insignia on my collar and quickly swept down my embarrassingly clean uniform. Through the glance he sent a message: You're new out here, aren't you? He knew what a lieutenant was and I knew what a corporal was. We both knew that in war a difference in combat experience is for a while more telling than a difference in rank. Until I had some time in the bush, until I had walked through adversity and close to death, I was to him a "newby," not a lieutenant. I kept my distance.

Since that was my first day in a field unit, I felt it would be both inappropriate and self-deceiving for me to make too many assumptions based on my mostly irrelevant experience. The only assumption I allowed myself about Mr. Real Grunt was that since I did not always look the same as I did on that day, he too did not always look the same. And there was some evidence to support my assumption. Under the corporal's worn and torn uniform, the dirt, the scratches, and the sunburn, one could still discern the outlines of a high school athlete's build. Probably only six or eight months before, this young man who was beginning to look old and knowing was wearing a different kind of uniform, was engaging in a different kind of combat. He was probably wearing spiked shoes, a stretch jersey over shoulder pads, and a shiny helmet with a number stamped on the back. And he was probably running down a grassy field on a Friday night under bright lights, carrying an oblong ball across white lines, bringing hundreds of people to their feet, and making a dozen cheerleaders scream with joy and jump up and down and show their soft, white thighs. And after he dove into the end zone and won the big game, he probably met his girl and drove her out to the cemetery, and with the cheers of the crowd still ringing in his ears he saw another pair of soft, white thighs and lunged into another end zone. But today in the 3d Marine Division rear, with a convoy forming up and a war going on, all of that was far behind him. Today he looked very filthy, perfectly functional, and very deadly.

After fifteen minutes Mr. Real Grunt and I were no longer alone. The rest of the grunts going north arrived in groups of four and five. Most were new and wore clean uniforms like mine. Then a jeep drove up past the line of trucks and stopped where we waited. Through a massive cloud of dust a sergeant wearing goggles and holding a shotgun yelled from the front seat, "Moving out, saddle up!" The corporal came alive now. He jammed the toothbrush into a corner of his pack, spit out a mass of white froth, led us to the roadside, and showed us how to climb up into a six-by. When we climbed up into the trucks we crossed the biggest boundary in our young lives: the wide river separating things known and secure from things unknown and insecure. The convoy commander leaned out of a jeep several vehicles to the front, gave an arm signal, and three tanks, fifty-six trucks, and two helicopters moved out on a dusty road. We were off now, up north to where it was all happening.